CIMA

Subject BA4

Fundamentals of Ethics, Corporate Governance and Business Law

Study Text

CIMA Certificate in Business Accounting

CIMA
PUBLISHING

KAPLAN
PUBLISHING

Published by: Kaplan Publishing UK

Unit 2 The Business Centre, Molly Millars Lane, Wokingham, Berkshire RG41 2QZ

Acknowledgements

We are grateful to the CIMA for permission to reproduce past examination questions. The answers to CIMA Exams have been prepared by Kaplan Publishing, except in the case of the CIMA November 2010 and subsequent CIMA Exam answers where the official CIMA answers have been reproduced. Questions from past live assessments have been included by kind permission of CIMA,

Notice

British Library Cataloguing in Publication Data

A catalogue record for this book is available from the British Library.

ISBN: 978-1-78740-489-2

Printed and bound in Great Britain

Contents

Introduction

How to Use the Materials

These Kaplan Publishing learning materials have been carefully designed to make your learning experience as easy as possible and to give you the best chances of success in your CIMA Cert BA Objective Test Examination.

The product range contains a number of features to help you in the study process. They include:

- a detailed explanation of all syllabus areas

- extensive 'practical' materials

- generous question practice, together with full solutions.

This Study Text has been designed with the needs of home-study and distance-learning candidates in mind. Such students require very full coverage of the syllabus topics, and also the facility to undertake extensive question practice. However, the Study Text is also ideal for fully taught courses.

The main body of the text is divided into a number of chapters, each of which is organised on the following pattern:

- **Detailed learning outcomes.** These describe the knowledge expected after your studies of the chapter are complete. You should assimilate these before beginning detailed work on the chapter, so that you can appreciate where your studies are leading.

- **Step-by-step topic coverage.** This is the heart of each chapter, containing detailed explanatory text supported where appropriate by worked examples and exercises. You should work carefully through this section, ensuring that you understand the material being explained and can tackle the examples and exercises successfully. Remember that in many cases knowledge is cumulative: if you fail to digest earlier material thoroughly, you may struggle to understand later chapters.

- **Activities.** Some chapters are illustrated by more practical elements, such as comments and questions designed to stimulate discussion.

- **Question practice.** The text contains exam-style objective test questions (OTQs).

- **Solutions.** Avoid the temptation merely to 'audit' the solutions provided. It is an illusion to think that this provides the same benefits as you would gain from a serious attempt of your own. However, if you are struggling to get started on a question you should read the introductory guidance provided at the beginning of the solution, where provided, and then make your own attempt before referring back to the full solution.

If you work conscientiously through this Official CIMA Study Text according to the guidelines above you will be giving yourself an excellent chance of success in your Objective Text Examination. Good luck with your studies!

Quality and accuracy are of the utmost importance to us so if you spot an error in any of our products, please send an email to mykaplanreporting@kaplan.com with full details, or follow the link to the feedback form in MyKaplan.

Our Quality Coordinator will work with our technical team to verify the error and take action to ensure it is corrected in future editions.

Icon explanations

 Definition – These sections explain important areas of knowledge which must be understood and reproduced in an assessment environment.

 Key point – Identifies topics which are key to success and are often examined.

 Supplementary reading – These sections will help to provide a deeper understanding of core areas. The supplementary reading is **NOT** optional reading. It is vital to provide you with the breadth of knowledge you will need to address the wide range of topics within your syllabus that could feature in an assessment question. **Reference to this text is vital when self-studying.**

 Test your understanding – Following key points and definitions are exercises which give the opportunity to assess the understanding of these core areas.

 Illustration – To help develop an understanding of particular topics. The illustrative examples are useful in preparing for the Test your understanding exercises.

 Exclamation mark – This symbol signifies a topic which can be more difficult to understand. When reviewing these areas, care should be taken.

Study technique

In this section we briefly outline some tips for effective study during the earlier stages of your approach to the Objective Test Examination. We also mention some techniques that you will find useful at the revision stage. Use of effective study and revision techniques can improve your chances of success in the CIMA Cert BA and CIMA Professional Qualification examinations.

Planning

To begin with, formal planning is essential to get the best return from the time you spend studying. Estimate how much time in total you are going to need for each subject you are studying. Remember that you need to allow time for revision as well as for initial study of the material.

With your study material before you, decide which chapters you are going to study in each week, and which weeks you will devote to revision and final question practice.

Prepare a written schedule summarising the above and stick to it!

It is essential to know your syllabus. As your studies progress you will become more familiar with how long it takes to cover topics in sufficient depth. Your timetable may need to be adapted to allocate enough time for the whole syllabus.

Students are advised to refer to the CIMA website, www.cimaglobal.com, to ensure they are up-to-date.

Students are advised to consult the syllabus when allocating their study time. The percentage weighting shown against each syllabus topic is intended as a guide to the proportion of study time each topic requires.

Tips for effective studying

(1) Aim to find a quiet and undisturbed location for your study and plan as far as possible to use the same period of time each day. Getting into a routine helps to avoid wasting time. Make sure that you have all the materials you need before you begin so as to minimise interruptions.

(2) Store all your materials in one place, so that you do not waste time searching for items every time you want to begin studying. If you have to pack everything away after each study period, keep your study materials in a box, or even a suitcase, which will not be disturbed until the next time.

(3) Limit distractions. To make the most effective use of your study periods you should be able to apply total concentration, so turn off all entertainment equipment, set your phones to silent mode, and put up your 'do not disturb' sign.

(4) Your timetable will tell you which topic to study. However, before diving in and becoming engrossed in the finer points, make sure you have an overall picture of all the areas that need to be covered by the end of that session. After an hour, allow yourself a short break and move away from your Study Text. With experience, you will learn to assess the pace you need to work at. Each study session should focus on component learning outcomes – the basis for all questions.

(5) Work carefully through a chapter, making notes as you go. When you have covered a suitable amount of material, vary the pattern by attempting a practice question. When you have finished your attempt, make notes of any mistakes you made, or any areas that you failed to cover or covered more briefly. Be aware that all component learning outcomes are examinable.

(6) Make notes as you study, and discover the techniques that work best for you. Your notes may be in the form of lists, bullet points, diagrams, summaries, 'mind maps' or the written word, but remember that you will need to refer back to them at a later date, so they must be intelligible. If you are on a taught course, make sure you highlight any issues you would like to follow up with your lecturer.

(7) Organise your notes. Make sure that all your notes, calculations etc. can be effectively filed and easily retrieved later.

Progression

There are two elements of progression that we can measure: how quickly students move through individual topics within a subject; and how quickly they move from one course to the next. We know that there is an optimum for both, but it can vary from subject to subject and from student to student. However, using data and our experience of student performance over many years, we can make some generalisations.

A fixed period of study set out at the start of a course with key milestones is important. This can be within a subject, for example 'I will finish this topic by 30 June', or for overall achievement, such as 'I want to be qualified by the end of next year'.

Your qualification is cumulative, as earlier papers provide a foundation for your subsequent studies, so do not allow there to be too big a gap between one subject and another. For example, E1 *Managing finance in a digital world* builds on your knowledge of the finance function from certificate level and lays the foundations for E2 *Managing performance* and all strategic papers particularly E3 *Strategic management* and P3 *Risk management*.

We know that exams encourage techniques that lead to some degree of short term retention, the result being that you will simply forget much of what you have already learned unless it is refreshed (look up Ebbinghaus Forgetting Curve for more details on this). This makes it more difficult as you move from one subject to another: not only will you have to learn the new subject, you will also have to relearn all the underpinning knowledge as well. This is very inefficient and slows down your overall progression which makes it more likely you may not succeed at all.

In addition, delaying your studies slows your path to qualification which can have negative impacts on your career, postponing the opportunity to apply for higher level positions and therefore higher pay.

You can use the following diagram showing the whole structure of your qualification to help you keep track of your progress. Make sure you carefully review the 2019 CIMA syllabus transition rules and seek appropriate advice if you are unsure about your progression through the qualification.

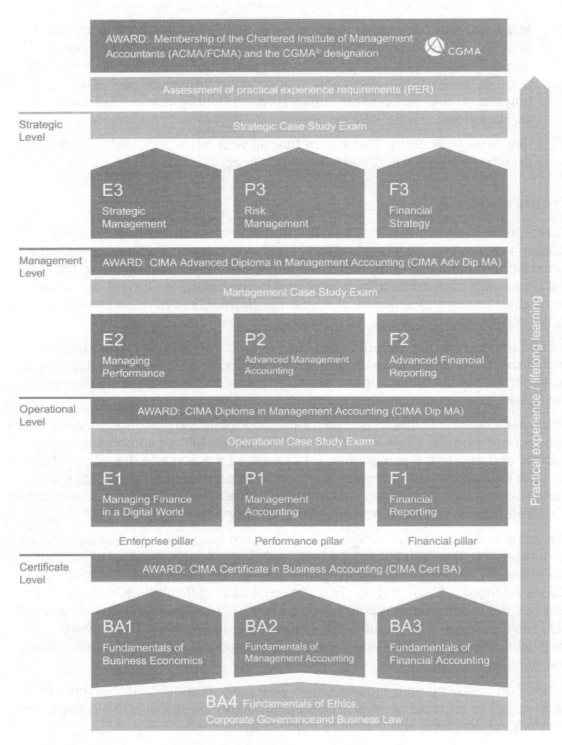

Reproduced with permission from CIMA

Objective Test

Objective Test questions require you to choose or provide a response to a question whose correct answer is predetermined.

The most common types of Objective Test question you will see are:

- multiple choice, where you have to choose the correct answer(s) from a list of possible answers – this could either be numbers or text

- multiple response with more choices and answers, for example, choosing two correct answers from a list of five available answers – this could be either numbers or text

- number entry, where you give your numeric answer to one or more parts of a question, for example, gross profit is $25,000 and the accrual for heat and light charges is $750.

- drag and drop, where you match one or more items with others from the list available, for example, matching several accounting terms with the appropriate definition

- drop down, where you choose the correct answer from those available in a drop down menu, for example, choosing the correct calculation of an accounting ratio, or stating whether an individual statement is true or false

- hot spot, where, for example, you use your computer cursor or mouse to identify the point of profit maximisation on a graph

- other types could be matching text with graphs and labelling/indicating areas on graphs or diagrams.

CIMA has provided the following guidance relating to the format of questions and their marking:

- questions which require narrative responses to be typed will not be used

- for number entry questions, a small range of answers will be accepted. Clear guidance will usually be given about the format in which the answer is required e.g. 'to the nearest $' or 'to two decimal places'

- item set questions provide a scenario which then forms the basis of more than one question (usually 2–4 questions). These sets of questions would appear together in the test and are most likely to appear in BA2 and BA3

- all questions are independent so that, where questions are based on a common item set scenario, each question will be distinct and the answer to a later question will not be dependent upon answering an earlier question correctly

- all items are equally weighted and, where a question consists of more than one element, all elements must be answered correctly for the question to be marked correct.

Throughout this Study Text we have introduced these types of questions, but obviously we have had to label answers A, B, C etc. rather than using click boxes. For convenience we have retained quite a few questions where an initial scenario leads to a number of sub-questions. There will be questions of this type in the Objective Test Examination but they will rarely have more than three sub-questions.

Guidance re CIMA on-screen calculator

As part of the CIMA Objective Test software, candidates are provided with a calculator. This calculator is on-screen and is available for the duration of the assessment. The calculator is available in Objective Test Examinations for BA1, BA2 and BA3 (it is not required for BA4).

Guidance regarding calculator use in the Objective Test Examinations is available online at: https://connect.cimaglobal.com/

CIMA Cert BA Objective Tests

The Objective Tests are a two-hour assessment comprising compulsory questions, each with one or more parts. There will be no choice and all questions should be attempted. The numbers of questions in each assessment are as follows:

BA1 Fundamentals of Business Economics – 60 questions

BA2 Fundamentals of Management Accounting – 60 questions

BA3 Fundamentals of Financial Accounting – 60 questions

BA4 Fundamentals of Ethics, Corporate Governance and Business Law – 85 questions

All questions are equally weighted. All parts of a question must be answered correctly for the question to be marked correct. Where questions are based upon a common scenario, each question will be independent, and answers to later questions will not be dependent upon answering earlier questions correctly.

Structure of subjects and learning outcomes

Each subject within the syllabus is divided into a number of broad syllabus topics. The topics contain one or more lead learning outcomes, related component learning outcomes and indicative syllabus content.

A learning outcome has two main purposes:

(a) to define the skill or ability that a well prepared candidate should be able to exhibit in the examination

(b) to demonstrate the approach likely to be taken in examination questions.

The learning outcomes are part of a hierarchy of learning objectives. The verbs used at the beginning of each learning outcome relate to a specific learning objective e.g.

Calculate the break-even point, profit target, margin of safety and profit/volume ratio for a single product or service.

The verb **'calculate'** indicates a level three learning objective. The following table lists the learning objectives and the verbs that appear in the CIMA Cert BA syllabus learning outcomes.

CIMA VERB HIERARCHY

CIMA place great importance on the definition of verbs in structuring objective tests. It is therefore crucial that you understand the verbs in order to appreciate the depth and breadth of a topic and the level of skill required. The objective tests will focus on levels one, two and three of the CIMA hierarchy of verbs. However, they will also test levels four and five, especially at the management and strategic levels.

Skill level	Verbs used	Definition
Level 3 **Application** How you are expected to apply your knowledge	Apply	Put to practical use
	Calculate	Ascertain or reckon mathematically
	Conduct	Organise and carry out
	Demonstrate	Prove with certainty or exhibit by practical means
	Prepare	Make or get ready for use
	Reconcile	Make or prove consistent/compatible
Level 2 **Comprehension** What you are expected to understand	Describe	Communicate the key features of
	Distinguish	Highlight the differences between
	Explain	Make clear or intelligible/state the meaning or purpose of
	Identify	Recognise, establish or select after consideration
	Illustrate	Use an example to describe or explain something
Level 1 **Knowledge** What you are expected to know	List	Make a list of
	State	Express, fully or clearly, the details/facts of
	Define	Give the exact meaning of
	Outline	Give a summary of

CIMA Cert BA resources

Access to CIMA Cert BA resources including syllabus information is available online at www.cimaglobal.com.

Additional resources

This Study Text is designed to be comprehensive and therefore sufficient to meet the needs of students studying this subject. However, CIMA recognises that many students also want to read around particular topic(s), either to extend their knowledge and understanding, or because it is particularly relevant to their work environment.

CIMA has therefore produced a related reading list for those students who wish to extend their knowledge and understanding, whether for personal interest or to help support work activities as follows:

BA1 – Fundamentals of Business Economics

Principles of Economics 3rd ed.	McDowell & Thom
Applied Economics 12th ed.	Griffiths & Wall
Mathematics for Economists: An Introductory Textbook 4th ed.	Pemberton & Rau

BA2 – Fundamentals of Management Accounting

Management and Cost Accounting	Colin Drury
Management Accounting	Catherine Gowthorpe

BA3 – Fundamentals of Financial Accounting

Financial Accounting – An Introduction	Pauline Weetman
Frank Wood's Business Accounting 1 & 2	Frank Wood & Alan Sangster

BA4 – Fundamentals of Ethics, Corporate Governance and Business Law

Students can find out about the specific law and regulation in their jurisdiction by referring to appropriate texts and publications for their country.

Managing Responsible Business	CGMA Report 2015
Global Management Accounting Principles	CIMA 2015
Embedded Ethical Values: A guide for CIMA Partners	CIMA Report 2014
Business Ethics for SMEs: A Guide for CIMA Partners	CIMA Report 2014
Ethics: Ethical Checklist	CIMA 2014
Ethics Support Guide	CIMA 2014
Acting under Pressure: How management accountants manage ethical issues	CIMA 2012

SYLLABUS GRIDS

BA4: Fundamentals of Ethics, Corporate Governance and Business Law

Syllabus overview

The learning outcomes in this subject reflect the professional standards to be demonstrated for the benefit of all stakeholders. With this in mind, the place of ethics and ethical conflict is an essential underpinning for commercial activity. Ethics is more than just knowing the rules around confidentiality, integrity and objectivity. It's about identifying ethical dilemmas, understanding the implications and behaving appropriately. It includes the role of corporate governance, corporate social responsibility and audit; and their increasing impact in the management of organisations.

Wherever business is conducted the legal and administrative framework underpins commercial activity. With this in mind the areas of contract law, employment law, administration and management of companies is considered.

Assessment strategy

There will be a two hour computer based assessment, comprising 85 compulsory objective test questions.

Syllabus structure

The syllabus comprises the following topics and weightings:

Content area		Weighting
A	Business ethics and ethical conflict	30%
B	Corporate governance, controls and corporate social responsibility	45%
C	General principles of the legal system, contract and employment law	15%
D	Company administration	10%
		100%

BA4A: Business ethics and ethical conflict (30%)

Learning outcomes

On completion of their studies, students should be able to:

Lead	Component	Level	Indicative syllabus content
1. Demonstrate an understanding of the importance of ethics to society, business and the professional accountant.	a. Explain the nature of ethics and its application to society, business and the accountancy profession.	2	• The importance of ethics. • The nature of ethics and its relevance to society, business and the accountancy profession. • Values and attitudes for professional accountants. • Legal frameworks, regulations and standards for business. • The role of national 'Professional Oversight Boards for Accountancy' and 'Auditing Practices Boards'. • The role of international accounting bodies e.g. IFAC. • Rules-based and framework approaches to ethics. • Managing responsible businesses. • Organisational and personal values.
	b. Apply the values and attitudes that provide professional accountants with a commitment to act in the public interest and with social responsibility.	3	
	c. Explain the need for a framework of laws, regulations and standards in business and their application and why CIMA and IFAC each have ethical codes.	2	
	d. Distinguish between detailed rules-based and framework/principles approaches to ethics.	2	
	e. Identify the ethical issues significant to organisations and how CIMA partners with strategic bodies to assist its members with ethical tensions/synergies.	2	
	f. Describe how personal and organisational policies and values promote behaviour.	2	
2. Explain the need and requirements for CIMA students and members in adopting the highest standards of ethical behaviour.	a. Explain the need to develop the virtues of reliability, responsibility, timeliness, courtesy and respect.	2	• The personal qualities of reliability, responsibility, timeliness, courtesy and respect. • The fundamental ethical principles, and examples of their use for professional accountants in practice and professional accountants in business. • Continual Professional Development (CPD), personal development and lifelong learning. • Disclosure required by law (confidentiality). • The concepts of independence, scepticism, accountability and social responsibility. • The threats and safeguards approach to resolving ethical issues, including whistle-blowing, grievance, regulations and laws.
	b. Explain the fundamental ethical principles.	2	
	c. Identify concepts of independence, scepticism, accountability and social responsibility.	2	
	d. Illustrate the threats and safeguards to the fundamental ethical principles.	2	

Lead	Component	Level	Indicative syllabus content
3. Explain the various means of regulating ethical behaviour, recognising different parties' perspectives towards ethical dilemmas.	a. Explain the relationship between the CIMA Code of Ethics and the law.	2	• The relationship between the CIMA Code of Ethics and the law.
	b. Describe the consequences of ethical behaviour to society, business, the profession and the professional accountant.	2	• The distinction between CIMA's Code of Ethics, contracts, and the responsibilities of students and members when they conflict.
	c. Identify conflicting perspectives of interest when dealing with stakeholders in society, business and the values of professional accountants.	2	• The consequences of unethical behaviour: reputation, financial, legal and regulatory; and the benefits of good ethical behaviour • The concepts of corporate and personal ethical stances, in relation to multiple stakeholders.
4. Identify ethical dilemmas and how they may be resolved.	a. Identify situations where ethical dilemmas and conflicts of interest occur, based on CIMA's ethical checklist.	2	• The nature of ethical dilemmas, tensions and synergies. • Conflicts of interest and how they arise. • Issues of corporate confidentiality. • CIMA's Ethical Checklist.

BA4B: Corporate governance, controls and corporate social responsibility (45%)

Learning outcomes

On completion of their studies, students should be able to:

Lead	Component	Level	Indicative syllabus content
1. Explain the role of corporate governance in meeting the concerns of society and investors over the management of corporations.	a. Describe corporate governance.	2	• The role and key objectives of corporate governance, agency theory.
	b. Explain the interaction of corporate governance with business ethics and company law.	2	• Objectivity and independence.
	c. Explain the purpose, definition of the Organisation for Economic Co-operation and Development (OECD) principles of Corporate Governance.	2	• The interaction of corporate governance, ethics and the law. • The purpose, definition and status of the OECD Corporate Governance Code.
	d. Describe IFAC's main drivers of sustainable corporate success.	2	• IFAC's drivers for sustainable organisational success.
	e. Illustrate CIMA's practical proposals for better corporate governance.	2	• CIMA's proposals for better reporting of corporate governance.
	f. Distinguish between detailed rules-based and principles-based approaches to governance.	2	• Rules and principles based approaches to governance.
2. Explain the impact of corporate governance on the directors and management structures of corporations.	a. Describe the role of the board and different board structures.	2	• The role of the board in establishing corporate governance standards.
	b. Explain the effects of corporate governance on directors' powers and duties.	2	• Types of board structures and the role of the board as independent, objective, sceptical and resourceful.
	c. Describe the types of policies and procedures that constitute 'best practice'.	2	• The impact of corporate governance on directors' powers and duties.
	d. Describe the respective committees and their roles and responsibilities with regards monitoring and controlling the actions of the Executive.	2	• Policies and procedures for 'best practice' in companies. • Audit committee – controls, monitoring and relationships. • Appointments Committee. • Remuneration Committee.
3. Explain the role of external and internal audit.	a. Identify the requirements for external audit and the basic processes undertaken.	2	• External audit. • Fair presentation.
	b. Explain the meaning of fair presentation.	2	• Distinction between external and internal audit.
	c. Distinguish between external and internal audit.	2	• Internal audit.
	d. Explain the purpose and basic procedures of internal audit; the need for financial controls and the purpose of audit checks and audit trails.	2	• Financial controls, audit checks and audit trails. • The role of internal audit in providing a service to management.
	e. Explain the role of internal audit in non-financial monitoring and control activities.	2	• How internal audit plays an important and value added service throughout the corporation both in financial and non-financial processes.
	f. Illustrate the added value internal audit provides to both the board and management of the corporation.	2	

Lead	Component	Level	Indicative syllabus content
4. explain the nature of errors and frauds.	a. Explain the nature of errors.	2	• Errors including those of principle, omission, and commission.
	b. Explain the nature of fraud.	2	• Types of fraud.
	c. Describe the different methods of fraud prevention and detection.	2	• Methods for prevention of fraud including levels of authorisation, documentation and staff organisation.
			• Methods of detection of fraud including spot checks, comparison with external evidence, reconciliations and control accounts.
5. Explain Corporate Social Responsibility (CSR) – a political and corporate perspective.	a. Describe the OECD general policies.	2	• The OECD general policies.
			• The role of international frameworks.
	b. Explain the role of national and international laws and regulations.	2	• The demands of stakeholders, maximising shareholder return and enhancing the supply chain.
	c. Describe conflicting demands of stakeholders.	2	• Issues within the supply chain.
	d. Identify issues with CSR and the supply chain.	2	
6. Explain the role of CSR within company reporting.	a. Describe the guidelines of reporting CSR within annual reports.	2	• Disclosure guidelines and sources of best practice.
	b. Identify synergies and tensions with CSR and brand management.	2	• The link between CSR and a company's brand.

BA4C: General principles of the legal system, contract and employment law (15%)

Learning outcomes

On completion of their studies, students should be able to:

Lead	Component	Level	Indicative syllabus content
1. Explain how the law determines the point at which a contract is formed and the legal status of contractual terms.	a. Identify the essential elements of a valid contract and situations where the law requires the contract to be in a particular form.	2	• The essential elements of a valid contract.
	b. Explain how the law determines whether negotiating parties have reached agreement and the role of consideration in making that agreement enforceable.	2	• The legal status of statements made by negotiating parties. Offers and acceptances and the application of the rules to standard form contracts using modern forms of communication.
	c. Explain when the parties will be regarded as intending the agreement to be legally binding and how an agreement may be avoided because of misrepresentations.	2	• The principles for establishing that the parties intend their agreement to have contractual force and how a contract is affected by a misrepresentation.
	d. Explain how the terms of a contract are established and their status determined.	2	• Incorporation of express and implied terms, conditions and warranties.
	e. Explain the ability of a company to contract.	2	• Corporate capacity to contract.
2. Explain the essential elements of an employment contract and the remedies available following termination of the contract.	a. Explain how the contents of a contract of employment are established.	2	• The express and implied terms of a contract of employment.
	b. Explain what policies and procedures may be present in the workplace.	2	• The rights and duties of employers and employees.
	c. Explain the distinction between unfair and wrongful dismissal and the consequences.	2	• Diversity, discrimination, anti-bribery, gifts, conflicts of interest, whistle-blowing, money laundering, disciplinary, data protection, social media, health and safety.
			• Notice and dismissal, redundancy.
			• Unfair and wrongful dismissal.

BA4D: Company administration (10%)

Learning outcomes

On completion of their studies, students should be able to:

Lead	Component	Level	Indicative syllabus content
1. Explain the nature, legal status and administration of business organisations.	a. Describe the essential characteristics of the different forms of business organisations and the implications of corporate personality.	2	• The essential characteristics of sole traders, partnerships, companies limited by shares and corporate personality.
	b. Explain the differences between public and private companies.	2	• 'Lifting the corporate veil' both at common law and by statute.
	c. Explain the purpose and legal status of the Articles of Association.	2	• The distinction between public and private companies.
	d. Explain the main advantages and disadvantages of carrying on business through the medium of a company limited by shares.	2	• Company registration and the advantages of purchasing a company 'off the shelf'.
			• The purpose and contents of the Articles of Association.
			• The advantages and disadvantages of a company limited by shares.

Information concerning formulae and tables will be provided via the CIMA
website, www.cimaglobal.com.'

Business Ethics

Chapter learning objectives

Upon completion of this chapter you will be able to:

- explain the nature of ethics and its application to society, business and the accountancy profession

- apply the values and attitudes that provide professional accountants with a commitment to act in the public interest and with social responsibility

- explain the need for a framework of laws, regulations and standards in business and their application and why CIMA and IFAC each have ethical codes

- distinguish between detailed rules-based and framework/principles approaches to ethics

- identify the ethical issues significant to organisations and how CIMA partners with strategic bodies to assist its members with ethical tensions/synergies

- describe how personal and organisational policies and values promote behaviour

- explain the need to develop the virtues of reliability, responsibility, timeliness, courtesy and respect

- explain the fundamental ethical principles

- identify concepts of independence, scepticism, accountability and social responsibility

- illustrate the threats and safeguards to the fundamental ethical principles.

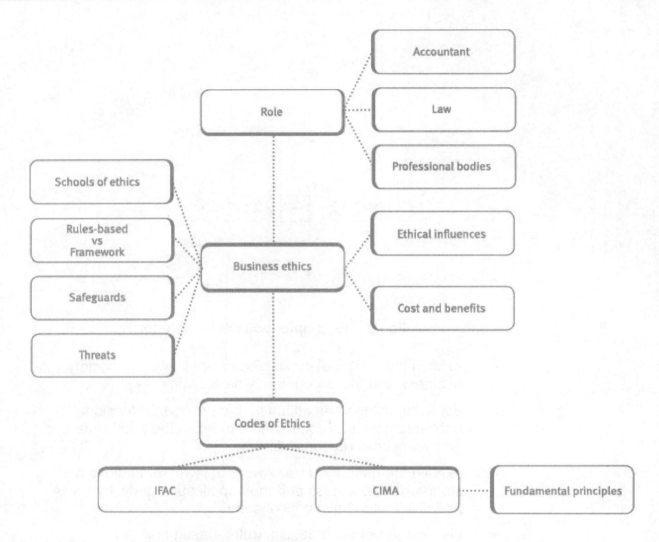

1   Introduction to business ethics

 Definition of Ethics

The Oxford English Dictionary defines ethics as the "moral principles that govern a person's behaviour of the conducting of an activity".

Ethics is thus concerned with how one should act in a certain situation, about 'doing the right thing' and is ultimately about morality – the difference between right and wrong.

Illustration 1

Ethical choices

Consider the following ethical dilemmas:

- You buy something in a shop and later discover that they have undercharged you for an item. Do you go back and tell them?

- You want a new designer label item of clothing but think it is too expensive. Would you buy a cheap fake copy if you saw one for sale while on holiday?

- Would you stop buying a particular product if you found out that the working conditions in the factories where they are made were far below 'acceptable' standards (such as low pay rates, excessive hours worked, use of child labour)?

Does the fact that you are a (student) member of a professional body affect your answers?

Schools of ethics

Virtue ethics, drawing on the work of Aristotle, holds that the virtues (such as justice, charity, and generosity) are dispositions to act in ways that benefit both the person possessing them and that person's society. This is the ethical school of the accountancy profession.

The second, deontological, defended particularly by Kant, makes the concept of duty central to morality: humans are bound, from a knowledge of their duty as rational beings, to obey the categorical imperative to respect other rational beings.

Thirdly, utilitarianism asserts that the guiding principle of conduct should be the greatest happiness or benefit of the greatest number.

2 Business ethics

Business ethics is the application of ethical principles to the problems typically encountered in a business setting.

Whether an action is considered to be right or wrong normally depends on a number of different factors, including:

- the consequences – does the end justify the means?
- the motivation behind the action
- guiding principles – e.g. 'treat others as you would be treated'
- key values – such as the importance of human rights.

Illustration 2

Typical issues in business ethics

Some typical issues addressed in business ethics include:

- 'creative accounting' to misrepresent financial performance
- misleading advertising
- aggressive personal selling (e.g. insurance or double glazing)
- data protection and privacy
- the difference between corporate hospitality and bribery
- the difference between business intelligence and industrial espionage
- political contributions to gain influence
- corporate crime, including insider trading and price fixing
- employee issues, such as discrimination or unfair dismissal
- environmental issues and related social concerns
- marketing, sales and negotiation techniques
- product issues such as patent and copyright infringement, planned obsolescence, product liability and product defects
- using legal loopholes to avoid paying tax.

3 The role of the accountant in promoting ethical behaviour

A management accountant's role is to provide the crucial information that forms the basis of decision-making within an organisation. If work is undertaken badly or in bad faith there can be wide-ranging consequences. Unethical behaviour can affect not only the accountant (perhaps resulting in disciplinary action against the employee or by CIMA), but may also affect the jobs, financial viability and business efficacy of an organisation in which the accountant works. Management accountants in the public sector are also dealing with tax-payers' money which, if poorly stewarded, might be wasted or misused.

At many business meetings, or on many Boards of Directors, it is only the professional accountant who belongs to a profession and therefore has a duty to act in the public interest.

Public interest refers to the common well-being or general welfare of society. Professional accountants must consider this, as they have a wider duty to act in the best interests of the public at large, as well as to the business and its owners.

The professional accountant therefore has a special role in promoting ethical behaviour throughout the business.

4 Ethical influences

Each of us has our own set of values and beliefs that we have evolved over the course of our lives through our education, experiences and upbringing. We all have our own ideas of what is right and what is wrong and these ideas can vary between individuals and cultures.

There are a number of factors that affect ethical obligations.

(i) The law

For example, deceptive advertising is illegal and violators of this law are liable to large fines, court action and/or loss of goodwill. Legislation hopefully makes it very clear what is acceptable as a minimum standard. However, ethics is more than just obeying the law. For example, using legal loopholes to minimise a global firm's tax bill may not be illegal but is increasingly viewed as unethical.

(ii) Government regulations

For example, regulations set standards on issues such as unfair competition, unsafe products, etc. Failure to comply with these regulations could lead to criminal charges, or fines etc. Unfortunately, some firms will still find ways to get round such regulations.

Artificial sweeteners

In 1970 cyclamates (a type of artificial sweetener) were banned in the USA following evidence that they were carcinogenic.

Following the ban a major US food manufacturer still sold 300,000 cases of cyclamate sweetened food overseas instead.

(iii) Ethical codes

Many organisations have codes that clearly state the ethical standards and principles an employee or member should follow.

Generally, written codes clarify the ethical issues and principles but leave the resolution to the individual conscience.

Ethical codes are usually followed if written down and enforced – say by disciplinary procedures. However, many companies have 'unwritten' codes of practice and/or have no method of enforcement.

(iv) Social pressure

Many people draw their values from what they see other people doing, whether on the news or people they know. However, social pressure can change, just as society changes.

Many protest groups and activists hope to change public values with the long term hope that new values become reflected in law. A good example of this is the change in discrimination laws over the last hundred years.

(v)   Corporate culture

Corporate culture is defined as "the sum total of all the beliefs, attitudes, norms and customs that prevail within an organisation" or "the way we do things around here".

Ideally we want a culture that supports and encourages ethical behaviour.

For example, if everyone else is exaggerating expense claims or covering up mistakes, then this can quickly become a norm of behaviour that new employees soon adopt.

Of particular importance is the example set by senior management – sometimes referred to as the 'tone at the top'.

(vi) Personal policies and values

An individual's personal characteristics such as gender, age and religious beliefs can also play a part in their approach to ethics.

5   The costs and benefits of business ethics

It can be argued that the primary purpose of a business is to try and earn a profit. In a company, for instance, the directors have been employed in order to earn the owners of the business a return on their investment.

Some have concluded from this that going beyond the legal minimum standard of behaviour is contrary to the directors' duty to make money and that behaving ethically increases costs and reduces profits.

For example:

- Increased cost of sourcing materials from ethical sources (e.g. Fairtrade products or free range eggs).

- Having to turn away business from customers considered to be unethical (e.g. an 'ethical' bank may choose not to invest in a company that manufactures weapons).

- The management time that can be taken up by planning and implementation of ethical practices.

However, as well as the moral argument to act ethically, there can be commercial benefits to firms from acting ethically:

- Having good ethics can attract customers.

  This can be because good ethics tend to enhance a company's reputation and therefore its brand. Given the choice, many customers will prefer to trade with a company they feel is ethical.

- Good ethics can result in a more effective workforce.

  A reputation for good business ethics is likely to involve good working conditions for employees, allowing the business to attract a higher calibre of staff.

Avoiding discrimination against workers is likely to give the company access to a wider human resource base.

Ethics programmes can cultivate strong teamwork and improve productivity.

- Ethics can give cost savings.

Avoiding pollution will tend to save companies in the long run – many governments are now fining or increasing taxes of more polluting businesses.

- Ethics can reduce risk.

Many firms have failed due to unethical practices within them.

 Approaches to ethics in practice

Imagine you are a company that runs a large chain of supermarkets. You have identified an opportunity to expand into country G. This expansion will create large numbers of local jobs and is expected to earn you significant profits.

Local officials in country G have made it clear that, in order to gain the appropriate planning permissions, you will need to pay them money as inducements (bribes). This is common practice for officials in country G, though it is illegal in your home country. What should you do?

The answer depends on your approach to ethics.

Consequentialists would argue that your decision depends on the consequences of paying the bribes.

If you were **egoist** (looking at your own needs), you would probably pay the bribes as you would still stand to earn a significant profit from the venture.

If you are a **utilitarian** company, you may also consider paying the bribe as doing so will not only mean that you can earn large profits, but will provide jobs for many locals. Paying the bribe will therefore be for the greater good. (However, it is worth noting that whatever the organisation may think about bribery, under UK law it is an illegal act.)

Pluralists would look at ensuring that the needs of none of the stakeholders are seriously compromised by paying the bribe. In this case, while the payment will involve some loss to our shareholders, paying the bribe will still allow us to expand into country G, benefiting everyone.

Relativists would look at the context of the decision to pay the bribe. In this case, bribery is a commonly accepted part of doing business in country G. Therefore, we can be flexible with our approach and may consider paying the bribe.

Absolutists would look at whether paying the bribe was fundamentally incorrect. In this case, bribery is illegal in our home country. An absolutist would therefore be likely to conclude that paying bribes to officials in country G would also be inappropriate, as doing so is always wrong.

6 The role of law in ethics

Legal and disciplinary frameworks do provide an effective means of challenging serious wrong-doing. They can provide deterrents to bad practice, through punishment and censure and remedies for some of the damage that results, for example by means of compensation. However, these means of controlling behaviour set the threshold for what amounts to unacceptable accounting practice at a fairly high level.

Thus, relying solely on the law and disciplinary frameworks to 'police' accounting ethics is not the most desirable way of preventing and detecting undesirable practices. Law by nature can be inflexible, therefore causing difficulty when trying to apply it to cases of ethical misconduct.

7 The role of professional bodies

There are a number of professional bodies, both international and national, that are relevant to the professional accountant's work.

The International Federation of Accountants (IFAC)

The International Federation of Accountants (IFAC) is an international body representing all major accountancy bodies across the world.

The role of the IFAC is to protect the public interest by developing high quality international standards, promoting strong ethical values and encouraging quality practice.

IFAC's International Ethics Standards Board for Accountants (IESBA)

IFAC's International Ethics Standards Board for Accountants (IESBA) is an independent standard-setting board that develops and issues, in the public interest, high-quality ethical standards and other pronouncements for professional accountants worldwide.

Through its activities, the IESBA develops the Code of Ethics for Professional Accountants, which establishes ethical requirements for professional accountants.

The board also provides adoption and implementation support, promotes good ethical practices globally, and fosters international debate on ethical issues faced by accountants.

The Financial Reporting Council (FRC)

The Financial Reporting Council (FRC) is the UK's independent regulator responsible for promoting high quality corporate governance and reporting to foster investment.

The main areas where most accountants experience the work of the FRC are in terms of accounting and auditing standards:

- The Board of the FRC issues UK versions of International Standards on Auditing where appropriate, taking advice from the Audit & Assurance Council (part of the FRC)

- The Board of the FRC also issues UK versions of International Financial Reporting Standards where appropriate, taking advice from the Accounting Council (part of the FRC).

Note: The Accounting Council replaced the Accounting Standards Board.

The Conduct Committee

The Conduct Committee is part of the FRC and provides independent oversight of professional disciplinary issues, together with oversight of the regulation of accountants and actuaries in the UK and Republic of Ireland.

Note: The Conduct Committee replaced the Professional Oversight Board.

 The Conduct Committee

The Conduct Committee's responsibilities include overseeing:

- Monitoring of Recognised Supervisory and Recognised Qualifying bodies

- Audit Quality Reviews

- Corporate Reporting Reviews

- Professional discipline

- Oversight of the regulation of accountants and actuaries.

---

8   Codes of Ethics

Each profession has its own specific code of ethics which form part of the identity of the profession i.e. the medical profession – sanctity of life.

Accountants have the ethical responsibility to be objective, independent in their representation of the accounts. These ethical principles create solidarity of the profession that society accepts within in its universalistic morality. Therefore, to maintain the benefit which accrue from the profession (status and financial benefits) it is the responsibility of the professional to ensure it acts within the ethical principles of the profession and ensuring the Public Interest is paramount within the ethical dimension of decision making both personally and within the organisation the professional is working. However, it is not the role of the individual accountant to work outside the law, therefore, in discerning the correct decision or action to take the rule of law should always take precedence.

Corporate codes of ethics

Most companies (especially if they are large) have approached the concept of business ethics by creating a set of internal policies and instructing employees to follow them. These policies can either be broad generalisations (a corporate ethics statement) or can contain specific rules (a corporate ethics code).

There is no standard list of content – it will vary between different organisations. Typically, however, it may contain guidelines on issues such as honesty, integrity and customer focus.

Many organisations appoint Ethics Officers (also known as Compliance Officers) to monitor the application of the policies and to be available to discuss ethical dilemmas with employees where needed.

The International Federation of Accountants (IFAC)

In June 2005, IFAC published their Code of Ethics for Professional Accountants which was prepared by the International Ethics Standards Board of the International Federation of Accountants. That Committee was charged with developing and issuing **high-quality ethical standards and other pronouncements for professional accountants around the world**. This reflected what has been seen as a growing crisis of confidence in accounting ethics internationally, following financial scandals with global implications. The Code has been revised over the years with the most recent version being issued in 2018.

IFAC is an umbrella organisation for accounting standards worldwide, the Code and its principles are shared by accounting bodies globally.

CIMA

In 2006, the CIMA Code of Ethics for Professional Accountants' was launched. Revised codes were issued in 2010 and 2015. In the revised 2015 Code, Part C was developed in co-operation with the American Institute of Certified Public Accountants (AICPA); and, like Parts A and B, the elements of the updated Part C which apply to CIMA members and students continue to reflect IFAC's fundamental principles and conceptual framework approach.

At the time of going to print CIMA are in consultation over their Code of Ethics and are proposing to publish an updated Code in 2019 to take effect from 1 January 2020. The purpose of the update is reflect the new structure, format and content adopted in the 2018 IFAC Code. Please refer to the CIMA website for progress on the updated Co

The CIMA Code reflects the standards CIMA expects of its members and students. It is aligned with global standards across the profession.

The CIMA Code reflects its status as a Chartered Institute and as a basis for any complaints or cases under CIMA's disciplinary procedures.

The CIMA Code of Ethics aims to:

(i)   identify the nature of the personal responsibility that the management accountant takes on as part of the price for getting a reasonable salary and status

(ii)   provide guidance on how to identify the practical situations where particular care might need to be taken because of the ethical pitfalls involved

(iii)   provide general guidance on how to address those difficult questions.

The CIMA Code itself is split into three parts with a list of definitions at the end:

Part A – General Application of the Code

This covers an introduction and the fundamental principles of integrity, objectivity, professional competence and due care, confidentiality and professional behaviour.

Part B – Professional Accountants in Public Practice

This covers particular issues identified as being of relevance to accountants in public practice such as professional appointment, conflicts of interest, second opinions, fees and other types of remuneration, marketing professional services, gifts and hospitality, custody of client assets, objectivity in all services and independence in assurance engagements.

Part C – Professional Accountants in Business

This covers issues such as potential conflicts, preparation and reporting of information, acting with sufficient expertise, financial interests and inducements.

The Code establishes ethical requirements for professional accountants and applies to all member firms or bodies of IFAC. Any such firm or **body may not apply less stringent standards than those stated in this Code**.

There is an override, should any firm or body be prohibited by law or regulation in complying with any parts of the Code. The expectation is that all parts of IFAC Code will be complied with otherwise. Professional accountants need to familiarise themselves with any differences if there are any, but to comply with the more stringent requirements and guidance unless prohibited.

Fundamental principles

CIMA's code lists five fundamental principles with which its members are expected to comply.

The fundamental principles are presented in Section 100.5.

Fundamental principles

100.5 A professional accountant shall comply with the following fundamental principles:

1   **Integrity** – to be straightforward and honest in all professional and business relationships.

2   **Objectivity** – to not allow bias, conflict of interest or undue influence of others to override professional or business judgments.

3   **Professional Competence and Due Care** – to maintain professional knowledge and skill at the level required to ensure that a client or employer receives competent professional services based on current developments in practice, legislation and techniques and act diligently and in accordance with applicable technical and professional standards.

4   **Confidentiality** – to respect the confidentiality of information acquired as a result of professional and business relationships and, therefore, not disclose any such information to third parties without proper and specific authority, unless there is a legal or professional right or duty to disclose, nor use the information for the personal advantage of the professional accountant or third parties.

5   **Professional Behaviour** – to comply with relevant laws and regulations and avoid any action that discredits the profession.

By 'fundamental' it is meant that these form the very foundations of reasoning and professional practice. The accountant should therefore not only know them, but use them as tools of reasoning and decision-making when judging their own work and that of fellow-professionals. Alongside checking the technical competence of a piece of work, the management accountant should ask, for example 'am I being objective and impartial in the way I am presenting these figures?'

Because they are fundamental, they merit further, deeper explanation, which you will find later on in this chapter. However, to sum up: CIMA has produced a Code of Ethics that states the fundamental values that accountants should work by, and a framework by which they can put these into practice in challenging practical situations, where there may be more than one course of action which may have undesirable consequences. For the time being, we need to understand the different tools available for regulating ethical behaviour.

9 Fundamental principles

CIMA's code lists five fundamental principles with which its members are expected to comply.

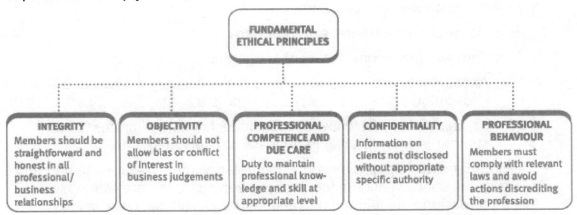

By 'fundamental' it is meant that these form the very foundations of reasoning and professional practice. The accountant should therefore not only know them, but use them as tools of reasoning and decision-making when judging their own work and that of fellow-professionals. Alongside checking the technical competence of a piece of work, the management accountant should ask, for example 'am I being objective and impartial in the way I am presenting these figures?'

More on fundamentals ethical principles

Integrity

Integrity implies fair dealing and truthfulness.

Members are also required not to be associated with any form of communication or report where the information is considered to be:

- materially false or to contain misleading statements

- provided recklessly

- incomplete such that the report or communication becomes misleading by this omission.

Objectivity

Accountants need to ensure that their business/professional judgement is not compromised because of bias or conflict of interest.

However, there are many situations where objectivity can be compromised, so a full list cannot be provided. Accountants are warned to always ensure that their objectivity is intact in any business/professional relationship.

Professional competence and due care

There are two main considerations under this heading:

1   Accountants are required to have the necessary professional knowledge and skill to carry out work for clients.

2   Accountants must follow applicable technical and professional standards when providing professional services.

Appropriate levels of professional competence must first be attained and then maintained. Maintenance implies keeping up to date with business and professional developments, and in many institutes completion of an annual return confirming that continuing professional development (CPD) requirements have been met.

Where provision of a professional service has inherent limitations (e.g. reliance on client information) then the client must be made aware of this.

Confidentiality

The principle of confidentiality implies two key considerations for accountants:

1   Information obtained in a business relationship is not disclosed outside the firm unless there is a proper and specific authority or unless there is a professional right or duty to disclose.

2   Confidential information acquired during the provision of professional services is not used to personal advantage.

The need to maintain confidentiality is normally extended to cover the accountant's social environment, information about prospective clients and employers and also where business relationships have terminated. Basically there must always be a reason for disclosure before confidential information is provided to a third party.

The main reasons for disclosure are when it is:

1   permitted by law and authorised by the client

2   required by law, e.g. during legal proceedings or disclosing information regarding infringements of law

3   there is professional duty or right to disclose (when not barred by law), e.g. provision of information to the professional institute or compliance with ethical requirements.

Professional behaviour

Accountants must comply with all relevant laws and regulations.

There is also a test whereby actions suggested by a third party which would bring discredit to the profession should also be avoided.

An accountant is required to treat all people contacted in a professional capacity with courtesy and consideration. Similarly, any marketing activities should not bring the profession into disrepute.

10   Threats and safeguards

Conceptual framework approach

- The circumstances in which management accountants operate may give rise to specific threats to compliance with the fundamental principles.

- It is impossible to define every situation that creates such threats and specify the appropriate mitigating action.

- A conceptual framework that requires a management accountant to identify, evaluate and address threats to compliance with the fundamental principles, rather than merely comply with a set of specific rules which may be arbitrary, is, therefore, in the public interest.

Threats

To apply the fundamental principles of the code (integrity, objectivity, professional competence and due care, confidentiality, and professional behaviour), you first need to be able to identify and evaluate existing or potential threats to them. If a threat exists that is anything other than trivial, you will need to take action to remove the threat or reduce it to an acceptable level.

Although it is impossible to define all the situations that could create a threat to the fundamental principles, the code does identify five categories of common threat:

- **Self-interest threats** can occur as a result of your own or your close family's interests – financial or otherwise. These threats often result in what is commonly called a 'conflict of interest' situation. Working in business, a self-interest threat could result from concern over job security, or from incentive remuneration arrangements. For those in practice it might be the possibility of losing a client or holding a financial interest in a client.

- **Self-review threats** occur when you are required to re-evaluate your own previous judgement, for example if you have been asked to review and justify a business decision you made, or if you are reporting on the operation of financial systems that you were involved in designing or implementing.

- **Familiarity threats** can be present when you become so sympathetic to the interests of others as a result of a close relationship that your professional judgement becomes compromised. Sometimes this can result from long association with business contacts who influence business decisions, long association with colleagues, or from accepting gifts or preferential treatment from a client.

- **Intimidation threats** occur when you are deterred from acting objectively by actual or perceived threats. It could be the threat of dismissal over a disagreement about applying an accounting principle or reporting financial information, or it could be a dominant personality attempting to influence the decision making process.

- **Advocacy threats** can be a problem when you are promoting a position or opinion to the point that your subsequent objectivity is compromised. It could include acting as an advocate on behalf of an assurance client in litigation or disputes with third parties. In general, promoting the legitimate goals of your employer does not create an advocacy threat, provided that any statements you make are not misleading.

Safeguards

So what should you do if there is a threat (or potential threat), to the principles of the code?

CIMA's code of ethics has a 'threats and safeguards' approach to resolving ethical issues. This means that if you are in a situation where there might be a threat to any of the code's fundamental principles you should first assess whether the threat is significant. If it is, you should to take action to remove or mitigate it.

The CIMA code does not describe all the safeguards that could be implemented, but instead gives general guidance for handling ethical issues, both for accountants working in business and for those in practice.

Safeguards created by the profession, legislation or regulation include, but are not restricted to:

- educational, training and experience requirements for entry into the profession
- continuing professional development requirements
- corporate governance regulations
- professional standards
- professional or regulatory monitoring and disciplinary procedures
- external review of the reports, returns, communications or information produced by a member and carried out by a legally empowered third party.

Safeguards in the work environment include, but are not restricted to:

- the employing organisation's systems of corporate oversight or other oversight structures
- the employing organisation's ethics and conduct programmes
- recruitment procedures in the employing organisation emphasising the importance of employing high calibre competent staff
- the employing organisation's grievance procedures
- strong internal controls
- appropriate disciplinary processes
- leadership that stresses the importance of ethical behaviour and the expectation that employees will act in an ethical manner
- policies and procedures to implement and monitor the quality of employee performance
- timely communication of the employing organisation's policies and procedures, including any changes to them, to all employees and appropriate training and education on such policies and procedures

- policies and procedures to empower and encourage employees to communicate to senior levels within the employing organisation any ethical issues that concern them without fear of retribution

- consultation with another appropriate professional. The nature of the safeguards to be applied will vary depending on the circumstances. In exercising professional judgement, a member should consider what a reasonable and informed third party, having knowledge of all relevant information, including the significance of the threat and the safeguards applied, would conclude to be unacceptable.

 Ethical threats and safeguards

Ethical threat	Safeguard
Conflict between requirements of the employer and the fundamental principles For example, acting contrary to laws or regulations or against professional or technical standards.	• Obtaining advice from the employer, professional organisation or professional advisor • The employer providing a formal dispute resolution process • Legal advice
Preparation and reporting on information Accountants need to prepare/report on information fairly, objectively and honestly. However, the accountant may be pressurised to provide misleading information.	• Consultation with superiors in the employing company • Consultation with those charged with governance • Consultation with the relevant professional body
Having sufficient expertise Accountants need to be honest in stating their level of expertise – and not mislead employers by implying they have more expertise than they actually possess. Threats that may result in lack of expertise include time pressure to carry out duties, being provided with inadequate information or having insufficient experience.	• Obtaining additional advice/training • Negotiating more time for duties • Obtaining assistance from someone with relevant expertise

Financial interests Situations where an accountant or close family member has financial interests in the employing company. Examples include the accountant being paid a bonus based on the financial statement results which he is preparing, or holding share options in the company.	• Remuneration being determined by other members of management • Disclosure of relevant interests to those charged with governance • Consultation with superiors or relevant professional body
Inducements – receiving offers Refers to incentives being offered to encourage unethical behaviour. Inducements may include gifts, hospitality, preferential treatment or inappropriate appeals to loyalty. Objectivity and/or confidentiality may be threatened by such inducements.	• Do not accept the inducement! • Inform relevant third parties such as senior management and professional association (normally after taking legal advice)
Inducements – giving offers Refers to accountants being pressurised to provide inducements to junior members of staff to influence a decision or obtain confidential information.	• Do not offer the inducement! If necessary, follow the conflict resolution process outlined in the next section
Confidential information Accountants should keep information about their employing company confidential unless there is a right or obligation to disclose, or they have received authorisation from the client. However, the accountant may be under pressure to disclose this information as a result of compliance with legal processes such as anti-money laundering/terrorism – in this situation there is a conflict between confidentiality and the need for disclosure.	• Disclose information in compliance with relevant statutory requirements, e.g. money laundering regulations

Whistleblowing	Follow the disclosure provisions of the employer. Otherwise disclosure should be based on assessment of: legal obligations, whether members of the public will be adversely affected, gravity of the matter, likelihood of repetition, reliability of the information, reasons why employer does not want to disclose
Situations where the accountant needs to consider disclosing information, where ethical rules have been broken by the client.	

11 Rules-based and framework approaches to ethics

There are two different approaches to formulating a code of ethics:

- a rules-based approach
- a framework approach.

Rules-based ethics

A rules-based approach to ethics is sometimes referred to as a compliance approach. It explicitly sets out what individuals can and cannot do, and specifies the sanctions that will be imposed for non-compliance.

A rules-based approach works because it instils a sense of fear. Individuals comply because they are required to and because they fear the consequences. However, the main disadvantage of this approach is the fact that the rules cannot cover every particular situation and rules may become out of date as circumstances change.

Rules based approach

Rules tend to be characterised by three things:

1. In theory, you are either inside a rule (compliant) or have broken it. This sometimes provides a harsh divide which is often more about the precise interpretation of the rule than the human activity it regulates.

2. Because of these attempts to make sharp distinctions in rules (so people know where the boundaries of self-preservation lie), there is always argument about the precise meaning of rules.

3. Rules require enforcement by an objective party to decide on things like interpretation and to ensure that breach of the rule has a consequence.

These factors make rules expensive, the source of contention and inflexible. Moreover, in ethics, rules seldom are capable of encompassing the rather difficult questions about behaviour that are involved, without becoming incredibly complicated. The Code-based approach blends the mandatory requirement to take account of the Code with a principles or values-based approach.

Framework approach

A framework approach to ethics provides a set of principles to help individuals arrive at the correct decision. It attempts to instil the idea of the 'correct' thing to do.

Its main advantage is that it can be applied more easily to new developments in business practice or to unique cases. However, its disadvantage is that it is left to the member to decide how best to deal with an ethical question within the framework laid down.

It is also much more difficult to monitor compliance than in a rules-based approach.

Framework approach

There has been a change in public and private attitudes to the performance of duties over the last five years that has moved against the idea of just doing what you can get away with towards continually striving to do the right thing. It is mirrored in the changes in management accounting trends from variance accounting, through activity-based to lean accounting. In management, it is reflected in the idea of performance management, rather than the management of labour. In public life, it is reflected in the change from a culture of trust and deference to those with authority, to a requirement for standards in public life and accountability.

The management accountant finds him or herself pushed by all three strands. Trends in management accounting look towards a more transparent approach to representing the life cycle of accounts. As an employee, the accountant is not there just to do a job and go home, but to do it well and continually improve. Ultimately, whether or not the accountant is employed in the public sector, the role of the accountant is to perform a public function in providing the truthful and independent account of finances that will be the basis of judgements by owners, shareholders, regulators, the government and so on.

The Seven Principles of Public Life

The publicly employed accountant is explicitly subject to the 'The Seven Principles of Public Life' issued by the Committee of Standards in Public Life, which arose out of the perceived crisis in public ethics of the 1990s in the United Kingdom. The Committee of Standards in Public Life is a body that was set up by the UK Government. The principles are reflected to a great extent in the professional standards for all accountants.

Selflessness

Holders of public office should act solely in terms of the public interest. They should not do so in order to gain financial or other benefits for themselves, their family or their friends.

Integrity

Holders of public office should not place themselves under any financial or other obligation to outside individuals or organisations that might seek to influence them in the performance of their official duties.

Objectivity

In carrying out public business, including making public appointments, awarding contracts, or recommending individuals for rewards and benefits, holders of public office should make choices on merit.

Accountability

Holders of public office are accountable for their decisions and actions to the public and must submit themselves to whatever scrutiny is appropriate to their office.

Openness

Holders of public office should be as open as possible about all the decisions and actions that they take. They should give reasons for their decisions and restrict information only when the wider public interest clearly demands.

Honesty

Holders of public office have a duty to declare any private interests relating to their public duties and to take steps to resolve any conflicts arising in a way that protects the public interest.

Leadership

Holders of public office should promote and support these principles by leadership and example.

Given the trends towards less trust and more desire for accountability, it is therefore of little surprise that management accountants are now expected to do more than merely follow the rules.

12 Contrasting compliance driven and principles based codes

The following table, contrasting the characteristics of a compliance-driven framework versus one primarily driven by values, principles and ethics.

Feature	Ethics	Compliance (Rules)
Objective	Prevention	Detection
Approach	Principles	Law based
Motivation	Values driven	Fear driven
Standards	Implicit	Explicit
Measure	Principles (values)	Rules
Choices	Judgement	Obedience/disobedience
Enforceability	Discretionary	Mandatory

An example of applying the different approaches above would be a company which has a strong rules-based culture, where individuals clearly have a sense of what they can and cannot do (letter of the law, black and white, mandatory, explicit) and what will happen if they do not (fear-driven, requires obedience, mandatory). However, if an employee is faced with a situation not covered by the 'rule book' they will be required to use their own judgement as to what to do. In most instances, the decision they take will be the right one but any potential for the wrong decision being made will be reduced if the employee has guiding values and principles which will underpin that difficult decision-making. So, an ethical framework of guidance is likely to be more wide-ranging in its applicability than a fully rules-based one.

A key aspect of compliance is measurement in addition to 'ticking boxes' that all is well. This, of course, is difficult with ethical issues which tend not to be conveniently black and white. There is therefore a need to develop and use proxy indicators by those assuring themselves that individuals are acting in a proper fashion.

In a wider context, the same is true in the public and private sectors, where organisations equally, as though they were individuals, seek to build trust with their employees, customers, suppliers, shareholders and all others who have a legitimate interest in how they perform.

But the essential question remains: Is trust better engendered by principled behaviour based on 'doing it because it is the right thing to do' or because the individual, the company or the public body has to?

13 Personal development and life-long learning

Every professional person has a duty in maintaining their role of acting in public interest by keeping themselves up to date professionally, that is technically as well developing their competencies to be better informed. It is also essential in a dynamic area of practice, where failure to keep oneself aware of developments may fundamentally undermine basic professional competence and leave the accountant open to accusations of negligence.

This has grown in importance as the pace of change develops and the role of the professional accountant grows more complex. It is now regarded as one of the fundamental principles in the CIMA 'Code of Ethics' (see Appendix for the complete code), where the professional accountant has the duty to maintain professional knowledge and skill at the level required to ensure that a client or employer receives competent professional service based on current developments in practice, legislation and techniques.

The concept of competent professional service is thus based not only on attaining professional competence but also in maintaining it. This requires a continuing awareness of up-to-date developments in the profession. This can be met through continuing professional development. CIMA has developed the CIMA Professional Development framework which addresses both the requirements on members and the institute regarding CPD, and the ways in which CIMA is supporting members in their professional development.

Personal qualities

Members of the profession need, or need to develop, certain qualities and virtues in order to meet the expectations of CIMA and the public, served in the wider context. In upholding the highest standards of ethical behaviour, members are contributing to the promotion of the integrity of CIMA's qualification and supporting CIMA's purpose.

The underlying reason has been explained earlier, in the context of 'virtue ethics'. The professional attitude being encouraged provides the ethical compass and personal motivation to act in accordance with the values of the profession and to make ethically sound decisions in everyday practice.

The particular qualities and virtues sought are reliability, responsibility, timeliness, courtesy and respect. These are taken from 'Approaches to the Development and Maintenance of Professional Values, Ethics and Attitudes in Accounting Education Programs,' published by the International Accounting Education Standards Board.

Reliability

This is the concept of being able to be trusted by others and to be dependable through the ability to deliver what and when it has been agreed with another. It is linked to the idea of providing a consistent approach to work, both in quality and in dependability. It is fairly clear that an unreliable accountant would almost certainly also be falling short of other basic standards of professional competence.

Responsibility

This is the concept of being accountable for one's actions and decisions. This also entails an individual's assumption of authority for making decisions. A responsible accountant addresses the decision-making processes that he needs to engage with and is willing and able to personally answer for those decisions. A management accountant is in a position of responsibility because he is being employed for his expertise in making professional judgements and will need to be able to explain and answer for their exercise to colleagues who may or may not share that expertise.

Timeliness

This is the concept of delivering in a timely manner without delay and meeting the expectations of others. The practical implications of poor timekeeping are self-evident, however there is a further reflection of the ethics of diligence in addressing tasks and responsibility in prioritising and managing work.

Courtesy

This is the virtue of demonstrating politeness and good manners towards others. While respect for clients and others is regarded as appropriate and professional, the increasing seriousness with which unacceptable forms of address (racist, sexist, homophobic and the like) are being tackled by law mean that it underpins a more fundamental set of societal values.

Respect

This is the virtue demonstrating an attitude of esteem, deference, regard or admiration of others in dealing with them, especially where their attitudes might differ. It is not to be mistaken for undue deference, merely that the accountant should listen to others, take account of their views and ideas, and if for no other reason than these may provide a broader base for making informed judgements.

Like a number of these qualities, it is easy to see reasons why respect might be practically useful and help avoid problems that might lead to sanction or censure, but the utility of respecting people is not the reason why you should respect them; it is not simply a case of respecting those who you think might have something useful to say, like each of these qualities they are aspects of professionalism to be cultivated for their own sake.

14 Independence

It is in the public interest, and required in CIMA's Code of Ethics that members of assurance engagement teams and their firms (and when applicable extended network firms too) be independent of the assurance clients. An audit should be performed with an attitude of professional scepticism which includes a questioning mind and being alert to conditions which may indicate fraud or error.

There are two key attributes to independence used in connection with the assurance engagement:

1   Of mind

It is required that the professional accountant has a state of mind that permits a conclusion to be expressed without being affected by influences that would compromise their professional judgement.

This allows the individual to act with integrity and exercise objectivity and professional scepticism. Bias is an insidious thing, and sometimes we are not fully aware of the influencing factors on our mind. Second opinions of close judgement calls can often help, but the accountant is ultimately responsible for his or her decisions. Keeping a clear, professional attitude and focusing on objective information, rather than over-relying on intuitions is a useful means of maintaining some independence of mind.

2   In appearance

This is a test reliant on the view that a reasonable and informed third party would conclude that a member of the assurance team's integrity, objectivity or professional scepticism was compromised if significant facts and circumstances were avoided or overlooked. The accountant often exercises judgements that have impacts on people's jobs, pay and progression. It is therefore of paramount importance that the exercise of professional judgement not only be just, but manifestly and undoubtedly be seen to be so.

It is impossible to define all situations where independence might be compromised, so it is in the public interest to prepare a conceptual framework requiring firms and member of assurance teams to identify, evaluate and address threats to independence. This can be based on identifying relationships between all the parties. For any threats so identified, safeguards can be introduced to eliminate or significantly reduce them to an acceptable level.

15 Accountability, social responsibility and professional scepticism

Accountability

The concept of accountability is that of the professional accountant being responsible to someone and for something or an action, and being able to explain those actions. It is an important aspect of the profession and of leadership in the wider business environment.

It is acknowledged that the professional accountant through CIMA, as a Chartered Institute, is accountable to the public in performing a public interest duty. That accountability is monitored by the FRC in the United Kingdom through the Conduct Committee and the Accounting Council.

Accountability is also to every client and employer too for whom the professional accountant is providing services. If that accountability fails then the client or employer can seek redress through complaint or disciplinary procedures.

Social responsibility

The professional accountant has a wider role in fulfilling their public duty, which is to be aware of their social or corporate responsibility. This is their role within the community, be it defined as their profession, their firm or place of work, where their place of work or home is located or howsoever the individual cares to define community.

Corporate Social Responsibility (CSR) is the outward manifestation of an ethical policy. CSR policies state the nature of the interaction between the company and its stakeholder base, employees, customers, suppliers and so forth (covered in more detail in Chapter 5). These CR policies need to be factored into risk management, which the better companies will report on in their reporting, internally and externally.

Typically, this is in relation to stakeholders listed as shareholders, employees, customers, suppliers and the wider community, to whom the company pays taxes and with whom it has a relationship as part of society. In upholding the principles of CIMA's 'Code of Ethics', the individual has a social responsibility to behave with integrity, courtesy, respect and with due care.

Professional scepticism

The application of an appropriate degree of professional scepticism is an essential skill for accountants, especially for those working in assurance and audit. Professional scepticism is an attitude of mind that ensures auditors are prepared to challenge management's assertions, and be alert to possible misstatements in the financial statements due to error or fraud. Auditors initially approach an audit without a strong belief that either the financial information is misstated or that management are other than honest and truthful. But if an auditor obtains information suggesting that the financial information could be misstated, they will step up their enquiries and look for more audit evidence to resolve issues, especially if they are concerned about the accuracy of the evidence or the integrity of those providing it.

A sceptical mind-set will be influenced by an individual's personality, their experience, their education and training, and by the culture of the firm where they work. It is through professional development and experience that an auditor learns the 'right' level of scepticism to be applied in different circumstances.

Professional accountants must recognise that scepticism is an integral part of their work and is closely interrelated to the fundamental concepts of independence and objectivity. Ethical Standards address the issue of auditors placing too much trust in their clients through requirements such as rotation of audit firms and partners and staff, and the prohibition of certain non-audit services, but ultimately it is the responsibility of individuals to perform their work with an appropriate degree of scepticism and challenge.

16   Ethical conflict: confidentiality

The following are circumstances where professional accountants are or may be required to disclose confidential information or when such disclosure may be appropriate:

(a)   **Disclosure is permitted by law and is authorised by the client or the employer:**

An example of this might be personal data. Personal data held by an accountant (for example, bank details of an individual) is covered by data protection legislation. This gives rise to particular responsibility on the accountant to maintain that data accurately and not to disclose it, except for the purposes it was disclosed. There are, however, some exceptions. One important one is that the person to whom that data pertains may have been given an authorisation for disclosure to third parties for marketing purposes. This would still need authorisation by the employer, but falls within the category of permissible disclosure.

(b) **Disclosure is required by law, for example:**

   (i)   Production of documents or other provision of evidence in the course of legal proceedings – numerous pieces of legislation allow investigative bodies, ranging from the national taxation authorities through to the police, the power to gain access to documents in the process of investigation. Strictly speaking, such access is limited to circumstances where the investigating agency has specific authorisation by a court, normally in the form of a warrant. In such circumstances, there is a duty to disclose that overrides any others.

   (ii)   Disclosure to the appropriate public authorities of infringements of the law that come to light – accountants are under some professional and ethical responsibility to disclose information which they believe tend to show illegal activity. This is a problematic area because such disclosures frequently run in the face of what an employer considers to be a duty of trust and confidence. A misplaced belief that an employer is doing wrong, which leads to an unauthorised disclosure will often end up as an acrimonious employment dispute.

Public interest disclosure legislation in the United Kingdom provides a means by which these two issues can be balanced. The accountant should first draw their manager's attention to the wrongdoing, or if it is inappropriate in the circumstances, a senior manager's attention may be drawn to it. If there is no adequate response or there is serious malfeasance which the accountant believes may be 'covered up', they may alert a professional body or an agency such as the police. Going to press is a risky and inadvisable course of action and carries with it few of the protections that are offered to those disclosing to professional bodies. In such circumstances, it is advisable to contact CIMA's Ethics Helpline. Members and students of CIMA can contact the Ethics Helpline for advice on whether and how to make a public interest disclosure. CIMA's Ethics Helpline can help any member or student facing an ethical conflict.

(c) **There is a professional duty or right to disclose, when not prohibited by law:**

   (i)   To comply with the quality review of a member body or professional body

   (ii)   To respond to an inquiry or investigation by a member body or regulatory body

   (iii)   To protect the professional interests of a professional accountant in legal proceedings; or

   (iv)   To comply with technical standards and ethics requirements.

All these examples in (c), above, relate to the regulation and disciplinary functions of CIMA and the profession more generally. It is important that disclosures are not only those necessary for the achievement of purpose of the inquiry but that they also cover all relevant aspects of the subject matter being inquired into. Partial disclosure is tantamount to deception and may give rise to disciplinary or legal penalties or consequences.

Disclosure is generally a question of professional discretion, as much as the application of rules. In identifying whether confidential information can be disclosed, it is necessary to consider whether any parties would be harmed by such disclosure, whether all relevant information is known and substantiated, and the type of disclosure and to whom it is to be made.

17 CGMA Report on Managing Responsible Business

Two of the world's most prestigious accounting bodies, AICPA and CIMA, have formed a joint venture to establish the Chartered Global Management Accountant (CGMA®) designation to elevate and build recognition of the profession of management accounting. This international designation recognises the most talented and committed management accountants with the discipline and skill to drive strong business performance. CGMA designation holders are either CPAs with qualifying management accounting experience or associate or fellow members of the Chartered Institute of Management Accountants.

Definitions (as used in the survey by CGMA)

Responsible business:

- is about an organisation's commitment to operating in a way that is economically, socially and environmentally sustainable

- means ensuring this commitment prevails while still upholding the interests of various stakeholder groups.

Business ethics:

- is the application of values such as integrity, fairness, respect and openness to organisational behaviour

- apply to all strategic and operational aspects of business conduct, including sales and marketing techniques, accounting practices and the treatment of suppliers, employees and customers

- may also be termed "business principles", and are usually set out in a code of ethics or similar policy document.

Ethical performance

- is the extent to which an organisation's behaviour aligns with its stated ethical values and commitments.

Ethical management information

- allows an assessment of the organisation's ethical performance, such as the efficacy of relevant policies and procedures, occurrence of breaches of relevant policies or codes, stakeholder opinion and other metrics

- may include specific ethics information, such as the number of employees attending ethics training or calls to an ethics helpline, as well as routine management and risk information

- will often originate from multiple sources within the business, and can be either quantitative or qualitative.

Integrated reporting

- describes an approach to corporate reporting. It is based on both financial and nonfinancial information that demonstrates the linkages between an organisation's strategy, governance and financial performance as well as the social, environmental and economic context within which it operates.

Ethical issues within organisations

- Security of information

- Safety and security in the workplace

- Discrimination

- Conflicts of interest

- Bribery

- Environmental

- Supply chain

- Responsible marketing

- Human rights

- Whistleblowing

- Fairness of remuneration.

18   Embedding ethical values: A guide for CIMA partners

CIMA and the Institute of Business Ethics have jointly produced two new guidance documents, the first of which is 'Embedding ethical values – a guide for CIMA partners'. The purpose of this guide is twofold: for organisations that don't yet have an ethical policy or equivalent, it provides the right resources and support to draw up a code or policy document. For organisations that already have a code in place, this guide directs to resources which helps address what else can be done to embed ethical values and make the code effective.

Below are extracts from the guide.

How does a company start to ensure that business behaviour reflects ethical values?

If an organisation wants to take ethics seriously, it first needs to identify the core values to which it is committed and wishes to be held accountable.

Core ethical values are those regarded by a company as non-negotiable – they form the foundation for a set of corporate ethical standards and commitments and the organisation's approach to corporate responsibility.

Commonly used value words found in introductions/preambles to codes of ethics include: responsibility, integrity, honesty, respect, trust, openness, fairness and transparency. Organisations may also articulate a set of business values, such as quality, profitability, efficiency, reliability and customer service.

Why produce a code?

Codes of ethics are critical to preventing misconduct and should not be developed merely as a reaction to a reputation crisis. They provide guidance for all employees on what is expected of them and how to act responsibly in different circumstances. Critically codes should be live documents that are referred to regularly by management to promote and support an ethical culture.

Is having a code enough?

Simply drawing up and publishing a code is never enough to influence behaviour and decision-making. Ethical values must be strongly embedded in an organisation's culture. To be effective the code should be supported by a programme of communication and training as well as leadership example. Ethical commitments need to be reflected through core business activities and policies and processes e.g. recruitment, appraisal, tendering, marketing, speak up etc. The organisation also needs to establish a monitoring programme which will assure its governing body that it is living up to its values.

Board agrees that a statement of corporate values and code of ethics is required

Board asks a senior manager to develop the statement of values and corporate code of ethics

| Senior manager consults with board members and employees at all levels about core values | Consults other business/experts on best practice | Consults with employees and other stakeholders to find out what ethical challenges and issues are material | Collates existing company policies on ethical issues | Works out an implementation programme |

Senior manager produces first draft of values statement and corporate code of ethics and implementation programme

| Circulates for comment to senior management | Has comparisons made with other company statements and codes | Organises cross company and all level 'focus' groups to comment on the draft | Considers standardising against an outside benchmark |

Final (draft) version goes to the board

When approved, a programme of familiarisation and integration is set in motion

| Ethical issues incorporated into all company training programmes | Regular reports to the board on how the code is working | Annual reporting process is put in place and a committee of the board is given overall oversight of the policy |

Based on Developing a Code of Business Ethics guide, p16, IBE, 2003

Ethical Values

| Code of Ethics | Communication and Awareness Campaigns | Training and Reinforcement | Supporting Context and Culture | Monitoring and Accountability |

Embed values ⟶ influence behaviour

Good practice:

- Root the code in core values e.g. trust, integrity
- Give a copy to all staff
- Provide a way to report breaches in a confidential manner
- Include ethical issues in corporate training programmes
- Set up a board committee to monitor the effectiveness of the code
- Report on the code's use in the annual report
- Make conformity to the code part of a contract of employment
- Make the code available in the language of those staff located overseas
- Make copies of the code available to business partners, including suppliers
- Make a named individual responsible for code implementation
- Review code in light of changing business challenges
- Make sure senior staff 'walk the talk'.

Poor practice:

- Just pinning the code to the notice board
- Failing to obtain board commitment to the code
- Leaving responsibility for the code's effectiveness to HR or any other department
- Failing to find out concerns of staff at different levels
- Failing to feature the code in induction training and management development activities
- Having no procedure for revising the code regularly
- Making exceptions to the code's application
- Failing to follow up on breaches of the code's standards
- Unhelpful example by corporate leaders
- Neglecting to have a strategy to integrate corporate values and standards into the running of the business
- Treating the code as confidential or a purely internal document
- Making it difficult for staff to have direct access to the code or the person who is responsible for it.

19 Test your understanding questions

Test your understanding 1

Are these statements true or false?

A   Professional accountants are expected to have regard to the public interest in performing their duties

B   Professional accountants are not expected to have regard to the public interest in performing their duties

C   Ethical values describe what an entity does, not how it does business

D   Ethical values describe how entity does its business, not what it does

Test your understanding 2

Are these statements true or false?

A   A rules based approach provides a set of principles

B   A framework approach explicitly sets out what individuals can or cannot do

C   'The Seven Principles of Public Life' govern only professional accountants

D   The CIMA 'Code of Ethics' includes reference to how a professional accountant can raise a concern about unprofessional or unethical behaviour

Test your understanding 3

Are these statements true or false?

A   An ethically based code is based on principles

B   A compliance based code is a rules-based framework

C   A characteristic of a compliance based code is that it takes a tick box approach

D   Compliance with legislation is mandatory

Test your understanding 4

Are these statements true or false?

A   The five qualities and virtues sought by CIMA are reliability, accountability, fairness, responsibility and timeliness

B   The five qualities and virtues sought by CIMA are reliability, responsibility, timeliness, courtesy and respect

C   The professional accountant is not bound by the principles of confidentiality after the end of the relationship with a client or employer

D   The professional accountant is bound by the principles of confidentiality after the end of the relationship with a client or employer

Test your understanding 5

Are these statements true or false?

A   Professional accountants are expected to exercise professional scepticism

B   Professional accountants are not expected to exercise professional scepticism

C   The IFAC code is mandatory for all member firms or bodies of IFAC

D   The IFAC code is a guide for all member firms or bodies of IFAC

Test your understanding 6

Which of the following is incorrect?

A   The IFAC Code of Ethics takes a rules-based approach

B   The CIMA Code of Ethics takes a framework-based approach

C   Company codes of ethics can take a framework-based or a rules-based approach

D   Code of ethics are often based on core values or principles

Test your understanding questions 7–9 are reflective questions and should be discussed or thought over. Answers to these have not been provided.

Test your understanding 7
Consider your work and, separately, everyday life. In what circumstances do you find the following compromised? A   Objectivity B   Courtesy C   Confidentiality D   The Appearance of Independence

Test your understanding 8
In relation to 7, above, consider whether each is because of: A   Something you have done B   Something you have failed to do C   Something you believe in D   Something outside your control

Test your understanding 9
Drawing on the discussions above, consider how and whether application of the ethical principles outlined might help you identify problems, and whether they might help you avoid them if you put them into practice.

Test your understanding answers

Test your understanding 1

A   **True.** Professional accountants, whether practicing in public or private practice have a leadership role and are expected to behave and act in the public interest. This is laid down in the Royal Charter which governs CIMA – *the Chartered Institute of Management Accountants.*

B   **False.**

C   **False.**

D   **True.**

Test your understanding 2

A   **False.** This applies to a framework approach.

B   **False.**

C   **False.** The Seven Principles of Public Life apply to all holders of public office.

D   **True.**

Test your understanding 3

A   **True.**

B   **True.**

C   **False.** A characteristic of compliance is detection.

D   **True.** Compliance with the law is mandatory.

Test your understanding 4

A   **False.**

B   **True.**

C   **False.**

D   **True.**

Test your understanding 5

A	**True.**
B	**False.**
C	**True.**
D	**False.**

Test your understanding 6

A

The CIMA and IFAC Codes both take a framework-based approach.

Test your understanding 7

There is no suggested solution.

Test your understanding 8

There is no suggested solution.

Test your understanding 9

There is no suggested solution.

Ethical Conflict

Chapter learning objectives

Upon completion of this chapter you will be able to:

- explain the relationship between the CIMA Code of Ethics and the law

- describe the consequences of unethical behaviour to the individual, the profession and the society

- identify conflicting perspectives of interest when dealing with stakeholders in society, business and the values of professional accountants

- identify situations where ethical dilemmas and conflicts of interest occur and apply CIMA's ethical check list to ethical dilemmas.

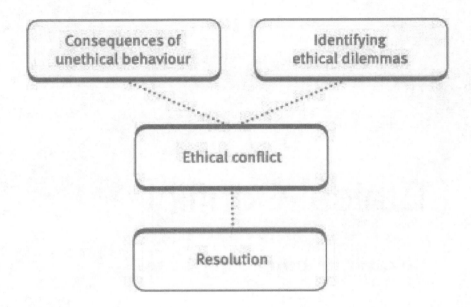

1   The relationship between ethics and the law

Ethical Codes vs Legislation

If the question of ethics is 'what to do for the best?' then the next natural question is 'why should I take responsibility for deciding what to do?' In effect, the key issues for all accountants are the linked questions of who should take responsibility for doing the right things and who picks up the pieces when it all goes wrong.

If there are problems of global or national significance that arise from a systematic failure, which in turn pressurises the individual into facing unpleasant choices, shouldn't the government or the profession step in to deal with the problem? The answer has to be 'yes'. This is why some aspects of professional conduct are regulated not by the profession, but by law.

The corporate and social responsibility agenda means that adherence to the ethics of the professions that support the business and the more general promotion of professionalism in the workplace is of paramount importance in the determination of the culture of organisations.

Laws do not, of themselves, help you out of general ethical problems. For example, you might feel that it is unethical to obey an immoral law. However, such difficulties do not arise in management accounting. If there is a conflict between a professional duty, such as confidentiality, and statute law, the CIMA Code explicitly states that the law is to be preferred. In the hierarchy of obligations, law overrides everything.

Ethical Codes v Contracts

But what about other legal obligations? Surely the contract you sign with your employer is a legal obligation and the contracts with clients have legal effects? Of course this is true. However, voluntarily assumed legal obligations are exactly that. You have made a choice to enter into that obligation. You have a choice not to comply with a contractual obligation and take instead the penalty for breach of that contract. This might be the appropriate course of action when performing the contract would bring you into serious breach of the CIMA Code.

Contractual duty vs professional duty

An example of where you might break with a contractual duty is where your employer instructed you to act in a way that is professionally unacceptable. Another might be where you are directed to follow a corporate policy that was devised to apply to general situations, but which you feel is inappropriate in a particular context because there are special ethical considerations.

From a purely ethical standpoint, if you are confronted by a choice of breach of professional ethics and a breach of your contract of employment, you are ultimately supposed to favour your profession over your employer.

CIMA support

A difficult situation can arise when you are expected to do something which is part of a contract with an outside client. Often, the management accountant has no direct relationship with the client. However, the repercussions of refusing to act in a certain way on your employer's client relationships can be considerable. Often, clients will simply take their business elsewhere, if they feel that your employer will not accommodate them. It may not cause a direct confrontation between you and your employer, but if clients won't work with your employer because of you, there is always the chance that you may feel that it is you who will be the first in line for redundancy!

Often, you will be trying to do the right thing, not for you, but for someone else. Resolving ethical conflict seldom has much more reward to the individual than the feeling that you know you have done the right thing. However, the accountant is not on his or her own. CIMA provides support for individuals faced with ethical conflict situations and the law 'helps' accountants and employers to make the right choice, often by imposing personal liability for the individual who acts unprofessionally or forces another to do so.

2 Consequences of unethical behaviour

The personal consequences of unethical behaviour can be dire, as typically it will entail a loss of reputation. For the individual, a loss of reputation may result in loss of earning potential, job, professional status, position in the community and so forth. For a professional body, a significant loss of reputation, if it were brought into disrepute, would undermine its credibility and, ultimately, potentially its loss of Chartered Institute status. For a corporation, loss of public confidence is likely to result in the failure and dissolution of the organisation.

In the wider context, when such unethical behaviour is identified there is a greater damage, as trust is undermined not only in the people and organisations directly affected but also in similar bodies or institutions on the fear that they also may be targeted or affected by scandal. This is the trust that society bears for its organisations.

Often however, the true economic and human consequences of unethical behaviour are diffuse and hard to pinpoint. Like a lot of 'victimless crimes', the indirect global effects of one person who is discourteous, slow and unreliable might be minimal, but the impact on the profession of a few thousand practitioners who are like that can be considerable, as the legal profession would have to acknowledge.

Volkswagen scandal

In 2015 Volkswagen became embroiled in one of the biggest corporate scandals of recent years.

The German car maker had been installing "defeat devices" – software that allows cars to cheat in emissions tests, making them appear cleaner than they actually are.

Volkswagen admitted to cheating the tests deliberately and revealed that 11 million cars worldwide were fitted with the device. The scandal caused much anger particularly amongst customers of Volkswagen. US customers are likely to receive monetary compensation from the company. The company could potentially face fines of up to $90 billion.

3 Ethical dilemmas and conflicts of interest

Introduction

There is an expectation in wider society that professional accountants have a leadership role in ensuring that companies, institutions, public bodies and all types of organisations where they work will behave ethically in carrying out their activities. Demonstrating such leadership by example can be achieved only if the individual professional concerned is sensitive enough to spot and to tackle ethical dilemmas. Without an 'inner guide' to ethical behaviour an individual may easily trip up.

For instance, a leader who fails to follow company procedures by deciding to appoint a friend to the board of the company is vulnerable to accusations of a conflict of interest if the appointment fails, or if there is a lack of transparency in making the appointment in the first instance. Governance procedures can add rigour to the appointment process, but it should be natural instinct to realise that business cannot be run without a core ethical values.

All individuals need to be able to recognise an ethical dilemma and deal with it appropriately. Pressures challenge personal integrity as well as business skills, which is why ethical acumen is an essential ingredient for a professional accountant.

Identifying ethical dilemmas

In identifying ethical dilemmas, it is important to understand how they arise.

Conflict can arise from any number of sources, however common ones include:

- societal values

- professional values

- personal values

- corporate values.

Individuals will recognise tensions if they are asked to condone the behaviour by their company which they feel to be wrong or inappropriate. If the tension is too great, they will leave the company. Before doing so, however, they may try to speak up, to voice their concerns. An example is where an employee is asked to 'overlook' improprieties carried out by their company, which would be counter to their professional code.

There are also tensions between corporate values and the values of society. If companies or individuals are deemed by society to be behaving or conducting their business inappropriately, then laws will be introduced to enforce minimum levels of behaviour. Such laws are wide ranging in order to cover the wide ranging activities of a business from employment practices to disposal of products in an environmentally friendly way, to banning cartels and unfair competitive activities and fraud, and the prevention of bribery and corruption.

Ethical dilemmas arise in many guises within an organisation – from those related to strategy and policy as faced by those running the organisation to those faced by middle managers or individuals in the course of their work. Dilemmas can occur at all levels.

How to identify an ethical dilemma

Behaving ethically or choosing how one wants to undertake business and achieve business goals is discretionary. Therefore, companies, as represented by the board, may or may not choose to encourage ethical behaviour by their staff.

Dilemmas arise when the boundaries of right and wrong are not clear; when an individual is faced with two options – the choice between making a better choice, or the least wrong. The individual must choose what to do. What makes ethical decisions hard is that they often are such unpalatable choices.

It is clear that what is not an ethical dilemma is when there is a choice between what is good for me and what is prescribed by professional standards. Doing what I want for my own reasons is not a professional choice but a personal preference, and therefore has no place in ethical reasoning.

Personal compromises include when friendships, families, loyalties and affiliations to organisations, political and other belief systems are involved. None of these are relevant to decision-making, except when they so strongly colour your perceptions that they make you incapable of objective judgement or where they so taint the outside perception of you that others think that you lack objectivity.

Dilemmas

Here are some examples of dilemmas which might occur:

- My wife has just got a great job as managing director of a successful business, which also happens to be one of my biggest clients. Does it matter?

- I have taken over a new account from my manager. In re-evaluating their work, I have come across a significant error, which nobody seems to have picked up on. I don't want to jeopardise my relationship with my manager. What should I do?

- I have had a client for many years who has always taken me for dinner after his year end to celebrate and say thank you. This year he says he's done rather well so he's offered to take me golfing for the weekend in St Andrews. Should I accept?

- Our firm has taken out an advert in the local paper to promote our services. However, it says that we are experts in tax and none of the partners have that expertise. I feel uncomfortable, but what can I do?

- Our firm is being taken over and there is talk of redundancies being made. I've been asked to review the accounting policies and see if I could 'make things look more favourable'; it was implied that my job would depend upon it. What should I do?

- I'm tendering for new business, and I bumped into the current accountants at a conference. They said they wouldn't be re-tendering for the business because of 'certain difficulties' with the client, but when pressed said that the information was confidential. What should I do?

In response to each of these instances, the CIMA Code gives guidance on how to avoid conflicts of interest and threats to independence, and how to deal with confidential issues.

Conflicts of interest

Individuals can often find that they face a conflict of interest between their professional and business lives. In such instances, it is important to follow guidelines laid down in the Code of Ethics. Some instances are obvious, others are subtle so the individual needs to be sensitive in spotting them.

Illustration 1: Conflicts of interest

Steve is the Management Accountant at the Head Office of EnviroServices Group. One of his best friends, Dan, works in another part of the group. They've been friends since university, their wives are also great friends and their families have been on holiday together once or twice. Steve and Dan often talk about work when their wives aren't listening, keeping each other abreast of developments in the respective parts of the group, although neither of them puts pressure on the other to divulge any sensitive information.

Restructuring is taking place throughout EnviroServices. Steve is a member of an internal working party mandated to ensure that the internal communications policies and practices of the group fully support the changes that will take place in the course of the restructuring. As a member of the working party, Steve is privy to plans for the restructuring. This is price-sensitive information available only to a few people apart from top management. This includes information about the proposed selling off of one part of the group, which is no longer seen as core business. It is the part of the group where Dan works.

There are bound to be redundancies, especially at Dan's middle manager level. When Steve and Dan had last got together, he'd been talking about moving his house, taking on a substantial new mortgage in the process, in order to be able to send his daughter to a special school for children with learning disabilities.

In this situation Steve may feel that there is a conflict of interest between his friendship with Dan and his role as a member of the internal working party.

Steve must follow the CIMA Code of Ethics in dealing with this conflict of interest.

Conflicts of interest are not wrong in themselves, but they do become a problem when a professional continues to engage in a course of action being, aware of that conflict. When you think you may have a conflict of interest, it is always a sensible idea to declare it. It is normal that an individual will withdraw from a course of dealing when a conflict arises.

Resolving ethical dilemmas/conflicts

The code is clear that the professional accountant should respond to an ethical conflict. Inaction or silence may well be a further breach of the code.

A professional accountant may be called upon to resolve a dilemma in the application of the CIMA Code of Ethics' Fundamental Principles.

CIMA's Ethical Checklist

CIMA is committed to upholding the highest ethical and professional standards and to maintaining public confidence in management accounting. CIMA members and students are required to comply with the CIMA Code of Ethics and to adopt its five fundamental principles to their working lives.

CIMA's Ethical Checklist provides an approach for when dealing with issues.

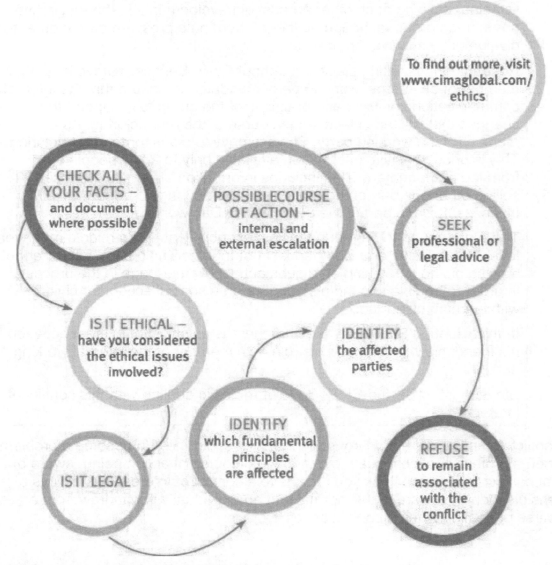

http://www.cimaglobal.com/Global/Images/standards-and-ethics/ethics_checklist_web_June2015_update.pdf

Guidance is given in the Code in Sections 100.19–100.24.

Ethical Conflict Resolution

100.19 – A professional accountant may be required to resolve a conflict in complying with the fundamental principles.

100.20 – When initiating either a formal or informal conflict resolution process, the following factors, either individually or together with others, may be relevant to the resolution process:

(a)   Relevant facts

(b)   Ethical issues involved

(c)   Fundamental principles related to the matter in question

(d)   Established internal procedures; and

(e)   Alternative courses of action.

Having considered the relevant factors, a professional accountant shall determine the appropriate course of action, weighing the consequences of each possible course of action. If the matter remains unresolved, the professional accountant may wish to consult with other appropriate persons within the firm or employing organisation for help in obtaining resolution.

100.21 – Where a matter involves a conflict with, or within, an organisation, a professional accountant shall determine whether to consult with those charged with governance of the organisation, such as the board of directors or the audit committee.

100.22 – It may be in the best interests of the professional accountant to document the substance of the issue, the details of any discussions held, and the decisions made concerning that issue.

100.23 – If a significant conflict cannot be resolved, a professional accountant may consider obtaining professional advice from the relevant professional body or from legal advisors. The professional accountant generally can obtain guidance on ethical issues without breaching the fundamental principle of confidentiality if the matter is discussed with the relevant professional body on an anonymous basis or with a legal advisor under the protection of legal privilege. Instances in which the professional accountant may consider obtaining legal advice vary. For example, a professional accountant may have encountered a fraud, the reporting of which could breach the professional accountant's responsibility to respect confidentiality. The professional accountant may consider obtaining legal advice in that instance to determine whether there is a requirement to report.

100.24 – If, after exhausting all relevant possibilities, the ethical conflict remains unresolved, a professional accountant shall, where possible, refuse to remain associated with the matter creating the conflict. The professional accountant shall determine whether, in the circumstances, it is appropriate to withdraw from the engagement team or specific assignment, or to resign altogether from the engagement, the firm or the employing organisation.

You need to act quickly when facing an ethical dilemma. The longer you leave it, the more chance there is for repercussions for the organisation, yourself and the standing of the profession. CIMA's Code of Ethics can help you identify and deal with situations where professional integrity may not exist.

CIMA is committed to upholding the highest ethical and professional standards and to maintaining public confidence in management accounting. CIMA members and students are required to comply with the CIMA Code of Ethics and to adopt its five fundamental principles to their working lives.

1   Check all your facts – and document where possible

–   Identify all relevant facts.

–   Do not rely on word of mouth, or assumptions. Is it really your problem?

–   Can anybody else help?

2   Is it ethical – have you considered the ethical issues involved?

–   Does it feel right?

–   How would you feel if you saw it in a newspaper?

–   How would you feel about your peers, friends, family knowing about it?

–   Have you referred to the CIMA Code of Ethics?

–   Have you referred to your internal Code of Ethics/Conduct and other internal policies?

3   Is it legal?

–   Is the issue in question regulated by the law – national and international?

–   Does it comply with rules, policies, standards and contracts imposed by relevant regulators/bodies and by your employer?

4   Identify which fundamental principles are affected

–   Integrity

–   Objectivity

–   Professional competence and due care

–   Confidentiality

–   Professional behaviour.

5   Identify the affected parties

- Who are the individuals, organisations and key stakeholders affected?
- In what way are they affected?
- Are there conflicts between different stakeholders?
- Understand the effects of non-action – to the organisation, to yourself and to society.

6   Possible course of action – internal and external escalation

- Escalate internally; consider grievance procedures.
- Document every action you take to resolve the conflict.
- Escalate externally to auditor, legal advisors, professional body.

7   Seek professional or legal advice

- Your internal whistle-blowing or speak up helpline.
- Legal advisors.
- CIMA ethics helpline: free to members and students.

8   Refuse to remain associated with the conflict

- If resolution seems unlikely, disassociate yourself from the issue – in writing if necessary.
- Legal advice may be needed if this affects your employment status or if you are implicated in any way with the issue.

Ethical values may include

- Integrity
- Honesty
- Openness
- Respect
- Fairness
- Responsibility.

Examples of business ethics issues

- Bullying and harassment
- Use of social media
- Paying suppliers on time
- Health and safety
- Conflicts of interest
- Tax avoidance
- Religious practices in workplace.

4 Business ethics for SME's: A guide for CIMA partners

Alongside 'Embedding ethical values' discussed in chapter 1, CIMA and the Institute of Business Ethics have produced a second guidance document, 'Business Ethics for SMEs', which explores what business ethics means for small to medium-sized business enterprises and how they can introduce and support high standards of business practice. Although both guides are aimed at CIMA partners, they are also relevant to members or students who seek to embed ethical values to their organisation or want to find out more about introducing a Code of Ethics.

Below is an extract:

Owners and managers can often encounter ethical challenges.

Examples include:

- Do I meet a deadline with my customer and ship out products even though I know there is a possibility they might be faulty, or do I openly discuss my difficulties with the customer

- How do I ensure that my employees do their work properly and do the right thing?

- How do I deal with my employees' desire to balance their work obligations with their personal ones?

- How do I respond when securing an important contract seems to require the payment of a kickback?

- Do I delay payment to suppliers and the Inland Revenue when my cash flow is currently limited?

Some benefits of making ethical values explicit

- Increased employee loyalty, higher commitment and morale as well as lower staff turnover

- Reputational benefits (customers and suppliers)

- Attraction of 'high-quality' staff

- More open and innovative culture

- Generation of goodwill in the communities in which the business operates

- Decreased cost of borrowing and insurance

- Supports employees to act ethically and raise concerns which reduces integrity risks.

Business values may include

- Customer service
- Quality
- Innovation
- Reliability
- Efficiency
- Value for money.

Ethics and CIMA

Going downhill fast

CIMA's ethics manager shares the true story of a CIMA member who contacted the institute's ethics helpline for advice. His problem stemmed from allowing what seemed, on the face of it, a minor issue to snowball into a job-threatening situation.

Andrew was the management accountant of a small firm that was part of a plc. His boss, Chris, was the firm's CEO. Several months ago Chris has approached him with a query about the month-end figures that Andrew has produced, saying that they must be wrong. At the time there was a certain amount of confusion, because their firm had just taken over another small company, so Andrew adjusted them as instructed.

Next month Chris questioned the numbers again, and Andrew duly changed them once more. This happened at several more month-ends until he began to suspect that Chris's reasons for changing the numbers might not be valid – and that the business was simply not performing. He raised the issue with his boss, who assured him that he would sort everything out. Relieved that Chris recognized that the matter needed to be dealt with, Andrew dropped it.

At the end of the firm's financial year, Chris announced that he had, as promised, found a solution to the problem of the ongoing adjustments. Unfortunately, this was very different from what Andrew was expecting. Chris proposed that he own up to the discrepancies, admit that they were the result of a simple error and then resign to prevent any further questions from being asked. In return for carrying the can, Andrew would receive a glowing reference – on the understanding, of course, that he kept quiet about the whole affair.

Shocked and unsure about what to do, Andrew contacted CIMA's ethics helpline. He had gone from accepting a small month-end adjustment to his figures to finding himself about to lose a job. Our guidance to Andrew was that he should consider taking the problem to more senior people in the group, since raising it with Chris wasn't an option. Andrew had some concerns about the possible repercussions of doing this, particularly because Chris was well respected in the group, and he was worried that his version of events would not be believed. The lack of an internal grievance or whistle blowing procedure made it hard for him to predict how his case would be handled.

Given all these factors, Andrew questioned whether quitting was an acceptable solution. A good reference had been promised, but was this pledge worth anything coming from Chris? And how would he explain to any future employer why he had left? And what would happen if a colleague were to complain to CIMA about his lack of competence? If this were to happen, he could potentially lose his membership. Even worse, lying to accept responsibility that wasn't his would be another breach of CIMA's code of ethics. If discovered, this would also have consequences for his membership.

After further discussion, Andrew identified a potential ally (a financial controller) at group level. He arranged a meeting through a trusted colleague in order to minimize the chances of discovery by Chris.

We suggested that Andrew should speak to the institute's legal advice line for expert guidance on his legal obligations and employment rights, and also to the whistle-blowing advice line for free, confidential, independent advice on raising his concerns.

Andrew spoke to the financial controller and Chris was eventually forced to resign. But Andrew's ongoing compliance with his boss's wishes was enough to have tarnished his reputation. A few months later he resigned of his own accord.

Andrew's case is a reminder of how crucial it is to use your professional judgment, heed the warning signs and establish the facts at the first sign of an ethical dilemma. Armed with these and CIMA's code of ethics, you can decide whether or not you need to act and, if so, what that action should be.

So how exactly do you know when an ethical dilemma is an ethical dilemma? As Oscar Wilde observed: 'Morality, like art, means drawing a line someplace.' When the amount of money is not material, the report is only for internal purposes or when no one else seems to think there's an issue, how can you be sure where that line is?

Taking time to consider the situation from all angles will help you to know for sure. In the code of ethics, the line is where a threat to our fundamental principles is anything more than trivial. Although the changes that Andrew made to the numbers in that first month might not have been material, the pattern that they established was. If he had stood up to Chris the first time he was asked to adjust the figures, the situation might never have developed.

This article appeared in Financial Management, November 2007.

Nike

Nike is one of the famous franchises in the world that sells sportswear for all ages. But is mostly famous for their athlete shoes and apparel and Nike is also one of the major manufacturers of sport equipment as well. The slogan for Nike is "Just Do It". Nike was founded in January 1962 in Oregon, United States by Philip Knight and Bill Bowerman. Nike has somewhere around 700 or more retail outlets spread all over the world, and has approximately 45 offices outside the United States. And it employs 30,000 people all over the world. Nike had a revenue excess of $16 billion in 2007. Nike's factories are mostly located in Asian countries like Pakistan, India, Malaysia, China, Indonesia, Philippines, Taiwan, Vietnam and Thailand.

The primary stakeholders of the company would be the shareholders, business partners, the employees, and the customers/consumers. What the shareholders and the investors want from the company is that the company achieves its profits, the employees of the expect work satisfaction, pay along with good supervision and the customers are concerned with quality, safety and availability of services when they require it. And when any primary stakeholder group is not satisfied the organisation's progress becomes questionable.

The secondary stakeholders of the company would be the community. Most companies like Nike exist under a charter or licenses and operate within the limits of safety laws, environmental protection and other laws and regulations. The socially responsible organisations like Nike should consider the effect of their actions upon all stakeholders. What all of these stakeholders want from the company is that the company is ethically and socially responsible and when this secondary stakeholder group becomes dis-satisfied, the reputation of the company gets tarnished (for example, the debate of sweatshops tarnished the reputation of Nike).

Issues faced by Nike:

- Child labour and the sweat shop problem

- Workers given a very low wage, and overtime in countries like Vietnam, China and Indonesia under a subcontract

- Poor working conditions, squalid working conditions and forced labour in the factories that manufacture their products

- Environmental damage done to society by air and water pollution, noise, and change in the climate due to pollution. (Stockdale & Crosby, 2004)

There are different kinds of guiding principles that can prevent Nike type scandals, and this is what the company did:

PR campaign

Nike decided to use a PR campaign so that it was able to repair its social image due to the sweatshop debate. The PR campaign covered the following actions:

Employment Practices

The management of Nike took a look at its employment practices; they made sure that the company was following the policies on recruitment, training, health, safety and welfare. The management of the company also oversaw their environmental practices – to make sure that the company follows procedures that are responsible in terms of waste disposal and avoidance and energy inputs.

Training Plan

They conducted and designed a training program for the employees. The management remembered that training and development programs are not universal solutions to every need of the company. Effective job designs, selection, placement and other activities of the HR department are also very important.

Assessing Performance

They set targets and identified performance measure standards. If performance is to be rated accurately, the performance of the company would require the management to assess each and every relevant performance dimension.

Ethical Responsibility

The management of Nike understood that ethical responsibility is needed within the company because it is the obligation of organisation's management to make decisions and take actions that will grow the welfare and interest of the society and the organisation. It would include activities and commitments that are related to human rights, governance and ethics, development, working conditions of the employees, community involvement, customer satisfaction, relations with the company's suppliers and customers and lastly respect for diverse cultures and different people.

5 Test your understanding questions

Test your understanding 1

Which of the following are possible consequences to the accounting profession if unethical behaviour is widespread?

(i)   The introduction of legislation.

(ii)   Loss of its reputation.

(iii)   Loss of its chartered institute status.

A   (i) and (ii) only

B   (ii) and (iii) only

C   (i) and (iii) only

D   (i), (ii) and (iii)

Test your understanding 2

Which statements are true or false?

A   Unethical behaviour will lead to financial loss

B   Codes of ethics are voluntary

C   Governance refers to how an organisation is run

D   Social responsibility refers to a company's relationship with its shareholders

Test your understanding 3

Which of the following is not an example of a familiarity threat?

A   Accepting gifts or preferential treatment from a client

B   Having a close business relationship with a client

C   Having a close family relationship with a director of a client

D   A former partner of the company being a director of the client

Test your understanding 4

An old friend has asked you to tender for accounting work. You are keen to assist. From an ethical as well as a business perspective, what is the most appropriate action for you to take?

A   Tender for the work

B   Suggest to your friend that they approach more than one company to create a competitive tender

C   Suggest to your friend that they assign the work to a different company instead

D   Ask a colleague to handle the client

Test your understanding answers

Test your understanding 1

D

They are all possible outcomes.

Test your understanding 2

A   **False.** Unethical behaviour may have consequences when it is highlighted. Not all ethical behaviour is highlighted.

B   **True.** A company may require its employees to comply with its code of ethics as part of the employee's contract of employment, but it is a voluntary decision of a company to set up a code of ethics initially.

C   **True.** This is the generic manner in which the term governance is used.

D   **False.** A company's social responsibility is a wider responsibility to ALL stakeholders of the company, not just the shareholders.

Test your understanding 3

B

Having a close business relationship with a client is an example of a self-interest threat.

Test your understanding 4

D

Accountants need to demonstrate both independence of mind and independence in appearance. You should therefore declare the potential conflict of interest and ask a colleague to handle the client.

Corporate Governance

Chapter learning objectives

Upon completion of this chapter you will be able to:

- describe corporate governance

- explain the interaction of corporate governance with business ethics and company law

- explain the purpose, definition of the Organisation for Economic Co-operation and Development (OECD) principles of Corporate Governance

- describe IFAC's main drivers of sustainable corporate success

- illustrate CIMA's practical proposals for better corporate governance

- distinguish between detailed rules-based and principles based approaches to governance.

- describe the role of the board and different board structures

- explain the effects of corporate governance on directors' powers and duties

- describe the types of policies and procedures that constitute 'best practice'

- describe the respective committees and their roles and responsibilities with regards monitoring and controlling the actions of the Executive.

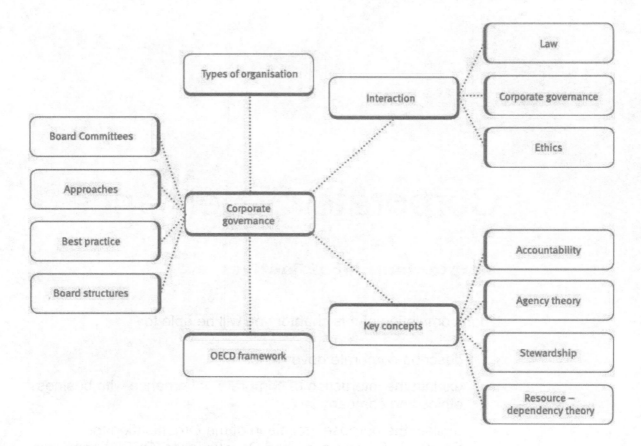

1 Introduction

This chapter deals with corporate governance which is contained in Section B of the syllabus.

You will be introduced to the concept of an 'organisation' within this chapter. This will be developed further in Chapter 8 which looks in more detail at the characteristics of particular types of organisations such as companies.

The rest of the chapter will look at the concept of corporate governance including its purpose and examples of policies and procedures.

2 Organisations

What is an organisation?

Defining an organisation is difficult as there are many types of organisations which are set up to meet a variety of needs, such as clubs, schools, companies, charities and hospitals.

What they all have in common is summarised in the definition produced by **Buchanan and Huczynski**.

 'Organisations are social arrangements for the controlled purpose of collective goals.'

What is an organisation?

Consider the three aspects of Buchanan and Huczynski's definition in more detail:

(a)   'Collective goals' – organisations are defined by their goals. The main goal of a school is to educate pupils. It will therefore be organised differently to a company that aims to make profits.

(b)   'Social arrangements' – someone working alone cannot be classed as an organisation. Organisations are structured to allow people to work together towards a common goal. Usually, the larger the organisation, the more formal its structures.

(c)   'Controlled performance' – an organisation will have systems and procedures in place to ensure that group goals are achieved. For a company this could involve setting sales targets, or periodically assessing the performance of staff members.

Different types of organisations

Different organisations have different goals. We can therefore classify them into several different categories.

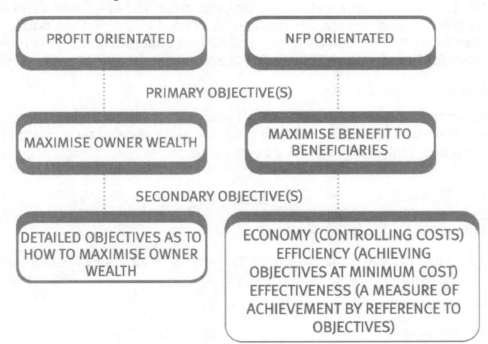

Profit-seeking organisations

Profit-seeking (or commercial) organisations see their main objective as maximising the wealth of their owners.

There are three common forms that a commercial company can take:

- **Sole traders** – the organisation is owned and run by one person.
- **Partnerships** – the organisation is owned and run by two or more individuals.

Note that in both of these organisations, the owner of the business is not legally separate from the business itself. If a partnership is sued by a customer, the customer is actually suing the owner of the business.

- **Limited liability companies** – a company has a separate legal identity to its owners (who are known as shareholders). The owner's liability is limited to the amount they have invested into the company.

  In the UK, there are two types of limited company:

  Private limited companies (with 'Ltd' after their name) – these tend to be smaller businesses, often owned by a few shareholders. Shares cannot be offered to the general public.

  Public limited companies (with 'plc' after their name) – these can be much larger businesses. Shares can be offered to the general public, meaning that there can be millions of different shareholders. This makes it easier for the company to raise finance, enabling further growth.

Not for profit organisations

Not-for-profit organisations (NFPs) do not see profitability as their main objective. Instead, they seek to satisfy the particular needs of their members or the sectors of society that they have been set up to benefit.

NFP's examples
NFPs include the following: - government departments and agencies (such as HM Revenue and Customs) - schools - hospitals - charities (such as the Red Cross, Oxfam and Doctors Without Borders) - clubs.

Public sector organisations

The public sector is the part of the economy that is concerned with providing basic government services and is controlled by government organisations.

Public sector organisations

The organisations that make up the public sector vary from country to country, but generally include:

- police
- military
- public transport
- primary education
- healthcare for the poor.

Private sector organisations

The private sector consists of organisations that are run by private individuals and groups rather than the government.

Private sector

The private sector will therefore normally include:

- businesses
- non-governmental organisations
- charities and
- clubs.

Within these will be both profit-seeking and not-for-profit organisations.

Non-governmental organisations (NGOs)

A non-governmental organisation is one which does not have profit as its primary goal and is not directly linked to the national government.

NGOs often promote political, social or environmental change within the countries they operate.

NGOs

Some of the largest NGOs operate in the humanitarian sphere and include:

- Oxfam
- the Red Cross
- World Vision
- Amnesty International.

Co-operatives

Co-operatives (or mutuals) are organisations that are owned and democratically controlled by their members – the people who buy their goods or services.

They are organised solely to meet the needs of the member-owners, who usually share any profits.

Co-operatives
In the UK, the largest example of a co-operative is the Co-operative Group, which has over 5.5 million members and operates in diverse markets, such as banking, travel and groceries.

3 What is corporate governance?

Definition of corporate governance

The Financial Reporting Council defines corporate governance as follows:

 The purpose of corporate governance is to facilitate effective, entrepreneurial and prudent management that can deliver the long-term success of the company.

Corporate governance is the system by which companies are directed and controlled. Boards of directors are responsible for the governance of their companies. The shareholders' role in governance is to appoint the directors and the auditors and to satisfy themselves that an appropriate governance structure is in place. The responsibilities of the board include setting the company's strategic aims, providing the leadership to put them into effect, supervising the management of the business and reporting to shareholders on their stewardship. The board's actions are subject to laws, regulations and the shareholders in general meetings.

The aim of corporate governance initiatives is to ensure that companies are run well in the interests of their shareholders and the wider community.

In response to major accounting scandals (e.g. Enron), regulators sought to change the rules surrounding the governance of companies, particularly publically owned ones.

There are different codes and practices around the world but they tend to cover similar areas:

- The role of the board of directors.

- The reliability of financial reports and the relationship between the company and its auditors.

- The interest of the company's shareholders in the company.

Importance of corporate governance

- In most developed countries, listed companies are required to operate systems of corporate governance laid down either by statute or by professional organisations (such as the Securities and Exchange Commission (SEC) in the US or the Financial Conduct Authority (FCA) in the UK).

- The requirements are often given the support of the stock exchanges, in that they are built into listing rules.

- The development of corporate governance codes is closely associated with the UK, hence this is a model to discuss best practice.

- The UK Corporate Governance Code follows a principles-based approach and is endorsed by the London Stock Exchange. The US system has been much more legislative with the introduction of the Sarbanes-Oxley Act of 2002.

Development of corporate governance

- Governance regulations have developed largely as a result of a series of corporate failures in the 1980s and early 1990s.

- The corporate governance themes that began to emerge from these collapses were:

  - poorly-run companies, especially companies with a board of directors dominated by a single chairman/chief executive figure, and companies with 'greedy' or 'fat cat' directors (demonstrating the agency problem of a company failing to operate in the best interests of its shareholders)

  - poor financial reporting, raising questions about auditing and internal control systems, and

  - an apparent lack of interest by the major investment institutions in the performance of the companies in which they invested.

- More recently the UK Corporate Governance Code has been developed further in accordance with the 2008–09 global financial crisis.

 Company collapses

Several issues or problems appear to emerge when there is a corporate governance 'scandal' and a company has collapsed.

- The company has not been well-run by its board of directors.

- In many cases, there has been an individual who has dominated the board and exerted excessive influence on decision-making by the board. In many cases, this individual held the positions of both chairman of the board and chief executive officer.

- A board of directors might have lacked sufficient breadth of knowledge and experience to appreciate the problems the company was in and the risks it faced.

- Companies were being run in the interests of the executive directors, who received high remuneration packages and generous bonuses, but the rewards were not being given for the achievement of objectives that were in the best interests of the shareholders. The interests of the directors were not properly aligned with those of the shareholders.

- Financial reporting was unreliable and the published accounts did not seem to give any indication of the true financial position of the company. In some cases there was a suspicion that the auditors were not sufficiently independent of the company and so not fulfilling their responsibilities adequately. Alternatively, the auditors were accused of doing their job badly or of being misled by the company's directors and management. (In 2002 audit firm Arthur Andersen collapsed from the consequences of its involvement in the Enron scandal.)

- Whenever a company collapsed unexpectedly, there have been suspicions that the internal control system was ineffective. There usually appears to have been inadequate risk management generally.

- Questions have also been asked about major institutional shareholders, and whether they could have done more to identify problems in companies and persuade or force the directors to make improvements.

Maxwell Communications Corporation

Robert Maxwell was born in to extreme poverty in Czechoslovakia in 1923. By the time of his death (accident or murder was never established) in 1991 he was a media mogul, having built a publishing empire that spanned the world. In the weeks that followed his death however, news emerged of the state of his company's finances.

After the Second World War he set up Pergamon Press publishing scientific journals. It became very profitable and he turned his attention to politics, later becoming a Member of Parliament for the Labour Party. His relationship with the Party was an uneasy one since anyone who criticised him was confronted in the courts. This was when signs emerged of his dishonesty.

In 1969, Maxwell agreed a takeover bid for Pergamon by Leasco (an American financial and data processing group). The profits of Pergamon were questioned by Leasco and eventually talks fell apart as a Department of Trade and Industry (DTI) enquiry ensued. Inspectors found that the profits depended on transactions with Maxwell family private companies. The DTI concluded that Maxwell 'is not a person... who can be relied upon to exercise proper stewardship of a publicly quoted company'.

In 1980 Maxwell took over the troubled British Printing Corporation renaming it Maxwell Communications Corporation. In 1984 he bought Mirror Group Newspapers (MGN) and Macmillan publishers, which put his company further into debt. In 1991 he floated MGN as a public company desperate to raise cash that would save the Group from bankruptcy (with debts over £2 billion). After Maxwell's death it transpired that he had taken money from the pension funds to keep the companies afloat and boost the share price.

Enron

In December 2001, US energy trader Enron collapsed. Enron was the largest bankruptcy in US history. Even though the United States was believed by many to be the most regulated financial market in the world, it was evident from Enron's collapse that investors were not properly informed about the significance of off-balance sheet transactions. US accounting rules may have contributed to this, in that they are concerned with the strict legal ownership of investment vehicles rather than with their control. By contrast, International Accounting Standards follow the principle of 'substance over form'. There were some indications that Enron may have actively lobbied against changing the treatment in US financial reporting of special purpose entities used in off-balance sheet financing. Overall, there was a clear need for greater transparency and trust in reporting.

The failure of Enron also highlighted the over-dependence of an auditor on one particular client, the employment of staff by Enron who had previously worked for the auditors, the process of audit appointments and re-appointments, the rotation of audit partners and how auditors are monitored and regulated.

As a consequence of the failure of Enron and WorldCom, the United States has introduced Sarbanes-Oxley legislation to address many of the criticisms of reporting and auditing practice. In their comments on the failure of Enron, the Association of Certified Chartered Accountants recommended the need for global financial markets to have a global set of principles-based financial reporting standards and a global code of corporate governance, arguing that legalistic, rules-based standards encourage creative, loophole-based practice.

Former chief executive Kenneth Lay died in 2006 before he could stand trial. Enron's former chief financial officer Andrew Fastow was sentenced in late 2006 to six years in prison for stealing from Enron and devising schemes to deceive investors about the energy company's true financial condition. Lawyers have to date won settlements totalling $US 7.3 billion from banks including JPMorgan Chase, Bank of America, Citigroup, etc.

Worldcom

WorldCom filed for bankruptcy protection in June 2002. It was the biggest corporate fraud in history, largely a result of treating operating expenses as capital expenditure.

WorldCom (now renamed MCI) admitted in March 2004 that the total amount by which it had misled investors over the previous 10 years was almost US$75 billion (£42 billion) and reduced its stated pre-tax profits for 2001 and 2002 by that amount.

WorldCom stock began falling in late 1999 as businesses slashed spending on telecom services and equipment. A series of debt downgrades had raised borrowing costs for the company, struggling with about US$32 billion in debt. WorldCom used accounting tricks to conceal a deteriorating financial condition and to inflate profits.

Former WorldCom chief executive Bernie Ebbers resigned in April 2002 amid questions about US$366 million in personal loans from the company and a federal probe of its accounting practices. Ebbers was subsequently charged with conspiracy to commit securities fraud, and filing misleading data with the Securities and Exchange Commission (SEC). Scott Sullivan, former chief financial officer, pleaded guilty to three criminal charges.

The SEC said WorldCom had committed 'accounting improprieties of unprecedented magnitude' – proof, it said, of the need for reform in the regulation of corporate accounting.

4 Governance, ethics and company law

Clearly there is an overlap between business ethics, company law and corporate governance. In many jurisdictions company law is made up of ethical principles and standards of behaviour which legislators and courts have thought appropriate to codify as law.

	Compliance requirements	Penalties
Law	The law must always be obeyed.	Penalties for infringement of the law may be civil or criminal.
		Civil remedies may allow the company to recover funds from directors who breach their legal obligations.
		A fine and/or imprisonment might result from certain criminal infringements.

	Compliance requirements	Penalties
Corporate governance	In the UK the stock exchange rules require listed companies to comply with the UK Corporate Governance Code. If a listed company does not comply, it must specify the provisions with which it has not complied, and give reasons for its non-compliance. Unlisted companies are under no obligation to comply, although it is considered best practice to do so.	There are no formal penalties for noncompliance. However, the company may suffer loss of reputation and receive bad publicity.
Ethics	It is said that ethics begin where the law ends. If an action is legal, individuals generally have freedom of choice as to their conduct. However, good ethical behaviour may be above that demanded by the law. CIMA students and members are expected to follow the code of ethics published by CIMA.	An individual who behaves unethically may suffer loss of reputation, dismissal from their job and sanctions may possibly be imposed by their professional body.

 Why does the law need to be supplemented?

It may be questioned therefore, if the law is so stringent, why has it proved necessary to have an additional body of rules and standards known as corporate governance? Why is it that the law has not prevented directors from paying themselves excessive salaries and/or involving their companies in major scandals?

The answer lies in the fact that, in many instances, the law provides for internal regulation of the activities of directors by:

(i)   requiring directors to fully disclose their dealings to the shareholders and

(ii)   by giving the shareholders the power to regulate the activities of the directors through their control of the company's constitution and, of course, by giving the shareholders the ultimate power, of appointing and dismissing the directors.

Why then does the law need to be supplemented? The short answer is that quite clearly these rules have not proved watertight, and in a number of high-profile instances directors have been able to circumvent the law. In general, this has happened for the following main reasons.

Firstly, persons and institutions who invest in shares in public limited companies mainly do so in order to achieve good capital growth, a good return on their investment in the form of dividends or a combination of the two. If that is what the investor is receiving, then he is less likely to be interested in the way that the company is being managed. In any event, the investors, particularly institutional investors, will be likely to have invested in a large number of companies throughout the world. It appears unrealistic in the extreme therefore, to suppose that fund managers will have the time to actively participate in the internal affairs of all the companies in which they invest.

Secondly, shares in public companies are potentially held by hundreds or even thousands of shareholders. It follows that shareholders in any particular company tend to be a disparate body, not united by any common objectives other than good returns on their investments. Such a group is likely to be difficult to organise behind a coherent policy and thus in a poor position to take on a relatively small powerful group like a board of directors. Even the ultimate power to remove directors may be difficult to use in practice. For example, it may be that the shareholders are concerned that if the market becomes aware of internal conflict within the company, that may have a detrimental effect on the share price. Additionally it may be that dismissing directors can be expensive in the extreme. Many directors of public companies would be entitled to large compensation payments in the event of their removal.

5 Key concepts

Accountability

Accountability means that people in a position of power can be held to account for their actions, i.e. they can be compelled to explain their decisions and can be criticised or punished if they have abused their position.

Accountability is central to the concept of good corporate governance – the process of ensuring that companies are well run.

The directors are accountable to the shareholders for the way in which they run the company.

 ### Agency theory

Agency theory is a group of concepts describing the nature of the agency relationship deriving from the separation between ownership and control.

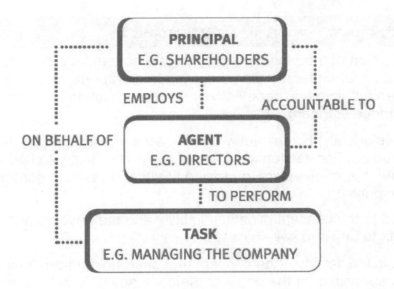

Agency theory and corporate governance

Agency theory can help to explain the actions of the various interest groups in the corporate governance debate.

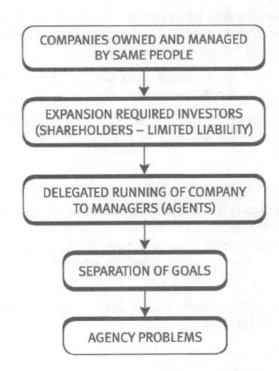

Agency theory and corporate governance

Examination of theories behind corporate governance provides a foundation for understanding the issue in greater depth and a link between an historical perspective and its application in modern governance standards.

- Historically, companies were owned and managed by the same people. For economies to grow it was necessary to find a larger number of investors to provide finance to assist in corporate expansion.

This led to the concept of limited liability and the development of stock markets to buy and sell shares.

- Limited liability – the concept that shareholders are legally responsible for the debts of the company only to the sum of the nominal value of their shares.

- Stock market – the "market" in which publicly held shares are issued and traded.

- Delegation of running the firm to the agent or managers.

- Separation of goals between wealth maximisation of shareholders and the personal objectives of managers. This separation is a key assumption of agency theory.

- Possible short-term perspective of managers rather than protecting long-term shareholder wealth.

- Divorce between ownership and control linked with differing objectives creates agency problems.

Stewardship

Stewardship is the responsibility to take good care of resources. A steward is a person entrusted with management of another person's property, for example, when one person is paid to look after another person's house while the owner goes abroad on holiday. The steward is **accountable** for the way he carries out his role.

This relationship, where one person has a duty of care towards someone else is known as a '**fiduciary relationship**'.

A **fiduciary relationship** is a relationship of 'good faith' such as that between the directors of a company and the shareholders of the company. There is a 'separation of ownership and control' in the sense that the shareholders own the company, while the directors make the decisions. The directors must make their decisions in the interests of the shareholders rather than in their own selfish personal interests.

In essence the directors are stewards of the company.

Resource-dependency theory

Resource-dependency theory is the study of how the external resources of organisations affect the behaviour of the organisation. The theory was formalised by Jeffrey Pfeffer and Gerald Salancik in 1978.

The ideology of resource dependence theory can be summarized as follows:

- Organisations depend on resources.

- These resources ultimately originate from an organisation's environment.

- The environment, to a considerable extent, contains other organisations.

- The resources one organisation needs are thus often in the hands of other organisations.

- Resources are a basis of power.

- Legally independent organisations can therefore depend on each other.

In the context of corporate governance, directors are responsible for developing appropriate strategies to exploit these resources in order to ensure the survival of their own organisation.

6 The OECD Principles of Corporate Governance

The OECD consists of 34 countries who want a free market economy with one set of rules for corporate governance.

Although there have always been well run entities as well as those where scandals have occurred, the fact that scandals do occur has led to the development of codes of practice for good corporate governance.

Often this is due to pressures exerted by stock exchanges. In 1999 the Organisation for Economic Co-operation and Development, OECD, assisted with the development of their 'Principles of Corporate Governance.' These were intended to:

- assist member and non-member governments in their efforts to evaluate and improve the legal, institutional and regulatory framework for corporate governance in their countries.

- provide guidance and suggestions for stock exchanges, investors, corporations, and other parties that have a role in the process of developing good corporate governance.

The OECD principles were first published in 1999 and were revised in 2004. Their focus is on publicly traded entities. However, to the extent they are deemed applicable, they are a useful tool to improve corporate governance in non-traded entities.

There are six principles, each backed up by a number of sub principles.

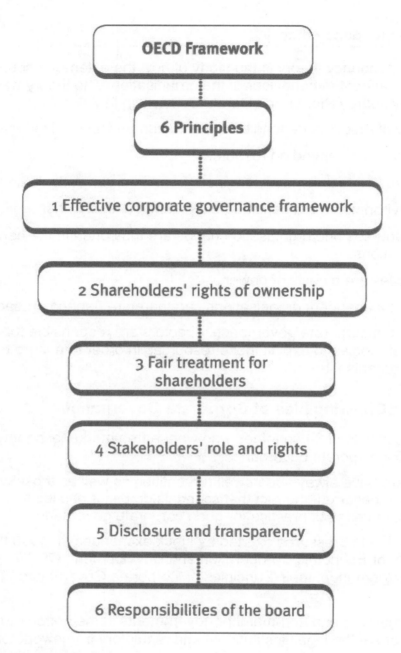

OECD Framework

6 Principles

1 Effective corporate governance framework

2 Shareholders' rights of ownership

3 Fair treatment for shareholders

4 Stakeholders' role and rights

5 Disclosure and transparency

6 Responsibilities of the board

The principles in detail

The six principles:

(i) **Ensuring the basis for an effective corporate governance framework**

The corporate governance framework should promote transparent and efficient markets, be consistent with the rule of law and clearly articulate the division of responsibilities among different supervisory, regulatory and enforcement authorities. In other words, making sure everyone involved is aware of their individual responsibilities so no party is in doubt as to what they are accountable for.

(ii) **The rights of shareholders and key ownership functions**

The corporate governance framework should protect and facilitate the exercise of shareholders' rights. The directors are the stewards of the entity and should be acting in the best interests of the shareholders. However, the existence of the corporate collapses mentioned above proves that this isn't always the case and shareholders need protecting from such people.

(iii) **The equitable treatment of shareholders**

The corporate governance framework should ensure the equitable treatment of all shareholders, including minority and foreign shareholders. All shareholders should have the opportunity to obtain effective redress for violation of their rights.

(iv) **The role of stakeholders in corporate governance**

The corporate governance framework should recognise the rights of stakeholders established by law or through mutual agreements and encourage active co-operation between corporations and stakeholders in creating wealth, jobs, and the sustainability of financially sound enterprise.

(v) **Disclosure and transparency**

The corporate governance framework should ensure that timely and accurate disclosure is made on all material matters regarding the corporation, including the financial situation, performance, ownership and governance of the entity. Therefore, the annual financial statements should be produced on a timely basis and include all matters of interest to the shareholders. For any matters of significance arising during the year, these should be communicated to the shareholders as appropriate.

(vi) **The responsibilities of the board**

The corporate governance framework should ensure the strategic guidance of the entity, the effective monitoring of management by the board, and the board's accountability to the entity and the shareholders. The introduction of audit committees and non executive directors on the board is the usual way for monitoring management. Non executive directors are not involved in the day to day running of the entity and are therefore more independent. They can evaluate the effectiveness of the executive board on its merits and make sure they are carrying out their duties properly.

The status of the OECD principles

- The principles represent a common basis that OECD Member countries consider essential for the development of good governance practice.

- They are intended to be concise, understandable and accessible to the international community.

- They are not intended to be a substitute for government or private sector initiatives to develop more detailed 'best practice' in governance.

7 IFAC's main drivers of sustainable corporate success

The Professional Accountants in Business (PAIB) Committee published a paper to support the global accountancy profession in responding to changing expectations of society, financial markets, and organisations, and promotes the value of professional accountants in business to their organisations.

The paper lists eight drivers of sustainable organisational success which provide the basis for understanding how the global accountancy profession needs to support the development of professional accountants, so that they can help organisations achieve sustainable value creation.

Customer and stakeholder focus

- Understanding and satisfying customer or service-user needs.
- Aligning all parts of an organisation to these needs.

Effective leadership and strategy

- Providing ethical and strategic leadership focused on sustainable value creation.
- Facilitating key performance drivers, including strong corporate values, ethical culture, and organisational structures and processes.

Integrated governance, risk and control

- Deploying effective governance structures and processes with integrated risk management and internal control.
- Balancing performance and conformance in governance.

Innovation and adaptability

- Innovating processes and products to improve reputation and performance.
- Adapting the organisation to changing circumstances.

Financial management

- Ensuring financial leadership and strategy support sustainable value creation.
- Implementing good practices in areas such as tax and treasury, cost and profitability improvement, and working capital management.

People and talent management

- Enabling people and talent management as a strategic function.
- Applying talent management to the finance function so it better serves the needs of the wider organisation.

Operational excellence

- Aligning resource allocation with strategic objectives and the drivers of shareholder and stakeholder value.

- Supporting decision making with timely and insightful performance analysis.

Effective and transparent communication

- Engaging stakeholders effectively to ensure that they receive relevant communications.

- Preparing high-quality business reporting to support stakeholder understanding and decision making.

8 CIMA's practical proposals for better corporate governance

CIMA is a contributor to Report Leadership which is a multi-stakeholder group that aims to challenge established thinking on corporate reporting.

Report Leadership have published a report on simple practical proposals for better reporting of corporate governance.

http://www.cimaglobal.com/Documents/Thought leadership docs/ Governance/Report-Leadership-Corporate-Governance-Report. pdf

The aim is for better rather than more disclosure, and disclosure that is adapted to the circumstances of the company.

The proposals are:

1 **Tone from the top**

   Communicating the chairman's views on good governance and the culture of the board.

2 **How the board works as a team**

   Showing how the board 'fits together' with a complementary set of skills, experience and personal characteristics.

3 **The key actions of the board and its committees**

   Linking the activities of the board to the year's key corporate events.

4 **Board effectiveness**

   Using board evaluations to communicate board performance and priorities.

5 **Communication and engagement with shareholders**

   Explaining how the information needs of the shareholders have been met during the year.

9 Board structures

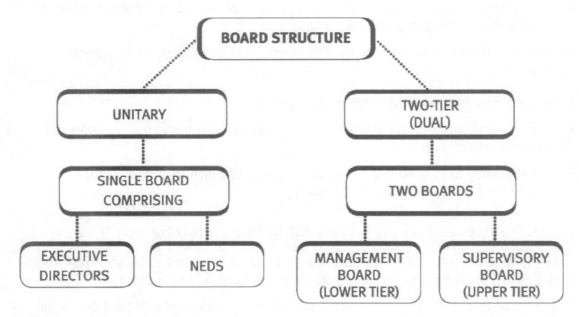

There are two kinds of board structure, unitary and two-tier (dual) boards.

Two-tier boards

These are predominantly associated with France and Germany. Using Germany as an example, there are two main reasons for their existence:

- Codetermination: the right for workers to be informed and involved in decisions that affects them. This is enshrined in the Codetermination Act (Germany) 1976.

- Relationships: banks have a much closer relationship with German companies than in the UK. They are frequently shareholders, and other shareholders often deposit their shares and the rights associated with them with their banks.

This creates a backdrop to creating structures where these parties are actively involved in company affairs, hence the two-tier structure.

Lower tier: management (operating) board:

- responsible for day-to-day running of the enterprise

- generally only includes executives

- the CEO co-ordinates activity.

Upper tier: supervisory (corporate) board:

- appoints, supervises and advises members of the management board

- strategic oversight of the organisation

- includes employee representatives, environmental groups and other stakeholders' management representatives (these NEDs are not considered to be 'independent NEDs')

- the chairman co-ordinates the work

- members are elected by shareholders at the annual general meeting (AGM)

- receives information and reports from the management board.

Advantages of a two-tier board

- Clear separation between those that manage the company and those that own it or must control it for the benefit of shareholders.

- Implicit shareholder involvement in most cases since these structures are used in countries where insider control is prevalent.

- Wider stakeholder involvement implicit through the use of worker representation.

- Independence of thought, discussion and decision since board meetings and operation are separate.

- Direct power over management through the right to appoint members of the management board.

Problems with a two-tier board

- Dilution of power, confusion over authority and hence a perceived lack of accountability. (NB Due to codeterm i nation, reference page 60, there is a right for many different stakeholders to be involved in decisions which affect them).

- Isolation of supervisory board through non-participation in management meetings.

- Agency problems between the boards where one will be acting on behalf of another e.g. the Management Board meetings excluding the Supervisory Board resulting in confusion over authority.

- Increased bureaucracy which may result in slower decisions being made.

- Lack of transparency over appointment of supervisory board members leading to inefficient monitoring and governance.

Additional advantages of a unitary board

Issues specific to the unitary board tend to relate to the role of NEDs.

- NED expertise: the implied involvement of NEDs in the running of the company rather than just supervising.

- NED empowerment: they are as responsible as the executives and this is better demonstrated by their active involvement at an early stage.

- Compromise: less extreme decisions developed prior to the need for supervisory approval.

- Responsibility: a cabinet decision-making unit with wide viewpoints suggests better decisions.

- Reduction of fraud, malpractice: this is due to wider involvement in the actual management of the company.

- Improved investor confidence: through all of the above.

10   The development of corporate governance codes

The development of corporate governance codes is closely associated with the UK, therefore this model is used to illustrate best practice.

Report	Focus	Outcome
Cadbury (1992)	Board of directors	Chairman/CEO role should be split, and Chairman independence necessary
	Institutional investors	Need for greater dialogue
	Audit and accountability	Good communication and disclosure
	Formed part of stock exchange listing rules – **comply or explain**	
Greenbury (1995)	Directors' remuneration	Reporting balance between salary and performance
Hampel (1998)	Deal with criticisms of previous reports	Consolidation in a **Combined Code**
Turnbull (1999)	Need for directors to review internal control systems and report on them	Framework for establishing systems of internal control
Higgs (2003)	Role of non-executive directors (NEDs)	Specific guidelines regarding NEDs and their role
Tyson (2003)	Recruitment and development of NEDs	Additional guidance
Smith (2003)	Auditors and audit committee	Relationship between auditors and the company and the role of the audit committee
Sir David Walker & the FRC (2010)	Complete review of Corporate Governance following the financial crisis 2008 – 2009	The Code was found to be 'fit for purpose' and the name changed to 'UK Corporate Governance Code'

11 Best Practice – policies and procedures

The UK Corporate Governance Code

In the UK for listed companies, the most important issues of best practice are contained in the UK Corporate Governance Code. This was first issued in 1998 and has been updated at regular intervals since then, most recently in 2018.

The UK Corporate Governance Code can be seen in full on the FRC website at

https://www.frc.org.uk/Our-Work/Codes-Standards/Corporategovernance/UK-Corporate-Governance-Code.aspx

The Code is not a rigid (or enforced) set of rules. Instead it consists of principles (main and supporting) and provisions. In the UK all companies quoted on the stock exchange have to comply with the FSA listing rules and these include a requirement that all companies include in their annual report:

- a statement of how the company has applied the main principles set out in the Code; and

- a statement as to whether the company has complied with all relevant provisions set out in the Code.

The main principles of the Code are:

Board leadership and company purpose

- A successful company is led by an effective board whose role is to promote long-term sustainable success thereby generating value for shareholders and contributing to wider society.

- The board should establish the company's purpose, values and strategy. The directors should lead by example and promote the desired culture.

- The board should ensure that the necessary resources are in place for the company to meet its objectives. The board should establish a framework of effective controls to enable risk to be assessed and managed.

- The board should ensure effective engagement with, and encourage participation from shareholders and stakeholders.

- The board should ensure that workforce policies and practices are consistent with the company's values. The workforce should be able to raise matters of concern.

Board roles

The chair's role

- Leads the board of directors.
- Enables flow of information and discussion at board meetings.
- Ensures satisfactory channels of communication with the external auditors.
- Ensures effective operation of board sub-committees.
- The chair should be independent to enhance effectiveness.

The chief executive's role

- Ensures the effective operation of the company.
- Head of the executive directors.
- Clear division of responsibilities between the chair and chief executive.

Executive directors

The executive directors have responsibility for running the company on a day to day basis.

Non-executive directors (NEDs)

The NEDs monitor the executive directors and contribute to the overall strategy and direction of the organisation. They are usually employed on a part-time basis and do not take part in the routine executive management of the company.

NEDs will:

- participate at board meetings.
- bring experience, insight and contacts to assist the board.
- sit on sub-committees as independent, knowledgeable parties.

Division of responsibilities

- The chair leads the board and is responsible for its overall effectiveness.
- The chair should ensure effective contribution of all board members.
- The chair should ensure that directors receive clear, accurate and timely information.
- The board should be balanced so that no individual or small group of individuals can dominate board decisions.

- NEDs should have sufficient time to meet their board responsibilities and should hold management to account.
- The board should ensure it has the policies, processes, information, time and resources it needs to function effectively and efficiently.

Composition, succession and evaluation

- Appointments to the board should be subject to a formal, rigorous and transparent procedure.
- An effective succession plan should be maintained for board and senior management.
- Appointments and succession should be based on merit and objective criteria and should promote diversity.
- The board and its committees should have a combination of skills, experience and knowledge.
- Annual evaluation of the board should consider its composition, diversity and how effectively members work together to achieve objectives.

Audit, risk and internal control including audit committees

- The board should establish formal and transparent policies and procedures to ensure the independence and effectiveness of internal and external audit functions and satisfy itself on the integrity of financial and narrative statements.
- The board should present a fair, balanced and understandable assessment of the company's position and prospects.
- The board should establish procedures to manage risk, oversee the internal control framework, and determine the nature and extent of the principal risks the company is willing to take in order to achieve its long-term strategic objectives.

Remuneration

- Remuneration should be designed to promote the long-term sustainable success of the company. Executive remuneration should be aligned to the company purpose, values and long-term strategy.
- The board should establish formal and transparent procedures for developing the policy for executive directors' remuneration.
- No director should be involved in setting their own pay.
- Directors should exercise independent judgment and discretion when authorising remuneration, taking account of company and individual performance, and wider circumstances.

Sarbanes-Oxley (SOX)

In 2002, following a number of corporate governance scandals such as Enron and WorldCom, tough new corporate governance regulations were introduced in the US by SOX.

- SOX is a rules-based approach to governance.

- SOX is extremely detailed and carries the full force of the law.

- SOX includes requirements for the Securities and Exchange Commission (SEC) to issue certain rules on corporate governance.

- It is relevant to US companies, directors of subsidiaries of US-listed businesses and auditors who are working on US-listed businesses.

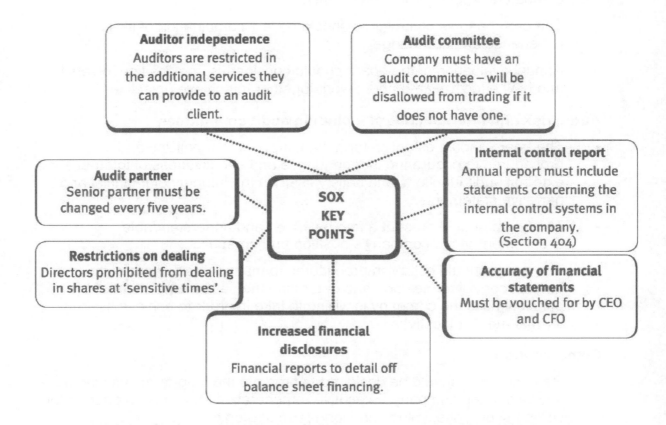

 Measures introduced by SOX

Measures introduced by SOX include:

- All companies with a listing for their shares in the US must provide a signed certificate to the SEC vouching for the accuracy of their financial statements (signed by CEO and CFO).

- If a company's financial statements are restated due to material noncompliance with accounting rules and standards, the CEO and chief finance officer (CFO) must forfeit bonuses awarded in the previous 12 months.

- Restrictions are placed on the type of non-audit work that can be performed for a company by its firm of auditors.

- The senior audit partner working on a client's audit must be changed at least every five years (i.e. audit partner rotation is compulsory).

- An independent five-man board called the Public Company Oversight Board has been established, with responsibilities for enforcing professional standards in accounting and auditing.

- Regulations on the disclosure of off-balance sheet transactions have been tightened up.

- Directors are prohibited from dealing in the shares of their company at 'sensitive times'.

King Report III

The Institute of Directors in Southern Africa (IoDSA) formally introduced the King Code of Governance Principles and the King Report on Governance (King III).

King III was published on 1 September 2009. Previous versions were issued in 1994 and 2002.

It applies to all entities regardless of the manner and form of incorporation. Principles are drafted on the basis that, if they are adhered to, any entity would have practiced good governance.

In addressing the link between governance principles and law, the introduction to the Report observes:

"The ultimate compliance officer is the company's stakeholders who will let the board know by their continued support of the company if they accept the departure from a recommended practice and the reasons furnished for doing so."

The Code of governance should be used in conjunction with the Report in which recommendations of best practices are provided.

The Code is divided into nine sections which address:

- ethical leadership and corporate citizenship

- boards and directors

- audit committees

- the governance of risk

- the governance of information technology

- compliance with laws, rules, codes and standards

- internal audit

- governing stakeholder relationships

- integrated reporting and disclosure.

King III has opted for an 'apply or explain' governance framework. Where the board believes it to be in the best interests of the company, it can adopt a practice different from that recommended in King III, but must explain it.

King III can be seen in full at:

http://www.iodsa.co.za

12 Rules and principles based approaches to corporate governance

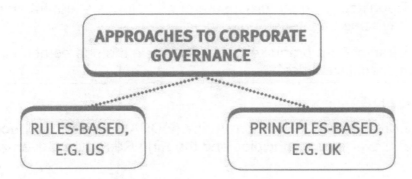

- A rules-based approach instils the code into law with appropriate penalties for transgression.

- A principles-based approach requires the company to adhere to the spirit rather than the letter of the code. The company must either comply with the code or explain why it has not through reports to the appropriate body and its shareholders.

The UK model is principles based and although it requires the company to adhere to the spirit of the code, and therefore best adopt best practice, it is governed by the Stock Exchange Listing Rules.

The listing rules provide statutory authority (via the Financial Service and Markets Act 2000) and require public listed companies to state how they have complied or explain why they have not under the "comply or explain" clause noted above. This provides a basis for comparing Corporate Statements.

There is no such requirement for disclosure of compliance in private company accounts.

The framework recommended by King III is principles-based and there is no 'one size fits all' solution. Entities are encouraged to tailor the principles of the Code as appropriate to the size, nature and complexity of their organisation.

The US model is enshrined into law by virtue of SOX. It is, therefore, a rules-based approach.

Choice of governance regime

The decision as to which approach to use for a country can be governed by many factors:

- dominant ownership structure (bank, family or multiple shareholder)
- legal system and its power/ability
- government structure and policies
- state of the economy
- culture and history
- levels of capital inflow or investment coming into the country
- global economic and political climate.

Comply or explain

A principles-based code requires the company to state that it has complied with the requirements of the code or to explain why it could not do so in its annual report. This will leave shareholders to draw their own conclusions regarding the governance of the company.

Arguments in favour of a rules-based approach (and against a principles-based approach)

Organisation's perspective:

- Clarity in terms of what the company must do – the rules are a legal requirement, clarity should exist and hence no interpretation is required.
- Standardisation for all companies – there is no choice as to complying or explaining and this creates a standardised and possibly fairer approach for all businesses.
- Binding requirements – the criminal nature makes it very clear that the rules must be complied with.

Wider stakeholder perspective:

- Standardisation across all companies – a level playing field is created.
- Sanction – the sanction is criminal and therefore a greater deterrent to transgression.
- Greater confidence in regulatory compliance.

Arguments against a rules-based approach (and in favour of a principles-based approach)

Organisation's perspective:

- Exploitation of loopholes – the exacting nature of the law lends itself to the seeking of loopholes.

- Underlying belief – the belief is that you must only play by the rules set. There is no suggestion that you should want to play by the rules (i.e. no 'buy-in' is required).

- Flexibility is lost – there is no choice in compliance to reflect the nature of the organisation, its size or stage of development.

- Checklist approach – this can arise as companies seek to comply with all aspects of the rules and start 'box-ticking'.

Wider stakeholder perspective:

- 'Regulation overload' – the volume of rules and amount of legislation may give rise to increasing costs for businesses and for the regulators.

- Legal costs – to enact new legislation to close loopholes.

- Limits – there is no room to improve, or go beyond the minimum level set.

- 'Box-ticking' rather than compliance – this does not lead to well governed organisations.

Issues in corporate governance relate to companies, and in particular listed companies whose shares are traded on major stock markets. However, similar issues might apply to smaller companies, and certainly to many large not-for-profit organisations.

	Large listed company	Private company	Not-for-profit organisation
Primary accountability	Shareholders and regulators	Shareholders	Fund providers, regulators, general public, members (where applicable).
Principal stakeholders	Shareholders	Shareholders	Donors, grant providers, regulators, general public, service users, members (if applicable).
Main methods of monitoring performance	Financial statements	Financial statements	Financial statements, other financial and nonfinancial measures.

Governance/ board structure	Executive and NEDs Appointment through formal process in line with governance requirements.	Executive directors Appointment may be the result of shareholding or other recruitment processes.	Volunteer trustees, paid and unpaid management team. Appointments through recruitment, recommendation or word of mouth, or election process.
Openness and transparency	In line with corporate governance requirements.	Limited disclosure requirements.	Limited requirements but large demand due to methods of funding.

- Corporate governance is a matter of great importance for large public companies, where the separation of ownership from management is much wider than for small private companies.

- Public companies raise capital on the stock markets, and institutional investors hold vast portfolios of shares and other investments. Investors need to know that their money is reasonably safe.

- Should there be any doubts about the integrity or intentions of the individuals in charge of a public company, the value of the company's shares will be affected and the company will have difficulty raising any new capital should it wish to do so.

- The scope of corporate governance for private and not-for-profit organisations will be much reduced when compared with a listed company, especially as there are no legal or regulatory requirements to comply with.

- The ownership and control, organisational objectives, risks and therefore focus may be different from a listed company. However, many of the governance principles will still be applicable to other entities.

- The public and not-for-profit sectors have voluntary best practice guidelines for governance which, while appreciating the differences in organisation and objective, cover many of the same topics (composition of governing bodies, accountability, risk management, transparency, etc.) included within the UK Corporate Governance Code.

- In not-for-profit organisations, a key governance focus will be to demonstrate to existing and potential fund providers that money is being spent in an appropriate manner, in line with the organisations' objectives.

Other governance codes

The Code of Governance for the Voluntary and Community Sector

- **Principle 1: Board leadership** – every organisation should be led and controlled by an effective board of trustees which collectively ensures delivery of its objects, sets its strategic direction and upholds its values.

- **Principle 2: The board in control** – the trustees as a board should collectively be responsible and accountable for ensuring and monitoring that the organisation is performing well, is solvent, and complies with all its obligations.

- **Principle 3: The high performance board** – the board should have clear responsibilities and functions, and should compose and organise itself to discharge them effectively.

- **Principle 4: Board review and renewal** – the board should periodically review its own and the organisation's effectiveness, and take any necessary steps to ensure that both continue to work well.

- **Principle 5: Board delegation** – the board should set out the functions of sub-committees, officers, the chief executive, other staff and agents in clear delegated authorities, and should monitor their performance.

- **Principle 6: Board and trustee integrity** – the board and individual trustees should act according to high ethical standards, and ensure that conflicts of interest are properly dealt with.

- **Principle 7: Board openness** – the board should be open, responsive and accountable to its users, beneficiaries, members, partners and others with an interest in its work.

The Good Governance Standard for Public Services

- Good governance means focusing on the organisation's purpose and on outcomes for citizens and service users.

- Good governance means performing effectively in clearly defined functions and roles.

- Good governance means promoting values for the whole organisation and demonstrating the values of good governance through behaviour.

- Good governance means taking informed, transparent decisions and managing risk.

- Good governance means developing the capacity and capability of the governing body to be effective.

- Good governance means engaging stakeholders and making accountability real.

13 Advantages and disadvantages of a governance code

Reasons for developing a code

- It should reduce instances of fraud and corruption improving shareholder perception and market confidence.

- There is statistical evidence that poor governance equates to poor performance.

- Management consultancy, McKinseys, found that global investors were willing to pay a significant premium for companies that are well governed.

- The existence of good governance is a decision factor for institutional investors.

- Even if it does not add value, it reduces risk and huge potential losses to shareholders.

Practical problems with a governance code

- The process is reactionary rather than proactive, responding to major failures in governance rather than setting the agenda.

- The impact varies depending on the nature of the company and the global viewpoint.

- Directors complain that it restricts or even dilutes individual decision-making power.

- It adds red tape and bureaucracy in the use of committees and disclosure requirements.

- Adherence to governance requirements harms competitiveness and does not add value.

- It cannot stop fraud.

14 Board committees

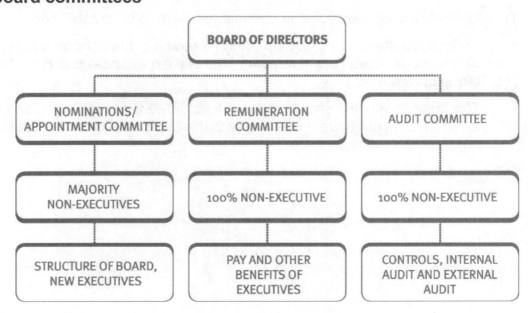

Importance of committees

Board sub-committees are a generally accepted part of board operations.

Positives that come out of the creation and use of such structures are:

- Reduces board workload and enables them to improve focus on other issues.

- Creates structures that can use inherent expertise to improve decisions in key areas.

- Communicates to shareholders that directors take these issues seriously.

- Increase in shareholder confidence.

- Communicates to stakeholders the importance of remuneration and risk.

- Satisfy requirements of the UK Corporate Governance Code (or other governance requirements).

Audit committee

Audit committees were first required under the Cadbury Code (and are now required by the UK Corporate Governance Code) in response to criticisms of the relationship between the directors and the auditors.

It was felt that the auditors were not sufficiently independent of the board of directors and that, as a result, the auditors were not providing their monitoring and reporting role as they should be.

Particular criticisms of the relationship were about:

- Remuneration of the auditors – decided by the directors.

- Appointment of the auditors – at the discretion of the directors in practice.

- Reports of the auditors – received by the directors.

- The directors had the power to give other lucrative work to auditors.

To address these concerns, audit committees were to be established.

- Audit committees are made up of non-executive directors (at least one of which should have recent relevant financial experience) and have formal terms of reference.

- The audit committee should meet at least three times per year, and also at least once a year have a meeting with the auditors without the presence of any executive directors.

Responsibilities of an audit committee

The responsibilities of the audit committee would typically include:

- Review of the financial statements, and any interim reports produced.

- Review of the company's system of internal financial controls.

- Discussion with the auditors about any significant matters that arose on the audit.

- Review of the internal audit programme and significant findings of the internal auditors.

- Recommendations on the appointment and removal of the auditors.

- The setting of the audit fee in discussion with the auditors.

- Review of the audit report and any management letter provided by the external auditors.

- Review all the company's internal control and risk management systems (unless this is delegated to a separate risk committee).

- Ensure that a system is in place for whistleblowing.

Nominations/Appointments Committee

The need for nominations committee is identified in many codes of best practice.

As an example, the UK Corporate Governance Code requires that **there should be a formal, rigorous and transparent procedure for the appointments of new directors to the board:**

- Creation of a nominations committee.

- This should have a majority of NEDs, the chairman should chair except when considering his successor.

- Evaluation of candidate's skills, knowledge and expertise is vital.

- Chairman's other commitments should be noted in the annual report.

- NED terms and conditions available for inspection, other commitments stated.

- Executives should not be members of any other FTSE 100 company board.

- A separate section of the annual report should describe the work of the committee.

Responsibilities of nominations committee

The main responsibilities and duties of the nominations committee are to:

- Review regularly the structure, size and composition of the board and make recommendations to the board.

- Consider the balance between executives and NEDs on the board of directors.

- Ensure appropriate management of diversity to board composition.

- Provide an appropriate balance of power to reduce domination in executive selection by the CEO/chairman.

- Regularly evaluate the balance of skills, knowledge and experience of the board.

- Give full consideration to succession planning for directors.

- Prepare a description of the role and capabilities required for any particular board appointment including that of the chairman.

- Identify and nominate for the approval by the board candidates to fill board vacancies as and when they arise.

- Make recommendations to the board concerning the standing for reappointment of directors.

- Be seen to operate independently for the benefit of shareholders.

Remuneration committee

The role of the remuneration committee

The role of the remuneration committee is to have an appropriate reward policy that attracts, retains and motivates directors to achieve the long-term interests of shareholders.

Objectives of the committee

- The committee is, and is seen to be, independent with access to its own external advice or consultants.

- It has a clear policy on remuneration that is well understood and has the support of shareholders.

- Performance packages produced are aligned with long-term shareholder interests and have challenging targets.

- Reporting is clear, concise and gives the reader of the annual report a bird's-eye view of policy payments and the rationale behind them.

The whole area of executive pay is one where trust must be created or restored through good governance and this is exercised through the use of a remuneration committee.

Responsibilities of the remuneration committee

The overall responsibilities of the remuneration committee are to:

- Determine and regularly review the framework, broad policy and specific terms for the remuneration and terms and conditions of employment of the chairman of the board and of executive directors (including design of targets and any bonus scheme payments).

- Recommend and monitor the level and structure of the remuneration of senior managers.

- Establish pension provision policy for all board members.

- Set detailed remuneration for all executive directors and the chairman, including pension rights and any compensation payments.

- Ensure that the executive directors and key management are fairly rewarded for their individual contribution to the overall performance of the company.

- Demonstrate to shareholders that the remuneration of the executive directors and key management is set by individuals with no personal interest in the outcome of the decisions of the committee.

- Agree any compensation for loss of office of any executive director.

15 The effects of corporate governance on directors' powers and duties

Directors' powers and duties can generally be determined by reference to the company's constitution and shareholder agreement. In addition, they may be derived from individual contracts of service and company law.

A director owes his duties to the company itself, that is to the shareholders as a body and those duties are enforceable by the company.

One of the ways in which corporate governance affects a director's duties and powers is by having a board with non-executive directors. Non-executive directors can scrutinise decisions made by executive directors. They can also take responsibility for monitoring the performance of executive management, especially with regard to the progress made towards achieving the determined company strategy and objectives.

The board sub-committees discussed above (nominations/remunerations/audit) can also detach a director from making decisions which in the past would have been within their powers.

The rules and standards which make up corporate governance are aimed at a much wider audience than just shareholders. The rules are intended to benefit stakeholders. It can therefore be argued that the legal duties a director has and the rules and standards which make up corporate governance have different aims. A director could be in breach of his legal duty yet still be complying with the principles of corporate governance.

16   Test your understanding questions

Test your understanding 1

List examples of profit-seeking organisations.

Test your understanding 2

What does a code of corporate governance cover?

Test your understanding 3

Which of the following is correct?

A   It is a criminal offence for listed companies to fail to comply with the UK Corporate Governance Code.

B   A listed public company has complied with the UK Corporate Governance Code if it produces a report explaining why it has not implemented its recommendations.

C   The UK Corporate Governance Code has no status and may be ignored by all companies.

D   A public company may be sued for breach of statutory duty if it fails to comply with the UK Corporate Governance Code.

Test your understanding 4

Which of the following apply a rules-based approach to corporate governance?

A   Sarbanes-Oxley

B   UK Corporate Governance Code

C   King III

D   All of the above

Test your understanding 5

How often should the audit committee meet?

Test your understanding answers

Test your understanding 1

Sole traders

Partnerships

Limited liability companies

Test your understanding 2

A code will tend to cover:

- The role of the board of directors

- The reliability of financial reports and the relationship between the company and its auditors

- The interest of the company's shareholders in the company.

Test your understanding 3

B

The UK Corporate Governance Code is not contained in any statute. The code is effectively a 'comply or explain' code. It follows that a company which explains why it has not taken up the recommendations of the Code would nonetheless be complying with it.

Test your understanding 4

A

Sarbanes-Oxley follows a rules-based approach.

Test your understanding 5

The audit committee should meet at least three times per year, and also at least once a year have a meeting with the auditors without the presence of any executive directors.

Controls

Chapter learning objectives

Upon completion of this chapter you will be able to:

- identify the requirements for external audit and the basic processes undertaken

- explain the meaning of fair presentation

- distinguish between external and internal audit

- explain the purpose and basic procedures of internal audit; the need for financial controls and the purpose of audit checks and audit trails

- explain the role of internal audit in non-financial monitoring and control activities

- illustrate the added value internal audit provides to both the board and management of the corporation

- explain the nature of errors

- explain the nature of fraud

- describe the different methods of fraud prevention and detection.

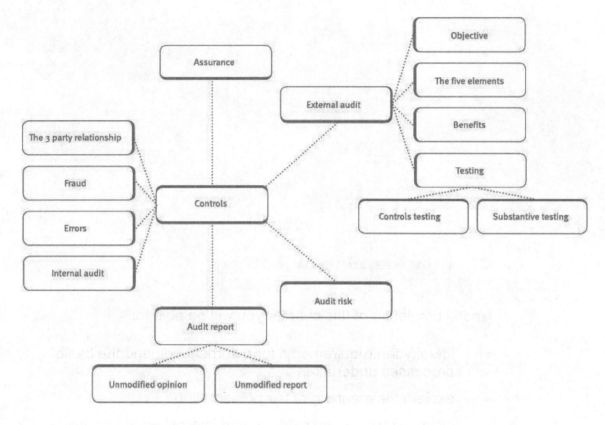

1   Assurance

An assurance engagement is one in which a **practitioner** expresses a conclusion designed to enhance the degree of confidence the **intended users** other than the **responsible party** have about the outcome of the evaluation or measurement of a subject matter against **criteria**.

The 3 party relationship

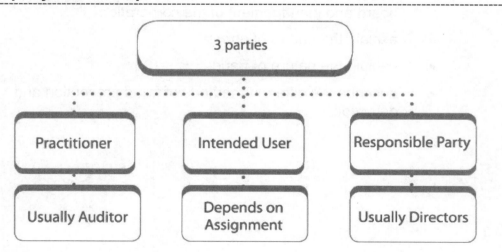

Examples of assurance engagements

- Statutory/external audit
- Fraud investigations
- Due diligence
- Internal controls assessment
- Business plan/projection reviews
- Environmental audits.

The objectives and processes of an external audit engagement will now be considered in more detail.

2 External audit engagement

Objective of an external audit engagement

The objective of an **external audit engagement** is to enable the auditor to express an opinion on whether the financial statements

- Give a fairly presented view (or fairly presented in all material respects).
- Are prepared, in all material respects, in accordance with an applicable financial reporting framework.

The financial reporting framework to be applied will vary from country to country.

The objectives of an **auditor** are to:

- Obtain reasonable assurance about whether the financial statements as a whole are free from material misstatement, whether due to fraud or error.
- Express an opinion on whether the financial statements are prepared, in all material respects, in accordance with an applicable financial reporting framework.
- Report on the financial statements, and communicate in accordance with the auditor's findings.

The purpose of an audit is to enhance the degree of confidence of the intended users in the financial statement. This is not 100% guarantee, but reasonable assurance.

The five elements of an external audit engagement

1   The three parties involved:

   –   the preparers – management/directors

   –   the users – shareholders

   –   the practitioner – the auditors.

2   The subject matter: the financial statements (prepared by management).

3   Sufficient appropriate evidence: obtained by performing audit procedures and reviewing the financial statements.

   –   **Sufficiency** relates to the **quantity** of evidence.

   –   **Appropriateness** relates to the **quality** or relevance and reliability of evidence.

4   This includes evaluating whether the financial statements are prepared in accordance with a relevant financial reporting framework (i.e. suitable criteria).

5   The audit report: which is presented to the shareholders. This report summarises the auditor's opinion as to whether the financial statements are fairly presented i.e. "true and fair".

An external audit is when an independent expert examines and checks the financial statements. The auditor will then prepare a report to present to the shareholders.

Some organisations are required by law to have their financial statements audited by an independent, qualified accountant. Others choose to have their financial statements audited on a voluntary basis, as the existence of an audit report may be beneficial to them.

The objective of an audit is for the auditor to express an opinion as to whether the financial statements are fairly presented, i.e. that they

•   show a true (accurate) and fair (unbiased) view

•   have been prepared in accordance with 'specific legislation' (thus will vary internationally).

The purpose of an audit is to give users confidence in the financial statements. This is not 100% guarantee, but reasonable assurance.

Need for external audit

- Shareholders provide the finance for a company and may or may not be involved in the day to day running of the company.

- Directors manage the company on behalf of the shareholders in order to achieve the objectives of that company (normally the maximisation of shareholder wealth).

- The directors must prepare financial statements to provide information on performance and financial position to the shareholders.

- The directors have various incentives to manipulate the financial statements and show a different level of performance.

- Hence the need for an independent review of the financial statements to ensure they give a true and fair view – the external audit.

In most developed countries, publicly quoted companies and large companies are required by law to produce annual financial statements and have them audited by an external auditor.

Companies that are not required to have a statutory audit may choose to have an external audit because the company's shareholders or other influential stakeholders want one and because of the benefits of an audit.

Benefits of an audit

- Improves the quality and reliability of information, giving investors faith in and improving the reputation of the market.

- Independent scrutiny and verification may be valuable to management.

- May reduce the risk of management bias, fraud and error by acting as a deterrent.

- May detect bias, fraud and error.

- Enhances the credibility of the financial statements, e.g. for tax authorities or lenders.

- Deficiencies in the internal control system may be highlighted by the auditor.

Expectations gap

Some users incorrectly believe that an audit provides absolute assurance; that the audit opinion is a guarantee the financial statements are 'correct'. This and other misconceptions about the role of an auditor are referred to as the **'expectations gap'**.

Examples of the expectations gap

- a belief that auditors test **all** transactions and balances; they test on a sample basis.

- a belief that auditors are required to detect **all** fraud; auditors are required to provide reasonable assurance that the financial statements are free from **material** misstatement, which may be caused by fraud.

- a belief that auditors are responsible for **preparing** the financial statements; this is the responsibility of management.

Auditors provide reasonable assurance which is not absolute assurance. The **limitations of an audit** mean that it is not possible to provide a 100% guarantee.

Limitations of an audit

- **F**inancial statements include subjective estimates and other judgemental matters.

- **I**nternal controls may be relied on which have their own inherent limitations.

- **R**epresentations from management may have to be relied upon as the only source of evidence in some areas.

- **E**vidence is often persuasive not conclusive.

- **D**o not test all transactions and balances. Auditors test on a sample basis.

Rights of auditors

In order to carry out their duties, auditors are given certain rights:

- access to accounting records

- access to information and explanations as necessary

- to receive notice of, attend and speak at general meetings of shareholders

- rights relating to their removal, resignation and retirement.

Fair presentation or true and fair

Fair presentation or 'true and fair' means that financial statements prepared for external publication should fairly reflect the financial position of the organisation. They should be free of material misstatements arising from negligence or deliberate manipulation. It may not be economically viable to test every single transaction, or to ensure 100 per cent accuracy, but fair presentation assumes that the financial statements do not contain any significant errors that would affect the actions of those reading them. This is based on the materiality convention discussed below. It is the duty of the registered auditor to test the financial statements for material misstatement and to report on whether they are presented fairly.

The materiality convention and the auditor

The purpose of an audit is to allow the auditor to form an opinion and to report accordingly on whether or not the financial statements fairly present the position and performance of a company.

To achieve this the auditor tests the transactions, accounting balances and disclosures reported in the financial statements. They cannot test everything so they select samples for testing based upon their assessment of where the greatest risk of material misstatement lies.

Following testing the auditor considers the results and conclusions of the tests, evaluating in particular any identified misstatements.

Testing

On the whole auditors perform two broad forms of tests.

The first is known as controls testing, which involves assessing the reliability of accounting systems, procedures and controls. If these appear to be working satisfactorily, the auditors can place a degree of reliance on them and that means that they do not need to test those areas in detail.

If there are areas of doubt, areas of high risk or items of a material nature, the auditors choose to carry out more detailed testing designed to detect material misstatement, known as substantive testing.

Audit risk

- Auditors usually adopt a risk–based approach to auditing.
- Effective risk assessment should:
  - Make the audit more efficient with work directed to likely problem areas.
  - Lead to fewer inappropriate opinions.
  - Result in fewer negligence claims against auditor.

Risk the auditor comes to an incorrect opinion = AUDIT RISK

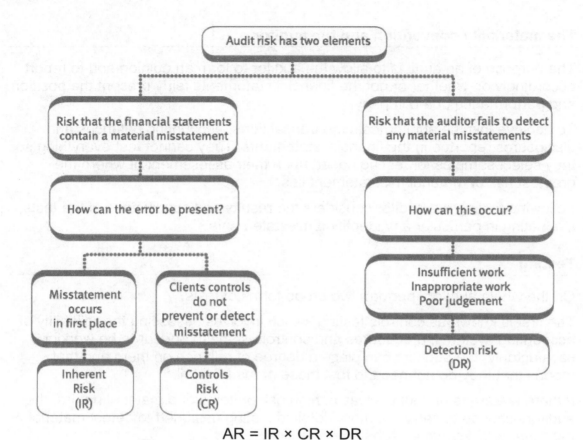

$$AR = IR \times CR \times DR$$

Inherent risk

The susceptibility of a transaction, account balance or disclosure to material misstatement irrespective of the internal controls in place.

Inherent risk can be considered at the:

- Industry level
  - Affects the whole industry
  - e.g. highly regulated industries such as banking.

- Entity level
  - Affects the whole entity
  - e.g. Company may not be a going concern, management get profit related bonuses.

- Balance level
  - Inherent risk is isolated to one balance
  - e.g. items which are complex or subjective.

Control risk

The risk that a material misstatement would not be prevented, detected or corrected by the accounting and internal control systems.

Detection risk

The risk that the auditor's procedures will not detect a misstatement that exists in an account balance or class of transactions that could be material, either individually or when aggregated with misstatements in other balances or classes.

Example:

Audit risk =   Inherent risk   ×   Control risk   ×   Detection risk

$\downarrow$ $\downarrow$

Highly regulated business   Poor controls

HIGH   ×   HIGH   ×   LOW

As the auditor has little or no control over the levels of inherent risk or control risk, this means that the only way to ensure the overall audit risk is acceptable is for the auditor to manipulate the detection risk, by increasing or reducing substantive testing.

In order for the auditor's opinion to be considered trustworthy auditors must come to their conclusions having completed a thorough examination of the books and records of their clients and they must document the procedures performed and evidence obtained, to support the conclusions reached.

As discussed earlier the auditor needs to obtain sufficient appropriate evidence.

Sufficiency relates to the quantity of evidence.

Appropriateness relates to the **quality** or relevance and reliability of evidence.

Sufficient evidence

There needs to be 'enough' evidence to support the auditor's conclusion. This is a matter of professional judgement. When determining whether there is enough evidence the auditor must consider:

- the risk of material misstatement
- the materiality of the item
- the nature of accounting and internal control systems
- the auditor's knowledge and experience of the business
- the results of controls tests
- the size of a population being tested
- the size of the sample selected to test
- the reliability of the evidence obtained.

Appropriate evidence

Appropriateness of evidence breaks down into two important concepts:

- reliability
- relevance.

Reliability

Auditors should always attempt to obtain evidence from the most trustworthy and dependable source possible. Evidence is considered more reliable when it is:

- obtained from an independent external source
- generated internally but subject to effective control
- obtained directly by the auditor
- in documentary form
- in original form.

Broadly speaking, the more reliable the evidence the less of it the auditor will need. However, if evidence is unreliable it will never be appropriate for the audit, no matter how much is gathered.

Relevance

To be relevant audit evidence has to address the objective/purpose of a procedure. For example, when attending an inventory count, the auditor will:

- select a sample of items from physical inventory and trace them to inventory records to confirm the **completeness** of accounting records
- select a sample of items from inventory records and trace them to physical inventories to confirm the **existence** of inventory assets.

Whilst the procedures are perhaps similar in nature their purpose (and relevance) is to test different **assertions** regarding inventory balances.

3 Agency and stewardship

The concepts of agency and stewardship were discussed in the previous chapter. We will now consider how these concepts apply to the role of the auditor.

Agency

The relationship of the company with its auditors is a principal-agent relationship.

- The audit is seen as a key component of corporate governance, providing an independent review of the financial position of the organisation.
- Auditors act as agents to principals (shareholders) when performing an audit and this relationship brings similar concerns with regard to trust and confidence as the director-shareholder relationship.

- Like directors, auditors will have their own interests and motives to consider.

- Auditor independence from the board of directors is of great importance to shareholders and is seen as a key factor in helping to deliver audit quality. However, an audit necessitates a close working relationship with the board of directors of a company.

- This close relationship has led (and continues to lead) shareholders to question the perceived and actual independence of auditors so tougher controls and standards have been introduced to protect them.

Stewardship

Auditors can be seen as stewards of a company. They are directly accountable to the shareholders for their period of office and hence owe a duty of care to the company's existing shareholders as a body i.e. to the company as a whole.

The Audit Firm Governance Code (explained in more detail later on in this chapter) requires auditors to engage regularly with the owners of the companies which they audit.

4 The engagement letter

The engagement letter specifies the nature of the **contract** between the audit firm.

Its purpose is to

- minimise the risk of any misunderstanding between the auditor and client

- confirm acceptance of the engagement

- set out the terms and conditions of the engagement.

The letter will be **sent before the audit commences**.

It should be **reviewed every year** to ensure that it is up to date but does not need to be reissued every year unless there are changes to the terms of the engagement. The auditor must issue a **new engagement letter if the scope or context** of the assignment **changes** after initial appointment.

The contents of the engagement letter

The main contents should include:

- the objective and scope of the audit.

- the responsibilities of the auditor.

- the responsibilities of management.

- the identification of an applicable financial reporting framework.

- reference to the expected form and content of any reports to be issued.

In addition the following items will be included:

- Reference to professional standards, regulations and legislation applicable to the audit.
- Limitations of an audit.
- Expectation that management will provide written representations.
- Basis on which the fees are calculated.
- Agreement of management to notify the auditor of subsequent events after the audit report is signed.
- Agreement of management to provide draft financial statements in time to allow the audit to be completed by the deadline.
- Form (and timing) of any other communication during the audit.

Other matters that the engagement letter may cover include:

- Arrangements concerning the involvement of internal auditors and other staff of the entity.
- Limitations to the auditor's liability.

5 Planning an audit

Audits are potentially complex, risky and expensive processes. It is vital that engagements are planned to ensure that the auditor:

- devotes appropriate attention to important areas of the audit
- identifies and resolves potential problems on a timely basis
- organises and manages the audit so that it is performed in an effective and efficient manner
- selects team members with appropriate capabilities and competencies
- directs and supervises the team and reviews their work
- effectively coordinates the work of others, such as experts and internal audit.

Planning ensures that the risk of performing a poor quality audit (and ultimately giving an inappropriate audit opinion) is reduced to an acceptable level.

The planning process

Planning consists of a number of elements. They can be summarised as:

- Preliminary engagement activities:
  - evaluating compliance with ethical requirements
  - establishing the terms of the engagement.
- Planning activities:
  - developing the audit strategy
  - developing an audit plan.

The audit strategy

The audit strategy sets the scope, timing and direction of the audit. It allows the auditor to determine the following:

- the resources to deploy for specific audit areas (e.g. experience level, external experts)

- the amount of resources to allocate (i.e. number of team members)

- when the resources are to be deployed

- how the resources are managed, directed and supervised, including the timings of meetings, debriefs and reviews.

The audit plan

Once the audit strategy has been established, the next stage is to develop a specific, detailed plan to address how the various matters identified in the overall strategy will be applied.

The strategy sets the overall approach to the audit, the plan fills in the operational details of how the strategy is to be achieved.

6   Reporting to those charged with governance

'Those charged with governance' includes the directors of a company and the members of its Audit Committee where one exists.

Matters to be communicated to those charged with governance include

- The responsibilities of the auditor in relation to the financial statements audit

- An overview of the planned scope and timing of the audit

- Significant findings of the audit

- For listed clients, matters that have a bearing on auditor Independence and the safeguards that have been put in place to eliminate them.

Communication shall be in any appropriate form, although the matters that must be communicated with regards to independence for listed clients must be communicated in writing.

Communicating deficiencies in internal control to those charged with governance

This covers reporting deficiencies in internal control that have been identified during the course of the audit. It is a by-product of the audit and may not be a comprehensive list of deficiencies.

This report, traditionally known as a management letter, is usually sent at the end of the audit process.

The report would generally include:

- A covering letter.

- Appendices showing, typically in tabular format, the control deficiencies, implications and recommendations for improvement.

The table in the appendix would normally have 3 sections:

Deficiency	Consequences	Recommendations
Statement of fact – in the exam this is normally given to you so does not need to be repeated	Cost to the business (e.g. losses, adverse impact on cash flow, loss of customer goodwill) Possibility of misstatements in the financial statements	Specific (who/what/when/how) Commercially feasible

When the auditor reports deficiencies, it should be made clear that:

- The report is not a comprehensive list of deficiencies, but only those that have come to light during normal audit procedures.

- The report is for the sole use of the company.

- No disclosure should be made to a third party without the written agreement of the auditor.

- No responsibility is assumed to any other parties.

7 Written representation letter

 A **written representation** is: a written statement by management provided to the auditor to confirm certain matters or to support other audit evidence.

The purpose of obtaining this form of evidence is:

- to obtain evidence that management, and those charged with governance, have fulfilled their responsibility (as agreed and acknowledged in the terms of the audit engagement) for the preparation of the financial statements, including:

  - preparing the financial statements in accordance with an applicable financial reporting framework

  - providing the auditor with all relevant information and access to records

  - recording all transactions and reflecting them in the financial statements.

- to support other audit evidence relevant to the financial statements if determined necessary by the auditor.

A representation to support other audit evidence may be appropriate where more reliable forms of evidence are not available, particularly in relation to matters requiring management judgement or knowledge restricted to management. Examples include:

- plans or intentions that may affect the carrying value of assets or liabilities

- confirmation of values where there is a significant degree of estimation or judgement involved, e.g. provisions and contingent liabilities

- formal confirmation of the directors' judgement on contentious issues, e.g. the value of assets where there is a risk of impairment

- aspects of laws and regulations that may affect the financial statements, including compliance.

A written representation should be in the form of a representation letter addressed to the auditor.

Note that written representations cannot substitute for more reliable evidence that should be available and do not constitute sufficient appropriate evidence on their own, about any of the matters with which they deal.

Written representations should only be sought to support other audit evidence.

In practice, the auditor will often draft the written representations letter but it must be printed on client headed paper and signed by the client.

The letter must be signed by an appropriate senior member of client management, with appropriate responsibilities for the financial statements and knowledge of the matters concerned. This would normally be the chief executive and chief financial officer.

The date of the written representation letter should be the same as the date the financial statements are authorised. It must be obtained (and signed) before the audit report is finalised.

8 Audit report

As discussed above one of the objectives of an auditor is to express an opinion which is executed through a written report.

When the auditor concludes that the financial statements are prepared, in all material respects, in accordance with the applicable financial reporting framework they issue an **unmodified opinion** in the audit report.

If there are no other matters which the auditor wishes to draw to the attention of the users, they will issue an **unmodified report**.

Contents of an unmodified audit report

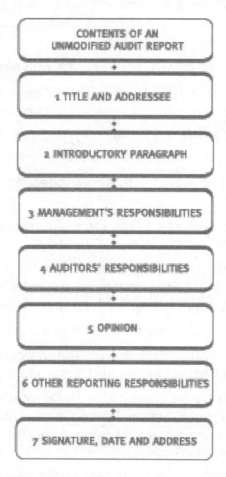

CONTENTS OF AN
UNMODIFIED AUDIT REPORT

1 TITLE AND ADDRESSEE

2 INTRODUCTORY PARAGRAPH

3 MANAGEMENT'S RESPONSIBILITIES

4 AUDITORS' RESPONSIBILITIES

5 OPINION

6 OTHER REPORTING RESPONSIBILITIES

7 SIGNATURE, DATE AND ADDRESS

The other types of audit report are:

- Modified without modifying the opinion – the financial statements show a true and fair view but there is something that needs to be brought to the attention of the user by way of an additional paragraph.

- Modified with a modified opinion – the financial statements don't fully show a true and fair view or the auditor has not obtained sufficient appropriate evidence to make that conclusion.

9 Audit Firm Governance Code

In January 2010 the FRC and Institute of Chartered Accountants in England and Wales (ICAEW) published the Audit Firm Governance Code.

The Code is the result of a recommendation in the October 2007 report of the FRC's Market Participants Group that "every firm that audits public interest entities should comply with the provisions of a Combined Code-style best practice corporate governance guide or give a considered explanation".

The Working Group recommended that the code should be applicable to those firms that audit more than 20 listed companies and that it should apply to financial years beginning on or after 1 June 2010.

The Code applies to seven audit firms that together audit about 95% of the companies listed on the Main Market of the London Stock Exchange.

The purpose of the Code is to provide a formal benchmark of good governance practice against which firms which audit listed companies can report for the benefit of the shareholders in such companies.

The full code can be accessed here:

https://www.frc.org.uk/Our-Work/Codes-Standards/Audit-andassurance/Audit-Firm-Governance-Code.aspx

Contents

The Code is split into five sections. It comprises twenty principles which are supported by thirty-one provisions.

The main principles of each section are outlined below (reference to 'a firm' means 'a firm that audits listed companies'):

Leadership

1   The management of a firm should be accountable to the firm's owners and no individual should have unfettered powers of decision.

2   A firm should have effective management which has responsibility and clear authority for running the firm.

Values

1   A firm should perform quality work by exercising judgement and upholding values of integrity, objectivity, professional competence and due care, confidentiality and professional behaviour in a way that properly takes the public interest into consideration.

2   A firm should publicly commit itself to this Audit Firm Governance Code.

3   A firm should maintain a culture of openness which encourages people to consult and share problems, knowledge and experience in order to achieve quality work in a way that properly takes the public interest into consideration.

Independent Non-Executives

1   A firm should appoint independent non-executives who through their involvement collectively enhance shareholder confidence in the public interest aspects of the firm's decision making, stakeholder dialogue and management of reputational risks including those in the firm's businesses that are not otherwise effectively addressed by regulation.

2   The independent non-executives' duty of care is to the firm. They should command the respect of the firm's owners and collectively enhance shareholder confidence by virtue of their independence, number, stature, experience and expertise.

3   Independent non-executives of a firm should have rights consistent with their role including a right of access to relevant information and people to the extent permitted by law or regulation, and a right to report a fundamental disagreement regarding the firm to its owners and, where ultimately this cannot be resolved and the independent non-executive resigns, to report this resignation publicly.

Operations

1   A firm should comply with professional standards and applicable legal and regulatory requirements.

2   A firm should maintain a sound system of internal control and risk management over the operations of the firm as a whole to safeguard the owners' investment and the firm's assets.

3   A firm should apply policies and procedures for managing people across the whole firm that support its commitment to the professionalism, openness and risk management principles of this Audit Firm Governance Code.

4   A firm should establish and apply confidential whistleblowing policies and procedures across the firm which enable people to report, without fear, concerns about the firm's commitment to quality work and professional judgement and values in a way that properly takes the public interest into consideration.

Reporting

1   The management team of a firm should ensure that members of its governance structures, including owners and independent non-executives, are supplied with information in a timely manner and in a form and of a quality appropriate to enable them to discharge their duties.

2   A firm should publish audited financial statements prepared in accordance with a recognised financial reporting framework such as International Financial Reporting Standards or UK GAAP.

3   The management of a firm should publish on an annual basis a balanced and understandable commentary on the firm's financial performance, position and prospects.

4   A firm should publicly report how it has applied in practice each of the principles of the Audit Firm Governance Code and make a statement on its compliance with the Code's provisions or give a considered explanation for any non-compliance.

5   A firm should establish formal and transparent arrangements for monitoring the quality of external reporting and for maintaining an appropriate relationship with the firm's auditors.

Dialogue

1   A firm should have dialogue with listed company shareholders, as well as listed companies and their audit committees, about matters covered by this Audit Firm Governance Code to enhance mutual communication and understanding and ensure that it keeps in touch with shareholder opinion, issues and concerns.

2   Shareholders should have dialogue with audit firms to enhance mutual communication and understanding.

3   Shareholders should have dialogue with listed companies on the process of recommending the appointment and re-appointment of auditors and should make considered use of votes in relation to such recommendations.

10   Internal audit

Function and importance of internal audit

- Internal audit is a management control. The department reviews the effectiveness of other controls within a company.

- It is part of the control systems of a company, with the aim of ensuring that other controls are working correctly.

- In some regimes, it is a statutory requirement to have internal audit. In others, codes of corporate governance strongly suggest that an internal audit department is necessary.

- The work of internal audit is varied – from reviewing financial controls through to checking compliance with legislation.

- The department is normally under the control of a chief internal auditor who reports to the audit committee.

Roles of internal audit

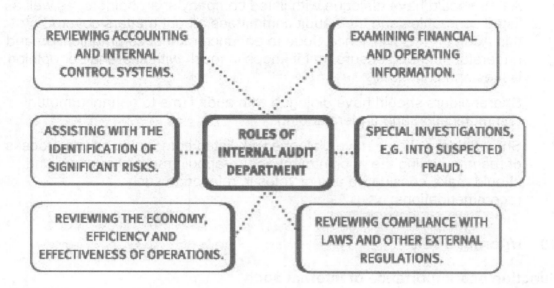

Companies must create a strong system of internal control in order to fulfil their responsibilities.

However, it is not sufficient to simply have mechanisms in place to manage a business; their effectiveness must be regularly evaluated. All systems need some form of monitoring and feedback. This is the role of internal audit.

Having an internal audit department is generally considered to be 'best practice,' but is not required by law. This allows flexibility in the way internal audit is established to suit the needs of a business.

In small, or owner managed businesses there is unlikely to be a need for internal audit because the owners are able to exercise more direct control over operations, and are accountable to fewer stakeholders.

The need for internal audit, therefore will depend on:

- Scale and diversity of activities. In a larger, diversified organisation there is a risk that controls don't work as effectively because of the delegation of responsibility down the organisation. Internal audit can report back to the audit committee if controls are not as effective as they should be.

- Complexity of operations. The more complex the organisation is, the more benefit can be obtained from having an internal audit function to evaluate as there is greater risk of things going wrong. With a larger organisation the consequences of poor controls/risk management/corporate governance practices are likely to be greater.

- Number of employees. The greater the number of employees the greater the risk of fraud.

- Cost/benefit considerations. It will only be worth establishing an internal audit function if the benefits outweigh the costs. For example a company might be losing money as a result of fraud, not using the most cost effective or reliable suppliers, incurring fines for noncompliance with laws and regulations. If these costs outweigh the cost of employing an internal audit function it will be beneficial to the company to establish a department.

- The desire of senior management to have assurance and advice on risk and control. The directors may wish to have the comfort that there is ongoing monitoring of the organisation to help them discharge their responsibilities.

Roles of internal audit department

Work area	Comment
Reviewing accounting and internal control systems (financial audit)	This is the traditional view of internal audit. The internal auditor checks the financial controls in the company, possibly assisting or sharing work with the external auditor. The internal auditor would comment on whether appropriate controls exist as well as whether they are working correctly. In this work, the internal auditor does not manage risk, but simply reports on controls.
Assisting with the identification of significant risks	In this function, the internal auditor does start to work on risks. The auditor may be asked to investigate areas of risk management, with specific reference on how the company identifies, assesses and controls significant risks from both internal and external sources.
Reviewing the economy, efficiency and effectiveness of operations (operational audit)	This is also called a value for money (VFM) audit. The auditor checks whether a particular activity is cost effective (economical), uses the minimum inputs for a given output (efficient) and meets its stated objectives (effective).
Examining financial and operating information	Internal auditors ensure that reporting of financial information is made on a timely basis and that the information in the reports is factually accurate.
Special investigations	Investigations into other areas of the company's business, e.g. checking the cost estimates for a new factory.
Reviewing compliance with laws and other external regulations	This objective is particularly relevant regarding SOX where the internal auditor will be carrying out detailed work to ensure that internal control systems and financial reports meet stock exchange requirements.

Types of audit work

The internal audit department will carry out many different types of audit, as highlighted by the department's varied roles.

Examples of audit types are:

- financial audit
- operational audit
- project audit
- value for money audit
- social and environmental audit
- management audit.

Types of audit

Financial audit

Financial auditing is traditionally the main area of work for the internal audit department. It embraces:

- the conventional tasks of examining records and evidence to support financial and management reporting in order to detect errors and prevent fraud
- analysing information, identifying trends and potentially significant variations from the norm.

Operational auditing covers:

- examination and review of a business operation
- the effectiveness of controls
- identification of areas for improvement in efficiency and performance including improving operational economy, efficiency and effectiveness – the three Es of value for money auditing.

There are four main areas where such an approach is commonly used

- procurement
- marketing
- treasury
- human resources.

Project auditing

Best value and IT assignments are really about looking at processes within the organisation and asking:

- were things done well?
- did the organisation achieve value for money?

Project auditing is about looking at a specific project:

- commissioning a new factory
- implementing new IT systems

and asking whether these were done well. So the focus is different and has more to do with:

- were the objectives achieved?
- was the project implemented efficiently.
- what lessons can be learned from any mistakes made?

A number of projects when taken together can become a programme.

Value for money audit

An area that internal auditors have been getting increasingly involved in is the value for money audits. These have been replaced in terminology more recently by "best value" audits, but many of the principles remain the same.

In a value for money audit the auditor assesses three main areas.

- Economy

  The economy of a business is assessed by looking at the inputs to the business (or process), and deciding whether these are the most economical that are available at an acceptable quality level. For example, if assessing the economy of a commercial company the inputs would be capital (plant and machinery, buildings, etc.), raw materials, the workforce and any administrative function required to run the business.

- Efficiency

  The efficiency of an operation is assessed by considering how well the operation converts inputs to outputs. In a manufacturing company this might involve looking at wastage in production or quality control failures for example.

- Effectiveness

  The effectiveness of an organisation is assessed by examining whether the organisation is achieving its objectives. To assess effectiveness there must be clear objectives for the organisation that can be examined. In some organisations, particularly not for profit and public service organisations, deciding suitable objectives can be one of the most difficult parts of the value for money exercise.

Social and environment audit

An environment audit is defined as:

'A management tool comprising a systematic, documented, periodic, and objective evaluation of how well organisations, management, and equipment are performing, with the aim of contributing to safeguarding the environment by facilitating management control of environmental practices, and assessing compliance with company policies, which would include meeting regulatory requirements and standards applicable.'

The social audit would look at the company's contribution to society and the community. The contributions made could be through:

- Donations.
- Sponsorship.
- Employment practices.
- Education.
- Health and safety.
- Ethical investments, etc.

A social audit could either confirm statements made by the directors, or make recommendations for social policies that the company should perform.

Management audit

A management audit is defined as 'an objective and independent appraisal of the effectiveness of managers and the corporate structure in the achievement of the entities' objectives and policies. Its aim is to identify existing and potential management weaknesses and recommend ways to rectify them.'

Limitations of internal audit

- Internal auditors may be employees of the company they are reporting on and therefore may not wish to raise issues in case they lose their job.

- In smaller organisations in particular, internal audit may be managed as part of the finance function. They will therefore have to report upon the effectiveness of financial systems that they form a part of and may be reluctant to say their department (and manager) has deficiencies.

- If the internal audit staff have worked in the organisation for a long time, possibly in different departments, there may be a familiarity threat as they will be audited the work of long standing colleagues and friends.

It is therefore difficult for internal audit to remain truly objective. However, acceptable levels of independence can be achieved through one, or more, of the following strategies:

- Reporting channels separate from the management of the main financial reporting function.

- Reviews of internal audit work by managers independent of the function under scrutiny.

- Outsourcing the internal audit function to a professional third party.

Qualities of an effective internal audit function

If the internal audit department is to be effective in providing assurance it needs to be:

- Sufficiently resourced, both financially and in terms of qualified, experienced staff.

- Well organised, so that it has well developed work practices.

- Independent and objective.

- Chief internal auditor appointed by the audit committee to reduce management bias.

- No operational responsibilities.

- Work plan agreed by the audit committee.

- No limitation on the scope of their work i.e. full access to every part of the organisation.

Outsourcing the internal audit function

In common with other areas of a company's operations, the directors may consider that outsourcing the internal audit function represents better value than an in-house provision.

Outsourcing is where the company uses an external company to perform its internal audit service instead of employing its own staff.

Advantages

- Greater focus on cost and efficiency of the internal audit function.
- Staff may be drawn from a broader range of expertise.
- Risk of staff turnover is passed to the outsourcing firm.
- Specialist skills may be more readily available.
- Costs of employing permanent staff are avoided.
- May improve independence.
- Access to new market place technologies, e.g. audit methodology software without associated costs.
- Reduced management time in administering an in-house department.

Disadvantages

- Possible conflict of interest if provided by the external auditors (In some jurisdictions – e.g. the UK, ethics rules specifically prohibit the external auditors from providing internal audit services where significant reliance will be placed on the work of the internal auditor).
- Pressure on the independence of the outsourced function due to, e.g. threat by management not to renew contract.
- Risk of lack of knowledge and understanding of the organisation's objectives, culture or business.
- The decision may be based on cost with the effectiveness of the function being reduced.
- Flexibility and availability may not be as high as with an in-house function.
- Lack of control over standard of service.
- Risk of blurring of roles between internal and external audit, losing credibility for both.

Reporting

Unlike an external audit report, the internal audit report does not have a formal reporting structure. It is likely that the format is agreed with the audit committee or board of directors prior to commencing the assignment.

These reports will generally be for internal use only. The external auditors may inspect them if they are intending on placing reliance on the work of internal audit.

A typical report will include:

- Terms of reference – the requirements of the assignment.

- Executive summary – the key risks and recommendations that are described more fully in the body of the report.

- Body of the report – a detailed description of the work performed and the results of that work.

- Appendix – containing any additional information that doesn't belong in the body of the report but which is relevant to the assignment.

11 Distinction between external and internal audit

Distinction between external and internal audit

	External audit	Internal audit
Objective	Express an opinion on the truth and fairness of the financial statements in a written report.	Improve the company's operations by reviewing the efficiency and effectiveness of internal controls.
Reporting	Reports to shareholders.	Reports to management or those charged with governance.
Availability of report	Publicly available.	Not publicly available. Usually only seen by management or those charged with governance.
Scope of work	Verifying the truth and fairness of the financial statements.	Wide in scope and dependent on management's requirements.
Appointment and removal	By the shareholders of the company.	By the audit committee or board of directors.
Relationship with company	Must be independent of the company.	May be employees (which limits independence) or an outsourced function (which enhances independence).

12 Errors

No bookkeeping system can be guaranteed to be entirely free of errors. Human beings are fallible, and even automated and computerised systems are less than perfect. For example, a computer cannot possibly know that a supplier has sent you an invoice that never arrived.

The following are types of errors:

- Errors of omission, where a transaction has been completely omitted from the ledger account.

- Errors of commission, where one side of the transaction has been entered in the wrong account (but of a similar type to the correct account, for example, entered in the wrong receivable's account, or in the wrong expense account). An error of commission would not affect the calculation of profit, or the position shown by the statement of financial position.

- Errors of principle, where the correct and incorrect accounts are of different types, for example, entered in the purchases account instead of a non-current asset account. This type of error would affect the calculation of profit, and the position shown by the statement of financial position.

Preventing errors

There are a number of ways in which errors can be prevented, or at least limited in their number and effect. Many of these also prevent deliberate fraud.

Authorisation procedures

Transactions should be authorised at an appropriate level. For example,

- the purchase of major non-current assets should be justified/agreed by senior management and recorded in the minutes of meetings

- cheques for large amounts should require two signatures

- new receivable and payable accounts should be authorised by a senior person

- all purchase orders should be authorised by a responsible officer

- all payments made should be approved. In particular
    - payments to suppliers should be checked against goods received, invoices and credit notes
    - refunds to customers should be authorised
    - payrolls should be checked and authorised prior to making payment.

Documentation

Documentation should be used to give evidence of transactions, and should be properly filed and referenced. This helps to provide an 'audit trail' of transactions through the system. As an example, consider the ordering of goods for resale, and the documentation involved.

- Raising of the order. On official order forms, properly authorised, after obtaining several quotations.

- Receipt of goods. Checked on arrival, checked with order, shortages and breakages recorded.

- Receipt of invoice. Checked with order and receipt of goods; prices, discounts and calculations checked.

- Payment of invoice. Only after all credit notes have been received, and checked with purchase ledger account prior to payment.

Organisation of staff

Staff should be properly recruited, trained and supervised. No one person should have complete control over any section of the bookkeeping system. Duties should be shared out between different members of staff. This is known as **segregation of duties**.

This can be illustrated by considering the procedures arising from selling goods on credit. In summary the tasks involved are:

- issuing sales invoices

- issuing credit notes

- credit control

- banking receipts from customers.

If one person were to be solely responsible for all (or even more than one) of these tasks, it would be easy for money to be diverted and the corresponding paperwork destroyed or falsified. Staff should also rotate their duties from time to time.

Safeguarding assets

Assets should be properly maintained, insured, utilised, valued and recorded.

Detecting errors

Some errors may come to light purely by chance, and some are never found at all. For example, if you receive a cheque from a customer who has no outstanding balance on his account, it is possible that an invoice has been omitted from the books. If you never receive the cheque, the error might never come to light.

It would be extremely unwise to trust to chance, and therefore there are several checks that can be incorporated to help detect errors.

Spot checks

These are particularly useful in detecting fraud. For example, spot checks on petty cash balances may uncover 'teeming and lading' activities, whereby an employee borrows money from the petty cash on a regular basis, but puts it back when the imprest is being checked, only to remove it again afterwards.

Spot checks are also commonly carried out on bank balances, ledger accounts and inventories.

13 Fraud

 What is fraud?

Fraud is an intentional act involving the use of deception to obtain an unjust or illegal advantage – essentially 'theft by deception'.

 Fraud or error

Fraud is a crime, but does not have a precise legal definition. The term 'fraud' refers to an intentional act by one or more individuals among management, those charged with governance, employees or third parties, involving the use of deception to obtain an unjust or illegal advantage. (International Standard of Auditing 240 *The Auditor's Responsibility to Consider Fraud in an Audit of Financial Statements*).

A distinction is made between:

- fraud, which is deliberate falsification, and

- errors, which are unintentional mistakes.

Note that fraud may be carried out by management, employees or third parties. For example:

- Managers may deliberately select inappropriate accounting policies.

- Employees may steal the proceeds of cash sales and omit to enter the sale into the accounting records.

- Third parties may send bogus invoices to the company, hoping that they will be paid in error.

> ### Findings about Fraud
>
> The CIMA publication "Fraud risk management: a guide to good practice" mentions that various surveys have highlighted the following facts about fraud:
>
> - organisations may be losing as much as 7% of their annual turnover as a result of fraud
>
> - corruption is estimated to cost the global economy about $1.5 trillion each year
>
> - only a small percentage of losses from fraud are recovered by organisations
>
> - a high percentage of frauds are committed by senior management and executives
>
> - greed is one of the main motivators for committing fraud
>
> - fraudsters often work in the finance function
>
> - fraud losses are not restricted to a particular sector or country
>
> - the prevalence of fraud is increasing in emerging markets.

Different types of fraud

Examples of fraud include:

- the theft of cash or other assets

- false accounting: this includes concealing or falsifying accounting records with a view to personal gain or providing false information that is misleading or deceptive

- crimes against consumers or clients, e.g. misrepresenting the quality of goods; pyramid trading schemes; selling counterfeit goods

- employee fraud against employers, e.g. payroll fraud; falsifying expense claims; theft of cash

- crimes against investors, consumers and employees, e.g. financial statement fraud

- crimes against financial institutions, e.g. using lost and stolen credit cards; fraudulent insurance claims

- crimes against government, e.g. social security benefit claims fraud; tax evasion

- crimes by professional criminals, e.g. money laundering; advance fee fraud

- e-crime by people using computers, e.g. spamming; copyright crimes; hacking.

Pyramid schemes

Pyramid schemes are also known as multi-level plans and network marketing plans. Although the law on these schemes varies between countries, as a general rule some pyramid schemes are legitimate and some are illegal.

The nature of a pyramid scheme is for the originator of the scheme to offer other people the opportunity to become a distributor for a product or service, which could range in size and value from vitamins to car leases. The distributor is given the opportunity to sell the product or service from home, in return for a commission.

In addition, a person who becomes a distributor is encouraged to sign up other people as distributors, and in return receives a commission for each new distributor they persuade to join the scheme.

The concept of the pyramid is that the originator of the scheme signs up a few distributors, who then sign up new distributors themselves. These new distributors in turn sign up more distributors, who then sign up more distributors.

Each new distributor signing up to the scheme is asked to make a payment, for an initial amount of products to sell, or for marketing material. Sometimes, new distributors might be persuaded to pay to go on a training course in the product or service.

If a pyramid scheme is intended primarily to sell the product or service to outside customers, it could well be legal. In the UK, for example, these schemes are legal provided they comply with certain regulations.

However, **these schemes are illegal** if their primary purpose is to sign up new distributors rather than to sell products or services to external customers.

When distributors earn money mainly by signing up more distributors, the pyramid selling scheme is illegal (in many countries) because there is a limit to the number of new distributors. At some stage, there will be no more distributors willing to sign up to the scheme. The distributors at the bottom of the pyramid will have spent money buying inventory and/or marketing material, with very little prospect of getting any money back. The scheme is then likely to be wound up, possibly with many commissions still unpaid, having made a large amount of money for its originator.

Fraud prevention

The aim of preventative controls is to reduce opportunity and remove temptation from potential offenders. Prevention techniques include the introduction of policies, procedures and controls, and activities such as training and fraud awareness to stop fraud from occurring.

The existence of a fraud strategy is itself a deterrent. This can be achieved through:

- An anti-fraud culture

  Where minor unethical practices are overlooked, for example, expenses or time recording, this may lead to a culture in which larger frauds occur. High ethical standards bring long term benefits as customers, suppliers, employees and the community realise they are dealing with a trustworthy organisation.

- Risk awareness

  Fraud should never be discounted, and there should be awareness among all staff that there is always the possibility that fraud is taking place. It is important to raise awareness through training programmes. Particular attention should be given to training and awareness among those people involved in receiving cash, purchasing and paying suppliers.

  Publicity can also be given to fraud that has been exposed. This serves as a reminder to those who may be tempted to commit fraud and a warning to those responsible for the management of controls.

- Whistleblowing

  Fraud may be suspected by those who are not personally involved. People must be encouraged to raise the alarm about fraud.

- Sound internal control systems

  Sound systems of internal control should monitor fraud by identifying risks and then putting into place procedures to monitor and report on those risks.

Fraud detection

A common misbelieve is that external auditors find fraud. This is actually rarely the case. Their letters of engagement typically state that it is not their responsibility to look for fraud.

Most frauds are discovered accidentally, or as a result of information received (whistleblowing).

Some methods of discovering fraud are:

- Performing regular checks

  For example stocktaking and cash counts.

- Warning signals

  For example:

  - Failures in internal control procedures.
  - Lack of information provided to auditors.
  - Unusual behaviour by individual staff members.
  - Accounting difficulties.
  - Whistleblowers.

Fraud response

- The fraud response plan sets out the arrangements for dealing with suspected cases of fraud, theft or corruption.

- It provides procedures for evidence-gathering that will enable decision-making and that will subsequently be admissible in any legal action.

- The fraud response plan also has a deterrent value and can help to restrict damage and minimise losses to the organisation.

The organisation's response to fraud may include:

- Internal disciplinary action, in accordance with personnel policies.

- Civil litigation for the recovery of loss.

- Criminal prosecution through the police.

Responsibilities

Within the response plan responsibilities should be allocated to:

- **Managers**, who should take responsibility for detecting fraud in their area.

- **Finance Director**, who has overall responsibility for the organisational response to fraud including the investigation. This role may be delegated to a **fraud officer** or internal security officer.

- **Personnel** (Human Resources Department), who will have responsibility for disciplinary procedures and issues of employment law and practice.

- **Audit committee**, who should review the details of all frauds and receive reports of any significant events.

- **Internal auditors**, who will most likely have the task of investigating the fraud.

- **External auditors**, to obtain expertise.

- **Legal advisors**, in relation to internal disciplinary, civil or criminal responses.

- **Public relations**, if the fraud is so significantly large that it will come to public attention.

- **Police**, where it is policy to prosecute all those suspected of fraud.

- **Insurers**, where there is likely to be a claim.

14 Test your understanding questions

Test your understanding 1

Which of the following is not an objective of an auditor?

A   To confirm that no fraud has occurred

B   Obtain reasonable assurance that the financial statements are free from material misstatement

C   Express an opinion whether the financial statements are prepared in accordance with an applicable financial reporting framework

D   Report on the financial statements

Test your understanding 2

In relation to assurance who are the three parties?

Test your understanding 3

Who are the users in an external audit engagement?

Test your understanding 4

List the contents of an unmodified audit report.

Test your understanding 5

Which of the following statements regarding internal audit is incorrect?

A   It should improve the company's operations

B   The reports are publicly available

C   The staff are appointed by the audit committee or board of directors

D   They report to management

Test your understanding answers

Test your understanding 1

A

This is not an objective of an auditor. It is management's responsibility to detect fraud.

Test your understanding 2

The 3 parties are:

* Practitioner
* Intended user
* Responsible party

Test your understanding 3

Shareholders

Test your understanding 4

The contents of an unmodified audit report are:

1   Title and addressee
2   Introductory paragraph
3   Management's responsibilities
4   Auditor's responsibilities
5   Opinion
6   Other reporting responsibilities
7   Signature, date and address

Test your understanding 5

B

The reports are not publicly available. They are usually only seen by management or those charged with governance.

Corporate Social Responsibility

Chapter learning objectives

Upon completion of this chapter you will be able to:

- describe the OECD general policies
- explain the role of national and international laws and regulations
- describe conflicting demands of stakeholders
- identify issues with CSR and the supply chain
- describe the guidelines of reporting CSR within annual reports
- identify synergies and tensions with CSR and brand management.

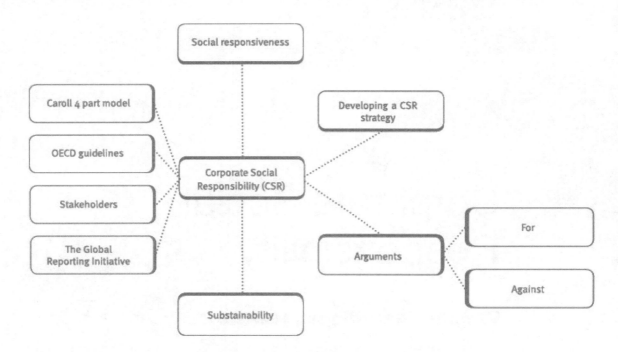

1 Corporate social responsibility (CSR)

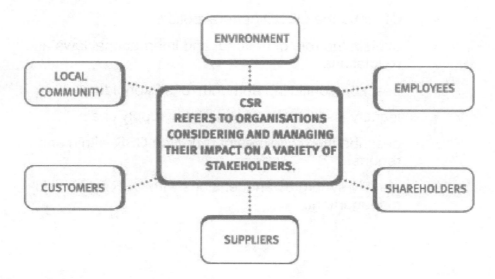

A corporation:

- Is an artificial person in law. It has the same rights and responsibilities as human beings.

- Is notionally owned by shareholders but exists independently of them. The shareholder has a right to vote and be paid a dividend but the company owns its assets.

- Managers have a fiduciary right to protect shareholder investment.

Milton Friedman argued that, in relation to this definition, a corporation has no responsibility outside of making profit for shareholders:

- Only human beings have moral responsibility for their actions.

- It is the managers' duty to act solely in the interest of shareholders:

    – this is a point of law. Any other action is shareholder betrayal.

- Social issues are the province of the state and not corporations.

The argument against this viewpoint needs to provide the organisation with an alternative view that leads to the same outcome of profit.

Enlightened self-interest

- Corporations perceived as ethically sound are rewarded with extra customers.

- Corporations which are ethically unsound are boycotted.

- Employees are more attracted to work for, and are more committed to, socially responsible companies.

- Voluntarily committing to social actions and programmes may forestall legislation and promote independence from government.

- Positive contribution to society may be a long-term investment in a safer, better educated and more equitable community creating a more stable context in which to do business.

What is CSR?

A formal definition of CSR has been proposed by the World Business Council for Sustainable Development (WBCSD):

'CSR is the continuous commitment by business to behave ethically and contribute to economic development while improving the quality of life of the workforce and their families as well as the local community and society at large'.

WBSCD meeting in the Netherlands, 1998

From the same source, perceptions of CSR from different societies and cultures were given as:

- 'CSR is about capacity building for sustainable livelihoods. It respects cultural differences and finds the business opportunities in building the skills of employees, the community and the government' (Ghana).

- 'CSR is about business giving back to society' (Philippines).

We can see that there is no one definition, or theory, of corporate social responsibility. However, it is certain that there will be increasing pressure on organisations to play an increasing role in the solution to social issues. This will be particularly true of those that have a global presence. This means that multinationals and non governmental organisations (NGOs) will increasingly be expected to take a lead in addressing those issues where a national government or local firm has not been able, or willing, to arrive at a solution.

Carroll's 4 Part Model

Economic

Economic responsibilities must be satisfied by organisations. Responsibilities relate to the ability of the organisation to stay in business and therefore provide for its stakeholders. For example:

- shareholders requiring a return on their investments

- employees to be provided with safe and fairly paid jobs

- customers to be able to obtain good quality products at a fair price.

The responsibilities are connected with why the organisation was established. The economic responsibility must be achieved in order to attain higher level responsibilities.

Legal

Legal responsibility implies that an organisation will follow the laws of the jurisdiction in which it is based as well as any internal moral views or objectives that the organisation has set. As with economic responsibility it is assumed that the organisation must act within the law to show that it is socially responsible.

Not complying with the law results in lack of social responsibility. For example:

- anti-competitive behaviour focusing on maximising market share and profits may be seen as lacking in social responsibility by limiting competition and charging excessively high prices (e.g. antitrust actions against Microsoft)

- price fixing by collusion (operation of cartels – always thought to be the case in the oil industry).

Legal responsibilities may therefore limit economic responsibilities by providing some social stance to organisations.

Ethical

Ethical responsibilities relate to what is expected by society from organisations compared with what those organisations have to do from an economic or legal viewpoint. Ethical responsibilities therefore relate to doing what is seen to be right compared with doing what is simply legal. For example:

- a company may decide to limit carbon emissions from its factory to a level below the legal maximum because this is seen to be acting in the interests of society

- Shell disposed of an oil platform on land rather than sinking it at sea (as it legally could have done) due to concern about the environmental consequences of this action.

Ethical responsibilities are therefore higher than both economic and legal responsibilities.

Philanthropic

Philanthropic responsibilities generally concern actions desired of organisations rather than those required by organisations. For example, organisations may:

- make donations to charities
- provide sports facilities for employees
- sponsor the arts (e.g. Tate & Lyle sponsoring the Tate Gallery in London).

These activities are carried out more because the organisation believes it is the correct thing to do rather than because it must. The term 'philanthropic' derives from the Greek 'love of society', so there is no obligation to act.

It has been argued that philanthropic responsibilities are less important than the other three levels because they are simply desired, not required, of organisations.

 The meaning of CSR

Marks and Spencer

Marks and Spencer promotes itself as a responsible business that takes the challenge of CSR seriously. It aims to listen and respond to the needs of its shareholders and build up good relationships with its employees, suppliers and society at large.

Marks and Spencer approach CSR by following three basic principles:

- products – throughout the three stages of each product's life (production, selling and usage), the aim is to encourage ethically and environmentally responsible behaviour
- people – everyone who works at the company is entitled to a mix of benefits. This approach is also encouraged amongst the company's suppliers, franchisees and other business partners
- places – the company recognises its obligations to the communities in which it trades. Successful retailing requires economically healthy and sustainable communities.

Social responsiveness

This refers to the capacity of the corporation to respond to social pressure, and the manner in which it does so.

Carroll suggests four possible strategies: reaction, defence, accommodation and proaction.

Reaction

The corporation denies any responsibility for social issues.

Defence

The corporation admits responsibility but fights it, doing the very least that seems to be required.

Accommodation

The corporation accepts responsibility and does what is demanded of it by relevant groups.

Proaction

The corporation seeks to go beyond industry norms.

Developing a CSR strategy

Strategic CSR

Organisations are now, more than ever before, under the watchful eye of their stakeholders.

By taking a strategic approach to CSR organisations can determine what activities they have the resources to devote to being socially responsible and therefore choose those that will strengthen their competitive advantage.

Including CSR as part of an organisation's strategic planning process can ensure that the pursuit of profit does not sideline or overshadow the need to behave ethically to their stakeholders.

In summary, strategic CSR provides companies with the structure for:

- Identifying and responding to threats and opportunities facing their stakeholders.

- Determining how to manage their stakeholder relationships.

- Development of sustainable business practices.

- Balancing the creation of economic value with societal value.

- Determining the organisations capacity for philanthropic activities.

The details on stakeholders will be covered in the following section.

Developing a CSR strategy in more detail

"What gets planned gets done." – Peter Drucker

Business Leaders understand that to achieve their company's goals, they need strategies to ensure that everyone in the organisation is headed in the right direction at the right time and that resources are available to support these goals when and where required.

For example, Hewlett-Packard's (HP) 2006 strategy to "Establish HP as the world's leading information technology company" was both clear and at the same time inspirational to the company's employees. The three subsidiary strategies established to achieve this goal were similarly very clear i.e. targeted growth, capital strategy, and efficiency.

HP personnel knew that if you contribute to one or more of these three strategies, you are helping the company achieve its greater goal of information technology supremacy. Therefore as an employee, you know that every year, your performance will be measured on your success in contributing to one or more of these strategies.

Unfortunately, few CSR strategies are as clear and compelling largely because the actual goals for most CSR efforts aren't in support of typical corporate functions such as marketing, manufacturing, sales, etc. so many companies are not exactly certain of what goals to set for them, or what strategies to pursue. This often results in unrelated strategies acting against rather than toward achieving corporate goals.

A suggested approach to develop a CSR strategy:

- The board make a firm published commitment to CSR, e.g. Marks and Spencer Plan A.

Senior executives must commit to and engage in CSR. A clear vision of CSR needs to be embedded within and reflect the core values of the firm, and be linked to the mission, vision and values of the organisation – recognizing that it creates not only social or environmental value, but that it creates business value as well. CSR should be managed as a core business strategy like for example marketing or research & development. CSR should report to a top-level executive in the company.

For example, innovative companies like Timberland have board committees overseeing corporate responsibility, and Gap takes board members on factory tours in China so they can see the value of supplier codes of conduct and audits. Generally the higher up CSR reports in the company, the more closely linked to providing value it is as a strategy.

- Determine the critical business objectives and priorities of the company, and develop a CSR strategy that will contribute to the achievement of those objectives.

To develop a CSR strategy, the company's leaders must first determine what specific business objectives this strategy must support. Defining business objectives is not as easy as it might appear and you're likely to get different answers from each business leader you ask.

For example, CSR can be used as a talent attraction and retention strategy if it is communicated clearly to potential and current employees, and they can engage in its principles. Similarly CSR can be used as a strategy to open up new markets for energy efficient products, penetrating new customer segments or grabbing market share from competitors whose customers care about environmentally friendly product lines.

- Align CSR strategy with the firm's core competencies.

CSR can be implemented in many businesses is typically executed in a non-integrated fashion. CSR initiatives originate from all parts of an organisation, and are often not directly linked to what the firm actually knows, does, or is expert in. Firms should, however, seek causes and social/ environmental strategies for which they own part of the solution. This requires focus and discipline and sticking true to that you know despite the myriad worthy causes and issues in our world.

For example, Ford Motor Company Foundation's support for breast cancer research which is approximately $100,000 each year.

There is no argument that this is a worthy cause with significant need, but there is no strategic link between the company's support for breast cancer research and the building of cars and trucks. Automotive companies know cars, transportation engineering, and design. It makes far more sense for an automobile manufacturer like Ford to support research in alternatively-fuelled vehicles or to address the global and environmental challenges around gasoline dependency because these initiatives fit the firm's core competencies and business objectives of selling more cars while potentially creating new products and revenue streams.

- Integrate CSR into the culture, governance and strategy development of the company.

CSR can be both a risk mitigation strategy and an opportunity-seeking strategy providing an intersection between business and social/ environmental returns.

- Develop key performance indicators to measure the impact of their CSR strategies.

CSR performance metrics should be both internal – such as reputation improvements, gains in market share, brand perception, increased sales, decreased operational expenditures, and employee satisfaction – as well as external ones focused on society and the environment.

CSR will not be fully embraced and executed with as much precision as are the more commonly measured functions such as sales and staff management until it is built into the recognition and performance appraisal system for a company's employees For example, Johnson and Johnson measures its employees on both their functional performance as well as their performance against their well respected ethical stance. Walmart in the supplier selection process measure them against price, quality, stock availability and sustainability.

Arguments against CSR

It can be argued that companies should not pursue corporate social responsibility. Milton Friedman argues that:

'The business of business is business.'

This means that the primary purpose of a business is to try and earn a profit. In a company, for instance, the managers have been employed in order to earn the owners of the business a return on their investment.

As such, it is a manager's duty to act in a way that maximises shareholder wealth, while conforming to all relevant laws and customs. If a manager does anything that is not directly related to wealth maximisation, he is failing in his responsibilities to the owners and therefore acting unethically.

For example, it can be argued that it is not right for a manager to donate any company funds to charity. The manager should instead work to maximise the return to the owner. If the owner wishes to make donations to charity, he can do so out of his earnings from the business.

In addition, it can be argued that maximising the wealth of business owners is, in itself, socially responsible. This is because:

- Increased returns will lead to increased tax payments made to the state. These can then be passed on to 'worthy causes'.

- A high proportion of company shares are owned by pension funds. This means that any gains will go to help provide pensions to individuals who may well be disadvantaged.

Don't forget that there may also be practical reasons why a business chooses not to pursue CSR. These can include:

- Increased cost of sourcing materials from ethical sources (e.g. Fairtrade products or free-range eggs).

- Having to turn away business from customers considered to be unethical (e.g. an 'ethical' bank may choose not to invest in a company that manufactures weapons).

- The management time that can be taken up by CSR planning and implementation.

Arguments for CSR

Not everyone agrees with Friedman's statements. There are a number of reasons why many businesses feel that CSR is a vital part of their strategy. These include:

- A key part of running a successful business is the ability to offer customers and consumers what they need. One of those needs is often a requirement for socially responsible behaviour from the organisation.

  Basically, **having good CSR can attract customers!** This can be because good CSR tends to enhance a company's reputation and therefore its brand. It can also be used a basis for differentiation in the market place – given the choice, many customers will prefer to trade with a company they feel is ethical.

- Good CSR is likely to involve good working conditions for employees, allowing the business to **attract a higher calibre of staff**.

- Avoiding discrimination against workers is likely to give the company **access to a wider human resource base**.

- Avoiding pollution will tend to save companies in the long run – many governments are now **fining or increasing taxes of more polluting businesses**.

- Sponsorship and charitable donations are tax deductible, improve staff morale and can be seen as a **form of advertising**.

Sustainability

One aspect of CSR that is also becoming increasingly important is sustainability.

Sustainability is the use of resources in such a way that they do not compromise the needs of future generations. It also involves not polluting the environment at a rate faster than they can be absorbed.

There are many examples of this. For example, some logging companies plant a tree for every one they fell.

Other companies try to make their products easy to recycle, helping to ensure that materials are reused rather than wasted. The computer manufacturer Apple has used this as part of its marketing approach for some years.

The reason that sustainability is so important for many businesses is that acting in a sustainable manner not only helps look after the environment and the wider community, but it strengthens the business and helps ensure its long-term survival.

It is worth noting that sustainability is increasingly being seen as important within the public sector. Ensuring that goods and services procured by the public sector are sustainable can help meet environmental goals across government, save considerable amounts of public money; and help support innovation and economic growth. This will involve taking account of a wide range of costs, such as pollution impacts, carbon emissions and waste disposal.

The difficulty for many businesses is that many companies focus on short term gains, rather than the long-term sustainability of the business and its environment. This is often evident in businesses that offer senior managers bonuses based on short-term or annual performance.

However, it should be noted that sustainability can lead to cost savings for an organisation in the short term. For example, an organisation that reduces packaging on its products may have a positive impact on the environment by generating less waste, but it will also reduce its costs, thereby improving profits.

Incorporating ethics and CSR into strategy

CIMA itself has been heavily involved in identifying and discussing the implications of sustainability for the business. To this end, in 2010 they published a research article discussing this.

http://www.cimaglobal.com/Documents/Professional%20ethics%20docs/Incorporatingethicsintostrategyweb 1.pdf

The article came to six key conclusions:

- Strong ethical principles that go beyond upholding the law can add great value to a brand, whereas failure to do the right thing can cause social, economic and environmental damage, undermining a company's long–term prospects in the process.

- Once they have adopted an ethical approach, companies will often find there are bottom-line benefits from demonstrating high ethical standards.

- The ethical tone comes from the top.

- High-quality management information on social, environmental and ethical performance is vital for monitoring the environmental and social impacts of a company and for compiling connected reports showing how effective its governance arrangements are.

- Corporate communications and reporting on sustainability need to do more than just pay lip service to the green agenda. They need to provide hard evidence of the positive impact on society, the environment and the strategic returns for the business, and how any negative effects are being addressed.

- Management accountants have a particular ethical responsibility to promote an ethics-based culture that doesn't permit practises such as bribery.

Championing sustainability

Rather than taking a reactive, passive approach to sustainability, finance professionals should take the initiative in raising awareness of social responsibility and the need to consider the impact of decisions and actions on sustainability. However, they need to remain objective while doing this.

This will involve promoting sustainable practices through the organisation in relation to the following:

Products and services

- Does making the product use inputs/materials/ingredients from renewable sources only?

- Does the firm source raw materials in ways that support their replenishment, safeguard natural habitats and ensure good animal welfare standards?

- What is the expected life of the product?

- How much of the product (including packaging) can be recycled?

- Is the level of packaging excessive?

Customers

- Does the firm have a recycling programme?

- What incentives are given to customers to encourage them to recycle?

- Does the firm encourage/help customers reduce their carbon footprint?

The supply chain

- Does the firm incorporate environmental considerations when selecting suppliers? For example, would it use a supplier with a poor record on pollution?

- Does the firm use suppliers who are geographically close to reduce the impact of transportation in terms of fuel used and exhaust emissions?

- Does the firm pay fair prices to suppliers or does it use its buying powers to drive prices down to very low levels?

- Does the firm encourage/help suppliers reduce their carbon footprint?

- Does the firm help suppliers reduce waste sent to landfill?

The workplace

- Does the firm have measurable targets for energy/water usage?

- Is the building energy efficient?

Employees

- Does the firm look after its employees in terms of working conditions, employment rights, job security, etc. or are staff 'hired and fired' when necessary?

- Does the firm contribute to community projects?

Other business functions and processes

- Does the firm take into account environmental impacts of activities when making decisions?

- Does the firm measure the impact of social initiatives?

Further CIMA information on sustainability

In December 2010, CIMA collaborated with the American Institute of Certified Public Accountants and the Canadian Institute of Chartered Accountants in a report entitled 'Evolution of corporate sustainability practices'.

Some key issues that this report raised include:

General

Business sustainability is about ensuring that organisations implement strategies that contribute to long–term success. Organisations that act in a sustainable manner not only help to maintain the well–being of the planet and people, they also create businesses that will survive and thrive in the long run.

The accounting profession can play an important role in this. Accountants can serve as leading agents for change by applying their skills and competencies to develop sustainability strategies, facilitate effective implementation, accurate measurement and credible business reporting.

Why do businesses have sustainability plans?

According to research conducted by CIMA, the key reasons include:

- **Compliance** – the need to comply with laws and regulations.

- **Reputational risk** – companies are concerned with how stakeholders will view them if they fail to act in a sustainable manner.

- **Cost-cutting and efficiency** – acting in a sustainable manner (for example becoming more energy-efficient) can help to reduce business expenditure. This is especially valuable for smaller companies.

Ten elements of organisational sustainability

The following areas are considered crucial to the successful embedding of sustainability within an organisation. It is worth noting that the accounting function will be useful in a number of these areas.

Strategy and oversight

- Board and senior management commitment.

- Understanding and analysing the key sustainability drivers for the organisation.

- Integrating the key sustainability drivers into the organisation's strategy.

Execution and alignment

- Ensuring that sustainability is the responsibility of everyone within the organisation (not just a specific department).

- Breaking down the sustainability targets and objectives for the organisation as a whole into targets and objectives which are meaningful for individual subsidiaries, divisions and departments.

- Processes that enable sustainability issues to be taken into account clearly and consistently in day-to-day decision-making.

- Extensive and effective sustainability training.

Performance and reporting

- Including sustainability targets and objectives in performance appraisal.

- Champions to promote sustainability and celebrate success.

- Monitoring and reporting sustainability performance.

Corporate social responsibility in action

Corporate social responsibility is seen as vital for many organisations. One company that is often hailed as a leader in this area is Ben & Jerry's – a US based manufacturer of ice-cream, frozen yoghurt and sorbet. The company has stated that 'business has a responsibility to the community and the environment'.

Ben & Jerry's CSR has included the following:

- Fair Trade ingredients – this ensures that suppliers of many of the company's raw materials enjoy safe working conditions, reasonable work hours and are paid fairly.

- Ethically sourced supplies – as well as a commitment to Fair Trade, the company also ensures, where possible, that it sources ingredients from suppliers who share its values. For example, Ben & Jerry's has historically sourced free-range eggs and sustainably produced dairy for its products.

- Community work – the company has engaged with communities to improve sustainability. Ben & Jerry's Vermont Dairy Farm Sustainability Project was launched in 1999 and sought to develop practical methods for dairy farms to reduce nitrogen and phosphorous run-off in order to prove water quality and overall sustainability.

- Corporate philanthropy – the company donates a portion of its pre-tax profits to corporate philanthropy via, in part, the Ben & Jerry's Foundation.

How sustainability impacts operations management

Operations management might contribute to achieving an organisation's sustainability targets in a number of ways:

Process design

The process should be designed to minimise waste, reduce energy use and reduce carbon emissions.

Product design

The product design should consider factors such as:

- Use of recycled inputs.

- Use of sustainable inputs.

- Ability to recycle product or dispose of it safely.

- Minimising wastage, e.g. unnecessary packaging.

Quality management

Higher quality should help to improve efficiency and reduce waste.

Supply chain management

Supply chain management is an important part of a company's CSR policy. It is common place to have policies in place to prevent slavery in the supply chain, lower carbon footprint and promote sustainable sourcing. Companies are expected to be able to track the carbon footprint not only of their own manufacturing activities but also their transportation, distribution and procurement activities.

The following are examples of practices adopted:

- **Purchasing:** Only products from a sustainable and ethical source should be purchased, e.g. a furniture manufacturer may purchase timber from sustainable forests only.

- **Supplier selection:** One of the key criteria to use when choosing between suppliers should be their adoption of sustainable development policies.

- **Location:** The distance between the supplier and the company should be minimised.

Brand image

A strong brand is what differentiates a company and/or its products in a competitive industry. A company can link unique characteristics and images to its brand name and passing its message to consumers, so that their distinct feelings about the brand are positively affected. As a result, brand image management is a key point in marketing strategy.

In recent times CSR has become a key element in the promotion of brand images. Customers have expectations that companies are implementing CSR policies. When CSR policies are communicated, it becomes a strategic branding tool. CSR initiatives can therefore strengthen a company's brand image and is therefore becoming a strategic necessity.

 Danger of poor supply chain management

Companies doing business in China have had difficulties maintaining quality throughout the supply chain, as illustrated by recent food and product recalls. For example, in 2008 there was a melamine-tainted baby milk scandal, which caused the death of at least six infants. Inherent problems in manufacturing processes and supply chains led to a breakdown of quality assurance. The scandal severely damaged China's dairy industry and shattered consumer confidence.

Managing Responsible Business 2015 Edition

This CGMA report draws on insight from nearly 2,500 Chartered Global Management Accountant designation holders and CIMA students working in both private and public sectors to review how the ethical landscape has changed since 2012.

The following is an extract from the report:

Four in five organisations view ethical issues concerning the supply chain as relevant to their business. In the last few years, regulation and legislation, media attention and public demand for greater transparency have all grown significantly. Today, this means that companies need to consider carefully not only their own business strategies and activities, but also those of the organisations who work with them and even those whom they supply.

2 The Global Reporting Initiative (GRI)

GRI is an international independent organisation that helps businesses, governments and other organisations understand and communicate the impact of business on critical sustainability issues such as climate change, human rights, corruption and many others.

Their vision is "to create a future where sustainability is integral to every organisation's decision making process."

GRI has produced The G4 Sustainability Reporting Guidelines. The Guidelines provide Reporting Principles, Standard Disclosures and an Implementation Manual for the preparation of sustainability reports by organisations, regardless of their size, sector or location.

The Guidelines sets out the following categories and aspects which should be addressed through sustainability reporting.

Category Economic	**Environmental**
Aspects • Economic Performance	• Materials
• Market Presence	• Energy
• Indirect Economic Impacts	• Water
• Procurement Practices	• Biodiversity
	• Emissions
	• Effluents and Waste
	• Products and Services
	• Compliance
	• Transport
	• Overall
	• Supplier Environmental
	• Assessment
	• Environmental Grievance
	• Mechanisms

Category Sub-categories	Social Labour Practices and Decent Work	Human Rights	Society	Product Responsibility
Aspects	• Employment • Labour/ Management Relations • Occupational Health and Safety • Training and Education • Diversity and Equal Opportunity • Equal Remuneration for Women and Men • Supplier Assessment for Labour Practices • Labour Practices Grievance Mechanisms	• Investment • Non-discrimination • Freedom of Association and Collective Bargaining • Child Labour • Forced or Compulsory Labour • Security Practices • Indigenous Rights • Assessment • Supplier Human • Rights Assessment • Human Rights Grievance Mechanisms	• Local Communities • Anticorruption • Public Policy • Anti-competitive Behaviour • Compliance • Supplier Assessment for Impacts on Society • Grievance Mechanisms for Impacts on Society	• Customer Health and Safety • Product and Service Labelling • Marketing Communications • Customer Privacy • Compliance

The Guidelines sets out Principles for Defining Report Content and Principles for Defining Report Quality.

Principles for Defining Report Content

Stakeholder Inclusiveness

Principle: The organisation should identify its stakeholders, and explain how it has responded to their reasonable expectations and interests.

Sustainability Context

Principle: The report should present the organisation's performance in the wider context of sustainability.

Materiality

Principle: The report should cover Aspects that:

• Reflect the organisation's significant economic. environmental and social impacts; or

• Substantively influence the assessments and decisions of stakeholders.

Completeness

Principle: The report should include coverage of material Aspects and their Boundaries, sufficient to reflect significant economic, environmental and social impacts, and to enable stakeholders to assess the organisation's performance in the reporting period.

Principles for Defining Report Quality

Balance

Principle: The report should reflect positive and negative aspects of the organisation's performance to enable a reasoned assessment of overall performance.

Comparability

Principle: The organisation should select, compile and report information consistently. The reported information should be presented in a manner that enables stakeholders to analyse changes in the organisation's performance over time, and that could support analysis relative to other organisations.

Accuracy

Principle: The reported information should be sufficiently accurate and detailed for stakeholders to assess the organisation's performance.

Timeliness

Principle: The organisation should report on a regular schedule so that information is available in time for stakeholders to make informed decisions.

Clarity

Principle: The organisation should make information available in a manner that is understandable and accessible to stakeholders using the report.

Reliability

Principle: The organisation should gather, record, compile, analyse and disclose information and processes used in the preparation of a report in a way that they can be subject to examination and that establishes the quality and materiality of the information.

The full set of guidelines can be accessed here:
https://www.globalreporting.org/standards/g4/Pages/default.aspx

3   Stakeholders

A stakeholder is a group or individual, who has an interest in what the organisation does, or an expectation of the organisation.

Types of stakeholder

Stakeholders can be broadly categorised into three categories; internal, connected and external.

Internal stakeholders

Internal stakeholders are intimately connected to the organisation, and their objectives are likely to have a strong influence on how it is run. Internal stakeholders include:

Stakeholder	Need/expectation
Employees managers/directors	pay, working conditions and job security status, pay, bonus, job security

Connected stakeholders

Connected stakeholders either invest in or have dealings with the firm. They include:

Stakeholder	Need/expectation
shareholders	dividends and capital growth and the continuation of the business
customers	value-for-money products and services
suppliers	paid promptly
finance providers	repayment of finance

External stakeholders

These stakeholders tend to not have a direct link to the organisation but can influence or be influenced by its activities.

Stakeholder	Need/expectation
community at large	will not want their lives to be negatively impacted by business decisions
environmental pressure groups	the organisation does not harm the external environment
government	provision of taxes and jobs and compliance with legislation
trade unions	to take an active part in the decision making process

Stakeholder needs analysis

Stakeholder needs analysis involves an organisation undertaking research to determine:

- Who its key stakeholders are, and

- What their needs are.

Each company must sit down with a blank sheet of paper and identify the stakeholders of their business.

For example, if a company has $1 m in the bank earning modest interest, then the bank is probably not a key stakeholder. In another company with a $100m debt to the bank and large interest payments, the bank is clearly an extremely important stakeholder.

Once the organisation has identified its stakeholders, it needs to understand what their needs and wants are. There is no better way of accomplishing this than asking them directly. Possible methods include:

- questionnaires

- focus groups

- direct interviews or interviews with representatives.

Stakeholders needs analysis

Car manufacturers

As well as being sensitive to the requirements of customers with respect to factors such as price and performance, a car manufacturer should also consider the following:

- public attitudes to pollution

- government policies on road tax and fuel tax.

As a result it may choose to develop more environmentally-friendly vehicles as part of its long term strategy even if current demand is for larger cars, say.

To some stakeholders, the company owes obligations arising from the law (e.g. to pay employees their salary each month, or to compensate them if they are made redundant). However, other obligations arise voluntarily due to the company's commitment to CSR (e.g. to discuss their plans with interested pressure groups before a particular plan is adopted).

Responsibilities of business to stakeholders

888.com

888.com is an internet gambling site that is listed on the London Stock Exchange. It is headquartered in Gibraltar and operates under a licence granted by the Government of Gibraltar. It has responsibilities to the following stakeholders:

- Shareholders – since it is listed on the London Stock Exchange it must comply with the rules of that exchange, including adopting the Corporate Governance Code.

- Employees – to be a good employer to all its members of staff.

- Customers – to offer a fair, regulated and secure environment in which to gamble.

- Government – to comply with the terms of its licence granted in Gibraltar.

- The public – the company chooses to sponsor several sports teams as part of strengthening its brand. The company also tries to address public concerns about the negative aspects of gambling, e.g. by identifying compulsive gamblers on their site and taking appropriate action.

4 CSR initiatives

In 2009 the OECD published an Overview of Selected Initiatives and Instruments Relevant to Corporate Social Responsibility.

The report "provides an overview of the unique status and characteristics of the OECD Guidelines for Multinational Enterprises, the ILO Tripartite Declaration of Principles Concerning Multinational Enterprises and Social Policy and the UN Global Compact".

The following is an extract from the report:

The Universal Declaration of Human Rights states that "every individual and organ of society" has the responsibility to strive "to promote respect for these rights and freedoms" and "by progressive measures, national and international, to secure their universal and effective recognition and observance". As important "organs" of society, businesses have a responsibility to promote worldwide respect for human rights.

The ILO Conventions establish norms covering all aspects of working conditions and industrial relations. Some of the most important cover core labour standards (i.e. basic human rights in the workplace). These include the right to freedom of association, the right to organise and to collective bargaining, and freedom from forced labour. ILO conventions are binding on all countries that have ratified them.

The ILO Tripartite Declaration of Principles Concerning Multinational Enterprises and Social Policy is a global instrument designed to provide guidance to government, employer and worker organisations in areas of employment, training, conditions of work and industrial relations. All core labour standards are covered. Although it is a non-binding instrument, its implementation is nevertheless the object of regular reviews.

The ILO Declaration on Fundamental Principles and Rights at Work is based on the core labour standards outline in the ILO Conventions. The Declaration is not binding but applies to all ILO member states. As part of a strategy to help countries to have well-functioning labour markets, it provides for a mechanism for annual review of the efforts made by member states that have not yet ratified the core labour standards. The Declaration also reinforces the application of core labour standards in private voluntary instruments.

The 1992 Rio Declaration sets out 27 principles defining the rights and responsibilities of states in relation to human development and well-being. The Agenda 21 agreement provides guidance for governments, business and individuals on how to contribute to efforts to make development socially, economically and environmentally sustainable. Its Chapter 30 recognises the value of promoting "responsible entrepreneurship". The Millennium Development Goals identify a series of government-agreed targets and timetables in relation to issues such as poverty reduction, improvement of child health care and education, and the promotion of gender equality.

The Johannesburg Declaration on Sustainable Development (2002) states that the private sector has "a duty to contribute to the evolution of equitable and sustainable communities and societies", and that "there is a need for private sector corporations to enforce corporate accountability". Its Plan of Implementation notes the need to "enhance corporate environmental and social responsibility and accountability". The UN Framework Convention on Climate Change and Convention on Biodiversity were also signed by a majority of governments.

The 2005 World Summit Outcome reiterated the importance of full respect for existing labour, human rights and environmental commitments and encouraged "responsible business practices, such as those promoted by the Global Compact".

Under the 2003 UN Convention Against Corruption, ratifying countries undertook to: criminalise an array of corrupt practices; develop national institutions to prevent corrupt practices and to prosecute offenders; cooperate with other governments to recover stolen assets; and help each other to fight corruption.

ILO Tripartite Declaration of Principles Concerning Multinational Enterprises and Social Policy.

The main areas covered by the Declaration are:

- General policies (obey national laws and respect international standards).

- Employment (employment promotion; equality of opportunity and treatment; security of employment).

- Training (policy development for vocational training, skills formation).

- Conditions of Work and Life (wages, benefits, conditions of work; minimum age; safety and health).

- Industrial Relations (freedom of association and right to organise; collective bargaining; consultation; grievances; settlement of disputes).

UN Global Compact

The UN Global Compact invites companies to embrace, support and enact, within their sphere of influence, the following ten principles:

Human Rights

Principle 1: Businesses should support and respect the protection of internationally proclaimed human rights; and

Principle 2: Make sure that they are not complicit in human rights abuses.

Labour Standards

Principle 3: Businesses should uphold the freedom of association and the effective recognition of the right to collective bargaining

Principle 4: The elimination of all forms of forced and compulsory labour

Principle 5: The effective abolition of child labour; and

Principle 6: The elimination of discrimination in respect of employment and occupation.

Environment

Principle 7: Businesses should support a precautionary approach to environmental challenges

Principle 8: Undertake initiatives to promote greater environmental responsibility; and

Principle 9: Encourage the development and diffusion of environmentally friendly technologies.

Anti-Corruption

Principle 10: Businesses should work against corruption in all its forms, including extortion and bribery.

5   OECD Guidelines

The OECD Guidelines for Multinational Enterprises (referred to here as the OECD Guidelines), were adopted in 1976, at a time when there was growing concern about the negative impact of corporate practices, particularly on developing countries.

The OECD Guidelines are non-binding recommendations addressed by governments to multinational enterprises operating in or from adhering countries. The Guidelines are signed by the 30 OECD participating countries and nine non-member countries (Argentina, Brazil, Chile, Estonia, Israel, Latvia, Lithuania, Romania and Slovenia).

The OECD Guidelines provide voluntary principles and standards for responsible business conduct in areas such as:

- Information disclosure

- Respect for labour standards

- Contribution to sustainable development

- Respect for human rights

- Supply chain responsibility

- Consumer interests

- Science and technology

- Competition

- Taxation

- Environment

- Bribery and corruption

- Whistleblower protection.

This is set out in the ten "chapters" of the OECD Guidelines. The OECD Guidelines have application to all sectors of business and cover companies operating in or from OECD member states worldwide and addresses their supply chain responsibilities.

The full set of guidelines can be accessed here:
http://mneguidelines.oecd.org/text/

General policies

Enterprises should take fully into account established policies in the countries in which they operate, and consider the views of other stakeholders. In this regard:

Enterprises should:

1   Contribute to economic, environmental and social progress with a view to achieving sustainable development.

2   Respect the internationally recognised human rights of those affected by their activities.

3   Encourage local capacity building through close co-operation with the local community, including business interests, as well as developing the enterprise's activities in domestic and foreign markets, consistent with the need for sound commercial practice.

4   Encourage human capital formation, in particular by creating employment opportunities and facilitating training opportunities for employees.

5   Refrain from seeking or accepting exemptions not contemplated in the statutory or regulatory framework related to human rights, environmental, health, safety, labour, taxation, financial incentives, or other issues.

6   Support and uphold good corporate governance principles and develop and apply good corporate governance practices, including throughout enterprise groups.

7   Develop and apply effective self-regulatory practices and management systems that foster a relationship of confidence and mutual trust between enterprises and the societies in which they operate.

8   Promote awareness of and compliance by workers employed by multinational enterprises with respect to company policies through appropriate dissemination of these policies, including through training programmes.

9   Refrain from discriminatory or disciplinary action against workers who make bona fide reports to management or, as appropriate, to the competent public authorities, on practices that contravene the law, the Guidelines or the enterprise's policies.

10 Carry out risk-based due diligence, for example by incorporating it into their enterprise risk management systems, to identify, prevent and mitigate actual and potential adverse impacts as described in paragraphs 11 and 12, and account for how these impacts are addressed. The nature and extent of due diligence depend on the circumstances of a particular situation.

11 Avoid causing or contributing to adverse impacts on matters covered by the Guidelines, through their own activities, and address such impacts when they occur.

12   Seek to prevent or mitigate an adverse impact where they have not contributed to that impact, when the impact is nevertheless directly linked to their operations, products or services by a business relationship. This is not intended to shift responsibility from the entity causing an adverse impact to the enterprise with which it has a business relationship.

13   In addition to addressing adverse impacts in relation to matters covered by the Guidelines, encourage, where practicable, business partners, including suppliers and sub-contractors, to apply principles of responsible business conduct compatible with the Guidelines.

14   Engage with relevant stakeholders in order to provide meaningful opportunities for their views to be taken into account in relation to planning and decision making for projects or other activities that may significantly impact local communities.

15   Abstain from any improper involvement in local political activities.

Enterprises are encouraged to:

1   Support, as appropriate to their circumstances, cooperative efforts in the appropriate fora to promote Internet Freedom through respect of freedom of expression, assembly and association online.

2   Engage in or support, where appropriate, private or multi-stakeholder initiatives and social dialogue on responsible supply chain management while ensuring that these initiatives take due account of their social and economic effects on developing countries and of existing internationally recognised standards.

6 Test your understanding questions

Test your understanding 1

List the stakeholders which organisations would consider as part of their CSR strategy.

Test your understanding 2

Explain the elements of Carroll's four-part model.

Test your understanding 3

What are the steps of developing a CSR strategy?

Test your understanding 4

Which of the following is the responsiveness strategy where the corporation denies any responsibility for social issues?

A   Reaction

B   Defence

C   Accommodation

D   Proaction

Test your understanding 5

Which of the following category would a shareholder be classified as?

A   Internal stakeholder

B   External stakeholder

C   Connected stakeholder

D   None of the above

Test your understanding answers

Test your understanding 1

Environment

Employees

Shareholders

Suppliers

Customers

Local community

Test your understanding 2

Carroll's four-part model is made up of:

- Economic responsibility
- Legal responsibility
- Ethical responsibility
- Philanthropic responsibility

Test your understanding 3

1   Identify stakeholders

2   Classify stakeholders

3   Establish stakeholders' claims

4   Assess importance of stakeholders

5   Decide upon response to social pressure

Test your understanding 4

A

Test your understanding 5

C

The Law of Contract

Chapter learning objectives

Upon completion of this chapter you will be able to:

- identify the essential elements of a valid contract and situations where the law requires the contract to be in a particular form

- explain how the law determines whether negotiating parties have reached agreement and the role of consideration in making that agreement enforceable

- explain when the parties will be regarded as intending the agreement to be legally binding and how an agreement may be avoided because of misrepresentations

- explain how the terms of a contract are established and their status determined

- explain the ability of a company to contract.

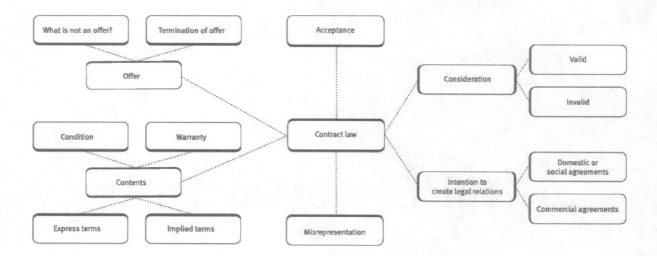

1 Introduction

This is the first chapter which deals with the business law part of the syllabus. The primary focus of this chapter is on general principles of contract law. The following two chapters look at general principles of employment law and company law.

Law in itself is quite a big topic and can vary from country to country. CIMA would like its students to have a general understanding of key legal principles without learning the details of any particular legal system.

Throughout this chapter and the following two chapters there will be some illustrations used to demonstrate legal principles in action. These are based on English case law, however, it must be noted that there is no requirement to learn these cases. They are included to help students understand how the law is applied.

2 Definition of law

 The Oxford Dictionary defines law as "The system of rules which a particular country or community recognizes as regulating the actions of its members and which it may enforce by the imposition of penalties."

3 Definition of a contract

A contract is a legally binding agreement between two or more parties.

Contract law is of vital importance in business life, and forms the basis of most commercial transactions such as dealings in land and goods, credit, insurance, carriage of goods, the formation and sale of business organisations, and employment.

For example, all of the following everyday transactions are contracts: purchasing a newspaper, buying a bus or rail ticket, purchasing a sandwich and a drink at lunchtime, buying a book or a CD, going to the cinema, the theatre or a football game.

Form of a contract

There is a general misconception that for there to be a valid contract it must be in writing. A contract can be in any form. It may be written, or oral or inferred from the conduct of the parties. However, in some situations the law may stipulate that in order for the contract to be enforceable it must be in a particular form e.g. in England any agreements for the transfer of land must be in writing.

Subject to contract

Where the words 'subject to contract' are used this means the parties to an agreement are not legally bound until a contract has been executed. Even though the parties have agreed terms, the matter effectively remains in a state of negotiation. Furthermore, either party can withdraw from the transaction without liability.

Standard form contracts

In many instances, rather than individually negotiating contracts, it is now common business practice for a customer to be presented with a written contract, the terms of which have already been set down in print. In these cases all that remains is for the customer to accept the terms by signing the contract. Examples of the use of such standard form contracts include contracts for gas and electricity services, telephone services, television packages, credit agreements and insurance etc.   Although such contracts are beneficial in that they save time and set down the terms of the agreement, they may be open to abuse by some unscrupulous businesses who seek to include terms of particular benefit to the business and to the detriment of the consumer. Thus although these contracts are subject to all the following principles regarding the essential elements of a valid contract, many jurisdictions have introduced additional consumer protection such as requiring terms in such contracts to be "fair" or allowing the consumer a "cooling – off" period after his initial acceptance during which it can be cancelled.

4   The essential elements of a valid contract

In most jurisdictions, the law provides that a contract cannot come into existence without the following:

An offer

- A definite and unequivocal statement of willingness to be bound on specified terms without further negotiation.

An acceptance

The unqualified and unconditional assent to all the terms of the offer.

Consideration

- Each party must provide something of value.

Intention to be legally bound

- Both parties must intend to enter into a legal relationship.

Each of these essential elements will be considered below.

 ### What is an offer?

An offer is a definite promise to be bound on specific terms made by the offeror to the offeree.

The offer can be made in any form but must be communicated to the offeree.

The offeree can be a particular person, a class of persons or even the whole world.

 English case law example

CARLILL v CARBOLIC SMOKE BALL 1893

Facts:

The manufacturers of a medicinal 'smoke ball' advertised in a newspaper that anyone who bought and used the ball as directed and still contracted influenza would be paid a £100 reward. Mrs. Carlill used the ball in accordance with the instructions and still caught flu. The manufacturers said there was no contract with Mrs. Carlill because an offer could not be made to the whole world.

Held:

An offer could be made to the whole world, the wording of the advert amounted to such an offer and Mrs Carlill had accepted it by using the ball correctly.

A legally binding offer includes:

- clearly stated terms
- an intention to enter into a contract
- communication of that intention.

What is not an offer?

Some countries may have rules on what is not an offer. The following are some general examples.

An invitation to treat

- An "invitation to treat" is an indication by one party that he is prepared to receive an offer from another party with a view to entering into a binding contract; it is not an offer.

Examples of invitations to treat

- most adverts (Carlill v Carbolic Smoke Ball is an exception to this)
- shop window displays
- goods on shop shelves
- company prospectus
- circulation of a price list or displays on a website
- tenders (a person asking for tenders is making an invitation to treat, the person submitting the tender is making the offer).

Jane offered to sell one of her paintings to John for £50. She also advertised some of her paintings in the local newspaper and put one on display in the window of her shop with a price tag attached to it. Jane has made an offer to John, but the advert in the local paper and the shop window display would not be offers but invitations to treat.

A supply of information or a statement of intention

A statement made early in the negotiations is unlikely to be held to be a valid offer and a statement of an intention to sell is not an offer.

Vague statements

A statement cannot constitute an offer if it is not sufficiently specific. For example, an offer to sell someone a car for £5,000 is valid, but a statement that a person will sell '...one of my cars for about £5,000' is not an offer: it is vague and uncertain.

Termination of the offer

In many jurisdictions, once an offer has been terminated it cannot be accepted and can only be revived by the person who originally made the offer.

An offer can be terminated in the following ways:

- Rejection and counter offer
- Revocation
- Lapse of time
- Failure of a pre-condition.

Rejection

An offer can be terminated by a rejection, either outright, by the offeree stating that they will not accept it, or by a counter offer.

A counter offer is an offer made in response to an offer. The most obvious example of this is where the offeree tries to negotiate the price downwards. For example where X offers his car to Y for £5,000 and Y responds by saying "I'll give you £4,500 for it." Y has made a counter offer and the effect at law is to terminate the original offer. A less obvious example perhaps, would be if Y in the above example had said "I accept and I'll pay you over the next 3 months." Even though Y has used the word "accept" this is also a counter offer, as Y has not unconditionally accepted X's offer but has added other conditions ("I'll pay you over the next 3 months").

English case law example

HYDE v WRENCH 1840

Facts: Wrench offered to sell Hyde a farm for £1,000. Hyde made a counter offer by offering £900.

Wrench rejected this counter offer. Later, Hyde came back to Wrench and said that he now accepted the offer at £1,000.

Held: Hyde could no longer accept the original offer as it no longer existed and was not capable of acceptance. Hyde's statement that he would pay the original £1,000 was a new offer, which Wrench did not accept.

A request for more information is not a rejection of an offer.

Request for information about an offer

Jack offered to sell some goods to Jill for £4,000 and some machinery to Bill for £6,000. Jill asked Jack if she could take half of the goods now and the remainder in one month's time. Jack didn't reply so Jill accepted his original offer. Bill replied by offering Jack £5,500 for the machinery. Jack didn't reply so Bill accepted Jack's original offer.

Jill has not made a counter offer. Had she done so then her attempt to accept the original offer would have been ineffective. She had simply requested more details of the terms of the offer and her subsequent acceptance was valid.

Bill's reply amounted to a counter offer which had the effect of terminating Jack's original offer. Bill was unable to accept the original offer which no longer existed. Bill's offer of £5,500 was a new offer made to Jack which he was free to accept or reject.

Revocation

An offer will be terminated if it is revoked (withdrawn) by the offeror. It can be revoked by the offeror or a person authorised to act on their behalf at any time before it has been accepted by the offeree.

The revocation may be by express words or it may be implied from the offeror's conduct. It must be communicated to the offeree by the offeror or by a reliable third party.

Revocation of an offer

Fred offered to sell his car to Emma and agreed to keep his offer open for two days. However, Fred changed his mind and, before the two days had expired, sold his car to Lucy, and informed Emma of the sale. Emma attempted to accept Fred's original offer arguing that he had given her two days to accept. However, Fred was not obliged to keep the offer open for two days as an offeror may revoke an offer at any time before it is accepted.

If however the offeree pays the offeror to keep the offer open, this creates a collateral contract and whilst the offeror can still revoke the original offer this would be a breach of that collateral contract. The offeree could claim damages (the most usual remedy for a breach of contract) for the loss of the opportunity to accept the original offer.

It may not be possible to revoke an offer where there is a unilateral contract. A unilateral contract arises where an offer has been made to the whole world that performing a particular act will result in a certain benefit. For example where a notice is published offering a reward for the return of a lost dog (or for using a carbolic smoke ball). In such cases it is impossible to notify everyone who may have seen the offer that it has been revoked (withdrawn). Also if an offeree had started to carry out the required act it is thought that it would be unjust to simply allow the offeror to withdraw the offer at that stage. It follows that a revocation is ineffective where an offeree is in the process of completing the required act.

Lapse of time

An offer ceases to exist if not accepted within a specified time limit and, if no time limit is specified, then it will lapse after a reasonable time. What is reasonable may depend on the subject matter of the contract. The time for an offer to purchase perishable goods is likely to be shorter than for non perishable goods.

An offer will also lapse on the death of the offeree or of the offeror unless the offeree accepts in ignorance of the death.

Failure of a pre-condition

A 'conditional' offer is one which is dependent on a specified event or change in circumstances. A conditional offer may not be accepted unless and until the condition or change of circumstances is met.

5 Acceptance

 Acceptance is the unequivocal and unconditional assent to all the terms of the offer.

Acceptance can be oral, in writing or by conduct

The acceptance can be express or implied by the conduct of the offeree (Carlill case). If an offeror stipulates the type of acceptance then that form of acceptance must be used.

Acceptance must be communicated

As a general rule acceptance must always be communicated to the offeror.

If a fax or telephone message is received during normal business hours then it is communicated when received. A fax or voicemail received outside of normal business hours is communicated once the business opens.

The law is unclear as to when a communication by email is received but there seems little reason to distinguish between this form and other types of instantaneous communication such as fax or telephone calls. It appears therefore, that the contract will be formed when the acceptance is received by the offeror's email system during business hours. If received outside business hours then it is communicated when the business reopens.

Acceptance must involve some act on the part of the offeree

An offeror cannot impose silence as the means of acceptance. There must be some words or action by the offeree to indicate acceptance.

 An offeror cannot impose silence as the means of acceptance

Rosie wrote to Jim that she was interested in buying his boat. She stated that she would assume the boat was hers for £1,000 if she did not hear from Jim. Jim didn't reply. Can Jim's silence amount to acceptance? The answer is "no". Rosie was unable to impose a contract on Jim by stating that his silence amounted to acceptance.

The Postal Rule

In some jurisdictions there is an exception to the rule that acceptance must always be communicated and this is known as the "Postal Rule". The postal rule states that acceptance is complete as soon as the letter is posted.

The rule only applies where the letter is properly stamped and addressed and if it would not be unreasonable to use the post (it would be unreasonable, for example, during a postal strike).

The postal rule applies even if the letter is never received by the offeror but not if the offeror states he must actually receive acceptance.

Carrying out an act in ignorance of an offer

A person must know of an offer before it can be accepted. For example, where a reward is offered, acceptance will only be effective where the offeree is aware of the offer.

Acceptance of a reward

Tilly offers a reward to anyone who finds and returns her cat. Tom, unaware of this offer, finds and returns her cat.

Did Tom accept Tilly's offer?

Tom cannot have "accepted" her offer since he was unaware of it and he is therefore not entitled to the reward.

6   Consideration

The third essential element of a valid contract is consideration.

In most jurisdictions a valid contract requires consideration. There may be some exceptions to this for example in English law a contract made by deed does not require consideration unless its terms require it.

Consideration is the price by which one party bought the other party's act or promise.

Valid consideration

Executed consideration

- means that the consideration is in the form of an act carried out at the time the contract was made, such as payment for goods at the time the goods are delivered.

  For example handing over payment and receiving coffee. Both the payment and the handing over of the coffee are executed at the time of the contract.

Executory consideration

- means that there is an exchange of promises to do something in the future such as a promise to pay for goods to be delivered and paid for at a later date.

  For example when a person agrees to pay for some goods 'cash on delivery'. Both the payment and the delivery are 'executory', i.e. to be completed at a later date.

  If a buyer pays now for the seller to deliver in the future, then the buyer's consideration is executed and the seller's executory.

Sufficient consideration

- the consideration must have some monetary value; but

- there is no need for each party's consideration to be equal in value.

  The parties have freedom to contract under any terms they wish and a court will not attempt to make a contract a fair bargain as long as there is some identifiable value.

 Adequacy of consideration

If John agrees to rent out his house for £1 a year to Janet there would be sufficient (and therefore valid) consideration even though the nominal figure of £1 would hardly be considered adequate.

Invalid consideration

Past consideration

Consideration is past if it involved something which had already been done at the time the promise is made.

 English case law example

RE MCARDLE 1951

Facts:

A husband and wife carried out improvements to a house. At a later date a promise was made to reimburse the couple.

Held:

The works had been carried out before the promise to pay had been made. Past consideration is no consideration.

If a person requests a service and no price is mentioned, then there is an implied promise to pay a reasonable sum. In practice this usually means the market rate for the goods or services.

Existing statutory duty

Generally, performance of an existing statutory duty i.e. legal duty is not good consideration.

However, if it can be shown that some extra service over and above that statutory duty is required this will constitute good consideration.

Existing contractual duty

The same principle as above applies. If there is only performance of an agreed contractual duty then this will not be considered good consideration.

However, if the original contractor asks for more than the original work required by the contract, then carrying out that additional work amounts to consideration.

Existing contractual duty

The following two English case law examples demonstrate the difference between what will not constitute sufficient consideration and what will.

STILK v MYRICK 1809

Facts:

A captain promised to share the wages of deserting seamen with the rest of the crew if they completed the voyage.

Held:

The promise was not binding as there was no extra consideration from the seamen who, by completing the voyage, were doing no more than they were contractually bound to do.

HARTLEY v PONSONBY 1857

Facts:

A large number of seamen deserted from a ship making the ship undermanned and hence unseaworthy. The captain offered extra pay to the remaining seamen if they would complete the voyage.

Held:

The promise of more money was recoverable by the seamen as they were involved in a dangerous situation and were doing more than they had originally contracted to do.

Illegal acts

An illegal act cannot amount to consideration.

7 Intention that the agreement should be legally binding

The final essential element in a valid contract is the intention to create legal relations.

If a contract is to be created both parties must intend to enter into a legal relationship. If it is not clear from the contract that the parties intended legal consequences then the law presumes the intention of the parties based on the type of agreement.

Domestic or social agreements

It is presumed there is no intention to be legally bound in a social or domestic arrangement.

This presumption can be rebutted or overturned by showing that there was clear evidence that the parties did intend to create legal relations.

English case law examples

BALFOUR v BALFOUR 1919

Facts:

Mr B, who was about to go abroad, promised to pay his wife £30 per month in consideration of her agreeing to support herself without calling on him for any further maintenance. The wife said the husband was contractually bound by the promise.

Held:

There was no legally binding contract between the parties. It was a domestic arrangement and it was presumed the parties did not intend to be legally bound.

But compare this case with the following where the parties were not living together happily.

MERRITT v MERRITT 1970

Facts:

A husband who was separated from his wife promised to transfer the house into her name if she paid off the outstanding mortgage debt. The wife paid off the debt but the husband refused to transfer the house.

Held:

In this case, the husband's promise was enforceable, the agreement having been made when the parties were not living together amicably.

Commercial agreements

It is presumed that there is an intention to be legally bound, unless it can be shown otherwise.

This is a strong presumption that can only be rebutted by clear evidence to the contrary.

Transactions binding in honour only

If the parties state that an agreement is 'binding in honour only', this amounts to an express denial of the intention to create a legal relationship.

8 Misrepresentation

During the negotiations preceding a contract, statements are often made with a view to inducing the other party to enter into a contract. If any such statement is false, the party thereby misled is not agreeing to what is the true state of affairs and the contract may be voidable for misrepresentation.

Misrepresentation, therefore, may be defined as a false statement of fact or law (but not a mere expression of opinion), made by one party to the other before the contract, and made with a view to inducing the other party to enter into it.

The statement must have been intended:

- to be acted upon, and
- it must actually have deceived the other party and induced him to make the agreement.

As a **general rule**, silence cannot amount to misrepresentation and there is no duty to disclose facts.

A contract entered into on the basis of a misrepresentation is said to be voidable on the part of the innocent party. "Voidable" means that the contract is valid and will continue until the innocent party takes steps to cancel the contract. Voidable must be distinguished from "void". If a contract is declared void that effectively means that it never existed.

The contract may be ended by the innocent party and the parties restored to their pre-contract positions. For example any money paid should be handed back and any goods recovered.

The right to be restored to the pre-contract position will be lost if the innocent party waits too long or it is not possible to recover property, as where for example, it has been destroyed.

9 The contents of the contract

In many jurisdictions the terms of the contract will be both express and implied terms.

Express terms

These can be written, oral or a combination of the two.

Such terms are specifically inserted into the contract by either or both parties.

They must be clear for them to be enforceable.

Implied terms

These are terms which are not expressly included but are still part of the contract. They can be implied by:

- the nature of the contract

  The courts can imply terms that are required by the contractual relationship. These terms may be implied into all similar contractual relationships, unless excluded or inconsistent with the express terms.

  The courts may imply a term where the parties have failed to provide for a particular matter which, unless remedied, would make the contract unworkable. Such implied terms are based on the presumed but unexpressed intention of the parties.

- custom and usage

  Any contract may be deemed to incorporate any relevant custom of the market, trade or locality in which it is made, unless the custom is inconsistent with the express terms or the nature of the contract.

  A term may be implied on the basis of what the particular parties have done in the past – this is called usage.

- legislation

  Many countries will have legislation which implies terms into contracts. This can happen for many reasons, for example implying terms into contracts for the sale of goods and services to provide better consumer protection, and implying terms into employment contracts to ensure greater health and safety protection.

Conditions and warranties

If there is a breach of contract and the innocent party seeks a remedy, it may be important to determine whether the breached term is considered to be a condition or a warranty.

Condition

A condition is a vital term of the contract, breach of which may be treated as a substantial failure to perform a basic element of the agreement.

The innocent party has the choice of cancelling the contract and claiming damages or continuing with the contract and claiming damages. "Damages" refers to monetary compensation for any loss or injury.

Warranty

A warranty is a less important term which is incidental to the main purpose of the contract.

The remedy for a breach of warranty is a claim for damages only.

It may not be obvious from the contract whether the parties intend a particular term to be a condition or warranty. In this situation the courts will classify the term according to the consequences of a breach of the term. If the breach would cause the parties to be deprived of the main benefit of the contract then the clause is a condition, if only minor loss was caused the term is a warranty.

The difference between a condition and a warranty

Compare the following two English cases:

POUSSARD v SPIERS 1876

Facts:

Madame Poussard agreed to sing in a series of operas for Spiers. She failed to appear on the opening night and Spiers refused her services for subsequent nights.

Held:

The obligation to appear on the opening night was a condition. Since Madame Poussard was in breach of this condition. Spiers was entitled to treat the contract as at an end and was therefore not himself in breach by refusing her services for the remaining nights.

BETTINI v GYE 1876

Facts:

Bettini, who agreed to sing in a series of concerts and to attend six days of rehearsals beforehand failed to appear for the first four rehearsal days. Gye in consequence refused Bettini's services for the balance of the rehearsals and performances.

Held:

The obligation to appear for rehearsals was a warranty and therefore Bettini's breach did not entitle Gye to treat the contract as at an end. Gye was accordingly in breach of contract when he refused Bettini's services for the remainder of the contract.

10 The ability of a company to contract

The legal concept of a company will be discussed in chapter 8. For the purposes of contract law, a company can enter into contracts in its own company name when it comes into existence. Nowadays companies can contract for any business purpose. If a company wishes to restrict its ability to enter into particular contracts then it will restrict the directors from doing so by internal arrangements.

If a company has restricted the ability of its directors to contract on its behalf and the directors ignore the restriction the consequences are as follows:

- If the directors are about to take the company into a contract in excess of their authority, shareholders may be able to apply to court for an injunction to stop them

- If the directors enter into the contract in excess of their authority then it is usually still enforceable by both parties but the directors may be sued for breach of their duty.

11 Test your understanding questions

Test your understanding 1

List the essential elements necessary for the formation of a contract.

Test your understanding 2

What effect will a counter offer have on an offer?

Test your understanding 3

Dennis wrote to Mark, offering to sell him a Renoir painting for £100,000. One week later, Mark wrote back saying he would pay that amount but not for another 2 months. Dennis did not respond and Mark, who decided that he wanted the painting, then heard that Dennis had sold the painting to Tom. Was there a contract between Dennis and Mark?

A   Yes. Dennis has made a valid offer which Mark has accepted

B   Yes. Mark's response was a request for further information and he was able to accept the offer afterwards

C   No. Mark's response constitutes a counter-offer which effectively destroyed Dennis's original offer

D   No. Dennis's letter to Mark constituted an invitation to treat, not an offer

Test your understanding 4

In contract law, once an offer has been terminated it cannot be accepted.

Which of the following does not terminate an offer?

A   A request for further information

B   Revocation by the offeror

C   Lapse of reasonable time

D   Rejection by the offeree

Test your understanding 5

Which of the following is incorrect?

A   A term may be implied into a contract by legislation

B   A term may be implied into a contract by a court on the ground that the term is customary in the parties' trade

C   A term may be implied into a contract by a court on the ground that it would make the contract more fair

D   A term may be implied into a contract due to the nature of the contract

Test your understanding 6

Which of the following is incorrect?

A   A condition is a term which the parties intend to be of vital importance

B   A warranty is a term which the parties do not intend to be of vital importance

C   If a condition is breached, then the contract must be cancelled

D   If a warranty is breached, then the injured party cannot terminate the contract

Test your understanding 7

Beryl enters a shop to purchase a new dress. She tells the shop assistant that she would like to buy the blue dress which is displayed in the shop window and priced at £100. The assistant removes the dress from the window for Beryl, but when she tries to pay for it at the till, the manager informs her that it is not for sale. He tells her that the dress is for display purposes only.

Required:

Delete as appropriate and complete the following sentences:

Beryl **is/is not** entitled to the dress because the display of the dress in the shop window constitutes an .... (3 words) and not an....(1 word). It follows that Beryl **does not have/has** a contract with the shop owners who **have/have not** acted in breach of contract.

Test your understanding answers

Test your understanding 1

The essential elements necessary for the formation of a contract are:

- offer

- acceptance

- consideration

- the intention to be legally bound.

Test your understanding 2

A counter offer has the effect of terminating the original offer. The counter offer itself constitutes a new offer which can either be rejected or accepted.

Test your understanding 3

C

C is the correct answer, because Mark is trying to impose his own terms, and thus is making a counter offer which is capable in turn of acceptance, and which destroys Dennis's original offer.

Test your understanding 4

A

A request for further information does not terminate an offer.

Test your understanding 5

C

A, B and D are all ways in which a term can be implied into a contract.

Test your understanding 6

C

C is the correct answer because whilst a breach of condition can result in the contract being terminated, it is wrong to say the contract must be terminated.

Test your understanding 7

Beryl **is not** entitled to the dress because the display of the dress in the shop window with a price tag constitutes an **invitation to treat** and not an **offer**. It follows that Beryl **does not have** a contract with the shop owners, who **have not** acted in breach of contract.

The Law of Employment

Chapter learning objectives

Upon completion of this chapter you will be able to:

- explain how the contents of a contract of employment are established

- explain what policies and procedures may be present in the workplace

- explain the distinction between unfair and wrongful dismissal and the consequences.

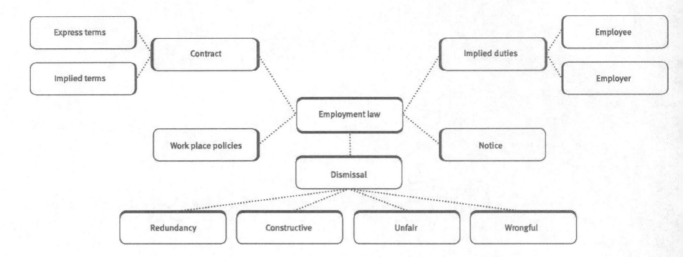

1 The contract of employment

An employment contract is like any other contractual relationship. The basic rules of contract will apply.

To be valid there must be agreement (offer and acceptance), consideration and intention to create legal relations. Therefore, in a contract of employment, the following applies:

- The employer offers employment.

- The employee accepts the offer of employment.

- Consideration is present in the form of the remuneration package provided by the employer in return for the work of the employee.

- Clearly this is a business agreement (as opposed to a social or domestic arrangement) and the parties are presumed to intend legal relations.

An employment contract is usually made in writing although it can be created orally. It is likely to contain a mixture of express and implied terms.

Express terms

Express terms are those agreed by the parties themselves. Their agreement may be written or oral.

A change in terms generally requires the consent of both parties, unless it is introduced by new legislation.

Sometimes an express term will give the employer the right to vary the terms of employment. For example, a mobility clause allows the employer to change the location of the employment. Such changes must, however, be reasonable.

Implied terms

Terms can be implied into a contract of employment from any of the following sources:

Sources of terms

- The courts

  A court may imply terms into an employment contract. Examples of terms implied in the past include a duty of good faith on the part of the employee, a duty of mutual co-operation on the part of the employer and employee and other duties noted below.

- Legislation

  For example terms in relation to the right to equal pay; the right not to be discriminated against; the right to be paid a minimum wage.

- Custom and practice

  Relevant business practices either nationally or locally can be implied into a contract of employment. Such practices must be reasonable, certain and not unlawful. This source of terms has diminished with the increased formalisation of employment contracts and if there is any conflict then, of course, the contract prevails.

- Collective agreements between employers and trade unions or staff associations

  The terms of an agreement between union and employer may expressly or impliedly form part of a contract of employment.

It should be noted that works and staff rules e.g. in an employee handbook or on staff notice boards may not be implied as terms of the employment contract, but a failure to obey them could be treated as evidence of a failure to obey reasonable orders. It may be more beneficial to the employer for these rules not to have the status of a contractual term since they can then be varied or introduced as the employer sees fit without the consent of the employee which would otherwise be necessary if they were contractual terms.

Different jurisdictions will imply different rights and duties on the employer and employee but many common ones are set out below.

Implied duties of the employee

- Duty to give honest and faithful service (fidelity)

  The duty of fidelity is of fundamental importance. It is breached if, for example, an employee works for a competitor in his spare time.

- Duty to obey lawful and reasonable orders.

English case law example

PEPPER v WEBB 1968

Facts: A gardener refused to plant the plants where instructed by the employer.

Held: He was in breach of the duty to obey lawful and reasonable orders and this, coupled with the fact that he was rude and surly, justified his dismissal.

- Duty to exercise reasonable care and skill

The employee must act with reasonable care in performing his duties. A single act of negligence will not usually justify dismissal, unless it is gross negligence.

An extension of this duty of care is a duty to indemnify the employer for any damages incurred as a result of the employee's negligence.

 English case law example

LISTER v ROMFORD ICE & COLD STORAGE LTD 1972

Facts: An employee negligently ran over another employee with a forklift truck.

Held: He was liable in damages to his employer for breach of contract.

- Duty not to misuse confidential information

An employee must not disclose trade secrets to a third party nor misuse confidential information he has acquired in the course of his employment. This duty can continue even after the employment has ended.

- Duty to give personal service

The employee must carry out his duties personally unless he has express or implied permission to delegate.

- Duty of mutual cooperation

This is a mutual obligation imposed on both parties and is based on respect and consideration for each other.

Implied duties of the employer

- To pay reasonable remuneration.
- To indemnify employees for properly incurred expenses.
- To take reasonable care for the safety of their employees e.g. safe plant and machinery, safe system of work and reasonably competent fellow employees.
- To give reasonable notice of termination of employment.
- To maintain mutual co-operation, trust and confidence.

Note that there is generally no duty to:

- provide work. However, such a duty may be implied where payment is by commission or piece work, or where the employee is skilled and needs practice to maintain those skills, there may be an obligation to provide a reasonable amount of work.

- provide a reference. However, if a reference is provided it must be truthful.

2 Notice and dismissal

Notice

Many contracts of employment will expressly state how much notice is to be given by either party in order to terminate the contract. Some jurisdictions have legislation which lays down certain minimum periods. These are usually based on the employee's length of continuous service with the employer.

Dismissal

Breach of a term of the contract, if it is serious enough, may entitle the innocent party to treat the contract as at an end and bring a claim for breach of contract. Breach by an employer may give the employee the right to bring a claim for wrongful and/ or unfair dismissal.

Employment law varies across different jurisdictions and not all terms have the same meaning. What follows is a general description of some common concepts but individual legal advice should always be sought in each jurisdiction.

Wrongful dismissal

This is the term often used where the employer terminates the contract:

- without giving proper notice, or
- during its fixed term.

Dismissal without notice is known as summary dismissal.

Summary dismissal is usually wrongful dismissal unless the employee:

- waives their rights or accepts payment in lieu of notice
- repudiates the contract themselves or is in fundamental breach (e.g. wilful refusal to obey lawful orders; failure to show professional skill; serious negligence; breach of duty of good faith).

Remedies

An individual who believes he has been wrongfully dismissed would sue for compensation in the form of damages (a monetary sum linked to the period of notice he failed to receive).

Wrongful dismissal

Bill employed Ben and Jack. Their contracts of employment provided that Bill must give a minimum of one week's notice to his employees. (This was also the minimum implied by legislation). Ben was a conscientious employee but Bill dismissed Ben with only one day's notice. Ben would have a claim for wrongful dismissal as he had not received the proper notice. Jack was not a conscientious employee and had been found by Bill committing a serious assault on his work colleagues in the staff canteen. Bill dismissed Jack on the spot. Jack's dismissal was a summary dismissal. It is however unlikely to be a wrongful dismissal as Jack was in very serious breach of his contract due to his gross misconduct.

Unfair dismissal

This is the term often used to describe the situation where an employer terminates an employee's contract of employment without justification.

A claim for unfair dismissal is usually governed by legislation and often requires the employee to have had a minimum length of service. The law usually provides that the employee must prove that he was dismissed. Dismissal for these purposes can be shown where the employer terminated the contract with or without notice, terminated before the expiry of a fixed term or terminated by constructive dismissal. Constructive dismissal occurs where an employee terminates the contract, with or without notice, by reason of the employer's conduct. The employer's conduct must be sufficiently serious for the employee to leave at once. If he continues for any length of time without leaving, he may be regarded as having affirmed the contract. Affirmation results in him losing the right to treat himself as discharged.

Once the employee has proved that he was dismissed the onus is placed upon the employer to prove that the dismissal was fair and that he acted reasonably in dismissing the employee.

Legislation often provides that some reasons for dismissal are "automatically" unfair (for example in England dismissal for pregnancy is automatically unfair) whereas other reasons may be "potentially fair".

When analysing whether dismissal is fair or a breach of contract, a number of issues are relevant:

- **Conduct** – a well documented and fair disciplinary procedure should be in place.

- **Capability** – the employer must demonstrate that the employee failed to meet the required standard and should detail formal/informal warnings given and any remedial actions attempted, for example the offer of extra training or transfer to another (more suitable) role.

- **Breach of statutory duty**– dismissal would be considered fair if continuing employment would breach statutory duty, e.g. health and safety legislation.

- **Some other suitable reason** – e.g. dishonesty, refusal to transfer within the organisation.

- **Redundancy** – see below.

Constructive dismissal

Even if the employer can prove that the reason for dismissal was fair he must also prove that he acted reasonably in dismissing the employee for that reason.

Unfair dismissal
The following examples might not be considered reasonable: - If an employee was dismissed without warning (except in the most flagrant cases). - If the dismissal was on the grounds of capability or qualifications and the employer did not allow time for improvement, training and consultation to discuss areas of difficulty. - If the employer is relying on the grounds of ill health and there is insufficient medical evidence to support that ground. - In the case of misconduct where the employer did not fully investigate the complaint and did not listen to what the employee had to say by way of explanation or mitigation. - If the employer is relying on redundancy and the employee was selected purely because of his trade union activities.

Remedies

If the employee is found to have been unfairly dismissed the legislation may provide a variety of remedies including the possible reinstatement or re-engagement of the employee or, more likely, some monetary compensation.

- Reinstatement

    This is an order that the employee may return to the same job without any break in continuity. It will only be ordered where requested by the applicant and practically achievable.

- Re-engagement

    This is an order that the employee must be re-engaged upon comparable employment.

Redundancy

In many jurisdictions, a dismissal on the grounds of redundancy may be justified on any of the following grounds:

- cessation of business

- cessation of business in the place where the employee was employed

- cessation of the type of work for which the employee was employed.

The place where a person is employed means in this context, the place where he is habitually employed and any place where, under his contract, he can be required to work. There will not, therefore, usually be a redundancy situation where the transfer of location is reasonable or where the contract gives the employer the right to move the employee in question from one place to another.

Redundancy should be fair and in some countries it is a requirement that consultation must take place, e.g. with employees and trade unions.

3 Workplace policies

There are many issues and many laws applying to matters that occur within the workplace. Some organisations may have specific policies which go beyond what is legally required as they have their own set of core values. A number of examples of workplace policies are included at the end of this chapter in order to illustrate how the policies may be worded. **Please note that you will not be examined on the wording of these examples.**

Diversity and discrimination (equal opportunities policy)

Many jurisdictions have legislation providing that an employee has the right not to be discriminated against in relation to their gender or sexual orientation, race, age, disabilities, or religion and beliefs.

There are two types of discrimination that an equal opportunities policy will attempt to prevent:

- **Direct discrimination** – this occurs when an employer treats an employee less favourably than another, due to their gender, race etc. For example, if a driving job was only open to male applicants.

    This may be allowed by law in certain, tightly defined circumstances.

- **Indirect discrimination** – this occurs when a working condition or rule disadvantages one group of people more than another. For example, a requirement for male employees to be clean-shaven would put some religious groups at a disadvantage.

    Indirect discrimination is often illegal, unless it is necessary for the working of the business and there is no way of avoiding it.

Diversity is about valuing and embracing the differences in people and reaping the benefits of a varied workforce that makes the best of people's talents whatever their backgrounds. Diversity encompasses visible and non-visible individual differences. It can be seen in the makeup of the workforce in terms of gender, ethnic minorities, and people with disabilities by looking at access to management positions, job opportunities and general terms and conditions in the workplace.

Disciplinary procedures

It is common practice for a company to have written disciplinary rules and procedures to deal with employee performance and conduct. Staff should be notified about these rules and procedures.

The rules should state what is acceptable and unacceptable behaviour in the workplace and what action will be taken if the rules are broken.

The rules should also clearly say when someone might face disciplinary action and what that action could be. Employees should also be provided with the name of someone they should appeal to if they are unhappy about a disciplinary decision.

The disciplinary rules should give examples of what will be treated as gross misconduct. This is misconduct judged so serious that it is likely to lead to dismissal without notice, e.g. fraud and theft.

Corruption and bribery

Corruption is now recognized to be one of the world's greatest challenges.

Kofi Annan, former Secretary General of the UN made the following statement:

"Corruption .. undermines democracy and the rule of law, leads to violations of human rights, distorts markets, erodes the quality of life and allows organised crime, terrorism and other threats to human security to flourish .. corruption hurts the poor disproportionately by diverting funds intended for development, undermining a government's ability to provide basic services, feeding inequality and injustice and discouraging foreign aid investment".

In 2013 The World Bank stated that "bribery has become a $1 trillion industry".

What is corruption?

Generally corruption is described as an abuse of trust in order to gain an unfair advantage.

Examples include but are not limited to:

- Bribery

  The giving or receiving of something of value (e.g. gift/loan/fee/reward or other advantage) to influence a transaction.

  Note: firms are allowed to provide hospitality, promotional or other business expenditure. For example, to provide tickets to sporting events, take clients to dinner, offer gifts to clients as a reflection of good relations, or pay for reasonable travel expenses in order to demonstrate goods or services to clients if that is reasonable and proportionate for the business.

  However where hospitality is really a cover for bribing someone, the authorities would look at such things as the level of hospitality offered, the way in which it was provided and the level of influence the person receiving it had on the business decision in question.

- Facilitation payments

  Facilitation payments are additional payments made to induce officials to perform routine functions that they are not otherwise obliged to perform. For example, additional payments to customs officials so they prioritise processing the import of particular goods.

  Some countries may perceive these facilitation payments as bribes if the sums involved are excessive.

- Conflict of interest

  This is where an employee has a duty to act on behalf of an employer and has an economic or personal interest in a transaction.

 English Bribery Act 2010

The bribery offences are as follows:

- bribing a person to induce or reward them to perform a relevant function improperly

- requesting, accepting or receiving a bribe as a reward for performing a relevant function improperly

- using a bribe to influence a foreign official to gain a business advantage

- corporate liability for failing to prevent bribery on behalf of a commercial organisation.

Evaluating anti-bribery and corruption procedures

Some countries have a requirement that firms have to ensure that they have adequate procedures and controls to prevent bribery and corruption.

What counts as adequate will depend on the bribery risks the organisation faces and the nature, size and complexity of the business.

Whistleblowing

Whistleblowing means disclosing information that a worker believes is evidence of illegality, gross waste, gross mismanagement, abuse of power, or substantial and specific danger to the public health and safety. The person who exposes the information is known as the whistleblower (from the sporting analogy of a referee blowing his whistle to indicate a foul). The information is often about the employer but it may be about a fellow worker. He may disclose as a matter of conscience or ethics or because he is following internal rules or procedures.

Sometimes whistleblowers are targeted in the workplace because they have disclosed information. Repercussions for the whistleblower could include termination/suspension/demotion/wage reduction and/or harsh treatment by his fellow workers.

In some countries there are laws which protect a whistleblower.

Generally, in order to be protected by law the whistleblower must:

- Reveal information of the right type: a 'qualifying disclosure'

- Reveal information to the right person and in the right way: this makes it a 'protected disclosure'.

Qualifying disclosures

To be protected the whistleblower needs to reasonably believe that malpractice is happening, has happened, or will happen. The malpractice can take the form of:

- a criminal offence, e.g. fraud

- someone's health and safety is in danger

- risk or actual damage to the environment

- a miscarriage of justice

- the company is breaking the law e.g. does not have the right insurance

- a belief that someone is covering up wrongdoing.

Protected disclosure

For a disclosure to a person to be protected the whistleblower must:

- Make the disclosure in good faith i.e. not acting out of revenge or spite or some other ulterior personal motive.

- Reasonably believe that the information is substantially true

- Reasonably believe that he is making the disclosure to the right person.

Most legislation encourages disclosure to be made internally in the first instance but also provides for external disclosure in certain circumstances to others such as:

- To a legal adviser

- To a government minister if the individual is a public sector worker

- To a professional body or in extreme circumstances the media (but in this case stricter rules apply).

Money Laundering

Money laundering is the process by which criminally obtained money or other assets (criminal property) are exchanged for 'clean' money or other assets with no obvious link to their criminal origins. It also covers money, however come by, which is used to fund terrorism.

There are three acknowledged phases to money laundering:

1   Placement

    The illegitimate funds generated from crime are placed in the financial system, for example cash paid into a bank account. This is the point when proceeds of crime are most apparent and at risk of detection.

2   Layering

    Once proceeds of crime are in the financial system, layering obscures their origins by passing the money through complex transactions. These often involve different entities like companies and trusts and can take place in multiple jurisdictions.

3   Integration

    Once the origin of the funds has been obscured, the criminal is able to make the funds reappear as legitimate funds or assets. They will invest funds in legitimate businesses or other forms of investment such as property.

Most financial institutions globally, and many non-financial institutions, are required to identify and report transactions of a suspicious nature to the financial intelligence unit in their country.

English Law

> Under English law an employee in a firm of accountants would be required to report to his firm's Money Laundering Reporting Officer (MLRO) if he knew or had reasonable grounds for suspecting that a person was engaged in, or attempting , money laundering. The MLRO and the firm would then report the matter to the National Crime Agency.

Data protection

Data protection laws exist to strike a balance between the rights of living individuals to privacy and the ability of an organisation to use data for the purposes of their business.

Some countries will have laws which give individuals the right to know what information is held about them. The law can provide a framework to ensure that personal information is handled properly.

The purpose of any such legislation is to:

- Give rules and principles concerning the use of data.

- Provide individuals with important rights concerning data held about them.

Data protection principles

Subject to certain exemptions, in general, anyone who processes personal information must ensure that the data is:

- processed fairly and lawfully.

- obtained only for specified and lawful purposes.

- adequate, relevant and not excessive.

- accurate and, where necessary, kept up to date.

- kept no longer than is necessary.

- processed in accordance with an individual's rights.

- kept secure; and

- not transferred to other countries without adequate protection.

Laws may provide individuals with important rights such as the right to find out what personal information is held on computer and most paper records, on payment of a reasonable fee.

Much of this legislation has impacted on the way in which organisations conduct business in terms of who can be contacted for marketing purposes, not only by telephone and direct mail but also by electronic means and this has led to the development of permission based marketing strategies.

Social Media

The impact of social media on the workplace is increasing. Social media is the broad term for internet-based tools used on PCs, laptops, tablets and smart phones to help people make contact, keep in touch and interact.

This trend can affect communications among managers, employees and job applicants, how organisations promote and control their reputation, and how colleagues treat one another. It can also distort what boundaries there are between home and work.

An organisation should ensure that it has a social media policy in place. Employers should include what is and what is not acceptable for general behaviour in the use at work of the internet, emails, smart phones and social media, such as networking websites, blogs and tweets. The employer needs to consider whether to use social media to evaluate applicants and whether to impose limits on use by employees due to loss of work time.

Health and Safety

The law typically puts the responsibility for health and safety on both the employer and the employee.

Generally speaking, the employer has a duty, amongst other things, to:

- provide a safe working environment

- provide adequate information, instruction, training and supervision to enable individuals to be safe

- prevent risks to health

- ensure that plant and machinery are safe to use and that safe working practices are set up and followed

- inform staff of any potential hazards

- provide adequate first aid facilities

- check that the right equipment is used and that it is regularly maintained

- set up emergency plans.

If employers fail to provide a safe and healthy working environment they may be liable to a claim from an employee or, even, the State.

Generally an employee has, amongst other things, a duty to:

- take reasonable care of their own health and safety

- take reasonable care not to put other people at risk

- cooperate with their employer to ensure they have adequate training and are familiar with their employer's health and safety policies

- report any injuries suffered as a result of performing their job

- inform their employer if anything affects their ability to work safely.

Examples of workplace policies

As mentioned earlier you will not be examined on the wording of these examples.

Examples of money laundering policy

The company is required under money laundering legislation to put in place appropriate systems and controls to prevent money laundering.

This policy contains the procedures that we have developed in order to comply with these obligations.

Money laundering is the process through which proceeds of crime and their true origin and ownership are changed so that the proceeds appear legitimate.

How do I know if my matter involves money laundering?

You do not have to behave like a police officer but you do have to remain alert to the warning signs of money laundering and make the sort of enquiries that a reasonable person (with the same qualifications, knowledge and experience as you) would make.

Typical signs of money laundering

- obstructive or secretive clients
- instructions outside our usual range of expertise, i.e. why is the client using us?
- clients based a long way from us with no apparent reason for using
- cases or instructions that change unexpectedly or for no logical reason, especially where:
  - the client has deposited funds with us; and
  - the source of funds changes at the last moment
  - you are asked to return funds or send funds to a third party
  - loss-making transactions where the loss is avoidable
- complex or unusually large transactions
- transactions with no apparent logical, economic or legal purpose
- large amounts of cash being used
- money transfers where there is a variation between the account holder and signatory

- payments to or from third parties where there is no logical connection to the client

- movement of funds between accounts, institutions or jurisdictions without reason

- large payment on account of fees with instructions terminated shortly after and the client requesting the funds are redirected.

Reporting suspicions

You have a strict duty to keep the affairs of our clients confidential. The circumstances in which you can disclose information about our clients are very limited.

However, legislation imposes obligations to report knowledge or suspicion of money laundering by way of a Suspicious Activity Report (SAR). These obligations can override your duty of confidentiality.

Any member of staff can submit a SAR form to the Nominated Officer.

What are knowledge and suspicion?

Knowledge means actual knowledge rather than wilfully shutting one's eyes to the truth.

Suspicion is a possibility which is more than fanciful. A vague feeling of unease will not suffice.

There is no requirement for the suspicion to be clear or firmly grounded on specific facts, but there must be a belief which is beyond mere speculation.

The test for whether you hold a suspicion is generally subjective. However, there is an objective element to the test i.e. would the reasonable solicitor, with the same knowledge, experience and information, have formed a suspicion.

The suspicion held must be that another person is engaged in money laundering and not simply that there is something 'fishy' about the client or the transaction.

If you have formed knowledge or suspicion that another person is engaged in money laundering you must complete the SAR form and send it to the Nominated Officer.

If you are suspicious but are not sure why, for instance there is something that just does not feel right about the client or the matter, you must discuss your concerns with the Nominated Officer, who may instruct you to complete the SAR form if he is satisfied that there are reasonable grounds to suspect money laundering or terrorist financing. You should keep a note of that discussion.

How do I make a report?

If you know or suspect that your matter involves money laundering, you must complete the SAR form.

What happens after I make a SAR?

On receiving your SAR form, the MLRO will consider the reasons for suspicion reported to him. He may ask you for more information.

The MLRO will then decide whether an external SAR is required. This decision rests only with the Nominated Officer.

You have discharged your reporting obligations under legislation by making the internal SAR.

What can I tell my client?

You must not tell the client that you have submitted a SAR. If you do you will be committing the offence of tipping-off and could be exposed to a criminal record.

There is very little, if anything, that you can tell the client after you have submitted a SAR. Always speak with the MLRO if you are in any doubt.

Example of data protection policy

The company is committed to the highest standards of document and information management and security and treat confidentiality and data security extremely seriously.

We take seriously our obligations under all relevant regulation and legislation.

Purpose

The purpose of this policy is to:

- protect against the potential breaches of confidentiality and failures of integrity or availability of information

- ensure all our information assets and IT facilities are protected against damage, loss or misuse

- increase awareness and understanding in the company of the requirements of information security and the responsibility of staff to protect the confidentiality and integrity of the information that they themselves handle.

Responsibility

Every member of staff is responsible for ensuring that information held is accurate and kept confidential and that the terms of this policy are adhered to.

In the event of a data security breach, the relevant person must be informed immediately.

Our obligations under data protection legislation include that:

- we only hold data with consent

- we keep that data confidential

- we use it only for authorised purpose(s)

- any data we hold is:
  - adequate
  - relevant
  - not excessive
  - accurate, and
  - up-to-date
  - we do not hold it for longer than is necessary.

Our Procedures

Information Management

- Records and information are owned by the company and not by any individual or team.

- Keeping accurate and up-to-date records is an integral part of all business activities.

- Complete and accurate records must be securely stored in the appropriate locations and be easily identifiable and accessible to those who need to see them. This means that:
  - files must be kept in accordance with our normal file management protocols and must be kept organised and up-to-date
  - substantive matter related emails must be placed on file and must not be stored solely in personal mailboxes
  - files must not be removed from the office except as permitted under this policy.

Access to Offices and Files

- All office access doors must be kept secure at all times and clients and visitors must not be given keys or pass-codes.

- Clients and visitors should never be left alone in areas where they could have access to confidential information.

Computers and IT

- Computers must be password protected. Passwords should not be written down or given to others.

- Computers and other devices should be locked when not in use to minimise the risk of accidental data loss or disclosure.

Backup of Data

- All electronic data must be securely backed up at the end of each working day.

- Backup media must be encrypted.

- Backup media that is retained on site prior to being sent for storage off site and must be stored securely in a locked safe and at a sufficient distance away from the original data to ensure both the original and backup copies are not compromised.

IT System Management and Development

- Our IT systems are managed by the IT manager who is responsible for overseeing day-to-day operation and to ensure continued security and integrity.

- Access controls will be maintained at appropriate levels for all systems by ongoing and proactive management. Any changes to permissions must be approved by the IT manager.

- New IT systems, or upgrades to existing systems, must be authorised by the IT manager and the authorisation process must take account of security requirements. The information assets associated with any proposed new or updated systems must be identified and a risk assessment undertaken.

- Any new equipment must have appropriate levels of resilience and fault tolerance and must be correctly maintained.

- Software and applications must be managed to ensure their smooth day-to-day running and to preserve data security and integrity. The purchase or installation of new or upgraded software must be planned and managed and any information security risks must be mitigated. Specifications for new software or upgrades of existing software must specify the required information security controls.

Reporting Breaches

All members of staff have an obligation to report actual or potential data protection compliance failures. This allows us to:

- investigate the failure and take remedial steps if necessary

- maintain a register of compliance failures.

Example of disciplinary

The Company requires good standards of conduct from its employees, together with satisfactory standards of work. The purpose of the disciplinary procedure is to ensure that any concerns over employees' conduct or performance are handled in a fair, consistent and timely manner, with the intention of bringing about an improvement, and to protect the proper operation of the Company's business and the health and safety of its employees.

Purpose and scope

Although line managers are encouraged to address conduct issues through coaching and other informal routes, a more formal approach is sometimes necessary. This would usually be the case where coaching has failed to result in the required improvements, or the issue is serious enough to warrant invoking the formal procedure in the first instance, for example a serious breach of your contract of employment.

Disciplinary offences

Matters that the Company views as amounting to disciplinary offences include (but are not limited to):

- persistent bad timekeeping, unauthorised absence or poor attendance
- minor damage to Company property
- failure to observe Company procedures
- abusive or disruptive behaviour
- unreasonable refusal to follow an instruction issued by a manager or supervisor
- smoking in non-designated areas of the Company's premises
- bribery offences
- and any breach of the Company's policies and procedures.

The Company reserves the right to implement the procedure at any stage as set out below taking into account the alleged misconduct of an employee.

Procedure for conducting formal disciplinary hearings

Depending on the offence, issues will normally be dealt with informally in the first instance. If it is felt that the issues cannot be dealt with informally, the employee will be invited to a disciplinary hearing. No formal disciplinary action will be taken against an employee until the issues have been investigated and in all cases the discipline and dismissal procedure will be adhered to. This procedure is as outlined below:

Step 1: The employee will be invited to attend a disciplinary hearing. The invite letter will set out the purpose of the hearing, when and where it is to take place, who will be in attendance and include details of the alleged misconduct, including any relevant supporting documentation (e.g.: investigation findings).

Step 2: A meeting will be held where the alleged misconduct will be discussed in detail.

Step 3: An outcome will be delivered at the end of the meeting or as soon as possible afterwards; this will either be a disciplinary sanction or a decision will be made to take no further action. This will be confirmed in writing.

In some cases further investigation may need to be carried out. In this case the meeting will be adjourned for investigating purposes. An outcome of the disciplinary hearing will be given at a later date. If further information is gathered, the employee will be allowed a reasonable period of time, to consider the new information prior to the reconvening of the disciplinary proceedings.

Step 4: Once received, the employee can appeal against the outcome of the meeting. Details of how to do so will be included in the outcome letter.

At any formal meeting, employees have the right to be accompanied by a colleague or Union Representative (if applicable). The employee must take all reasonable steps to attend the meeting.

At the hearing

Attendance

Where the employee is unable to attend a disciplinary hearing and provides a good reason for failing to attend, the hearing will be adjourned to another day. Except in exceptional circumstances, if the employee is unable to attend the rearranged hearing, the rearranged hearing will take place in the employee's absence. The employee's fellow worker or trade union official may attend in such circumstances and will be allowed the opportunity to present the employee's case. The employee will also be allowed to make written submissions in such a situation.

Witnesses

Employees must give advance warning if they wish to call his/her own relevant witnesses to the hearing to support their case, however, the Company will not allow the calling of witnesses for the purposes of cross-examination. Instead, where witnesses have provided evidence for an investigation, you will have an opportunity to respond to that evidence during the hearing.

Role of a companion

The employee's chosen companion has the right to address the hearing to put the employee's case, sum up the case and respond on the employee's behalf to any view expressed at the hearing. The companion may also confer with the employee during the hearing. However, there is no requirement for the employer to permit the companion to answer questions on behalf of the employee, or to address the hearing where the employee indicates that he/she does not wish this.

Gross misconduct and summary dismissal

Gross misconduct is misconduct of such a serious and fundamental nature that it breaches the contractual relationship between the employee and the Company. In the event that an employee commits an act of gross misconduct, the Company will be entitled to terminate summarily the employee's contract of employment without notice or pay in lieu of notice.

Matters that the Company views as amounting to gross misconduct include (but are not limited to):

- theft, fraud, deliberate falsification of records

- other offences of dishonesty

- absence without leave and unauthorised leave

- falsification of a qualification that is a stated requirement of the employee's employment or results in financial gain to the employee

- sexual misconduct at work

- fighting with or physical assault on members of staff or the public

- deliberate and/or damage to or misuse of the organisation's property

- serious incapability through alcohol or being under the influence of illegal drugs

- possession, custody or control of illegal drugs on the organisation's premises

- serious breach of the organisation's rules, including, but not restricted to, health and safety rules and rules on computer and social media use

- gross negligence

- imprisonment

- conduct that brings the Company's name into disrepute; and

- bullying, harassment and discrimination.

Appeal

An employee who wishes to appeal against a disciplinary decision must do so in writing within 7 calendar days. A relevant manager or a member of the Human Resources team will hold the appeal meeting and their decision is final. Wherever possible a manager of seniority to be capable of over-riding an original decision (if necessary) will hold the appeal meeting and their decision is final. At the appeal meeting, any disciplinary sanction that has been imposed will be reviewed.

When lodging an appeal, the employee should state:

(a)   the grounds of the appeal; and

(b)   whether he/she is appealing against the finding that he/she has committed that alleged act or acts of misconduct, or against the level of disciplinary sanction imposed.

Appeal hearings will normally take place within 14 days of receipt of the employee's written notice of appeal.

Extract from an equity, diversity and inclusion policy

Our core values define the Company's culture and provide the framework for what we deliver to our customers and employees each day. We are fully committed to providing services which embrace diversity and promote equality and inclusion. As an employer we celebrate and value equality, diversity and inclusion within our workforce. Our vision is to ensure that these commitments, reinforced by our values, are embedded in our day-to-day working practices with all our learners, colleagues and partners.

The Company expects all its managers and employees to be fully committed to the elimination of unlawful and unfair discrimination and to actively embrace the principles of equality, diversity and inclusion (EDI).

Purpose and scope

The Company is fully committed to providing a good and harmonious working environment where everyone is treated equally and with respect and dignity. Our aim is that remuneration, recruitment, promotion, and retention will not be affected by irrelevant considerations and stereotyping.

The Company is proudly committed to being an equal opportunities employer. Therefore, it is our policy that there will be no discrimination against or harassment of any employee, job applicant or supplier contractor either directly, indirectly or by association or perception, on the basis of any of the following:

- Race (including nationality & ethnicity)
- Sex
- Disability
- Gender reassignment
- Sexual orientation
- Religion or philosophical belief
- Age
- Marital or civil partnership status
- Pregnancy & maternity.

This policy has been developed to:

- Ensure the company fulfils its legal obligations
- Prevent and/or minimise the risk of any discrimination or unfair treatment to employees and job applicants
- Increase awareness of minimum acceptable standards amongst employees and workers
- Promote positive attitudes and behaviours with regard to EDI for the health, well-being and benefit of employees, learners, employers and other stakeholders
- Share good and best practice which leads to continuous improvement through embedding EDI into all the policies, strategies and procedures.

Our core values define the Company's culture, and as part of promoting that culture it is important to the Company that any fraud, misconduct or wrongdoing by workers is reported and dealt with properly.

Purpose and scope

This policy sets out the way in which individuals may raise any concerns they have about business malpractice and how those concerns will be dealt with.

Disclosure

Legislation provides protection for workers who raise legitimate concerns about a specified matter. These are called 'qualifying disclosures'. Legislation only covers qualifying disclosures that are made in the public interest under six categories; criminal offence, miscarriage of justice, endangerment of health and safety, damage to the environment, breach of any other legal obligation and any cover-up of these issues.

To obtain protection employees must first disclose the information to the employer using the internal procedures available.

A worker who makes such a protected disclosure has the right not to be dismissed, or subjected to victimisation, because they have made the disclosure.

This procedure should be used to disclose a concern that, in your honest, reasonable belief, wrongdoing has been committed, is being committed or is likely to be committed.

What is covered

Wrongdoing includes (but is not limited to):

- Serious breach of the Company's Code of Conduct

- An unlawful or criminal offence (e.g. fraud, corruption or theft)

- A breach of a legal obligation

- A miscarriage of justice

- A disregard of legislation governing health and safety at work

- Action that has led to or could lead to damage to the environment

- Breach of the Company's Anti-bribery & Corruption Policy

- The deliberate covering up of information in relation to any of the above.

Reporting a concern

A worker who reasonably believes that inappropriate business conduct has occurred, is occurring or is likely to occur should in the first instance raise the issue with member of the Senior Leadership Team or a Human Resources Manager. Alternatively, the conduct or activity may be reported anonymously by calling the Company's Ethics Hotline.

Every effort will be made to ensure confidentiality and if requested all reasonable steps will be taken to protect the anonymity of the whistleblower. However, under certain circumstances to assist with the investigation the individual's identity may become known or need to be revealed.

Investigation

Once an individual has raised a concern, the matter will be investigated by either the person to whom the matter was raised or, where more appropriate, the Company will appoint an alternative manager. It is not the responsibility of the individual raising the concern to investigate the wrongdoing in order to gather evidence.

The format of the investigation may vary depending upon the circumstances. However, the individual who raised the concern may be required to attend an investigation meeting.

Once the investigation is complete, the individual who raised the concern will be informed of the outcome and further steps that are to be taken.

If the individual who raised the concern is dissatisfied with the investigation or outcome they should raise the matter with a more senior member of the management team or HR.

Safeguards

The Company will not tolerate any negative behaviour towards an employee who has reported a possible wrongdoing. Victimisation of a worker for raising a concern may constitute a disciplinary offence.

No action will be taken against anyone who makes an allegation, reasonably believing it to be true, even if the allegation is not subsequently confirmed by the investigation. However, maliciously making a false allegation or misuse of the whistleblowing procedure is a disciplinary offence.

Examples of social media policy

Purpose and scope

This policy sets out how social media usage is managed in line with Company policy and guidelines, as well as legal obligations.

It is important all employees understand their obligations in line with ensuring appropriate use of social media whilst an employee of the Company.

Definition of social media

For the purposes of this policy, social media is a type of interactive online media that allows parties to communicate instantly with each other or to share data in a public forum. Social Media includes, but is not limited to, online social forums, blogs, wiki's, communities and sites such as Twitter, Facebook and LinkedIn, video- and image-sharing websites such as YouTube, Pinterest and Flickr, and any other web-based or virtual communities in which people may share and exchange information.

Employees should be aware that there are many more examples of social media than can be listed here and this is a constantly changing area. Employees should follow these guidelines in relation to any social media that they use.

Things you should know about your public information

Employees should be aware that many of the communications and information they post on social networking sites is neither private nor temporary. Employees should also be aware that when they choose to publish their opinions through a blog, social networking site or other openly accessible medium, they are legally responsible for those opinions. Ultimately, it is the responsibility of the employee to keep information private if desired.

Use of social media in your personal life and at work

The organisation encourages employees to make reasonable and appropriate use of social media websites as part of their work, as and when required. The Company recognises that when used in an appropriate capacity, social media allows our employees to share insight and add value for our customers. In addition, the organisation recognises that many employees may also make use of social media in a personal capacity.

Employees must be aware at all times that, if recognisable as a Company employee, or when contributing to the organisation's social media activities, they are representing the organisation. The Company recognises that employees may wish to state the Company as their employer on social media, however the employee's online profile (for example, the name of a blog or a Twitter name) must not contain the organisation's name, except in the case of LinkedIn or similar social media sites that are specifically designed for this purpose.

If employees do discuss their work on social media sites, other than via official Company channels, (for example, giving opinions on their specialism or the sector in which the organisation operates), they must include on their profile a statement along the following lines: "The views I express here are mine alone and do not necessarily reflect the views of my employer."

Employees may contribute to the organisation's social media activities, for example by writing for our blogs/managing a Facebook account/running an official Twitter account on behalf of the organisation, however only when authorised to do so within their role. Employees should use the same safeguards as they would with any other form of communication about the organisation in the public sphere.

Any communications that employees make in a professional or personal capacity through social media must not:

- bring the organisation into disrepute, for example by: – criticising or arguing with customers, colleagues or rivals

  - making defamatory comments about individuals or other organisations or groups; or

  - posting images that are inappropriate or links to inappropriate content

- breach confidentiality, for example by:

  - revealing trade secrets or information owned by the organisation

  - giving away confidential information about an individual (such as a colleague or customer contact) or organisation (such as a rival business); or

  - discussing the organisation's internal workings (such as deals that it is doing with a customer/client or its future business plans that have not been communicated to the public)

- breach copyright, for example by:

  - using someone else's images or written content without permission; or

  - failing to give acknowledgement where permission has been given to reproduce something; or

- do anything that could be considered discriminatory against, or bullying or harassment of, any individual, for example by:

  - making (or condoning others to make) offensive or derogatory comments relating to sex, gender reassignment, race (including nationality), disability, sexual orientation, religion or belief or age

- – using social media to bully another individual (such as an employee of the organisation); or

- – posting images that are discriminatory or offensive (or links to such content).

- make any false or misleading statements or claims about the Company's products or services.

- confirm, deny or make comment on issues that the employee is not authorised to handle, or for which the employee is not considered an expert.

Please note that this list is indicative and is not exhaustive. Be thoughtful and as considerate when communicating online as you would be in person. Any communication online that does not adhere to the Company's core values or internal policies may be determined to be inappropriate.

Excessive use of social media at work

Employees should not spend an excessive amount of time using social media websites while at work, even if they claim to be doing so as part of their work. This is likely to have a detrimental effect on employees' productivity. They should ensure that use of social media does not interfere with their other duties whilst at work and personal use of social media, whether on company equipment or on an employee's own equipment, should be limited to lunch hours, outside of normal working hours and very limited other occasions.

Consequences for breach of this policy

Employees should note that any breaches of this policy may lead to disciplinary action in line with the Company's Disciplinary Policy, and/or legal action if required. Serious breaches of this policy, for example incidents of bullying of colleagues or social media activity causing serious damage to the organisation, may constitute gross misconduct and lead to summary dismissal.

Monitoring use of social media during work time

The organisation reserves the right to monitor employees' internet usage in line with our IT Acceptable Use policy. The organisation considers that valid reasons for checking an employee's internet usage include suspicions that the employee has:

- been spending an excessive amount of time using social media websites for non-work-related activity; or

- acted in a way that is in breach of the rules set out in this policy; or

- breached any other policy or explicit contractual terms.

Access to particular social media websites may be withdrawn or prohibited, in any case of misuse.

This safety policy statement demonstrates the Company's absolute commitment and responsibility as an employer and educator for providing a safe and healthy environment within the work place, for all staff, contractors and visitors in accordance with the health and safety legislation and our responsibility to reduce our impact on the environment.

The company views managing health, safety, fire issues and the associated responsibilities as the highest priority.

Our statement of general policy is:

- to provide adequate control of the health and safety risks arising from our work activities

- to consult with our employees on matters affecting their health and safety

- to provide and maintain safe plant and equipment

- to ensure safe handling and use of substances

- to provide information, instruction and supervision for employees

- to ensure all employees are competent to do their tasks, and to give them adequate training

- to prevent accidents and cases of work-related ill health

- to maintain safe and healthy working conditions; and to review and revise this policy as necessary at regular intervals.

All employees have to:

- co-operate with supervisors and managers on health and safety matters

- not interfere with anything provided to safeguard their health and safety

- take reasonable care of their own health and safety; and

- report all health and safety concerns to an appropriate person.

4   Test your understanding questions

Test your understanding 1

An employer has an implied duty:

A   To provide facilities for smokers

B   To give employees who leave a reference

C   To provide work

D   To pay reasonable remuneration

Test your understanding 2

Which of the following does not constitute an implied term of an employment contract?

A   A decision of the court

B   Legislation

C   Custom and practice

D   Employee handbook

Test your understanding 3

Which of the following is not an implied duty owed by an employee towards his employer?

A   A duty not to misuse confidential information

B   A duty to provide faithful service

C   A duty to maintain trust and confidence

D   A duty to obey all orders given to him by his employer

Test your understanding 4

What is the remedy available to an employee who has been wrongfully dismissed?

Test your understanding 5

A summary dismissal occurs when:

A   The parties agree to end the contract immediately

B   The employer terminates the contract with notice but no investigation

C   The employer terminates the contract without notice

D   The employee resigns

Test your understanding 6

What is constructive dismissal?

Test your understanding 7

In the context of whistleblowing what is a 'qualifying disclosure'?

A   Revealing information of the right type

B   Revealing information within the appropriate time frame

C   Revealing information to the right person

D   Revealing information in the right way

Test your understanding 8

Which of the following is not a phase of money laundering?

A   Integration

B   Placement

C   Adjustment

D   Layering

Test your understanding answers

Test your understanding 1

D

This is an implied duty of an employer.

Test your understanding 2

D

The rules in a handbook would not be treated as implied terms, but a failure to obey them could be treated as evidence of a failure to obey reasonable orders.

Test your understanding 3

D

An employee is only under an obligation to obey orders which are lawful and reasonable.

Test your understanding 4

The remedy available would be compensation in the form of damages.

Test your understanding 5

C

Summary dismissal is dismissal without notice.

Test your understanding 6

Constructive dismissal is when an employee terminates the contract, with or without notice, by reason of the employer's conduct.

Test your understanding 7

A

A qualifying disclosure is revealing information of the right type.

Test your understanding 8

C

Placement, layering and integration are phases to money laundering.

Company Administration

Chapter learning objectives

Upon completion of this chapter you will be able to:

- describe the essential characteristics of the different forms of business organisations and the implications of corporate personality

- explain the differences between public and private companies

- explain the purpose and legal status of the articles of association

- explain the main advantages and disadvantages of carrying on business through the medium of a company limited by shares.

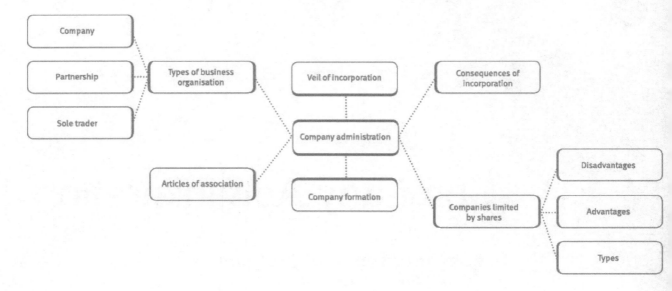

1 Introduction

Business may be carried on by many different forms of organisation. Each jurisdiction will have specific laws governing these organisations and such matters as their creation, their liability, their ownership. In this chapter we are seeking to introduce you to some common forms of business organisations and the general rules that may apply to them.

2 Types of business organisation

Essential characteristics

Sole trader

- The owner 'is' the business – owns the assets and is liable for all the debts.

- Generally no legal formalities are required to set up a sole trader business.

- This form of business is inappropriate for large businesses or those involving a degree of risk.

Partnership

- The relationship which subsists between persons carrying on a business in common with a view of profit.

- A partnership can be an informal arrangement or be formalised and regulated by a written agreement. This agreement is private to the partners.

- In many jurisdictions a partnership is not recognised as a separate legal entity so the partners as individuals are jointly and severally liable for the debts of the partnership. These are often known as ordinary or general partnerships.

- Some jurisdictions however allow the creation of a partnership where one or more partners has limited liability. These partnerships are often created by formal registration under statute and the partnership is recognised as a separate legal entity (e.g. in England the Limited Liability Partnerships Act 2000 allows the creation of limited liability partnerships which must have "LLP" at the end of their name so that a third party can distinguish it from an ordinary partnership).

- In some jurisdictions an LLP is an artificial legal entity with 'perpetual succession'. It can hold property in its own right, enter into contracts in its own name, sue and be sued.

- In some jurisdictions the liability of the members of a limited liability partnership (LLP) is limited to the amount of capital they have agreed to contribute. Requirements similar to that of a company.

Company

- A company is an artificial legal person created by registration with a written constitution (see below).

3   Companies

The doctrine of veil of incorporation

The term 'veil of incorporation' refers to the fact that a company is a separate legal entity (i.e. separate from its members, the owners and its directors, the managers). This separates the legal identity of the company from that of its members, and also its liability from that of the members.

English case law example

SALOMON v SALOMON & CO Ltd 1897

Facts:

S transferred his business to a limited company. He was the director and majority shareholder and a secured creditor. The company went into liquidation and the other creditors tried to obtain repayment from S personally.

Held:

S as shareholder and director had no personal liability to creditors, and he could be repaid in priority as a secured creditor. This enshrined the concepts of separate legal personality and limited liability in the law.

Consequences of incorporation for a company limited by shares

There are a number of consequences of being a separate legal entity:

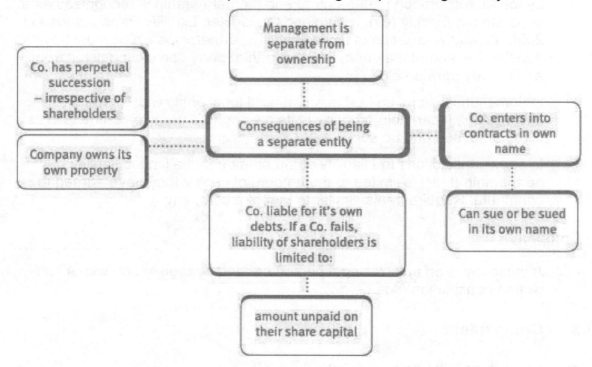

English case law example

MACAURA v NORTHERN LIFE ASSURANCE 1925

Facts:

M owned a forest. He formed a company in which he beneficially owned all the shares and sold his forest to it. He, however, continued to maintain an insurance policy on the forest in his own name. The forest was destroyed by fire.

Held:

He could not claim on the policy since the property damaged belonged to the company, not him, and as shareholder he had no insurable interest in the forest.

Lifting the veil of incorporation

'Lifting the veil of incorporation' means that in certain circumstances the courts can look through the company to the identity of the shareholders. This is intended to prevent inequitable results and expose the commercial reality of the situation.

The usual result of lifting the veil is that the members or directors become personally liable for the company's debts.

GILFORD MOTOR CO Ltd v HORNE 1933

Facts:

An employee had a covenant in his contract of employment which stated that he would not solicit his former employer's customers. After he left their employment he formed a company to solicit those customers and claimed it was the company approaching the customers and not him.

Held:

The court held that the company could be restrained from competition, as the previous employee had set it up to evade his own legal obligations. An injunction was granted against him and the company.

There may also be instances where statute will intervene to lift the veil, usually in order to confer a personal liability on those who run a company for breach of their obligations e.g. in England if a director participates in the management of a company in contravention of an order made under the Company Directors Disqualification Act 1986 he may be jointly or severally liable along with the company for the company's debts.

4 Companies limited by shares

Introduction

There are many different types of company but by far the most common are companies limited by shares. The company's capital is divided into "shares". Each member holds one or more share. Initially the shares are issued by the company in return for payment by the member. Such companies may be private or public.

Private company v public company

There will be differences between a private company and a public company. The differences can depend on the company law legislation of a particular country. The following table summarises the difference between a private company and a public company in the UK.

	Public companies	**Private (limited) companies**
Definition	Registered as a public company.	Any company that is not a public company.
Name	Ends with plc or public limited company.	Ends with Ltd or limited.
Capital	In order to trade, must have allotted shares of at least £50,000.	No minimum (or maximum) requirements.
Raising capital	May raise capital by advertising its shares as available for public subscription. This can be through a Stock Exchange.	Prohibited from offering its shares to the public.
Start of trading	Must obtain trading certificate from registrar before commencing trading.	Can begin from date of incorporation.
Directors	Minimum two.	Minimum one.
Secretary	Must have one. Must be qualified.	Need not have one.
Accounts	Must file accounts within 6 months.	Need not lay accounts before general meeting. Must file within 9 months.
Audit	Accounts must be audited.	Audit not required if turnover below £6.5m.
Annual General Meeting (AGM)	Must be held each year.	Need not hold an AGM.

5 Company formation

In order to form a company a procedure will need to be followed. Normally a number of documents will need to be submitted to a central registration office (e.g. in England the office of the Registrar of Companies) which includes the following type of information:

- the proposed name of the company

- the memorandum of association which records the intention of each initial subscriber to form a new limited company

- the type of company (e.g. private or public)

- details of the registered office (the address for delivery of legal documents which may need to be served on the company)

- the share capital (e.g. number and class of shares and their nominal value)

- the names of proposed directors and their consent to act

- the names of the first shareholders

- a registration fee.

If this information is satisfactory, then a certificate of incorporation or similar document is issued and the company exists from the date on that certificate.

Off-the-shelf companies

Rather than forming a new company themselves, those wishing to set up a company may buy one 'ready made' or 'off-the-shelf' from a company formation dealer.

The dealer will hold in stock a number of ready made companies with generally non-descriptive names. The company can either trade with an existing name, or have the existing name changed to one of the purchaser's choice, subject to availability.

Buying off the shelf has a number of advantages as follows:

- it may be cheaper and simpler

- the company may be able to trade immediately

- as the company exists, it can enter into contracts immediately.

6 Articles of association

Introduction

The Articles of Association (also known as the Articles of Incorporation or Memorandum of Incorporation in some jurisdictions) form part of the company's internal constitution along with the memorandum of association (in cases where a memorandum is required).

The Articles of Association:

- set out the manner in which the company is to be governed and

- regulate the relationship between the company, its shareholders and its directors.

Articles should contain rules on a number of areas, the most important of which are as follows:

- Appointment and dismissal of directors.

- Powers, responsibilities and liabilities of directors.

- Directors' meetings.

- Members' rights.

- Members' meetings.
- Payment of dividends.
- Communication with members.
- Issue of shares.
- Documents and records.

Companies often draft their own articles although in some jurisdictions the company can choose to adopt articles prescribed by law. These articles can usually be amended by the members although the law often prescribes that a certain percentage of members must approve any such amendment.

Legal effect of company's constitutional documents

Generally the provisions of a company's constitution bind the company and its members to the same extent as if there were covenants on the part of the company and of each member to observe those provisions. This means that the articles form a contract between the company and its members, and between the members themselves, even if they do not sign them. They do not however bind the company to third parties.

7 Advantages and disadvantages of companies limited by shares

Detailed below are the principal advantages and disadvantages of operating a business through the medium of a company limited by shares that are found in many jurisdictions.

Advantages

- Legal entity – separate from its members.
- Liability – the company is liable itself on its contracts.
- Limit on liability – the member's liability is limited to the amount he agreed to pay for his shares; the liability of the company is unlimited.
- Ownership – the company owns its assets and ownership is not affected by any change in members (perpetual succession of the company).
- Transferability of shares – members' shares are freely transferrable (subject to any provision in the articles).

Disadvantages

- Formation – detailed documents and administration procedures required on registration.

- Disclosure and loss of privacy – much information about the company, its officers and its financial affairs must be kept and much of this may have to be open for public inspection.

- Cost – complying with all the administrative requirements and the possible need for an audit.

- Management – a member cannot be directly involved in the management of the company unless he is also a director.

- Dissolution – formal procedure required.

8 Test your understanding questions

Test your understanding 1

Which of the following is an example of an artificial legal person?

A   A sole trader

B   A general partnership

C   A company

D   None of the above

Test your understanding 2

What are the characteristics of an LLP?

Test your understanding 3

A partnership is a significant form of business organisation.

Which one of the following statements is correct?

A   A partnership is an example of an incorporated business organisation

B   A partnership is recognised in law as an artificial legal person

C   Partners generally benefit from limited liability for any debts incurred as a result of their business activities

D   None of the above

Test your understanding 4

What does 'lifting the veil of incorporation' mean?

Test your understanding 5

What are the articles of association?

Test your understanding answers

Test your understanding 1

C

A company is an artificial legal person.

Test your understanding 2

An artificial legal entity with 'perpetual succession'.

It can hold property in its own right, enter into contracts in its own name, sue and be sued.

The liability of the members is limited to the amount of capital they have agreed to contribute.

Test your understanding 3

D

Test your understanding 4

'Lifting the veil of incorporation' means that in certain circumstances the courts can look through the company to the identity of the shareholders.

Test your understanding 5

The articles of association form part of the company's internal constitution. They set out the manner in which the company is to be governed and regulate the relationship between the company, its shareholders and its directors.

Appendix 1: CIMA Code of Ethics for Professional Accountants

Supplementary reading: Preface

CIMA CODE OF ETHICS FOR PROFESSIONAL ACCOUNTANTS

CIMA PREFACE

As Chartered Management Accountants CIMA members (and registered students) throughout the world have a duty to observe the highest standards of conduct and integrity, and to uphold the good standing and reputation of the profession. They must also refrain from any conduct which might discredit the profession. Members and registered students must have regard to these guidelines irrespective of their field of activity, of their contract of employment or of any other professional memberships they may hold.

CIMA upholds the aims and principles of equal opportunities and fundamental human rights worldwide, including the handling of personal information. The Institute promotes the highest ethical and business standards, and encourages its members to be good and responsible professionals. Good ethical behaviour may be above that required by the law. In a highly competitive, complex business world, it is essential that CIMA members sustain their integrity and remember the trust and confidence which is placed on them by whoever relies on their objectivity and professionalism. Members must avoid actions or situations which are inconsistent with their professional obligations. They should also be guided not merely by the terms but by the spirit of this Code.

CIMA members should conduct themselves with courtesy and consideration towards all with whom they have professional dealings and should not behave in a manner which could be considered offensive or discriminatory.

To ensure that CIMA members protect the good standing and reputation of the profession, members must report the fact to the Institute if they are convicted or disqualified from acting as an officer of a company or if they are subject to any sanction resulting from disciplinary action taken by any other body or authority.

CIMA has adopted the following code of ethics. Parts A and B of this code are based on the IFAC* Code of Ethics, that was developed with the help of input from CIMA and the global accountancy profession. Part C of the Code was developed in cooperation with the American Institute of Certified Public Accountants (AICPA).The AICPA and CIMA joined together to create a designation for management accountants, the Chartered Global Management Accountant (CGMA). The CGMA designation is designed to elevate management accounting and further emphasize its importance for businesses worldwide. Part C of the Code is designed to provide guidance to all CIMA members around the world who are members in business and professional accountants in business and, those who hold the CGMA credential. When a CGMA is also a member in public practice the CGMA should also comply with the applicable guidance of the CIMA Code of Ethics and apply the most restrictive provisions.

If a member cannot resolve an ethical issue by following this Code by consulting the ethics information on CIMA's website or by seeking guidance from CIMA's ethics helpline, he or she should seek legal advice as to both his or her legal rights and any obligations he or she may have. The CIMA Charter, Byelaws and Regulations give definitive rules on many matters.

For further information see: www.cimaglobal.com/ethics

Note: The CIMA Code of Ethics is a Law of the Institute (to which all members and registered students are required to comply) for the purpose of the definition of "misconduct" in Byelaw 1.

*International Federation of Accountants.

Parts A and B of the CIMA Code of Ethics are based on the IFAC Handbook of the Code of Ethics for Professional Accountants, of the International Ethics Standards Board of Accountants (IESBA), published by IFAC in July 2014 and is used with permission by IFAC.

Supplementary reading: Contents

CIMA CODE OF ETHICS FOR PROFESSIONAL ACCOUNTANTS

Contents

PREFACE

PART A – GENERAL APPLICATION OF THE CODE

100 Introduction and fundamental principles

110 Integrity

120 Objectivity

130 Professional competence and due care

140 Confidentiality

150 Professional behaviour

PART B – PROFESSIONAL ACCOUNTANTS IN PUBLIC PRACTICE

200 Introduction

210 Professional appointment

220 Conflicts of Interest

230 Second opinions

240 Fees and other types of remuneration

250 Marketing professional services

260 Gifts and Hospitality

270 Custody of client assets

280 Objectivity – All services

290 Independence – Audit and Review engagements: see Annex 1

291 Independence – Other assurance engagements: see Annex

PART C – PROFESSIONAL ACCOUNTANTS IN BUSINESS

300 Introduction

310 Ethical conflicts

320 Conflicts of interest

330 Gifts, entertainment and other forms of inducements

340 Preparing and reporting information

350 Educational services

360 General standards/Professional competence and due care

370 Acts discreditable/Professional behaviour/Confidentiality

DEFINITIONS

ANNEX 1

290 Independence – Audit and Review engagement

291 Independence – Other assurance engagements

Supplementary reading: Sections 100 and 110

PART A – GENERAL APPLICATION OF THE CODE

SECTION 100

Introduction and fundamental principles

100.1 A distinguishing mark of the accountancy profession is its acceptance of the responsibility to act in the public interest. Therefore, a professional accountant's responsibility is not exclusively to satisfy the needs of an individual client or employer. In acting in the public interest, a professional accountant shall observe and comply with this Code. If a professional accountant is prohibited from complying with certain parts of this Code by law or regulation, the professional accountant shall comply with all other parts of this Code.

100.2 This Code contains three parts. Part A establishes the fundamental principles of professional ethics for professional accountants and provides a conceptual framework that professional accountants shall apply to:

(a) Identify threats to compliance with the fundamental principles

(b) Evaluate the significance of the threats identified; and

(c) Apply safeguards, when necessary, to eliminate the threats or reduce them to an acceptable level.

Safeguards are necessary when the professional accountant determines that the threats are not at a level at which a reasonable and informed third party would be likely to conclude, weighing all the specific facts and circumstances available to the professional accountant at that time, that compliance with the fundamental principles is not compromised. A professional accountant shall use professional judgement in applying this conceptual framework.

100.3 Parts B and C describe how the conceptual framework applies in certain situations. They provide examples of safeguards that may be appropriate to address threats to compliance with the fundamental principles. They also describe situations where safeguards are not available to address the threats, and consequently, the circumstance or relationship creating the threats shall be avoided. Part B applies to professional accountants in public practice. Part C applies to professional accountants in business. Professional accountants in public practice may also find Part C relevant to their particular circumstances.

100.4 The use of the word 'shall' in this Code imposes a requirement on the professional accountant or firm to comply with the specific provision in which 'shall' has been used. Compliance is required unless an exception is permitted by this Code.

Fundamental principles

100.5 A professional accountant shall comply with the following fundamental principles:

(a) Integrity – to be straightforward and honest in all professional and business relationships.

(b) Objectivity – to not allow bias, conflict of interest or undue influence of others to override professional or business judgements.

(c) Professional Competence and Due Care – to maintain professional knowledge and skill at the level required to ensure that a client or employer receives competent professional services based on current developments in practice, legislation and techniques and act diligently and in accordance with applicable technical and professional standards.

(d) Confidentiality – to respect the confidentiality of information acquired as a result of professional and business relationships and, therefore, not disclose any such information to third parties without proper and specific authority, unless there is a legal or professional right or duty to disclose, nor use the information for the personal advantage of the professional accountant or third parties.

(e) Professional Behaviour – to comply with relevant laws and regulations and avoid any action that discredits the profession.

Each of these fundamental principles is discussed in more detail in Sections 110 –150.

Conceptual framework approach

100.6 The circumstances in which professional accountants operate may create specific threats to compliance with the fundamental principles. It is impossible to define every situation that creates threats to compliance with the fundamental principles and specify the appropriate action. In addition, the nature of engagements and work assignments may differ and, consequently, different threats may be created, requiring the application of different safeguards. Therefore, this Code establishes a conceptual framework that requires a professional accountant to identify, evaluate, and address threats to compliance with the fundamental principles. The conceptual framework approach assists professional accountants in complying with the ethical requirements of this Code and meeting their responsibility to act in the public interest. It accommodates many variations in circumstances that create threats to compliance with the fundamental principles and can deter a professional accountant from concluding that a situation is permitted if it is not specifically prohibited.

100.7 When a professional accountant identifies threats to compliance with the fundamental principles and, based on an evaluation of those threats, determines that they are not at an acceptable level, the professional accountant shall determine whether appropriate safeguards are available and can be applied to eliminate the threats or reduce them to an acceptable level. In making that determination, the professional accountant shall exercise professional judgement and take into account whether a reasonable and informed third party, weighing all the specific facts and circumstances available to the professional accountant at the time, would be likely to conclude that the threats would be eliminated or reduced to an acceptable level by the application of the safeguards, such that compliance with the fundamental principles is not compromised.

100.8 A professional accountant shall evaluate any threats to compliance with the fundamental principles when the professional accountant knows, or could reasonably be expected to know, of circumstances or relationships that may compromise compliance with the fundamental principles.

100.9 A professional accountant shall take qualitative as well as quantitative factors into account when evaluating the significance of a threat. When applying the conceptual framework, a professional accountant may encounter situations in which threats cannot be eliminated or reduced to an acceptable level, either because the threat is too significant or because appropriate safeguards are not available or cannot be applied. In such situations, the professional accountant shall decline or discontinue the specific professional activity or service involved or, when necessary, resign from the engagement (in the case of a professional accountant in public practice) or the employing organisation (in the case of a professional accountant in business).

100.10 Sections 290 and 291 contain provisions with which a professional accountant shall comply if the professional accountant identifies a breach of an independence provision of the Code. If a professional accountant identifies a breach of any other provision of the Code, the professional accountant shall evaluate the significance of the breach and the impact of the accountant's ability to comply with the fundamental principles. The accountant shall take whatever actions that may be available, as soon as possible, to satisfactorily address the consequences of the breach. The accountant shall determine whether to report the breach, for example, to those who may have been affected by the breach, a member body, relevant regulator or oversight authority.

100.11 When a professional accountant encounters unusual circumstances in which the application of a specific requirement of the Code would result in a disproportionate outcome or an outcome that may not be in the public interest, it is recommended that the professional accountant consult with a member body or the relevant regulator.

Threats and Safeguards

100.12 Threats may be created by a broad range of relationships and circumstances. When a relationship or circumstance creates a threat, such a threat could compromise, or could be perceived to compromise, a professional accountant's compliance with the fundamental principles. A circumstance or relationship may create more than one threat, and a threat may affect compliance with more than one fundamental principle. Threats fall into one or more of the following categories:

(a) Self-interest threat – the threat that a financial or other interest will inappropriately influence the professional accountant's judgement or behaviour

(b) Self-review threat – the threat that a professional accountant will not appropriately evaluate the results of a previous judgement made or activity or service performed by the professional accountant, or by another individual within the professional accountant's firm or employing organisation, on which the accountant will rely when forming a judgement as part of providing a current activity or providing a current service

(c) Advocacy threat – the threat that a professional accountant will promote a client's or employer's position to the point that the professional accountant's objectivity is compromised

(d) Familiarity threat – the threat that due to a long or close relationship with a client or employer, a professional accountant will be too sympathetic to their interests or too accepting of their work; and

(e) Intimidation threat – the threat that a professional accountant will be deterred from acting objectively because of actual or perceived pressures, including attempts to exercise undue influence over the professional accountant. Parts B and C of this Code explain how these categories of threats may be created for professional accountants in public practice and professional accountants in business, respectively. Professional accountants in public practice may also find Part C relevant to their particular circumstances.

100.13 Safeguards are actions or other measures that may eliminate threats or reduce them to an acceptable level. They fall into two broad categories:

(a) Safeguards created by the profession, legislation or regulation; and

(b) Safeguards in the work environment.

100.14 Safeguards created by the profession, legislation or regulation include:

- Educational, training and experience requirements for entry into the profession.

- Continuing professional development requirements.

- Corporate governance regulations.

- Professional standards.

- Professional or regulatory monitoring and disciplinary procedures.

- External review by a legally empowered third party of the reports, returns, communications or information produced by a professional accountant.

100.15 Parts B and C of this Code discuss safeguards in the work environment for professional accountants in public practice and professional accountants in business, respectively.

100.16 Certain safeguards may increase the likelihood of identifying or deterring unethical behaviour. Such safeguards, which may be created by the accounting profession, legislation, regulation, or an employing organisation, include:

- Effective, well-publicised complaint systems operated by the employing organisation, the profession or a regulator, which enable colleagues, employers and members of the public to draw attention to unprofessional or unethical behaviour.

- An explicitly stated duty to report breaches of ethical requirements.

Conflicts of interest

100.17 A professional accountant may be faced with a conflict of interest when undertaking a professional activity. A conflict of interest creates a threat to objectivity and may create threats to the other fundamental principles. Such threats may be created when:

- The professional accountant undertakes a professional activity related to a particular matter for two or more parties whose interest with respect to that matter are in conflict; or

- The interests of the professional accountant with respect to a particular matter and the interests of a party for whom the professional accountant provides a professional activity related to that matter are in conflict.

100.18 Parts B and C of this Code discuss conflicts of interest for professional accountants in public practice and professional accountants in business, respectively.

Ethical conflict resolution

100.19 A professional accountant may be required to resolve a conflict in complying with the fundamental principles.

100.20 When initiating either a formal or informal conflict resolution process, the following factors, either individually or together with other factors, may be relevant to the resolution process:

(a)   Relevant facts

(b)   Ethical issues involved

(c)   Fundamental principles related to the matter in question

(d)   Established internal procedures; and

(e)   Alternative courses of action.

Having considered the relevant factors, a professional accountant shall determine the appropriate course of action, weighing the consequences of each possible course of action. If the matter remains unresolved, the professional accountant may wish to consult with other appropriate persons within the firm or employing organisation for help in obtaining resolution.

100.21 Where a matter involves a conflict with, or within, an organisation, a professional accountant shall determine whether to consult with those charged with governance of the organisation, such as the board of directors or the audit committee.

100.22 It may be in the best interests of the professional accountant to document the substance of the issue, the details of any discussions held, and the decisions made concerning that issue.

100.23 If a significant conflict cannot be resolved, a professional accountant may consider obtaining professional advice from the relevant professional body or from legal advisors. The professional accountant generally can obtain guidance on ethical issues without breaching the fundamental principle of confidentiality if the matter is discussed with the relevant professional body on an anonymous basis or with a legal advisor under the protection of legal privilege. Instances in which the professional accountant may consider obtaining legal advice vary. For example, a professional accountant may have encountered a fraud, the reporting of which could breach the professional accountant's responsibility to respect confidentiality. The professional accountant may consider obtaining legal advice in that instance to determine whether there is a requirement to report.

100.24 If, after exhausting all relevant possibilities, the ethical conflict remains unresolved, a professional accountant shall, where possible, refuse to remain associated with the matter creating the conflict. The professional accountant shall determine whether, in the circumstances, it is appropriate to withdraw from the engagement team or specific assignment, or to resign altogether from the engagement, the firm or the employing organisation.

Communicating with those charged with governance

100.25 When communicating with those charged with governance in accordance with the provisions of this Code, the professional accountant or firm shall determine, having regard to the nature and importance of the particular circumstances and matter to be communicated, the appropriate person(s) within the entity's governance structure with whom to communicate. If the professional accountant or firm communicates with a subgroup of those charged with governance, for example, an audit committee or an individual, the professional accountant or firm shall determine whether communication with all of those charged with governance is also necessary so that they are adequately informed.

SECTION 110

Integrity

110.1 The principle of integrity imposes an obligation on all professional accountants to be straightforward and honest in all professional and business relationships. Integrity also implies fair dealing and truthfulness.

110.2 A professional accountant shall not knowingly be associated with reports, returns, communications or other information where the professional accountant believes that the information:

(a) Contains a materially false or misleading statement

(b) Contains statements or information furnished recklessly; or

(c) Omits or obscures information required to be included where such omission or obscurity would be misleading.

When a professional accountant becomes aware that the accountant has been associated with such information, the accountant shall take steps to be disassociated from that information.

110.3 A professional accountant will be deemed not to be in breach of paragraph 110.2 if the professional accountant provides a modified report in respect of a matter contained in paragraph 110.2.

Supplementary reading: Sections 120 to 150

SECTION 120

Objectivity

120.1 The principle of objectivity imposes an obligation on all professional accountants not to compromise their professional or business judgement because of bias, conflict of interest or the undue influence of others.

120.2 A professional accountant may be exposed to situations that may impair objectivity. It is impracticable to define and prescribe all such situations. A professional accountant shall not perform a professional service if a circumstance or relationship biases or unduly influences the accountant's professional judgement with respect to that service.

SECTION 130

Professional competence and due care

130.1 The principle of professional competence and due care imposes the following obligations on all professional accountants:

(a) To maintain professional knowledge and skill at the level required to ensure that clients or employers receive competent professional service; and

(b) To act diligently in accordance with applicable technical and professional standards when providing professional services.

130.2 Competent professional service requires the exercise of sound judgement in applying professional knowledge and skill in the performance of such service. Professional competence may be divided into two separate phases:

(a) Attainment of professional competence; and

(b) Maintenance of professional competence.

130.3 The maintenance of professional competence requires a continuing awareness and an understanding of relevant technical, professional and business developments. Continuing professional development enables a professional accountant to develop and maintain the capabilities to perform competently within the professional environment.

130.4 Diligence encompasses the responsibility to act in accordance with the requirements of an assignment, carefully, thoroughly and on a timely basis.

130.5 A professional accountant shall take reasonable steps to ensure that those working under the professional accountant's authority in a professional capacity have appropriate training and supervision.

130.6 Where appropriate, a professional accountant shall make clients, employers or other users of the accountant's professional services or activities aware of the limitations inherent in the services or activities.

SECTION 140

Confidentiality

140.1 The principle of confidentiality imposes an obligation on all professional accountants to refrain from:

(a)   Disclosing outside the firm or employing organisation confidential information acquired as a result of professional and business relationships without proper and specific authority or unless there is a legal or professional right or duty to disclose; and

(b)   Using confidential information acquired as a result of professional and business relationships to their personal advantage or the advantage of third parties.

140.2 A professional accountant shall maintain confidentiality, including in a social environment, being alert to the possibility of inadvertent disclosure, particularly to a close business associate or a close or immediate family member.

140.3 A professional accountant shall maintain confidentiality of information disclosed by a prospective client or employer.

140.4 A professional accountant shall maintain confidentiality of information within the firm or employing organisation.

140.5 A professional accountant shall take reasonable steps to ensure that staff under the professional accountant's control and persons from whom advice and assistance is obtained respect the professional accountant's duty of confidentiality.

140.6 The need to comply with the principle of confidentiality continues even after the end of relationships between a professional accountant and a client or employer. When a professional accountant changes employment or acquires a new client, the professional accountant is entitled to use prior experience. The professional accountant shall not, however, use or disclose any confidential information either acquired or received as a result of a professional or business relationship.

140.7 The following are circumstances where professional accountants are or may be required to disclose confidential information or when such disclosure may be appropriate:

(a)   Disclosure is permitted by law and is authorised by the client or the employer

(b)   Disclosure is required by law, for example:

(i)   Production of documents or other provision of evidence in the course of legal proceedings; or

(ii)   Disclosure to the appropriate public authorities of infringements of the law that come to light; an

(c)   There is a professional duty or right to disclose, when not prohibited by law:

(i)   To comply with the quality review of a member body or professional body

(ii)   To respond to an inquiry or investigation by a member body or regulatory body

(iii)   To protect the professional interests of a professional accountant in legal proceedings; or

(iv)   To comply with technical standards and ethics requirements.

140.8 In deciding whether to disclose confidential information, relevant factors to consider include:

(a)   Whether the interests of all parties, including third parties whose interests may be affected, could be harmed if the client or employer consents to the disclosure of information by the professional accountant

(b)   Whether all the relevant information is known and substantiated, to the extent it is practicable; when the situation involves unsubstantiated facts, incomplete information or unsubstantiated conclusions, professional judgement shall be used in determining the type of disclosure to be made, if any

(c)   The type of communication that is expected and to whom it is addressed; and

(d)   Whether the parties to whom the communication is addressed are appropriate recipients.

SECTION 150

Professional behaviour

150.1 The principle of professional behaviour imposes an obligation on all professional accountants to comply with relevant laws and regulations and avoid any action that the professional accountant knows or should know may discredit the profession. This includes actions that a reasonable and informed third party, weighing all the specific facts and circumstances available to the professional accountant at that time, would be likely to conclude adversely affects the good reputation of the profession.

150.2 In marketing and promoting themselves and their work, professional accountants shall not bring the profession into disrepute. Professional accountants shall be honest and truthful and not:

(a)   Make exaggerated claims for the services they are able to offer, the qualifications they possess, or experience they have gained; or

(b)   Make disparaging references or unsubstantiated comparisons to the work of others.

 Supplementary reading: Sections 200 and 210

PART B – PROFESSIONAL ACCOUNTANTS IN PUBLIC PRACTICE

Section 200 Introduction

Section 210 Professional appointment

Section 220 Conflicts of Interest

Section 230 Second opinions

Section 240 Fees and other types of remuneration

Section 250 Marketing professional services

Section 260 Gifts and Hospitality

Section 270 Custody of client assets

Section 280 Objectivity – All services

Section 290 Independence – Audit and Review engagements: see Annex 1

Section 291 Independence – Other assurance engagements: see Annex 1

NOTE: CIMA Code of Ethics: Annex 1

Sections 290 and 291 address the independence requirements for audit, review and other assurance engagements and apply a conceptual framework approach. They also include commentary on the independence requirements and the effective date and transitional provisions for public interest entities, partner rotation, non-assurance services, fees and compensation and evaluation policies.

SECTION 200

Introduction

200.1 This Part of the Code describes how the conceptual framework contained in Part A applies in certain situations to professional accountants in public practice. This Part does not describe all of the circumstances and relationships that could be encountered by a professional accountant in public practice that create or may create threats to compliance with the fundamental principles. Therefore, the professional accountant in public practice is encouraged to be alert for such circumstances and relationships.

200.2 A professional accountant in public practice shall not knowingly engage in any business, occupation, or activity that impairs or might impair integrity, objectivity or the good reputation of the profession and as a result would be incompatible with the fundamental principles.

- A firm being concerned about the possibility of losing a significant client.

- A member of the audit team entering into employment negotiations with the audit client.

- A firm entering into a contingent fee arrangement relating to an assurance engagement.

- A professional accountant discovering a significant error when evaluating the results of a previous professional service performed by a member of the professional accountant's firm.

200.5 Examples of circumstances that create self-review threats for a professional accountant in public practice include:

- A firm issuing an assurance report on the effectiveness of the operation of financial systems after designing or implementing the systems.

- A firm having prepared the original data used to generate records that are the subject matter of the assurance engagement.

- A member of the assurance team being, or having recently been, a director or officer of the client.

- A member of the assurance team being, or having recently been, employed by the client in a position to exert significant influence over the subject matter of the engagement.

- The firm performing a service for an assurance client that directly affects the subject matter information of the assurance engagement.

200.6 Examples of circumstances that create advocacy threats for a professional accountant in public practice include:

- The firm promoting shares in an audit client.

- A professional accountant acting as an advocate on behalf of an audit client in litigation or disputes with third parties.

200.7 Examples of circumstances that create familiarity threats for a professional accountant in public practice include:

- A member of the engagement team having a close or immediate family member who is a director or officer of the client.

- A member of the engagement team having a close or immediate family member who is an employee of the client who is in a position to exert significant influence over the subject matter of the engagement.

- A director or officer of the client or an employee in a position to exert significant influence over the subject matter of the engagement having recently served as the engagement partner.

- A professional accountant accepting gifts or preferential treatment from a client, unless the value is trivial or inconsequential.

- Senior personnel having a long association with the assurance client.

Threats and Safeguards

200.3 Compliance with the fundamental principles may potentially be threatened by a broad range of circumstances and relationships. The nature and significance of the threats may differ depending on whether they arise in relation to the provision of services to an audit client and whether the audit client is a public interest entity, to an assurance client that is not an audit client, or to a non-assurance client.

Threats fall into one or more of the following categories:

(a) Self-interest

(b) Self-review

(c) Advocacy

(d) Familiarity; and

(e) Intimidation.

These threats are discussed further in Part A of this Code.

200.4 Examples of circumstances that create self-interest threats for a professional accountant in public practice include:

- A member of the assurance team having a direct financial interest in the assurance client.

- A firm having undue dependence on total fees from a client.

- A member of the assurance team having a significant close business relationship with an assurance client.

200.8 Examples of circumstances that create intimidation threats for a professional accountant in public practice include:

- A firm being threatened with dismissal from a client engagement.

- An audit client indicating that it will not award a planned non-assurance contract to the firm if the firm continues to disagree with the client's accounting treatment for a particular transaction.

- A firm being threatened with litigation by the client.

- A firm being pressured to reduce inappropriately the extent of work performed in order to reduce fees.

- A professional accountant feeling pressured to agree with the judgement of a client employee because the employee has more expertise on the matter in question.

- A professional accountant being informed by a partner of the firm that a planned promotion will not occur unless the accountant agrees with an audit client's inappropriate accounting treatment.

200.9 Safeguards that may eliminate or reduce threats to an acceptable level fall into two broad categories:

(a) Safeguards created by the profession, legislation or regulation; and

(b) Safeguards in the work environment.

Examples of safeguards created by the profession, legislation or regulation are described in paragraph

100.14 of Part A of this Code.

200.10 A professional accountant in public practice shall exercise judgement to determine how best to deal with threats that are not at an acceptable level, whether by applying safeguards to eliminate the threat or reduce it to an acceptable level or by terminating or declining the relevant engagement. In exercising this judgement, a professional accountant in public practice shall consider whether a reasonable and informed third party, weighing all the specific facts and circumstances available to the professional accountant at that time, would be likely to conclude that the threats would be eliminated or reduced to an acceptable level by the application of safeguards, such that compliance with the fundamental principles is not compromised. This consideration will be affected by matters such as the significance of the threat, the nature of the engagement and the structure of the firm.

200.11 In the work environment, the relevant safeguards will vary depending on the circumstances. Work environment safeguards comprise firm-wide safeguards and engagement-specific safeguards.

200.12 Examples of firm-wide safeguards in the work environment include:

- Leadership of the firm that stresses the importance of compliance with the fundamental principles.

- Leadership of the firm that establishes the expectation that members of an assurance team will act in the public interest.

- Policies and procedures to implement and monitor quality control of engagements.

- Documented policies regarding the need to identify threats to compliance with the fundamental principles, evaluate the significance of those threats, and apply safeguards to eliminate or reduce the threats to an acceptable level or, when appropriate safeguards are not available or cannot be applied, terminate or decline the relevant engagement.

- Documented internal policies and procedures requiring compliance with the fundamental principles.

- Policies and procedures that will enable the identification of interests or relationships between the firm or members of engagement teams and clients.

- Policies and procedures to monitor and, if necessary, manage the reliance on revenue received from a single client.

- Using different partners and engagement teams with separate reporting lines for the provision of non-assurance services to an assurance client.

- Policies and procedures to prohibit individuals who are not members of an engagement team from inappropriately influencing the outcome of the engagement.

- Timely communication of a firm's policies and procedures, including any changes to them, to all partners and professional staff, and appropriate training and education on such policies and procedures.

- Designating a member of senior management to be responsible for overseeing the adequate functioning of the firm's quality control system.

- Advising partners and professional staff of assurance clients and related entities from which independence is required.

- A disciplinary mechanism to promote compliance with policies and procedures.

- Published policies and procedures to encourage and empower staff to communicate to senior levels within the firm any issue relating to compliance with the fundamental principles that concerns them.

200.13 Examples of engagement-specific safeguards in the work environment include:

- Having a professional accountant who was not involved with the non-assurance service review the non-assurance work performed or otherwise advise as necessary.

- Having a professional accountant who was not a member of the assurance team review the assurance work performed or otherwise advise as necessary.

- Consulting an independent third party, such as a committee of independent directors, a professional regulatory body or another professional accountant.

- Discussing ethical issues with those charged with governance of the client.

- Disclosing to those charged with governance of the client the nature of services provided and extent of fees charged.

- Involving another firm to perform or re-perform part of the engagement.

- Rotating senior assurance team personnel.

200.14 Depending on the nature of the engagement, a professional accountant in public practice may also be able to rely on safeguards that the client has implemented. However it is not possible to rely solely on such safeguards to reduce threats to an acceptable level.

200.15 Examples of safeguards within the client's systems and procedures include:

- The client requires persons other than management to ratify or approve the appointment of a firm to perform an engagement.

- The client has competent employees with experience and seniority to make managerial decisions.

- The client has implemented internal procedures that ensure objective choices in commissioning non-assurance engagements.

- The client has a corporate governance structure that provides appropriate oversight and communications regarding the firm's services.

SECTION 210

Professional appointment

Client acceptance

210.1 Before accepting a new client relationship, a professional accountant in public practice shall determine whether acceptance would create any threats to compliance with the fundamental principles. Potential threats to integrity or professional behaviour may be created from, for example, questionable issues associated with the client (its owners, management or activities).

210.2 Client issues that, if known, could threaten compliance with the fundamental principles include, for example, client involvement in illegal activities (such as money laundering), dishonesty or questionable financial reporting practices.

210.3 A professional accountant in public practice shall evaluate the significance of any threats and apply safeguards when necessary to eliminate them or reduce them to an acceptable level. Examples of such safeguards include:

- Obtaining knowledge and understanding of the client, its owners, managers and those responsible for its governance and business activities; or

- Securing the client's commitment to improve corporate governance practices or internal controls.

210.4 Where it is not possible to reduce the threats to an acceptable level, the professional accountant in public practice shall decline to enter into the client relationship.

210.5 It is recommended that a professional accountant in public practice periodically review acceptance decisions for recurring client engagements.

Engagement acceptance

210.6 The fundamental principle of professional competence and due care imposes an obligation on a professional accountant in public practice to provide only those services that the professional accountant in public practice is competent to perform. Before accepting a specific client engagement, a professional accountant in public practice shall determine whether acceptance would create any threats to compliance with the fundamental principles. For example, a self-interest threat to professional competence and due care is created if the engagement team does not possess, or cannot acquire, the competencies necessary to properly carry out the engagement.

210.7 A professional accountant in public practice shall evaluate the significance of threats and apply safeguards, when necessary, to eliminate them or reduce them to an acceptable level.

Examples of such safeguards include:

- Acquiring an appropriate understanding of the nature of the client's business, the complexity of its operations, the specific requirements of the engagement and the purpose, nature and scope of the work to be performed.

- Acquiring knowledge of relevant industries or subject matters.

- Possessing or obtaining experience with relevant regulatory or reporting requirements.

- Assigning sufficient staff with the necessary competencies.

- Using experts where necessary.

- Agreeing on a realistic time frame for the performance of the engagement.

- Complying with quality control policies and procedures designed to provide reasonable assurance that specific engagements are accepted only when they can be performed competently.

210.8 When a professional accountant in public practice intends to rely on the advice or work of an expert, the professional accountant in public practice shall determine whether such reliance is warranted. Factors to consider include: reputation, expertise, resources available and applicable professional and ethical standards. Such information may be gained from prior association with the expert or from consulting others.

Changes in a professional appointment

210.9 A professional accountant in public practice who is asked to replace another professional accountant in public practice, or who is considering tendering for an engagement currently held by another professional accountant in public practice, shall determine whether there are any reasons, professional or otherwise, for not accepting the engagement, such as circumstances that create threats to compliance with the fundamental principles that cannot be eliminated or reduced to an acceptable level by the application of safeguards. For example, there may be a threat to professional competence and due care if a professional accountant in public practice accepts the engagement before knowing all the pertinent facts.

210.10 A professional accountant in public practice shall evaluate the significance of any threats. Depending on the nature of the engagement, this may require direct communication with the existing accountant to establish the facts and circumstances regarding the proposed change so that the professional accountant in public practice can decide whether it would be appropriate to accept the engagement. For example, the apparent reasons for the change in appointment may not fully reflect the facts and may indicate disagreements with the existing accountant that may influence the decision to accept the appointment.

210.11 Safeguards shall be applied when necessary to eliminate any threats or reduce them to an acceptable level. Examples of such safeguards include:

- When replying to requests to submit tenders, stating in the tender that, before accepting the engagement, contact with the existing accountant will be requested so that inquiries may be made as to whether there are any professional or other reasons why the appointment should not be accepted

- Asking the existing accountant to provide known information on any facts or circumstances that, in the existing accountant's opinion, the proposed accountant needs to be aware of before deciding whether to accept the engagement; or

- Obtaining necessary information from other sources.

When the threats cannot be eliminated or reduced to an acceptable level through the application of safeguards, a professional accountant in public practice shall, unless there is satisfaction as to necessary facts by other means, decline the engagement.

210.12 A professional accountant in public practice may be asked to undertake work that is complementary or additional to the work of the existing accountant. Such circumstances may create threats to professional competence and due care resulting from, for example, a lack of or incomplete information. The significance of any threats shall be evaluated and safeguards applied when necessary to eliminate the threat or reduce it to an acceptable level. An example of such a safeguard is notifying the existing accountant of the proposed work, which would give the existing accountant the opportunity to provide any relevant information needed for the proper conduct of the work.

210.13 An existing accountant is bound by confidentiality. Whether that professional accountant is permitted or required to discuss the affairs of a client with a proposed accountant will depend on the nature of the engagement and on:

(a)   Whether the client's permission to do so has been obtained; or

(b)   The legal or ethical requirements relating to such communications and disclosure, which may vary by jurisdiction.

Circumstances where the professional accountant is or may be required to disclose confidential information or where such disclosure may otherwise be appropriate are set out in Section 140 of Part A of this Code.

210.14 A professional accountant in public practice will generally need to obtain the client's permission, preferably in writing, to initiate discussion with an existing accountant. Once that permission is obtained, the existing accountant shall comply with relevant legal and other regulations governing such requests. Where the existing accountant provides information, it shall be provided honestly and unambiguously. If the proposed accountant is unable to communicate with the existing accountant, the proposed accountant shall take reasonable steps to obtain information about any possible threats by other means, such as through inquiries of third parties or background investigations of senior management or those charged with governance of the client.

Supplementary reading: Sections 220 to 280

SECTION 220

Conflicts of Interest

220.1 A professional accountant in public practice may be faced with a conflict of interest when performing a professional service. A conflict of interest creates a threat to objectivity and may create threats to the other fundamental principles. Such threats may be created when:

- The professional accountant provides a professional service related to a particular matter for two or more clients whose interests with respect to that matter are in conflict

  or

- The interests of the professional accountant with respect to a particular matter and the interests of the client for whom the professional accountant provides a professional service related to that matter are in conflict.

A professional accountant shall not allow a conflict of interest to compromise professional or business judgement.

When the professional service is an assurance service, compliance with the fundamental principle of objectivity also requires being independent of assurance clients in accordance with Sections 290 or 291 as appropriate.

220.2 Examples of situations in which conflicts of interest may arise include:

- Providing a transaction advisory service to a client seeking to acquire an audit client of the firm, where the firm has obtained confidential information during the course of the audit that may be relevant to the transaction.

- Advising two clients at the same time who are competing to acquire the same company where the advice might be relevant to the parties' competitive positions.

- Providing services to both a vendor and a purchaser in relation to the same transaction.

- Preparing valuations of assets for two parties who are in an adversarial position with respect to the assets.

- Representing two clients regarding the same matter who are in a legal dispute with each other, such as during divorce proceedings or the dissolution of a partnership.

- Providing an assurance report for a licensor on royalties due under a license agreement when at the same time advising the licensee of the correctness of the amounts payable.

- Advising a client to invest in a business in which, for example, the spouse of the professional accountant in public practice has a financial interest.

- Providing strategic advice to a client on its competitive position while having a joint venture or similar interest with a major competitor of the client.

- Advising a client on the acquisition of a business which the firm is also interested in acquiring.

- Advising a client on the purchase of a product or service while having a royalty or commission agreement with one of the potential vendors of that product or service.

220.3 When identifying and evaluating the interests and relationships that might create a conflict of interest and implementing safeguards, when necessary, to eliminate or reduce any threat to compliance with the fundamental principles to an acceptable level, a professional accountant in public practice shall exercise professional judgement and take into account whether a reasonable and informed third party, weighing all the specific facts and circumstances available to the professional accountant at the time, would be likely to conclude that compliance with the fundamental principles is not compromised.

220.4 When addressing conflicts of interest, including making disclosures or sharing information within the firm or network and seeking guidance of third parties, the professional accountant in public practice shall remain alert to the fundamental principle of confidentiality.

220.5 If the threat created by a conflict of interest is not at an acceptable level, the professional accountant in public practice shall apply safeguards to eliminate the threat or reduce it to an acceptable level. If safeguards cannot reduce the threat to an acceptable level, the professional accountant shall decline to perform or shall discontinue professional services that would result in the conflict of interest; or shall terminate relevant relationships or dispose of relevant interests to eliminate the threat or reduce it to an acceptable level.

220.6 Before accepting a new client relationship, engagement, or business relationship, a professional accountant in public practice shall take reasonable steps to identify circumstances that might create a conflict of interest, including identification of:

- The nature of the relevant interests and relationships between the parties involved; and

- The nature of the service and its implication for relevant parties.

The nature of the services and the relevant interests and relationships may change during the course of the engagement. This is particularly true when a professional accountant is asked to conduct an engagement in a situation that may become adversarial, even though the parties who engage the professional accountant may not initially be involved in a dispute. The professional accountant shall remain alert to such changes for the purpose of identifying circumstances that might create a conflict of interest.

220.7 For the purpose of identifying interests and relationships that might create a conflict of interest, having an effective conflict identification process assists a professional accountant in public practice to identify actual or potential conflicts of interest prior to determining whether to accept an engagement and throughout an engagement. This includes matters identified by external parties, for example clients or potential clients. The earlier an actual or potential conflict of interest is identified, the greater the likelihood of the professional accountant being able to apply safeguards, when necessary, to eliminate the threat to objectivity and any threat to compliance with other fundamental principles or reduce it to an acceptable level. The process to identify actual or potential conflicts of interest will depend on such factors as:

- The nature of the professional services provided.

- The size of the firm.

- The size and nature of the client base.

- The structure of the firm, for example, the number and geographic location of offices.

220.8 If the firm is a member of a network, conflict identification shall include any conflicts of interest that the professional accountant in public practice has reason to believe may exist or might arise due to interests and relationships of a network firm. Reasonable steps to identify such interests and relationships involving a network firm will depend on factors such as the nature of the professional services provided, the clients served by the network and the geographic locations of all relevant parties.

220.9 If a conflict of interest is identified, the professional accountant in public practice shall evaluate:

- The significance of relevant interests or relationships; and

- The significance of the threats created by performing the professional service or services. In general, the more direct the connection between the professional service and the matter on which the parties' interests are in conflict, the more significant the threat to objectivity and compliance with the other fundamental principles will be.

220.10 The professional accountant in public practice shall apply safeguards, when necessary, to eliminate the threats to compliance with the fundamental principles created by the conflict of interest or reduce them to an acceptable level. Examples of safeguards include:

- Implementing mechanisms to prevent unauthorised disclosure of confidential information when performing professional services related to a particular matter for two or more clients whose interests with respect to that matter are in conflict. This could include:

    - Using separate engagement teams who are provided with clear policies and procedures on maintaining confidentiality.

    - Creating separate areas of practice for specialty functions within the firm, which may act as a barrier to the passing of confidential client information from one practice area to another within a firm.

    - Establishing policies and procedures to limit access to client files, the use of confidentiality agreements signed by employees and partners of the firm and/or the physical and electronic separation of confidential information.

- Regular review of the application of safeguards by a senior individual not involved with the client engagement or engagements.

- Having a professional accountant who is not involved in providing the service or otherwise affected by the conflict, review the work performed to assess whether the key judgements and conclusions are appropriate.

- Consulting with third parties, such as a professional body, legal counsel or another professional accountant.

220.11 In addition, it is generally necessary to disclose the nature of the conflict of interest and the related safeguards, if any, to clients affected by the conflict and, when safeguards are required to reduce the threat to an acceptable level, to obtain their consent to the professional accountant in public practice performing the professional services. Disclosure and consent may take different forms, for example:

- General disclosure to clients of circumstances where the professional accountant, in keeping with common commercial practice, does not provide services exclusively for any one client (for example, in a particular service in a particular market sector) in order for the client to provide general consent accordingly. Such disclosure might, for example, be made in the professional accountant's standard terms and conditions for the engagement.

- Specific disclosure to affected clients of the circumstances of the particular conflict, including a detailed presentation of the situation and a comprehensive explanation of any planned safeguards and the risks involved, sufficient to enable the client to make an informed decision with respect to the matter and to provide explicit consent accordingly.

- In certain circumstances, consent may be implied by the client's conduct where the professional accountant has sufficient evidence to conclude that clients know the circumstances at the outset and have accepted the conflict of interest if they do not raise an objection to the existence of the conflict.

The professional accountant shall determine whether the nature and significance of the conflict of interest is such that specific disclosure and explicit consent is necessary. For this purpose, the professional accountant shall exercise professional judgement in weighing the outcome of the evaluation of the circumstances that create a conflict of interest, including the parties that might be affected, the nature of the issues that might arise and the potential for the particular matter to develop in an unexpected manner.

220.12 Where a professional accountant in public practice has requested explicit consent from a client and that consent has been refused by the client, the professional accountant shall decline to perform or shall discontinue professional services that would result in the conflict of interest; or shall terminate relevant relationships or dispose of relevant interests to eliminate the threat or reduce it to an acceptable level, such that consent can be obtained, after applying any additional safeguards if necessary.

220.13 When disclosure is verbal, or consent is verbal or implied, the professional accountant in public practice is encouraged to document the nature of the circumstances giving rise to the conflict of interest, the safeguards applied to reduce the threats to an acceptable level and the consent obtained.

220.14 In certain circumstances, making specific disclosure for the purpose of obtaining explicit consent would result in a breach of confidentiality. Examples of such circumstances may include:

- Performing a transaction-related service for a client in connection with a hostile takeover of another client of the firm.

- Performing a forensic investigation for a client in connection with a suspected fraudulent act where the firm has confidential information obtained through having performed a professional service for another client who might be involved in the fraud.

The firm shall not accept or continue an engagement under such circumstances unless the following conditions are met:

- The firm does not act in an advocacy role for one client where this requires the firm to assume an adversarial position against the other client with respect to the same matter

- Specific mechanisms are in place to prevent disclosure of confidential information between the engagement teams serving the two clients; and

- The firm is satisfied that a reasonable and informed third party, weighing all the specific facts and circumstances available to the professional accountant in public practice at the time, would be likely to conclude that it is appropriate for the firm to accept or continue the engagement because a restriction on the firm's ability to provide the service would produce a disproportionate adverse outcome for the clients or other relevant third parties.

The professional accountant shall document the nature of the circumstances, including the role that the professional the professional accountant is to undertake, the specific mechanisms in place to prevent disclosure of information between the engagement teams serving the two clients and the rationale for the conclusion that it is appropriate to accept the engagement.

SECTION 230

Second opinions

230.1 Situations where a professional accountant in public practice is asked to provide a second opinion on the application of accounting, auditing, reporting or other standards or principles to specific circumstances or transactions by or on behalf of a company or an entity that is not an existing client may create threats to compliance with the fundamental principles. For example, there may be a threat to professional competence and due care in circumstances where the second opinion is not based on the same set of facts that were made available to the existing accountant or is based on inadequate evidence. The existence and significance of any threat will depend on the circumstances of the request and all the other available facts and assumptions relevant to the expression of a professional judgement.

230.2 When asked to provide such an opinion, a professional accountant in public practice shall evaluate the significance of any threats and apply safeguards when necessary to eliminate them or reduce them to an acceptable level. Examples of such safeguards include seeking client permission to contact the existing accountant, describing the limitations surrounding any opinion in communications with the client and providing the existing accountant with a copy of the opinion.

230.3 If the company or entity seeking the opinion will not permit communication with the existing accountant, a professional accountant in public practice shall determine whether, taking all the circumstances into account, it is appropriate to provide the opinion sought.

SECTION 240

Fees and other types of remuneration

240.1 When entering into negotiations regarding professional services, a professional accountant in public practice may quote whatever fee is deemed appropriate. The fact that one professional accountant in public practice may quote a fee lower than another is not in itself unethical. Nevertheless, there may be threats to compliance with the fundamental principles arising from the level of fees quoted. For example, a self-interest threat to professional competence and due care is created if the fee quoted is so low that it may be difficult to perform the engagement in accordance with applicable technical and professional standards for that price.

240.2 The existence and significance of any threats created will depend on factors such as the level of fee quoted and the services to which it applies. The significance of any threat shall be evaluated and safeguards applied when necessary to eliminate the threat or reduce it to an acceptable level. Examples of such safeguards include:

- Making the client aware of the terms of the engagement and, in particular, the basis on which fees are charged and which services are covered by the quoted fee.

- Assigning appropriate time and qualified staff to the task.

240.3 Contingent fees are widely used for certain types of non-assurance engagements. They may, however, create threats to compliance with the fundamental principles in certain circumstances. They may create a self-interest threat to objectivity. The existence and significance of such threats will depend on factors including:

- The nature of the engagement.

- The range of possible fee amounts.

- The basis for determining the fee.

- Whether the outcome or result of the transaction is to be reviewed by an independent third party.

240.4 The significance of any such threats shall be evaluated and safeguards applied when necessary to eliminate or reduce them to an acceptable level. Examples of such safeguards include:

- An advance written agreement with the client as to the basis of remuneration.

- Disclosure to intended users of the work performed by the professional accountant in public practice and the basis of remuneration.

- Quality control policies and procedures.

- Review by an independent third party of the work performed by the professional accountant in public practice.

240.5 In certain circumstances, a professional accountant in public practice may receive a referral fee or commission relating to a client. For example, where the professional accountant in public practice does not provide the specific service required, a fee may be received for referring a continuing client to another professional accountant in public practice or other expert. A professional accountant in public practice may receive a commission from a third party (for example, a software vendor) in connection with the sale of goods or services to a client. Accepting such a referral fee or commission creates a self-interest threat to objectivity and professional competence and due care.

240.6 A professional accountant in public practice may also pay a referral fee to obtain a client, for example, where the client continues as a client of another professional accountant in public practice but requires specialist services not offered by the existing accountant. The payment of such a referral fee also creates a self-interest threat to objectivity and professional competence and due care.

240.7 The significance of the threat shall be evaluated and safeguards applied when necessary to eliminate the threat or reduce it to an acceptable level. Examples of such safeguards include:

- Disclosing to the client any arrangements to pay a referral fee to another professional accountant for the work referred.

- Disclosing to the client any arrangements to receive a referral fee for referring the client to another professional accountant in public practice.

- Obtaining advance agreement from the client for commission arrangements in connection with the sale by a third party of goods or services to the client.

240.8 A professional accountant in public practice may purchase all or part of another firm on the basis that payments will be made to individuals formerly owning the firm or to their heirs or estates. Such payments are not regarded as commissions or referral fees for the purpose of paragraphs 240.5–240.7 above.

SECTION 250

Marketing professional services

250.1 When a professional accountant in public practice solicits new work through advertising or other forms of marketing, there may be a threat to compliance with the fundamental principles. For example, a self-interest threat to compliance with the principle of professional behaviour is created if services, achievements, or products are marketed in a way that is inconsistent with that principle.

250.2 A professional accountant in public practice shall not bring the profession into disrepute when marketing professional services. The professional accountant in public practice shall be honest and truthful, and not:

(a) Make exaggerated claims for services offered, qualifications possessed, or experience gained; or

(b) Make disparaging references or unsubstantiated comparisons to the work of another.

If the professional accountant in public practice is in doubt about whether a proposed form of advertising or marketing is appropriate, the professional accountant in public practice shall consider consulting with the relevant professional body.

SECTION 260

Gifts and Hospitality

260.1 A professional accountant in public practice, or an immediate or close family member, may be offered gifts and hospitality from a client. Such an offer may create threats to compliance with the fundamental principles. For example, a self-interest or familiarity threat to objectivity may be created if a gift from a client is accepted; an intimidation threat to objectivity may result from the possibility of such offers being made public.

260.2 The existence and significance of any threat will depend on the nature, value, and intent of the offer. Where gifts or hospitality are offered that a reasonable and informed third party, weighing all the specific facts and circumstances, would consider trivial and inconsequential, a professional accountant in public practice may conclude that the offer is made in the normal course of business without the specific intent to influence decision making or to obtain information. In such cases, the professional accountant in public practice may generally conclude that any threat to compliance with the fundamental principles is at an acceptable level.

260.3 A professional accountant in public practice shall evaluate the significance of any threats and apply safeguards when necessary to eliminate the threats or reduce them to an acceptable level. When the threats cannot be eliminated or reduced to an acceptable level through the application of safeguards, a professional accountant in public practice shall not accept such an offer.

SECTION 270

Custody of client assets

270.1 A professional accountant in public practice shall not assume custody of client monies or other assets unless permitted to do so by law and, if so, in compliance with any additional legal duties imposed on a professional accountant in public practice holding such assets.

270.2 The holding of client assets creates threats to compliance with the fundamental principles; for example, there is a self-interest threat to professional behaviour and may be a self interest threat to objectivity arising from holding client assets. A professional accountant in public practice entrusted with money (or other assets) belonging to others shall therefore:

(a)   Keep such assets separately from personal or firm assets

(b)   Use such assets only for the purpose for which they are intended

(c)   At all times be ready to account for those assets and any income, dividends, or gains generated, to any persons entitled to such accounting; and

(d)   Comply with all relevant laws and regulations relevant to the holding of and accounting for such assets.

270.3 As part of client and engagement acceptance procedures for services that may involve the holding of client assets, a professional accountant in public practice shall make appropriate inquiries about the source of such assets and consider legal and regulatory obligations. For example, if the assets were derived from illegal activities, such as money laundering, a threat to compliance with the fundamental principles would be created. In such situations, the professional accountant may consider seeking legal advice.

SECTION 280

Objectivity – All services

280.1 A professional accountant in public practice shall determine when providing any professional service whether there are threats to compliance with the fundamental principle of objectivity resulting from having interests in, or relationships with, a client or its directors, officers or employees. For example, a familiarity threat to objectivity may be created from a family or close personal or business relationship.

280.2 A professional accountant in public practice who provides an assurance service shall be independent of the assurance client. Independence of mind and in appearance is necessary to enable the professional accountant in public practice to express a conclusion, and be seen to express a conclusion, without bias, conflict of interest, or undue influence of others. Sections 290 and 291 provide specific guidance on independence requirements for professional accountants in public practice when performing assurance engagements.

280.3 The existence of threats to objectivity when providing any professional service will depend upon the particular circumstances of the engagement and the nature of the work that the professional accountant in public practice is performing.

280.4 A professional accountant in public practice shall evaluate the significance of any threats and apply safeguards when necessary to eliminate them or reduce them to an acceptable level. Examples of such safeguards include:

- Withdrawing from the engagement team.

- Supervisory procedures.

- Terminating the financial or business relationship giving rise to the threat.

- Discussing the issue with higher levels of management within the firm.

- Discussing the issue with those charged with governance of the client.

If safeguards cannot eliminate or reduce the threat to an acceptable level, the professional accountant shall decline or terminate the relevant engagement.

Supplementary reading: Sections 300 to 370

PART C – PROFESSIONAL ACCOUNTANTS IN BUSINESS (INCLUDING CGMA DESIGNATION HOLDERS)

300 Introduction

310 Ethical conflicts

320 Conflicts of interest

330 Gifts, entertainment and other forms of inducements

340 Preparing and reporting information

350 Educational services

360 General standards/Professional competence and due care

370 Acts discreditable/Professional behaviour/Confidentiality

SECTION 300

Introduction

300.1 This Part of the Code applies to members in business (AICPA) who hold the CGMA credential and all professional accountants in business (CIMA) including those who hold the CGMA credential (or are entitled to do so).

Conceptual framework for members in business

300.2 Members may encounter various relationships or circumstances that create threats to the member's compliance with the rules and fundamental principles. The rules, fundamental principles and interpretations seek to address many situations; however, they cannot address all relationships or circumstances that may arise. Thus, in the absence of an interpretation that addresses a particular relationship or circumstance, a member should evaluate whether that relationship or circumstance would lead a reasonable and informed third party who is aware of the relevant information to conclude that there is a threat to the member's compliance with the rules and fundamental principles that is not at an acceptable level. When making that evaluation, the member should apply the conceptual framework approach as outlined in this interpretation.

300.3 The CGMA code specifies that in some circumstances, no safeguards can reduce a threat to an acceptable level. For example, the code specifies that a member may not subordinate the member's professional judgement to others without violating the Integrity and Objectivity Rule and Principles. A member may not use the conceptual framework to overcome this or any other prohibition or requirement in the code.

Conceptual framework approach

300.4 Under the conceptual framework approach, members should identify threats to compliance with the rules and fundamental principles and evaluate the significance of those threats. Members should evaluate identified threats both individually and in the aggregate because threats can have a cumulative effect on a member's compliance with the rules and fundamental principles. Members should perform three main steps in applying the conceptual framework approach:

(a) **Identify threats.** The relationships or circumstances that a member encounters in various engagements and work assignments or positions will often create different threats to complying with the rules. When a member encounters a relationship or circumstance that is not specifically addressed by a rule, fundamental principle or an interpretation, under this approach, the member should determine whether the relationship or circumstance creates one or more threats, such as those identified in paragraphs .07–.12 that follow. The existence of a threat does not mean that the member is not in compliance with the rules and fundamental principles; however, the member should evaluate the significance of the threat.

(b) **Evaluate the significance of a threat.** In evaluating the significance of an identified threat, the member should determine whether a threat is at an acceptable level. A threat is at an acceptable level when a reasonable and informed third party who is aware of the relevant information would be expected to conclude that the threat would not compromise the member's compliance with the rules and fundamental principles. Members should consider both qualitative and quantitative factors when evaluating the significance of a threat, including the extent to which existing safeguards already reduce the threat to an acceptable level. If the member evaluates the threat and concludes that a reasonable and informed third party who is aware of the relevant information would be expected to conclude that the threat does not compromise a member's compliance with the rules and fundamental principles, the threat is at an acceptable level and the member is not required to evaluate the threat any further under this conceptual framework approach.

(c) **Identify and apply safeguards.** If, in evaluating the significance of an identified threat, the member concludes that the threat is not at an acceptable level, the member should apply safeguards to eliminate the threat or reduce it to an acceptable level. The member should apply judgement in determining the nature of the safeguards to be applied because the effectiveness of safeguards will vary depending on the circumstances. When identifying appropriate safeguards to apply, one safeguard may eliminate or reduce multiple threats. In some cases, the member should apply multiple safeguards to eliminate or reduce one threat to an acceptable level. In other cases, an identified threat may be so significant that no safeguards will eliminate the threat or reduce it to an acceptable level, or the member will be unable to implement effective safeguards. Under such circumstances, providing the specific professional services would compromise the member's compliance with the rules, and the member should determine whether to decline or discontinue the professional services or resign from the employing organisation.

Threats

300.5 Many threats fall into one or more of the following six broad categories: adverse interest, advocacy, familiarity, self-interest, self-review, and undue influence (also referred to as "intimidation threat").

300.6 Examples of threats associated with a specific relationship or circumstance are identified in the interpretations of the code. Paragraphs .07–.12 of this section define and provide examples, which are not all inclusive, of each of these threat categories.

300.7 Adverse interest threat. The threat that a member will not act with objectivity, because the member's interests are opposed to the interests of the employing organisation. Examples of adverse interest threats include the following:

(a) A member has charged, or expressed an intention to charge, the employing organisation with violations of law.

(b) A member or the member's immediate family or close relative has a financial or another relationship with a vendor, customer, competitor, or potential acquisition of the employing organisation.

(c) A member has sued or expressed an intention to sue the employing organisation or its officers, directors, or employees.

300.8 Advocacy threat. The threat that a member will promote an organisation's interests or position to the point that his or her objectivity is compromised. Examples of advocacy threats include the following:

(a) Obtaining favourable financing or additional capital is dependent upon the information that the member includes in, or excludes from, a prospectus, an offering, a business plan, a financing application, or a regulatory filing.

(b) The member gives or fails to give information that the member knows will unduly influence the conclusions reached by an external service provider or other third party.

300.9 Familiarity threat. The threat that, due to a long or close relationship with a person or an employing organisation, a member will become too sympathetic to their interests or too accepting of the person's work or organisation's product or service. Examples of familiarity threats include the following:

(a) A member uses an immediate family's or a close relative's company as a supplier to the employing organisation.

(b) A member may accept an individual's work product with little or no review because the individual has been producing an acceptable work product for an extended period of time.

(c) A member's immediate family or close relative is employed as a member's subordinate.

(d) A member regularly accepts gifts or entertainment from a vendor or customer of the employing organisation.

300.10 Self-interest threat. The threat that a member could benefit, financially or otherwise, from an interest in, or relationship with, the employing organisation or persons associated with the employing organisation. Examples of self-interest threats include the following:

(a) A member's immediate family or close relative has a financial interest in the employing organisation.

(b) A member holds a financial interest (for example, shares or share options) in the employing organisation, and the value of that financial interest is directly affected by the member's decisions.

(c) A member is eligible for a profit or other performance-related bonus, and the value of that bonus is directly affected by the member's decisions.

300.11 Self-review threat. The threat that a member will not appropriately evaluate the results of a previous judgement made or service performed or supervised by the member, or an individual in the employing organisation, and that the member will rely on that service in forming a judgement as part of another service. Examples of self-review threats include the following:

(a) When performing an internal audit procedure, an internal auditor accepts work that he or she previously performed in a different position.

(b) The member accepts the work previously performed by the member, alone or with others, that will be the basis for providing another professional service.

300.12 Undue influence threat (also referred to as "intimidation threat"). The threat that a member will subordinate his or her judgement to that of an individual associated with the employing organisation or any relevant third party due to that individual's position, reputation or expertise, aggressive or dominant personality, or attempts to coerce or exercise excessive influence over the member. Examples of undue influence threats include the following:

(a) A member is pressured to become associated with misleading information.

(b) A member is pressured to deviate from a company policy.

(c) A member is pressured to change a conclusion regarding an accounting or a tax position.

(d) A member is pressured to hire an unqualified individual.

Safeguards

300.13 Safeguards may partially or completely eliminate a threat or diminish the potential influence of a threat. The nature and extent of the safeguards applied will depend on many factors. To be effective, safeguards should eliminate the threat or reduce it to an acceptable level.

300.14 Safeguards that may eliminate a threat or reduce it to an acceptable level fall into two broad categories:

(a) Safeguards created by the profession, legislation, or regulation

(b) Safeguards implemented by the employing organisation.

300.15 The effectiveness of a safeguard depends on many factors, including those listed here:

(a)   The facts and circumstances specific to a particular situation

(b)   The proper identification of threats

(c)   Whether the safeguard is suitably designed to meet its objectives

(d)   The party(ies) who will be subject to the safeguard

(e)   How the safeguard is applied

(f)   The consistency with which the safeguard is applied

(g)   Who applies the safeguard

(h)   How the safeguard interacts with a safeguard from another category

(i)   Whether the employing organisation is a public interest entity.

300.16 Examples of safeguards within each category are presented in the following paragraphs. Because these are only examples and are not intended to be all inclusive, it is possible that threats may be sufficiently mitigated through the application of other safeguards not specifically identified herein.

300.17 The following are examples of safeguards created by the profession, legislation, or regulation:

- Education and training requirements on ethics and professional responsibilities

- Continuing education requirements on ethics

- Professional standards and the threat of discipline

- Legislation establishing prohibitions and requirements for entities and employees

- Competency and experience requirements for professional licensure and credentials

- Professional resources, such as hotlines, for consultation on ethical issues.

300.18 Examples of safeguards implemented by the employing organisation are as follows:

- A tone at the top emphasising a commitment to fair financial reporting and compliance with applicable laws, rules, regulations, and corporate governance policies

- Policies and procedures addressing ethical conduct and compliance with laws, rules, and regulations

- Audit committee charter, including independent audit committee members
- Internal policies and procedures requiring disclosure of identified interests or relationships among the employing organisation, its directors or officers, and vendors, suppliers, or customers
- Internal policies and procedures related to purchasing controls
- Internal policies and procedures related to customer acceptance or credit limits
- Dissemination of corporate ethical compliance policies and procedures, including whistle-blower hotlines, the reporting structure, dispute resolution, or other similar policies, to promote compliance with laws, rules, regulations, and other professional requirements
- Human resource policies and procedures safeguarding against discrimination or harassment, such as those concerning a worker's religion, sexual orientation, gender, or disability
- Human resource policies and procedures stressing the hiring and retention of technically competent employees
- Policies and procedures for implementing and monitoring ethical policies
- Assigning sufficient staff with the necessary competencies to projects and other tasks
- Policies segregating personal assets from company assets
- Staff training on applicable laws, rules, and regulations
- Regular monitoring of internal policies and procedures
- A reporting structure whereby the internal auditor does not report to the financial reporting group
- Policies and procedures that do not allow an internal auditor to monitor areas where the internal auditor has operational or functional responsibilities
- Policies for promotion, rewards, and enforcement of a culture of high ethics and integrity
- Use of third-party resources for consultation as needed on significant matters of professional judgement.

SECTION 310

Ethical conflicts

310.1 An ethical conflict arises when a member encounters one or both of the following:

(a)   Obstacles to following an appropriate course of action due to internal or external pressures

(b)   Conflicts in applying relevant professional and legal standards.

For example, a member suspects a fraud may have occurred, but reporting the suspected fraud would violate the member's responsibility to maintain the confidentiality of his or her employer's confidential information.

310.2 Once an ethical conflict is encountered, a member may be required to take steps to best achieve compliance with the rules, fundamental principles and law. In weighing alternative courses of action, the member should consider factors such as the following:

(a)   Relevant facts and circumstances, including applicable rules, laws, or regulations

(b)   Ethical issues involved

(c)   Established internal procedures.

310.3 The member should also be prepared to justify any departures that the member believes were appropriate in applying the relevant rules, fundamental principles and law. If the member was unable to resolve the conflict in a way that permitted compliance with the applicable rules, fundamental principles and law, the member may have to address the consequences of any violations.

310.4 Before pursuing a course of action, the member should consider consulting with appropriate persons within the organisation that employs the member.

310.5 If a member decides not to consult with appropriate persons within the organisation that employs the member, and the conflict remains unresolved after pursuing the selected course of action, the member should consider either consulting with other individuals for help in reaching a resolution or obtaining advice from an appropriate professional body or legal counsel. The member also should consider documenting the substance of the issue, the parties with whom the issue was discussed, details of any discussions held, and any decisions made concerning the issue.

310.6 If the ethical conflict remains unresolved, the member will in all likelihood be in violation of one or more rules or fundamental principles if he or she remains associated with the matter creating the conflict. Accordingly, the member should consider his or her continuing relationship with the specific assignment or employer.

Integrity and objectivity

310.7 Integrity and Objectivity Rule (AICPA): In the performance of any professional service, a member shall maintain objectivity and integrity, shall be free of conflicts of interest, and shall not knowingly misrepresent facts or subordinate his or her judgement to others.

310.8 Integrity Principle (CIMA): The principle of integrity imposes an obligation on all members to be straightforward and honest in all professional and business relationships.

Objectivity Principle (CIMA): The principle of objectivity imposes an obligation on all members not to compromise their professional or business judgement because of bias, conflict of interest or the undue influence of others.

Interpretations under the "Integrity and Objectivity Rule" and the "Integrity and Objectivity Principles"

Application of the conceptual framework for members in business and ethical conflicts

310.9 In the absence of an interpretation of the "Integrity and Objectivity Rule" and the Integrity and Objectivity principles that addresses a particular relationship or circumstance, a member should apply the "Conceptual Framework for Members in Business". (300.2–300.3).

310.10 A member will be considered in violation of the "Integrity and Objectivity Rule" and the Integrity and Objectivity principles if the member cannot demonstrate that safeguards were applied that eliminated or reduced significant threats to an acceptable level.

310.11 A member should consider the guidance in the "Ethical Conflicts" interpretation (310.1–310.6) when addressing ethical conflicts that may arise when the member encounters obstacles to following an appropriate course of action. Such obstacles may be due to internal or external pressures or to conflicts in applying relevant professional and legal standards, or both.

SECTION 320

Conflicts of interest

Conflicts of interest for members in business

320.1 A member in business may be faced with a conflict of interest when undertaking a professional service. In determining whether a professional service, relationship, or matter would result in a conflict of interest, a member should use professional judgement, taking into account whether a reasonable and informed third party who is aware of the relevant information would conclude that a conflict of interest exists.

320.2 A conflict of interest creates adverse interest and self-interest threats to the member's compliance with the "Integrity and Objectivity Rule" and the Integrity and Objectivity principles. For example, threats may be created when:

(a)   a member undertakes a professional service related to a particular matter involving two or more parties whose interests with respect to that matter are in conflict

   or

(b)   the interests of a member with respect to a particular matter and the interests of a party for whom the member undertakes a professional service related to that matter are in conflict.

320.3 A party may include an employing organisation, a vendor, a customer, a lender, a shareholder, or another party.

320.4 The following are examples of situations in which conflicts of interest may arise:

- Serving in a management or governance position for two employing organisations and acquiring confidential information from one employing organisation that could be used by the member to the advantage or disadvantage of the other employing organisation.

- Undertaking a professional service for each of two parties in a partnership employing the member to assist in dissolving their partnership.

- Preparing financial information for certain members of management of the employing organisation who are seeking to undertake a management buy-out.

- Being responsible for selecting a vendor for the member's employing organisation when the member or his or her immediate family member could benefit financially from the transaction.

- Serving in a governance capacity or influencing an employing organisation that is approving certain investments for the company in which one of those specific investments will increase the value of the personal investment portfolio of the member or his or her immediate family member.

Identification of a conflict of interest

320.5 In identifying whether a conflict of interest exists or may be created, a member should take reasonable steps to determine:

(a)   The nature of the relevant interests and relationships between the parties involved and

(b)   the nature of the services and its implication for relevant parties.

320.6 The nature of the relevant interests and relationships and the services may change over time. The member should remain alert to such changes for the purposes of identifying circumstances that might create a conflict of interest.

Evaluation of a conflict of interest

320.7 When an actual conflict of interest has been identified, the member should evaluate the significance of the threat created by the conflict of interest to determine if the threat is at an acceptable level. Members should consider both qualitative and quantitative factors when evaluating the significance of the threat, including the extent to which existing safeguards already reduce the threat to an acceptable level.

320.8 In evaluating the significance of an identified threat, members should consider the following:

(a) The significance of relevant interests or relationships.

(b) The significance of the threats created by undertaking the professional service or services. In general, the more direct the connection between the member and the matter on which the parties' interests are in conflict, the more significant the threat to compliance with the rule will be.

320.9 If the member concludes that the threat is not at an acceptable level, the member should apply safeguards to eliminate the threat or reduce it to an acceptable level. Examples of safeguards include the following:

(a) Restructuring or segregating certain responsibilities and duties

(b) Obtaining appropriate oversight

(c) Withdrawing from the decision making process related to the matter giving rise to the conflict of interest

(d) Consulting with third parties, such as a professional body, legal counsel, or another professional accountant.

320.10 In cases where an identified threat may be so significant that no safeguards will eliminate the threat or reduce it to an acceptable level, or the member is unable to implement effective safeguards, the member should:

(a) decline to perform or discontinue the professional services that would result in the conflict of interest; or

(b) terminate the relevant relationships or dispose of the relevant interests to eliminate the threat or reduce it to an acceptable level.

Disclosure of a conflict of interest and consent

320.11 When a conflict of interest exists, the member should disclose the nature of the conflict to the relevant parties, including to the appropriate levels within the employing organisation and obtain their consent to undertake the professional service. The member should disclose the conflict of interest and obtain consent even if the member concludes that threats are at an acceptable level.

320.12 The member is encouraged to document the nature of the circumstances giving rise to the conflict of interest, the safeguards applied to eliminate or reduce the threats to an acceptable level, and the consent obtained.

320.13 When addressing a conflict of interest, a member is encouraged to seek guidance from within the employing organisation or from others, such as a professional body, legal counsel, or another professional accountant. When making disclosures and seeking guidance of third parties, the member should remain alert to the requirements of the "Confidential Information Obtained From Employment or Volunteer Activities", interpretation of the "Acts Discreditable Rule" and the Integrity and Objectivity principles (370.1 and 310.8). In addition, federal, state, or local statutes, or regulations concerning confidentiality of employer information may be more restrictive than the requirements contained in the CGMA code.

320.14 A member may encounter other threats to compliance with the "Integrity and Objectivity Rule" and the Integrity and Objectivity principles. This may occur, for example, when preparing or reporting financial information as a result of undue pressure from others within the employing organisation or financial, business or personal relationships that close relatives or immediate family members of the member have with the employing organisation. Guidance on managing such threats is covered by the "Knowing Misrepresentations in the Preparation of Financial Statements or Records", interpretation (340.1–340.2) and the "Subordination of Judgement by a Member", interpretation (340.3– 340.13).

SECTION 330

Gifts, entertainment and other forms of inducements

Offering or accepting gifts or entertainment

330.1 For purposes of this interpretation, a customer or vendor of the member's employer includes a representative of the customer or vendor.

330.2 When a member offers to, or accepts gifts or entertainment from, a customer or vendor of the member's employer, self-interest, familiarity, or undue influence threats to the member's compliance with the "Integrity and Objectivity Rule" and the Integrity and Objectivity principles may exist.

330.3 Threats to compliance with the "Integrity and Objectivity Rule" and the "Integrity Principle" would not be at an acceptable level and could not be reduced to an acceptable level by the application of safeguards and the member would be presumed to lack integrity in violation of the "Integrity and Objectivity Rule" and the "Integrity Principle" in the following circumstances:

(a) The member offers to, or accepts gifts or entertainment from, a customer or vendor of the member's employer that violate applicable laws, rules, or regulations or the policies of the member's employer or the customer or vendor.

(b) The member knows of the violation or demonstrates recklessness in not knowing.

330.4 A member should evaluate the significance of any threats to determine if they are at an acceptable level. Threats are at an acceptable level when gifts or entertainment are reasonable in the circumstances. The member should exercise judgement in determining whether gifts or entertainment would be considered reasonable in the circumstances. The following are examples of relevant facts and circumstances:

- The nature of the gift or entertainment

- The occasion giving rise to the gift or entertainment

- The cost or value of the gift or entertainment

- The nature, frequency, and value of other gifts and entertainment offered or accepted

- Whether the entertainment was associated with the active conduct of business directly before, during, or after the entertainment

- Whether other customers or vendors also participated in the entertainment

- The individuals from the customer or vendor and a member's employer who participated in the entertainment.

330.5 Threats to compliance with the "Integrity and Objectivity Rule" and the "Objectivity Principle" would not be at an acceptable level and could not be reduced to an acceptable level through the application of safeguards if a member offers to, or accepts gifts or entertainment from, a customer or vendor of the member's employer that is not reasonable in the circumstances. The member would be considered to lack objectivity in violation of the "Integrity and Objectivity Rule" and the "Objectivity Principle" under these circumstances.

Offering or accepting other forms of inducements

330.6 Threats to compliance with the "Integrity and Objectivity Rule" and the Integrity and Objectivity principles may also exist when a member or his or her immediate family or close relative offer to, or accept from, a third party other forms of inducements such as, preferential treatment or inappropriate appeals to friendship or loyalty.

330.7 For example, self-interest threats are created when an inducement is made in an attempt to unduly influence actions or decisions, encourage illegal or unethical behaviour, or obtain confidential information, and undue influence threats are created if such an inducement is offered or accepted and it is followed by threats to make that offer public and damage the reputation of either the member or an immediate family member or close relative.

330.8 A member should evaluate the significance of any threats to determine if they are at an acceptable level. Threats are at an acceptable level when the inducement is reasonable in the circumstances [see 330.4] and not intended to encourage unethical behaviour.

330.9 Threats to compliance with the "Integrity and Objectivity Rule" and the Integrity and Objectivity principles would not be at an acceptable level and could not be reduced to an acceptable level through the application of safeguards if a member offers to, or accepts inducements from, a third party that are not reasonable in the circumstances or are intended to encourage unethical behaviour. The member would be considered to lack integrity and objectivity in violation of the "Integrity and Objectivity Rule" and the Integrity and Objectivity principles under these circumstances.

SECTION 340

Preparing and reporting information

Knowing misrepresentations in the preparation of financial statements or records

340.1 Members in business are often involved in the preparation and reporting of information that may either be made public or used by others inside or outside the employing organisation. Such information may include financial or management information, for example, forecasts and budgets, financial statements, management's discussion and analysis, and the management letter of representation provided to the auditors during the audit of the entity's financial statements.

340.2 Threats to compliance with the "Integrity and Objectivity Rule" and the Integrity and Objectivity principles would not be at an acceptable level and could not be reduced to an acceptable level by the application of safeguards, and the member would be considered to have knowingly misrepresented facts in violation of the "Integrity and Objectivity Rule" and the Integrity and Objectivity principles if the member:

(a) makes, or permits or directs another to make, materially false and misleading entries in an entity's financial statements or records

(b) fails to correct an entity's financial statements or records that are materially false and misleading when the member has the authority to record the entries; or

(c) signs, or permits or directs another to sign, a document containing materially false and misleading information.

Subordination of judgement

340.3 The "Integrity and Objectivity Rule" and the Integrity and Objectivity principles prohibit a member from knowingly misrepresenting facts or subordinating his or her judgement when performing professional services for an employer or on a volunteer basis. This interpretation addresses differences of opinion between a member and his or her supervisor or any other person within the member's organisation.

340.4 Self-interest, familiarity, and undue influence threats to the member's compliance with the "Integrity and Objectivity Rule" and the Integrity and Objectivity principles may exist when a member and his or her supervisor or any other person within the member's organisation have a difference of opinion relating to the application of accounting principles; auditing standards; or other relevant professional standards, including standards applicable to tax and consulting services or applicable laws or regulations.

340.5 A member should evaluate the significance of any threats to determine if they are at an acceptable level. Threats are at an acceptable level if the member concludes that the position taken does not result in a material misrepresentation of fact or a violation of applicable laws or regulations. If threats are not at an acceptable level, the member should apply the safeguards in paragraphs .06–.08 to eliminate or reduce the threat(s) to an acceptable level so that the member does not subordinate his or her judgement.

340.6 In evaluating the significance of any identified threats, the member should determine, after appropriate research or consultation, whether the result of the position taken by the supervisor or other person

(a) fails to comply with professional standards, when applicable

(b) creates a material misrepresentation of fact; or

(c) may violate applicable laws or regulations.

340.7 If the member concludes that threats are at an acceptable level the member should discuss his or her conclusions with the person taking the position. No further action would be needed under this interpretation.

340.8 If the member concludes that the position results in a material misrepresentation of fact or a violation of applicable laws or regulations, then threats would not be at an acceptable level. In such circumstances, the member should discuss his or her concerns with the supervisor.

340.9 If the difference of opinion is not resolved after discussing the concerns with the supervisor, the member should discuss his or her concerns with the appropriate higher level(s) of management within the member's organisation (for example, the supervisor's immediate superior, senior management, and those charged with governance).

340.10 If after discussing the concerns with the supervisor and appropriate higher level(s) of management within the member's organisation, the member concludes that appropriate action was not taken, then the member should consider, in no specific order, the following safeguards to ensure that threats to the member's compliance with the "Integrity and Objectivity Rule" and the Integrity and Objectivity principles are eliminated or reduced to an acceptable level:

- Determine whether the organisation's internal policies and procedures have any additional requirements for reporting differences of opinion.

- Determine whether he or she is responsible for communicating to third parties, such as regulatory authorities or the organisation's (former organisation's) external accountant. In considering such communications, the member should be cognizant of his or her obligations under the "Confidential Information Obtained from Employment or Volunteer Activities" interpretation (370.5-370.23) and the "Obligation of a Member to His or Her Employer's External Accountant" interpretation (340.14).

- Consult with his or her legal counsel regarding his or her responsibilities.

- Document his or her understanding of the facts, the accounting principles, auditing standards, or other relevant professional standards involved or applicable laws or regulations and the conversations and parties with whom these matters were discussed.

340.11 If the member concludes that no safeguards can eliminate or reduce the threats to an acceptable level or if the member concludes that appropriate action was not taken, then he or she should consider the continuing relationship with the member's organisation and take appropriate steps to eliminate his or her exposure to subordination of judgement.

340.12 Nothing in this interpretation precludes a member from resigning from the organisation at any time. However, resignation may not relieve the member of responsibilities in the situation, including any responsibility to disclose concerns to third parties, such as regulatory authorities or the employer's (former employer's) external accountant.

340.13 A member should use professional judgement and apply similar safeguards, as appropriate, to other situations involving a difference of opinion as described in this interpretation so that the member does not subordinate his or her judgement.

Obligation of a member to his or her employer's external accountant

340.14 The "Integrity and Objectivity Rule" and the Integrity and Objectivity principles require a member to maintain objectivity and integrity in the performance of a professional service. When dealing with an employer's external accountant, a member must be candid and not knowingly misrepresent facts or knowingly fail to disclose material facts. This would include, for example, responding to specific inquiries for which the employer's external accountant requests written representation.

SECTION 350

Educational services

350.1 Members who perform educational services, such as teaching full or part time at a university, teaching a continuing professional education course, or engaging in research and scholarship, are performing professional services and, therefore, are subject to the "Integrity and Objectivity Rule" and the Integrity and Objectivity principles.

SECTION 360

General standards/Professional competence and due care

General standards rule (AICPA)

360.1 A member shall comply with the following standards and with any interpretations thereof by bodies designated by Council.

(a) Professional Competence. Undertake only those professional services that the member or the member's firm can reasonably expect to be completed with professional competence.

(b) Due Professional Care. Exercise due professional care in the performance of professional services.

(c) Planning and Supervision. Adequately plan and supervise the performance of professional services.

(d) Sufficient Relevant Data. Obtain sufficient relevant data to afford a reasonable basis for conclusions or recommendations in relation to any professional services performed.

Professional competence and due care principle (CIMA)

360.2 The principle of Professional Competence and Due Care imposes the following obligations on all professional accountants:

(a) To maintain professional knowledge and skill at the level required to ensure that employers receive competent professional service

(b) To act diligently in accordance with applicable technical and professional standards when providing professional services.

Interpretations under the "General Standards Rule" and "Professional Competence and Due Care Principle"

Application of the conceptual framework for members in business and ethical conflicts

360.3 In the absence of an interpretation of the "General Standards Rule" and "Professional Competence and Due Care Principle" that addresses a particular relationship or circumstance, a member should apply the "Conceptual Framework for Members in Business" (300.2 – 300.3).

360.4 A member would be considered in violation of the "General Standards Rule" and "Professional Competence and Due Care Principle" if the member cannot demonstrate that safeguards were applied that eliminated or reduced significant threats to an acceptable level.

360.5 A member should consider the guidance in the "Ethical Conflicts" interpretation (310.1) when addressing ethical conflicts that may arise when the member encounters obstacles to following an appropriate course of action. Such obstacles may be due to internal or external pressures or to conflicts in applying relevant professional and legal standards, or both.

Professional competence and due care

360.6 Competence, in this context, means that the member or member's staff possesses the appropriate technical qualifications to perform professional services and, as required, supervises and evaluates the quality of work performed. Competence encompasses knowledge of the profession's standards, the techniques and technical subject matter involved, and the ability to exercise sound judgement in applying such knowledge in the performance of professional services.

360.7 A member's agreement to perform professional services implies that the member has the necessary competence to complete those services according to professional standards and to apply the member's knowledge and skill with reasonable care and diligence. However, the member does not assume a responsibility for infallibility of knowledge or judgement.

360.8 The member may have the knowledge required to complete the services in accordance with professional standards prior to performance. A normal part of providing professional services involves performing additional research or consulting with others to gain sufficient competence.

360.9 Threats to the member's compliance with the "General Standards Rule" and "Professional Competence and Due Care Principle" may exist if the member is performing professional services and the member has:

- insufficient time for properly performing or completing the relevant duties

- incomplete, restricted or otherwise inadequate information for performing the duties properly

- insufficient experience, training or education, or both; or

- inadequate resources for the proper performance of the duties.

360.10 The significance of the threats will depend on factors such as the extent to which the member is working with others, relative seniority in the business, and the level of supervision and review applied to the work. The member should evaluate the significance of any threats and apply safeguards, when necessary, to eliminate or reduce the threats to an acceptable level. Examples of such safeguards include:

- performing additional research or obtaining additional advice or training.

- ensuring that there is adequate time available for performing the relevant duties.

- obtaining assistance from someone with the necessary expertise.

- consulting, where appropriate, with
  - superiors within the employing organisation
  - independent experts; or
  - a relevant professional body.

360.11 If the member determines that the threats are so significant that no safeguards could eliminate or reduce the threats to an acceptable level, and therefore the member is unable to gain sufficient competence, the member should suggest the involvement of a competent person to perform the needed professional service, either independently or as an associate.

Submission of financial statements

360.12 When a member is a stockholder, a partner, a director, an officer, or an employee of an entity and, in this capacity, prepares or submits the entity's financial statements to third parties, the member should clearly communicate, preferably in writing, the member's relationship to the entity and should not imply that the member is independent of the entity. In addition, if the communication states affirmatively that the financial statements are presented in conformity with the applicable financial reporting framework, the member should comply with the "Accounting Principles Rule" and the "Professional Competence and Due Care Principle".

360.13 AICPA members should refer to the "Use of CPA Credential" interpretation (370.26) for additional guidance.

Compliance with standards/Professional competence and due care

Compliance with standards rule (AICPA)

360.14 A member who performs auditing, review, compilation, management consulting, tax, or other professional services shall comply with standards promulgated by bodies designated by Council.

Professional competence and due care principle (CIMA)

360.15 The principle of professional competence and due care imposes the following obligations on all professional accountants:

(a) To maintain professional knowledge and skill at the level required to ensure that employers receive competent professional service; and

(b) To act diligently in accordance with applicable technical and professional standards when providing professional services.

Interpretations under the "Compliance with Standards Rule" and the "Professional Competence and Due Care Principle"

Application of the conceptual framework for members in business and ethical conflicts

360.16 In the absence of an interpretation of the "Compliance with Standards Rule" and the "Professional Competence and Due Care Principle" that addresses a particular relationship or circumstance, a member should apply the "Conceptual Framework for Members in Business" (300.2–300.3).

360.17 A member would be considered in violation of the "Compliance with Standards Rule" and the "Professional Competence and Due Care Principle" if the member cannot demonstrate that safeguards were applied that eliminated or reduced significant threats to an acceptable level.

360.18 A member should consider the guidance in the "Ethical Conflicts" interpretation (310.1) when addressing ethical conflicts that may arise when the member encounters obstacles to following an appropriate course of action. Such obstacles may be due to internal or external pressures or to conflicts in applying relevant professional or legal standards, or both.

Accounting principles

Accounting principles rule (AICPA)

360.19 A member shall not (1) express an opinion or state affirmatively that the financial statements or other financial data of any entity are presented in conformity with generally accepted accounting principles or (2) state that he or she is not aware of any material modifications that should be made to such statements or data in order for them to be in conformity with generally accepted accounting principles, if such statements or data contain any departure from an accounting principle promulgated by bodies designated by Council to establish such principles that has a material effect on the statements or data taken as a whole. If, however, the statements or data contain such a departure and the member can demonstrate that due to unusual circumstances the financial statements or data would otherwise have been misleading, the member can comply with the rule by describing the departure, its approximate effects, if practicable, and the reasons why compliance with the principle would result in a misleading statement.

Professional competence and due care principle (CIMA)

360.20 The principle of professional competence and due care imposes the following obligations on all professional accountants:

(a)   To maintain professional knowledge and skill at the level required to ensure that employers receive competent professional service

(b)   To act diligently in accordance with applicable technical and professional standards when providing professional services.

Interpretations under the "Accounting Principles Rule" and the "Professional Competence and Due Care Principle"

Application of the Conceptual Framework for Members in Business and Ethical Conflicts

360.21 In the absence of an interpretation of the "Accounting Principles Rule" and the "Professional Competence and Due Care Principle" that addresses a particular relationship or circumstance, a member should apply the "Conceptual Framework for Members in Business" (30.2–300.3).

360.22 A member would be considered in violation of the "Accounting Principles Rule" and the "Professional Competence and Due Care Principle" if the member cannot demonstrate that safeguards were applied that eliminated or reduced significant threats to an acceptable level.

360.23 A member should consider the guidance in the "Ethical Conflicts" interpretation (310.1) when addressing ethical conflicts that may arise when the member encounters obstacles to following an appropriate course of action. Such obstacles may be due to internal or external pressures or to conflicts in applying relevant professional or legal standards, or both.

Responsibility for affirming that financial statements are in conformity with the applicable financial reporting framework (AICPA)

360.24 A member shall not state affirmatively that an entity's financial statements or other financial data are presented in conformity with generally accepted accounting principles (GAAP) if such statements or data contain any departure from an accounting principle promulgated by a body designated by Council to establish such principles. Members who affirm that financial statements or other financial data are presented in conformity with GAAP should comply with "Accounting Principles Rule". A member's representation in a letter or other communication that an entity's financial statements are in conformity with GAAP may be considered an affirmative statement within the meaning of this rule with respect to the member who signed the letter or other communication (for example, the member signed a report to a regulatory authority, a creditor, or an auditor).

Responsibility for affirming that financial statements are in conformity with the applicable financial reporting framework (CIMA)

360.25 A member of CIMA who has responsibility for the preparation or approval of the general purpose financial statements of an employing organisation shall be satisfied that those financial statements are presented in accordance with the applicable financial reporting standards.

Status of financial accounting standards board, Governmental accounting standards board, Federal accounting standards advisory board, and International accounting standards board interpretations (AICPA)

360.26 The "Accounting Principles Rule" authorizes Council to designate bodies to establish accounting principles. Council has designated the U.S. Financial Accounting Standards Board (FASB) as such a body and has resolved that FASB Accounting Standards Codification® (ASC) constitutes accounting principles as contemplated in the rule. Council designated the U.S. Governmental Accounting Standards Board (GASB), with respect to Statements of Governmental Accounting Standards issued in July 1984 and thereafter, as the body to establish financial accounting principles for state and local governmental entities, pursuant to the "Accounting Principles Rule". Council designated the U.S. Federal Accounting Standards Advisory Board (FASAB), with respect to Statements of Federal Accounting Standards adopted and issued in March 1993 and subsequently, as the body to establish accounting principles for federal government entities, pursuant to the "Accounting Principles Rule". Council designated the International Accounting Standards Board (IASB) as an accounting body for purposes of establishing international financial accounting and reporting principles.

360.27 Reference to GAAP in the "Accounting Principles Rule" means those accounting principles promulgated by bodies designated by Council, which are listed in paragraph .01 "Council Resolution Designating Bodies to Promulgate Technical Standards".

360.28 The AICPA Professional Ethics Division will look to the codification or statements and any interpretations thereof issued by FASB, GASB, FASAB, or IASB in determining whether a member of the AICPA has departed from an accounting principle established by a designated accounting standard-setter in FASB ASC, a Statement of Governmental Accounting Standards, a Statement of Federal Accounting Standards, or International Financial Reporting Standards (IFRS).

Departures from generally accepted accounting principles (AICPA)

360.29 It is difficult to anticipate all the circumstances in which accounting principles may be applied. However, there is a strong presumption that adherence to GAAP would, in nearly all instances, result in financial statements that are not misleading. The "Accounting Principles Rule" recognizes that, upon occasion, there may be unusual circumstances when the literal application of GAAP would have the effect of rendering financial statements misleading. In such cases, the proper accounting treatment to apply is that which will not render the financial statements misleading.

360.30 The question of what constitutes unusual circumstances, as referred to in the "Accounting Principles Rule" is a matter of professional judgement involving the ability to support the position that adherence to a promulgated principle within GAAP would be regarded generally by reasonable persons as producing misleading financial statements.

360.31 Examples of circumstances that may justify a departure from GAAP include new legislation or evolution of a new form of business transaction. Examples of circumstances that would not justify departures from GAAP include an unusual degree of materiality or conflicting industry practices.

360.32 If the statements or data contain such departures, see the "Accounting Principles Rule" for further guidance.

Financial statements prepared pursuant to financial reporting frameworks other than GAAP (AICPA)

360.33 Reference to GAAP in the "Accounting Principles Rule" means those accounting principles promulgated by bodies designated by Council. The bodies designed by Council to promulgate accounting principles are:

- FASAB
- FASB
- GASB, and
- IASB.

360.34 Financial statements prepared pursuant to other accounting principles would be considered financial reporting frameworks other than GAAP within the context of the "Accounting Principles Rule".

360.35 However, the "Accounting Principles Rule" does not preclude a member from preparing or reporting on financial statements that have been prepared pursuant to financial reporting frameworks other than GAAP, such as:

(a) financial reporting frameworks generally accepted in another country, including jurisdictional variations of IFRS such that the entity's financial statements do not meet the requirements for full compliance with IFRS, as promulgated by the IASB

(b) financial reporting frameworks prescribed by an agreement or a contract

or

(c) other special purpose frameworks, including statutory financial reporting provisions required by law or a U.S. or foreign governmental regulatory body to whose jurisdiction the entity is subject.

360.36 In such circumstances, however, the financial statements or member's reports thereon should not purport that the financial statements are in accordance with GAAP and the financial statements or reports on those financial statements, or both, should clarify the financial reporting framework(s) used.

SECTION 370

Acts discreditable/Professional behaviour/Confidentiality

Acts discreditable rule (AICPA)

370.1 A member shall not commit an act discreditable to the profession.

Professional behaviour principle (CIMA)

370.2 The principle of professional behaviour imposes an obligation on all members to comply with relevant laws and regulations and avoid any action that the member knows or should know may discredit the profession.

Confidentiality principle (CIMA)

370.3 The principle of confidentiality imposes an obligation on all members to respect the confidentiality of information acquired as a result of professional and business relationships and, therefore, not disclose any such information to third parties without proper and specific authority, unless there is a legal or professional right or duty to disclose, nor use the information for the personal advantage of the professional accountant or third parties.

Interpretations under the "Acts Discreditable Rule" and "Professional Behaviour and Confidentiality Principles"

Application of the conceptual framework for members in business and ethical conflicts

370.4 In the absence of an interpretation of the "Acts Discreditable Rule" and the Professional Behaviour and Confidentiality principles that addresses a particular relationship or circumstance, a member should apply the "Conceptual Framework for Members in Business" (300.2–300.3).

370.5 A member would be considered in violation of the "Acts Discreditable Rule" and the Professional Behaviour and Confidentiality principles if the member cannot demonstrate that safeguards were applied that eliminated or reduced significant threats to an acceptable level.

370.6 A member should consider the guidance in the "Ethical Conflicts" interpretation (310.1) when addressing ethical conflicts that may arise when the member encounters obstacles to follow an appropriate course of action. Such obstacles may be due to internal or external pressures or to conflicts in applying relevant professional standards or legal standards, or both.

Discrimination and harassment in employment practices

370.7 A member would be presumed to have committed an act discreditable to the profession, in violation of the "Acts Discreditable Rule" and the "Professional Behaviour Principle" if a final determination, no longer subject to appeal, is made by a court or an administrative agency of competent jurisdiction that a member has violated any antidiscrimination laws of the country, state, or municipality, including those related to sexual and other forms of harassment.

Solicitation or disclosure of CPA/CIMA examination questions and answers

370.8 A member who solicits or knowingly discloses the Uniform CPA Examination or the CIMA Examination question(s) or answer(s), or both, without the AICPA's or CIMA's respective written authorisation shall be considered to have committed an act discreditable to the profession, in violation of the "Acts Discreditable Rule" and the "Professional Behaviour Principle".

Failure to file a tax return or pay a tax liability

370.9 A member who fails to comply with applicable federal, state, or local laws or regulations regarding (a) the timely filing of the member's personal tax returns or tax returns for the member's employer that the member has the authority to timely file or (b) the timely remittance of all payroll and other taxes collected on behalf of others may be considered to have committed an act discreditable to the profession, in violation of the "Acts Discreditable Rule" and the "Professional Behaviour Principle".

Negligence in the Preparation of Financial Statements or Records

370.10 A member would be considered in violation of the "Acts Discreditable Rule" and the "Professional Behaviour Principle" if the member, by virtue of his or her negligence, does any of the following:

(a) Makes, or permits or directs another to make, materially false and misleading entries in the financial statements or records of an entity

(b) Fails to correct an entity's financial statements that are materially false and misleading when the member has the authority to record an entry

(c) Signs, or permits or directs another to sign, a document containing materially false and misleading information.

Governmental bodies, commissions or other regulatory agencies

370.11 Many governmental bodies, commissions, or other regulatory agencies have established requirements, such as standards, guides, rules, and regulations, that members are required to follow in the preparation of financial statements or related information.

370.12 If a member prepares financial statements or related information (for example, management's discussion and analysis) for purposes of reporting to such bodies, commissions, or regulatory agencies, the member should follow the requirements of such organisations in addition to the applicable financial reporting framework.

370.13 A member's material departure from such requirements would be considered a violation of the "Acts Discreditable Rule" and the "Professional Behaviour Principle" unless the member discloses in the financial statements or related information that such requirements were not followed and the applicable reasons.

Indemnification and limitation of liability provisions

370.14 Certain governmental bodies, commissions, or other regulatory agencies (collectively, regulators) have established requirements through laws, regulations, or published interpretations that:

(a)   prohibit entities subject to their regulation (regulated entity) from including certain types of indemnification and limitation of liability provisions in agreements for the performance of audit or other attest or assurance services on behalf of the employing organisation that are required by such regulators

or

(b)   provide that the existence of such provisions disqualifies a member from rendering such services to these entities.

370.15 If a member enters into, or directs or knowingly permits another individual to enter into, a contract for the performance of audit or other attest or assurance services that are subject to the requirements of these regulators, the member should not include, or knowingly permit or direct another individual to include, an indemnification or limitation of liability provision that would cause the regulated entity or a member to be in violation of such requirements or disqualify a member from providing such services to the regulated entity. A member who enters into, or directs or knowingly permits another individual to enter into, such an agreement for the performance of audit or other attest services would be considered in violation of the "Acts Discreditable Rule" and the "Professional Behaviour Principle".

Confidential information obtained from employment or volunteer activities

370.16 A member should maintain the confidentiality of his or her employer's confidential information and should not use or disclose any confidential employer information obtained as a result of an employment relationship, such as discussions with the employer's vendors, customers, or lenders (for example, any confidential information pertaining to a current or previous employer, subsidiary, affiliate, or parent thereof, as well as any entities for which the member is working in a volunteer capacity).

370.17 For purposes of this interpretation, confidential employer information is any proprietary information pertaining to the employer or any organisation for whom the member may work in a volunteer capacity that is not known to be available to the public and is obtained as a result of such relationships.

370.18 A member should be alert to the possibility of inadvertent disclosure, particularly to a close business associate or close relative or immediate family member. The member should also take reasonable steps to ensure that staff under his or her control or others within the employing organisation and persons from whom advice and assistance are obtained are aware of the confidential nature of the information.

370.19 When a member changes employment, a member should not use confidential employer information acquired as a result of a prior employment relationship to his or her personal advantage or the advantage of a third party, such as a current or prospective employer. The requirement to maintain the confidentiality of an employer's confidential information continues even after the end of the relationship between a member and the employer. However, the member is entitled to use experience and expertise gained through prior employment relationships.

370.20 A member would be considered in violation of the "Acts Discreditable Rule" and "Confidentiality Principle" if the member discloses or uses any confidential employer information acquired as a result of employment or volunteer relationships without the proper authority or specific consent of the employer or organisation for whom the member may work in a volunteer capacity, unless there is a legal or professional responsibility to use or disclose such information.

370.21 The following are examples of situations in which members are permitted or may be required to disclose confidential employer information or when such disclosure may be appropriate:

(a) Disclosure is permitted by law and authorised by the employer.

(b) Disclosure is required by law, for example, to

- comply with a validly issued and enforceable subpoena or summons or

- inform the appropriate public authorities of violations of law that have been discovered.

(c) There is a professional responsibility or right to disclose information, when not prohibited by law, to

- initiate a complaint with, or respond to any inquiry made by, the AICPA Professional Ethics Division or trial board of the AICPA or a duly constituted investigative or disciplinary body of a state CPA society, board of accountancy, or other regulatory body (AICPA)

– initiate a complaint with, or respond to any inquiry made by, the CIMA Professional Conduct Department or a duly constituted investigative or disciplinary body of CIMA, or other regulatory body (CIMA)

– protect the member's professional interests in legal proceedings

– comply with professional standards (for example, technical standards) and other ethics requirements; or

– report potential concerns regarding questionable accounting, auditing, or other matters to the employer's confidential complaint hotline or those charged with governance.

(d) Disclosure is permitted on behalf of the employer to

– obtain financing with lenders

– communicate with vendors and customers; or

– communicate with the employer's external accountant, attorneys, regulators, and other business professionals.

370.22 In deciding whether to disclose confidential employer information relevant factors to consider include the following:

(a) Whether all the relevant information is known and substantiated to the extent that it is practicable. When the situation involves unsubstantiated facts, incomplete information, or unsubstantiated conclusions, the member should use professional judgement in determining the type of disclosure to be made, if any.

(b) Whether the parties to whom the communication may be addressed are appropriate recipients.

370.23 A member may wish to consult with legal counsel prior to disclosing, or determining whether to disclose, confidential employer information.

370.24 Refer to the "Subordination of Judgement" interpretation (340.3–340.13) for additional guidance.

False, misleading, or deceptive acts in promoting or marketing professional services

370.25 A member would be in violation of the "Acts Discreditable Rule" and the "Professional Behaviour Principle" if the member promotes or markets the member's abilities to provide professional services or makes claims about the member's experience or qualifications in a manner that is false, misleading, or deceptive.

370.26 Promotional efforts would be false, misleading, or deceptive if they contain any claim or representation that would likely cause a reasonable person to be misled or deceived. This includes any representation about CPA licensure, CGMA credential or any other professional certification or accreditation that is not in compliance with the requirements of the relevant licensing authority or designating body.

Use of the CPA credential (AICPA)

370.27 A member should refer to applicable state accountancy laws and board of accountancy rules and regulations for guidance regarding the use of the CPA credential. A member who fails to follow the accountancy laws, rules, and regulations on use of the CPA credential in any of the jurisdictions in which the CPA practices would be considered to have used the CPA credential in a manner that is false, misleading, or deceptive and in violation of the "Acts Discreditable Rule".

 Supplementary reading: Definitions

DEFINITIONS (PARTS A AND B)

In the CIMA Code of Ethics for Professional Accountants, the following expressions have the following meanings assigned to them:

Acceptable level

A level at which a reasonable and informed third party would be likely to conclude, weighing all the specific facts and circumstances available to the professional accountant at that time, that compliance with the fundamental principles is not compromised.

Advertising

The communication to the public of information as to the services or skills provided by professional accountants in public practice with a view to procuring professional business.

Assurance client

The responsible party that is the person (or persons) who:

(a) In a direct reporting engagement, is responsible for the subject matter; or

(b) In an assertion-based engagement, is responsible for the subject matter information and may be responsible for the subject matter.

Assurance engagement

An engagement in which a professional accountant in public practice expresses a conclusion designed to enhance the degree of confidence of the intended users other than the responsible party about the outcome of the evaluation or measurement of a subject matter against criteria. (For guidance on assurance engagements see the International Framework for Assurance Engagements issued by the International Auditing and Assurance Standards Board which describes the elements and objectives of an assurance engagement and identifies engagements to which International Standards on Auditing (ISAs), International Standards on Review Engagements (ISREs) and International Standards on Assurance Engagements (ISAEs) apply.)

Assurance team

(a)   All members of the engagement team for the assurance engagement

(b)   All others within a firm who can directly influence the outcome of the assurance engagement, including:

   (i)   those who recommend the compensation of, or who provide direct supervisory, management or other oversight of the assurance engagement partner in connection with the performance of the assurance engagement

   (ii)   those who provide consultation regarding technical or industry specific issues, transactions or events for the assurance engagement; and

   (iii) those who provide quality control for the assurance engagement, including those who perform the engagement quality control review for the assurance engagement.

Audit client

An entity in respect of which a firm conducts an audit engagement. When the client is a listed entity, audit client will always include its related entities. When the audit client is not a listed entity, audit client includes those related entities over which the client has direct or indirect control.

Audit engagement

A reasonable assurance engagement in which a professional accountant in public practice expresses an opinion whether financial statements are prepared, in all material respects (or give a true and fair view or are presented fairly, in all material respects), in accordance with an applicable financial reporting framework, such as an engagement conducted in accordance with International Standards on Auditing. This includes a Statutory Audit, which is an audit required by legislation or other regulation.

Audit team

(a)   All members of the engagement team for the audit engagement

(b)   All others within a firm who can directly influence the outcome of the audit engagement, including:

(i)   Those who recommend the compensation of, or who provide direct supervisory, management or other oversight of the engagement partner in connection with the performance of the audit engagement including those at all successively senior levels above the engagement partner through to the individual who is the firm's Senior or Managing Partner (Chief Executive or equivalent)

(ii)   Those who provide consultation regarding technical or industry-specific issues, transactions or events for the engagement; and

(iii) Those who provide quality control for the engagement, including those who perform the engagement quality control review for the engagement; and

(c)   All those within a network firm who can directly influence the outcome of the audit engagement.

Close family

A parent, child or sibling who is not an immediate family member.

Contingent fee

A fee calculated on a predetermined basis relating to the outcome of a transaction or the result of the services performed by the firm. A fee that is established by a court or other public authority is not a contingent fee.

Direct financial interest

A financial interest:

(a)   Owned directly by and under the control of an individual or entity (including those managed on a discretionary basis by others); or

(b)   Beneficially owned through a collective investment vehicle, estate, trust or other intermediary over which the individual or entity has control, or the ability to influence investment decisions.

Director or officer

Those charged with the governance of an entity, or acting in an equivalent capacity, regardless of their title, which may vary from jurisdiction to jurisdiction.

Engagement partner

The partner or other person in the firm who is responsible for the engagement and its performance, and for the report that is issued on behalf of the firm, and who, where required, has the appropriate authority from a professional, legal or regulatory body.

Engagement quality control review

A process designed to provide an objective evaluation, on or before the report is issued, of the significant judgements the engagement team made and the conclusions it reached in formulating the report.

Engagement team

All partners and staff performing the engagement, and any individuals engaged by the firm or a network firm who perform assurance procedures on the engagement. This excludes external experts engaged by the firm or a network firm.

The term 'engagement team' also excludes individuals within the client's internal audit function who provide direct assistance on an audit engagement when the external auditor complies with the requirements of ASA 610 (Revised 2013) Using the work of internal auditors.

Existing accountant

A professional accountant in public practice currently holding an audit appointment or carrying out accounting, taxation, consulting or similar professional services for a client.

External expert

An individual (who is not a partner or a member of the professional staff, including temporary staff, of the firm or a network firm) or organisation possessing skills, knowledge and experience in a field other than accounting or auditing, whose work in that field is used to assist the professional accountant in obtaining sufficient appropriate evidence.

Financial interest

An interest in an equity or other security, debenture, loan or other debt instrument of an entity, including rights and obligations to acquire such an interest and derivatives directly related to such interest.

Financial statements

A structured representation of historical financial information, including related notes, intended to communicate an entity's economic resources or obligations at a point in time or the changes therein for a period of time in accordance with a financial reporting framework. The related notes ordinarily comprise a summary of significant accounting policies and other explanatory information. The term can relate to a complete set of financial statements, but it can also refer to a single financial statement, for example, a balance sheet, or a statement of revenues and expenses, and related explanatory notes.

Financial statements on which the firm will express an opinion

In the case of a single entity, the financial statements of that entity. In the case of consolidated financial statements, also referred to as group financial statements, the consolidated financial statements.

Firm

(a) A sole practitioner, partnership or corporation of professional accountants

(b) An entity that controls such parties, through ownership, management or other means; and

(c) An entity controlled by such parties, through ownership, management or other means.

Historical financial information

Information expressed in financial terms in relation to a particular entity, derived primarily from that entity's accounting system, about economic events occurring in past time periods or about economic conditions or circumstances at points in time in the past.

Immediate family

A spouse (or equivalent) or dependent.

Independence

Independence is:

(a) Independence of mind – the state of mind that permits the expression of a conclusion without being affected by influences that compromise professional judgement, thereby allowing an individual to act with integrity, and exercise objectivity and professional scepticism.

(b) Independence in appearance – the avoidance of facts and circumstances that are so significant that a reasonable and informed third party would be likely to conclude, weighing all the specific facts and circumstances, that a firm's, or a member of the audit or assurance team's, integrity, objectivity or professional scepticism has been compromised.

Indirect financial interest

A financial interest beneficially owned through a collective investment vehicle, estate, trust or other intermediary over which the individual or entity has no control or ability to influence investment decisions.

Key audit partner

The engagement partner, the individual responsible for the engagement quality control review, and other audit partners, if any, on the engagement team who make key decisions or judgements on significant matters with respect to the audit of the financial statements on which the firm will express an opinion. Depending upon the circumstances and the role of the individuals on the audit, 'other audit partners' may include, for example, audit partners responsible for significant subsidiaries or divisions.

Listed entity

An entity whose shares, stock or debt are quoted or listed on a recognised stock exchange, or are marketed under the regulations of a recognised stock exchange or other equivalent body.

Network

A larger structure:

(a)   That is aimed at co-operation; and

(b)   That is clearly aimed at profit or cost sharing or shares common ownership, control or management, common quality control policies and procedures, common business strategy, the use of a common brand-name, or a significant part of professional resources.

Network firm

A firm or entity that belongs to a network.

Office

A distinct sub-group, whether organised on geographical or practice lines.

Professional accountant

An individual who is a member of an IFAC member body.

Professional accountant in business

A professional accountant employed or engaged in an executive or non-executive capacity in such areas as commerce, industry, service, the public sector, education, the not for profit sector, regulatory bodies or professional bodies, or a professional accountant contracted by such entities.

Professional accountant in public practice

A professional accountant, irrespective of functional classification (for example, audit, tax or consulting) in a firm that provides professional services. This term is also used to refer to a firm of professional accountants in public practice.

Professional activity

An activity requiring accountancy or related skills undertaken by a professional accountant, including accounting, auditing, taxation, management consulting, and financial management.

Professional services

Professional activities performed for clients.

Public interest entity

(a)   A listed entity; and

(b)   An entity:

  (i)   Defined by regulation or legislation as a public interest entity; or

  (ii)   For which the audit is required by regulation or legislation to be conducted in compliance with the same independence requirements that apply to the audit of listed entities. Such regulation may be promulgated by any relevant regulator, including an audit regulator.

Related entity

An entity that has any of the following relationships with the client:

(a)   An entity that has direct or indirect control over the client if the client is material to such entity

(b)   An entity with a direct financial interest in the client if that entity has significant influence over the client and the interest in the client is material to such entity

(c)   An entity over which the client has direct or indirect control

(d)   An entity in which the client, or an entity related to the client under (c) above, has a direct financial interest that gives it significant influence over such entity and the interest is material to the client and its related entity in (c); and

(e)   An entity which is under common control with the client (a 'sister entity') if the sister entity and the client are both material to the entity that controls both the client and sister entity.

Review client

An entity in respect of which a firm conducts a review engagement.

Review engagement

An assurance engagement, conducted in accordance with International Standards on Review Engagements or equivalent, in which a professional accountant in public practice expresses a conclusion on whether, on the basis of the procedures which do not provide all the evidence that would be required in an audit, anything has come to the accountant's attention that causes the accountant to believe that the financial statements are not prepared, in all material respects, in accordance with an applicable financial reporting framework.

Review team

(a) All members of the engagement team for the review engagement; and

(b) All others within a firm who can directly influence the outcome of the review engagement, including:

    (i) Those who recommend the compensation of, or who provide direct supervisory, management or other oversight of the engagement partner in connection with the performance of the review engagement including those at all successively senior levels above the engagement partner through to the individual who is the firm's Senior or Managing Partner (Chief Executive or equivalent)

    (ii) Those who provide consultation regarding technical or industry specific issues, transactions or events for the engagement; and

    (iii) Those who provide quality control for the engagement, including those who perform the engagement quality control review for the engagement; and

    (iv) All those within a network firm who can directly influence the outcome of the review engagement.

Special purpose financial statements

Financial statements prepared in accordance with a financial reporting framework designed to meet the financial information needs of specified users.

Those charged with governance

The person(s) or organisation(s) (for example, a corporate trustee) with responsibility for overseeing the strategic direction of the entity and obligations related to the accountability of the entity. This includes overseeing the financial reporting process.

For some entities in some jurisdictions, those charged with governance may include management personnel, for example, executive members of a governance board of a private or public sector entity, or an owner-manager.

DEFINITIONS (PART C)

In Part C of the CIMA Code of Ethics for Professional Accountants, the following expressions have the following meanings assigned to them:

Acceptable level

An acceptable level is a level at which a reasonable and informed third party who is aware of the relevant information would be expected to conclude that a member's compliance with the rules or fundamental principles is not compromised.

Client

Any person or entity, other than the member's employer, that engages a member or member's firm to perform professional services and, if different, the person or entity with respect to which professional services are performed. For purposes of this definition for AICPA members, the term employer does not include the following:

(a) Person or entity engaged in public practice.

(b) Federal, state, and local government or component unit thereof, provided that the member performing professional services with respect to the entity is

   (i) directly elected by voters of the government or component unit thereof with respect to which professional services are performed

   (ii) an individual who is (1) appointed by a legislative body and (2) subject to removal by a legislative body; or

   (iii) appointed by someone other than the legislative body, so long as the appointment is confirmed by the legislative body and removal is subject to oversight or approval by the legislative body.

Close relative

A parent, sibling, or nondependent child.

Council

The AICPA Council.

Employing organisation

Any entity that employs the member or engages the member on a contractual or volunteer basis in an executive, a staff, a governance, an advisory, or an administrative capacity to provide professional services.

Financial interest

An ownership interest in an equity or a debt security issued by an entity, including rights and obligations to acquire such an interest and derivatives directly related to such interest.

Financial statements

A presentation of financial data, including accompanying disclosures, if any, intended to communicate an entity's economic resources or obligations, or both, at a point in time or the changes therein for a period of time, in accordance with the applicable financial reporting framework. Tax returns and supporting schedules do not, for this purpose, constitute financial statements. The statement, affidavit, or signature of preparers required on tax returns neither constitutes an opinion on financial statements nor requires a disclaimer of such opinion.

Immediate family

A spouse, spousal equivalent, or dependent (regardless of whether the dependent is related).

Institute

The AICPA or CIMA.

Interpretation

Pronouncements issued by the AICPA and CIMA to provide guidelines concerning the scope and application of the rules of conduct and fundamental principles.

Member

A member of the AICPA is a member, an associate or affiliate member or international associate of the AICPA. A member of CIMA is a Fellow or Associate of the Institute, and includes, for the purposes of the disciplinary powers and procedures of the Institute, a person who ceased to be a member on or after June 14, 2003. When used in this code, the term member means a member in business or professional accountant in business and who is a CGMA (or entitled to use the designation CGMA).

Member(s) in business or professional accountant(s) in business

A member who is employed or engaged on a contractual or volunteer basis in a(n) executive, staff, governance, advisory, or administrative capacity in such areas as industry, the public sector, education, the not-for-profit sector, and regulatory or professional bodies. This does not include a member engaged in public practice.

Professional services

Include all services requiring accountancy or related skills that are performed by a member for an employer, or on a volunteer basis. These services include, but are not limited to accounting, tax, bookkeeping, management consulting, financial management, corporate governance, business valuation and educational services. For AICPA members, it also includes those services for which standards are promulgated by bodies designated by AICPA Council.

Public interest entity(ies)

Public interest entities are (a) all listed entities, including entities whose shares, stock, or debt are quoted or listed on a recognised stock exchange or marketed under the regulations of a recognised stock exchange or other equivalent body, and (b) any entity for which an audit is required by regulation or legislation to be conducted in compliance with the same independence requirements that apply to an audit of listed entities. Members may wish to consider whether additional entities should also be treated as public interest entities because they have a large number and wide range of stakeholders. Factors to be considered may include (a) the nature of the business, such as the holding of assets in a fiduciary capacity for a large number of stakeholders; (b) size; and (c) number of employees.

Public practice

Consists of the performance of professional services for a client by a member or member's firm.

Safeguards

Actions or other measures that may eliminate a threat or reduce a threat to an acceptable level.

Those charged with governance

The person(s) or organisation(s) (for example, a corporate trustee) with responsibility for overseeing the strategic direction of the entity and the obligations related to the accountability of the entity. This includes overseeing the financial reporting process. Those charged with governance may include management personnel (for example, executive members of a governance board or an owner-manager).

When an interpretation requires communicating with those charged with governance, the member should determine, considering the nature and importance of the particular circumstances and matter to be communicated, the appropriate person(s) within the entity's governance structure with whom to communicate. If the member communicates with a subgroup of those charged with governance (for example, an audit committee or an individual), the member should determine whether communication with all of those charged with governance is also necessary, so that they are adequately informed.

Threat(s)

Relationships or circumstances that could compromise a member's compliance with the rules or fundamental principles.

Supplementary reading: Annex 1 Preface and Contents

CIMA CODE OF ETHICS for professional accountants – Annex 1 (Sections 290 and 291)

CIMA PREFACE

Annex 1 comprises section 290 and 291 of the CIMA Code of Ethics which address the independence requirement for audit, review and other assurance engagements and apply a conceptual framework approach.

Also included is commentary on the independence requirements and the effective date and transitional provisions for public interest entities, partner rotation, non-assurance services, fees and compensation and evaluation policies.

For CIMA members providing non-audit assurance services, the Code contains new modified independence requirements relating to certain audit and review reports that include a restriction on use and distribution (290.500–290.514). Similar provisions are included in 291.21–291.27

Section 290: Independence – Audit and Review engagements

Section 291: Independence – Other assurance engagements

SECTION 290

INDEPENDENCE – AUDIT AND REVIEW ENGAGEMENTS
CONTENTS

Structure of section

A conceptual framework approach to independence

Networks and Network firms

Public interest entities

Related entities

Those charged with governance

Documentation

Engagement period

Mergers and Acquisitions

Other considerations

Application of the conceptual framework approach to independence

Financial interests

Loans and Guarantees

Business relationships

Family and personal relationships

Employment with an audit client

Temporary staff assignments

Recent service with an audit client

Serving as a Director or Officer of an audit client

Long association of senior personnel (including partner rotation) with an audit client

Provision of non-assurance services to audit clients

    Management responsibilities

    Preparing accounting records and financial statements

    Valuation services

    Taxation services

    Internal audit services

    IT systems services

    Litigation support services

    Legal services

    Recruiting services

    Corporate finance services

> **Fees**
>> Fees – Relative size
>> Fees – Overdue
>> Contingent fees
>
> Compensation and Evaluation policies
>
> Gifts and Hospitality
>
> Actual or threatened litigation
>
> Reports that include a restriction on use and distribution
>
> Effective date

Supplementary reading: Annex 1 290.1 to 290.39

Structure of section

290.1 This section addresses the independence requirements for audit engagements and review engagements, which are assurance engagements in which a professional accountant in public practice expresses a conclusion on financial statements. Such engagements comprise audit and review engagements to report on a complete set of financial statements and a single financial statement.

Independence requirements for assurance engagements that are not audit or review engagements are addressed in Section 291.

290.2 In certain circumstances involving audit engagements where the audit report includes a restriction on use and distribution and provided certain conditions are met, the independence requirements in this section may be modified as provided in paragraphs 290.500 to 290.514. The modifications are not permitted in the case of an audit of financial statements required by law or regulation.

290.3 In this section, the term(s):

(a) 'Audit,' 'audit team,' 'audit engagement,' 'audit client' and 'audit report' includes review, review team, review engagement, review client and review report; and

(b) 'Firm' includes network firm, except where otherwise stated.

A conceptual framework approach to independence

290.4 In the case of audit engagements, it is in the public interest and, therefore, required by this Code, that members of audit teams, firms and network firms shall be independent of audit clients.

290.5 The objective of this section is to assist firms and members of audit teams in applying the conceptual framework approach described below to achieving and maintaining independence.

290.6 Independence comprises:

(a)   Independence of mind

   The state of mind that permits the expression of a conclusion without being affected by influences that compromise professional judgement, thereby allowing an individual to act with integrity and exercise objectivity and professional scepticism.

(b)   Independence in appearance

   The avoidance of facts and circumstances that are so significant that a reasonable and informed third party would be likely to conclude, weighing all the specific facts and circumstances, that a firm's, or a member of the audit team's, integrity, objectivity or professional scepticism has been compromised.

290.7 The conceptual framework approach shall be applied by professional accountants to:

(a)   Identify threats to independence

(b)   Evaluate the significance of the threats identified; and

(c)   Apply safeguards, when necessary, to eliminate the threats or reduce them to an acceptable level.

When the professional accountant determines that appropriate safeguards are not available or cannot be applied to eliminate the threats or reduce them to an acceptable level, the professional accountant shall eliminate the circumstance or relationship creating the threats or decline or terminate the audit engagement.

A professional accountant shall use professional judgement in applying this conceptual framework.

290.8 Many different circumstances, or combinations of circumstances, may be relevant in assessing threats to independence. It is impossible to define every situation that creates threats to independence and to specify the appropriate action. Therefore, this Code establishes a conceptual framework that requires firms and members of audit teams to identify, evaluate, and address threats to independence.

The conceptual framework approach assists professional accountants in practice in complying with the ethical requirements in this Code. It accommodates many variations in circumstances that create threats to independence and can deter a professional accountant from concluding that a situation is permitted if it is not specifically prohibited.

290.9 Paragraphs 290.100 and onwards describe how the conceptual framework approach to independence is to be applied. These paragraphs do not address all the circumstances and relationships that create or may create threats to independence.

290.10 In deciding whether to accept or continue an engagement, or whether a particular individual may be a member of the audit team, a firm shall identify and evaluate threats to independence. If the threats are not at an acceptable level, and the decision is whether to accept an engagement or include a particular individual on the audit team, the firm shall determine whether safeguards are available to eliminate the threats or reduce them to an acceptable level. If the decision is whether to continue an engagement, the firm shall determine whether any existing safeguards will continue to be effective to eliminate the threats or reduce them to an acceptable level or whether other safeguards will need to be applied or whether the engagement needs to be terminated. Whenever new information about a threat to independence comes to the attention of the firm during the engagement, the firm shall evaluate the significance of the threat in accordance with the conceptual framework approach.

290.11 Throughout this section, reference is made to the significance of threats to independence. In evaluating the significance of a threat, qualitative as well as quantitative factors shall be taken into account.

290.12 This section does not, in most cases, prescribe the specific responsibility of individuals within the firm for actions related to independence because responsibility may differ depending on the size, structure and organisation of a firm. The firm is required by International Standards on Quality Control (ISQCs) to establish policies and procedures designed to provide it with reasonable assurance that independence is maintained when required by relevant ethical requirements. In addition, International Standards on Auditing (ISAs) require the engagement partner to form a conclusion on compliance with the independence requirements that apply to the engagement.

Networks and Network firms

290.13 If a firm is deemed to be a network firm, the firm shall be independent of the audit clients of the other firms within the network (unless otherwise stated in this Code). The independence requirements in this section that apply to a network firm apply to any entity, such as a consulting practice or professional law practice, that meets the definition of a network firm irrespective of whether the entity itself meets the definition of a firm.

290.14 To enhance their ability to provide professional services, firms frequently form larger structures with other firms and entities. Whether these larger structures create a network depends on the particular facts and circumstances and does not depend on whether the firms and entities are legally separate and distinct. For example, a larger structure may be aimed only at facilitating the referral of work, which in itself does not meet the criteria necessary to constitute a network. Alternatively, a larger structure might be such that it is aimed at co-operation and the firms share a common brand name, a common system of quality control, or significant professional resources and consequently is deemed to be a network.

290.15 The judgement as to whether the larger structure is a network shall be made in light of whether a reasonable and informed third party would be likely to conclude, weighing all the specific facts and circumstances, that the entities are associated in such a way that a network exists. This judgement shall be applied consistently throughout the network.

290.16 Where the larger structure is aimed at co-operation and it is clearly aimed at profit or cost sharing among the entities within the structure, it is deemed to be a network. However, the sharing of immaterial costs does not in itself create a network. In addition, if the sharing of costs is limited only to those costs related to the development of audit methodologies, manuals, or training courses, this would not in itself create a network. Further, an association between a firm and an otherwise unrelated entity to jointly provide a service or develop a product does not in itself create a network.

290.17 Where the larger structure is aimed at cooperation and the entities within the structure share common ownership, control or management, it is deemed to be a network. This could be achieved by contract or other means.

290.18 Where the larger structure is aimed at co-operation and the entities within the structure share common quality control policies and procedures, it is deemed to be a network. For this purpose, common quality control policies and procedures are those designed, implemented and monitored across the larger structure.

290.19 Where the larger structure is aimed at co-operation and the entities within the structure share a common business strategy, it is deemed to be a network. Sharing a common business strategy involves an agreement by the entities to achieve common strategic objectives. An entity is not deemed to be a network firm merely because it co-operates with another entity solely to respond jointly to a request for a proposal for the provision of a professional service.

290.20 Where the larger structure is aimed at co-operation and the entities within the structure share the use of a common brand name, it is deemed to be a network. A common brand name includes common initials or a common name. A firm is deemed to be using a common brand name if it includes, for example, the common brand name as part of, or along with, its firm name, when a partner of the firm signs an audit report.

290.21 Even though a firm does not belong to a network and does not use a common brand name as part of its firm name, it may give the appearance that it belongs to a network if it makes reference in its stationery or promotional materials to being a member of an association of firms. Accordingly, if care is not taken in how a firm describes such memberships, a perception may be created that the firm belongs to a network.

290.22 If a firm sells a component of its practice, the sales agreement sometimes provides that, for a limited period of time, the component may continue to use the name of the firm, or an element of the name, even though it is no longer connected to the firm. In such circumstances, while the two entities may be practicing under a common name, the facts are such that they do not belong to a larger structure aimed at co-operation and are, therefore, not network firms. Those entities shall determine how to disclose that they are not network firms when presenting themselves to outside parties.

290.23 Where the larger structure is aimed at co-operation and the entities within the structure share a significant part of professional resources, it is deemed to be a network. Professional resources include:

- Common systems that enable firms to exchange information such as client data, billing and time records

- Partners and staff

- Technical departments that consult on technical or industry specific issues, transactions or events for assurance engagements

- Audit methodology or audit manuals; and

- Training courses and facilities.

290.24 The determination of whether the professional resources shared are significant, and therefore the firms are network firms, shall be made based on the relevant facts and circumstances. Where the shared resources are limited to common audit methodology or audit manuals, with no exchange of personnel or client or market information, it is unlikely that the shared resources would be significant. The same applies to a common training endeavour. Where, however, the shared resources involve the exchange of people or information, such as where staff are drawn from a shared pool, or a common technical department is created within the larger structure to provide participating firms with technical advice that the firms are required to follow, a reasonable and informed third party is more likely to conclude that the shared resources are significant.

Public interest entities

290.25 Section 290 contains additional provisions that reflect the extent of public interest in certain entities. For the purpose of this section, public interest entities are:

(a)   All listed entities; and

(b)   Any entity:

    (i)   Defined by regulation or legislation as a public interest entity; or

    (ii)   For which the audit is required by regulation or legislation to be conducted in compliance with the same independence requirements that apply to the audit of listed entities. Such regulation may be promulgated by any relevant regulator, including an audit regulator.

290.26 Firms and member bodies are encouraged to determine whether to treat additional entities, or certain categories of entities, as public interest entities because they have a large number and wide range of stakeholders. Factors to be considered include:

- The nature of the business, such as the holding of assets in a fiduciary capacity for a large number of stakeholders. Examples may include financial institutions, such as banks and insurance companies, and pension funds

- Size; and

- Number of employees.

Related entities

290.27 In the case of an audit client that is a listed entity, references to an audit client in this section include related entities of the client (unless otherwise stated). For all other audit clients, references to an audit client in this section include related entities over which the client has direct or indirect control.

When the audit team knows or has reason to believe that a relationship or circumstance involving another related entity of the client is relevant to the evaluation of the firm's independence from the client, the audit team shall include that related entity when identifying and evaluating threats to independence and applying appropriate safeguards.

Those charged with governance

290.28 Even when not required by the Code, applicable auditing standards, law or regulation, regular communication is encouraged between the firm and those charged with governance of the audit client regarding relationships and other matters that might, in the firm's opinion, reasonably bear on independence. Such communication enables those charged with governance to:

(a) Consider the firm's judgements in identifying and evaluating threats to independence

(b) Consider the appropriateness of safeguards applied to eliminate them or reduce them to an acceptable level, and

(c) Take appropriate action. Such an approach can be particularly helpful with respect to intimidation and familiarity threats.

Documentation

290.29 Documentation provides evidence of the professional accountant's judgements in forming conclusions regarding compliance with independence requirements. The absence of documentation is not a determinant of whether a firm considered a particular matter nor whether it is independent. The professional accountant shall document conclusions regarding compliance with independence requirements, and the substance of any relevant discussions that support those conclusions.

Accordingly:

(a) When safeguards are required to reduce a threat to an acceptable level, the professional accountant shall document the nature of the threat and the safeguards in place or applied that reduce the threat to an acceptable level; and

(b) When a threat required significant analysis to determine whether safeguards were necessary and the professional accountant concluded that they were not because the threat was already at an acceptable level, the professional accountant shall document the nature of the threat and the rationale for the conclusion.

Engagement period

290.30 Independence from the audit client is required both during the engagement period and the period covered by the financial statements. The engagement period starts when the audit team begins to perform audit services. The engagement period ends when the audit report is issued. When the engagement is of a recurring nature, it ends at the later of the notification by either party that the professional relationship has terminated or the issuance of the final audit report.

290.31 When an entity becomes an audit client during or after the period covered by the financial statements on which the firm will express an opinion, the firm shall determine whether any threats to independence are created by:

(a) Financial or business relationships with the audit client during or after the period covered by the financial statements but before accepting the audit engagement; or

(b) Previous services provided to the audit client.

290.32 If a non-assurance service was provided to the audit client during or after the period covered by the financial statements but before the audit team begins to perform audit services and the service would not be permitted during the period of the audit engagement, the firm shall evaluate any threat to independence created by the service. If a threat is not at an acceptable level, the audit engagement shall only be accepted if safeguards are applied to eliminate any threats or reduce them to an acceptable level. Examples of such safeguards include:

- Not including personnel who provided the non-assurance service as members of the audit team

- Having a professional accountant review the audit and non-assurance work as appropriate; or

- Engaging another firm to evaluate the results of the non-assurance service or having another firm re-perform the non-assurance service to the extent necessary to enable it to take responsibility for the service.

Mergers and Acquisitions

290.33 When, as a result of a merger or acquisition, an entity becomes a related entity of an audit client, the firm shall identify and evaluate previous and current interests and relationships with the related entity that, taking into account available safeguards, could affect its independence and therefore its ability to continue the audit engagement after the effective date of the merger or acquisition.

290.34 The firm shall take steps necessary to terminate, by the effective date of the merger or acquisition, any current interests or relationships that are not permitted under this Code. However, if such a current interest or relationship cannot reasonably be terminated by the effective date of the merger or acquisition, for example, because the related entity is unable by the effective date to effect an orderly transition to another service provider of a non-assurance service provided by the firm, the firm shall evaluate the threat that is created by such interest or relationship. The more significant the threat, the more likely the firm's objectivity will be compromised and it will be unable to continue as auditor.

The significance of the threat will depend upon factors such as:

- The nature and significance of the interest or relationship

- The nature and significance of the related entity relationship (for example, whether the related entity is a subsidiary or parent); and

- The length of time until the interest or relationship can reasonably be terminated.

The firm shall discuss with those charged with governance the reasons why the interest or relationship cannot reasonably be terminated by the effective date of the merger or acquisition and the evaluation of the significance of the threat.

290.35 If those charged with governance request the firm to continue as auditor, the firm shall do so only if:

(a) The interest or relationship will be terminated as soon as reasonably possible and in all cases within six months of the effective date of the merger or acquisition

(b) Any individual who has such an interest or relationship, including one that has arisen through performing a non-assurance service that would not be permitted under this section, will not be a member of the engagement team for the audit or the individual responsible for the engagement quality control review; and

(c) Appropriate transitional measures will be applied, as necessary, and discussed with those charged with governance. Examples of transitional measures include:

- Having a professional accountant review the audit or non-assurance work as appropriate

- Having a professional accountant, who is not a member of the firm expressing the opinion on the financial statements, perform a review that is equivalent to an engagement quality control review; or

- Engaging another firm to evaluate the results of the non-assurance service or having another firm re-perform the non-assurance service to the extent necessary to enable it to take responsibility for the service.

290.36 The firm may have completed a significant amount of work on the audit prior to the effective date of the merger or acquisition and may be able to complete the remaining audit procedures within a short period of time. In such circumstances, if those charged with governance request the firm to complete the audit while continuing with an interest or relationship identified in paragraph 290.33, the firm shall do so only if it:

(a) Has evaluated the significance of the threat created by such interest or relationship and discussed the evaluation with those charged with governance

(b) Complies with the requirements of paragraph 290.35(b)–(c); and

(c) Ceases to be the auditor no later than the issuance of the audit report.

290.37 When addressing previous and current interests and relationships covered by paragraphs 290.33 to 290.36, the firm shall determine whether, even if all the requirements could be met, the interests and relationships create threats that would remain so significant that objectivity would be compromised and, if so, the firm shall cease to be the auditor.

290.38 The professional accountant shall document any interests or relationships covered by paragraphs 290.34 and 36 that will not be terminated by the effective date of the merger or acquisition and the reasons why they will not be terminated, the transitional measures applied, the results of the discussion with those charged with governance, and the rationale as to why the previous and current interests and relationships do not create threats that would remain so significant that objectivity would be compromised.

Other considerations

290.39 There may be occasions when there is an inadvertent violation of this section. If such an inadvertent violation occurs, it generally will be deemed not to compromise independence provided the firm has appropriate quality control policies and procedures in place, equivalent to those required by ISQCs, to maintain independence and, once discovered, the violation is corrected promptly and any necessary safeguards are applied to eliminate any threat or reduce it to an acceptable level. The firm shall determine whether to discuss the matter with those charged with governance.

Paragraphs 290.40 to 290.99 are intentionally left blank.

Supplementary reading: Annex 1 290.100 to 290.133

Application of the conceptual framework approach to independence

290.100 Paragraphs 290.102 to 290.231 describe specific circumstances and relationships that create or may create threats to independence. The paragraphs describe the potential threats and the types of safeguards that may be appropriate to eliminate the threats or reduce them to an acceptable level and identify certain situations where no safeguards could reduce the threats to an acceptable level. The paragraphs do not describe all of the circumstances and relationships that create or may create a threat to independence. The firm and the members of the audit team shall evaluate the implications of similar, but different, circumstances and relationships and determine whether safeguards, including the safeguards in paragraphs 200.12 to 200.15, can be applied when necessary to eliminate the threats to independence or reduce them to an acceptable level.

290.101 Paragraphs 290.102 to 290.126 contain references to the materiality of a financial interest, loan, or guarantee, or the significance of a business relationship. For the purpose of determining whether such an interest is material to an individual, the combined net worth of the individual and the individual's immediate family members may be taken into account.

Financial interests

290.102 Holding a financial interest in an audit client may create a self-interest threat. The existence and significance of any threat created depends on:

(a)   The role of the person holding the financial interest

(b)   Whether the financial interest is direct or indirect, and

(c)   The materiality of the financial interest.

290.103 Financial interests may be held through an intermediary (for example, a collective investment vehicle, estate or trust). The determination of whether such financial interests are direct or indirect will depend upon whether the beneficial owner has control over the investment vehicle or the ability to influence its investment decisions. When control over the investment vehicle or the ability to influence investment decisions exists, this Code defines that financial interest to be a direct financial interest.

Conversely, when the beneficial owner of the financial interest has no control over the investment vehicle or ability to influence its investment decisions, this Code defines that financial interest to be an indirect financial interest.

290.104 If a member of the audit team, a member of that individual's immediate family, or a firm has a direct financial interest or a material indirect financial interest in the audit client, the self-interest threat created would be so significant that no safeguards could reduce the threat to an acceptable level. Therefore, none of the following shall have a direct financial interest or a material indirect financial interest in the client: a member of the audit team; a member of that individual's immediate family; or the firm.

290.105 When a member of the audit team has a close family member who the audit team member knows has a direct financial interest or a material indirect financial interest in the audit client, a self-interest threat is created. The significance of the threat will depend on factors such as:

•   The nature of the relationship between the member of the audit team and the close family member; and

•   The materiality of the financial interest to the close family member.

The significance of the threat shall be evaluated and safeguards applied when necessary to eliminate the threat or reduce it to an acceptable level. Examples of such safeguards include:

- The close family member disposing, as soon as practicable, of all of the financial interest or disposing of a sufficient portion of an indirect financial interest so that the remaining interest is no longer material

- Having a professional accountant review the work of the member of the audit team; or

- Removing the individual from the audit team.

290.106 If a member of the audit team, a member of that individual's immediate family, or a firm has a direct or material indirect financial interest in an entity that has a controlling interest in the audit client, and the client is material to the entity, the self-interest threat created would be so significant that no safeguards could reduce the threat to an acceptable level. Therefore, none of the following shall have such a financial interest: a member of the audit team; a member of that individual's immediate family; and the firm.

290.107 The holding by a firm's retirement benefit plan of a direct or material indirect financial interest in an audit client creates a self-interest threat. The significance of the threat shall be evaluated and safeguards applied when necessary to eliminate the threat or reduce it to an acceptable level.

290.108 If other partners in the office in which the engagement partner practices in connection with the audit engagement, or their immediate family members, hold a direct financial interest or a material indirect financial interest in that audit client, the self-interest threat created would be so significant that no safeguards could reduce the threat to an acceptable level. Therefore, neither such partners nor their immediate family members shall hold any such financial interests in such an audit client.

290.109 The office in which the engagement partner practices in connection with the audit engagement is not necessarily the office to which that partner is assigned. Accordingly, when the engagement partner is located in a different office from that of the other members of the audit team, professional judgement shall be used to determine in which office the partner practices in connection with that engagement.

290.110 If other partners and managerial employees who provide non-audit services to the audit client, except those whose involvement is minimal, or their immediate family members, hold a direct financial interest or a material indirect financial interest in the audit client, the self-interest threat created would be so significant that no safeguards could reduce the threat to an acceptable level. Accordingly, neither such personnel nor their immediate family members shall hold any such financial interests in such an audit client.

290.111 Despite paragraphs 290.108 and 290.110, the holding of a financial interest in an audit client by an immediate family member of:

(a)   A partner located in the office in which the engagement partner practices in connection with the audit engagement, or

(b)   A partner or managerial employee who provides non-audit services to the audit client, is deemed not to compromise independence if the financial interest is received as a result of the immediate family member's employment rights (for example, through pension or share option plans) and, when necessary, safeguards are applied to eliminate any threat to independence or reduce it to an acceptable level. However, when the immediate family member has or obtains the right to dispose of the financial interest or, in the case of a stock option, the right to exercise the option, the financial interest shall be disposed of or forfeited as soon as practicable.

290.112 A self-interest threat may be created if the firm or a member of the audit team, or a member of that individual's immediate family, has a financial interest in an entity and an audit client also has a financial interest in that entity. However, independence is deemed not to be compromised if these interests are immaterial and the audit client cannot exercise significant influence over the entity. If such interest is material to any party, and the audit client can exercise significant influence over the other entity, no safeguards could reduce the threat to an acceptable level. Accordingly, the firm shall not have such an interest and any individual with such an interest shall, before becoming a member of the audit team, either:

(a)   Dispose of the interest; or

(b)   Dispose of a sufficient amount of the interest so that the remaining interest is no longer material.

290.113 A self-interest, familiarity or intimidation threat may be created if a member of the audit team, or a member of that individual's immediate family, or the firm, has a financial interest in an entity when a director, officer or controlling owner of the audit client is also known to have a financial interest in that entity. The existence and significance of any threat will depend upon factors such as:

- The role of the professional on the audit team

- Whether ownership of the entity is closely or widely held

- Whether the interest gives the investor the ability to control or significantly influence the entity; and

- The materiality of the financial interest.

The significance of any threat shall be evaluated and safeguards applied when necessary to eliminate the threat or reduce it to an acceptable level. Examples of such safeguards include:

- Removing the member of the audit team with the financial interest from the audit team; or

- Having a professional accountant review the work of the member of the audit team.

290.114 The holding by a firm, or a member of the audit team, or a member of that individual's immediate family, of a direct financial interest or a material indirect financial interest in the audit client as a trustee creates a self-interest threat. Similarly, a self-interest threat is created when:

(a) A partner in the office in which the engagement partner practices in connection with the audit

(b) Other partners and managerial employees who provide non-assurance services to the audit client, except those whose involvement is minimal; or

(c) Their immediate family members, hold a direct financial interest or a material indirect financial interest in the audit client as trustee. Such an interest shall not be held unless:

- Neither the trustee, nor an immediate family member of the trustee, nor the firm are beneficiaries of the trust

- The interest in the audit client held by the trust is not material to the trust

- The trust is not able to exercise significant influence over the audit client; and

- The trustee, an immediate family member of the trustee, or the firm cannot significantly influence any investment decision involving a financial interest in the audit client.

290.115 Members of the audit team shall determine whether a self-interest threat is created by any known financial interests in the audit client held by other individuals including:

(a) Partners and professional employees of the firm, other than those referred to above, or their immediate family members; and

(b) Individuals with a close personal relationship with a member of the audit team.

Whether these interests create a self-interest threat will depend on factors such as:

- The firm's organisational, operating and reporting structure; and

- The nature of the relationship between the individual and the member of the audit team.

The significance of any threat shall be evaluated and safeguards applied when necessary to eliminate the threat or reduce it to an acceptable level. Examples of such safeguards include:

- Removing the member of the audit team with the personal relationship from the audit team

- Excluding the member of the audit team from any significant decision-making concerning the audit engagement; or

- Having a professional accountant review the work of the member of the audit team.

290.116 If a firm or a partner or employee of the firm, or a member of that individual's immediate family, receives a direct financial interest or a material indirect financial interest in an audit client, for example, by way of an inheritance, gift or as a result of a merger and such interest would not be permitted to be held under this section, then:

(a) If the interest is received by the firm, the financial interest shall be disposed of immediately, or a sufficient amount of an indirect financial interest shall be disposed of so that the remaining interest is no longer material

(b) If the interest is received by a member of the audit team, or a member of that individual's immediate family, the individual who received the financial interest shall immediately dispose of the financial interest, or dispose of a sufficient amount of an indirect financial interest so that the remaining interest is no longer material; or

(c) If the interest is received by an individual who is not a member of the audit team, or by an immediate family member of the individual, the financial interest shall be disposed of as soon as possible, or a sufficient amount of an indirect financial interest shall be disposed of so that the remaining interest is no longer material. Pending the disposal of the financial interest, a determination shall be made as to whether any safeguards are necessary.

290.117 When an inadvertent violation of this section as it relates to a financial interest in an audit client occurs, it is deemed not to compromise independence if:

(a)   The firm has established policies and procedures that require prompt notification to the firm of any breaches resulting from the purchase, inheritance or other acquisition of a financial interest in the audit client

(b)   The actions in paragraph 290.116 (a)–(c) are taken as applicable; and

(c)   The firm applies other safeguards when necessary to reduce any remaining threat to an acceptable level. Examples of such safeguards include:

–   Having a professional accountant review the work of the member of the audit team; or

–   Excluding the individual from any significant decision-making concerning the audit engagement.

The firm shall determine whether to discuss the matter with those charged with governance.

Loans and Guarantees

290.118 A loan, or a guarantee of a loan, to a member of the audit team, or a member of that individual's immediate family, or the firm from an audit client that is a bank or a similar institution may create a threat to independence. If the loan or guarantee is not made under normal lending procedures, terms and conditions, a self-interest threat would be created that would be so significant that no safeguards could reduce the threat to an acceptable level. Accordingly, neither a member of the audit team, a member of that individual's immediate family, nor a firm shall accept such a loan or guarantee.

290.119 If a loan to a firm from an audit client that is a bank or similar institution is made under normal lending procedures, terms and conditions and it is material to the audit client or firm receiving the loan, it may be possible to apply safeguards to reduce the self-interest threat to an acceptable level. An example of such a safeguard is having the work reviewed by a professional accountant from a network firm that is neither involved with the audit nor received the loan.

290.120 A loan, or a guarantee of a loan, from an audit client that is a bank or a similar institution to a member of the audit team, or a member of that individual's immediate family, does not create a threat to independence if the loan or guarantee is made under normal lending procedures, terms and conditions. Examples of such loans include home mortgages, bank overdrafts, car loans and credit card balances.

290.121 If the firm or a member of the audit team, or a member of that individual's immediate family, accepts a loan from, or has a borrowing guaranteed by, an audit client that is not a bank or similar institution, the self-interest threat created would be so significant that no safeguards could reduce the threat to an acceptable level, unless the loan or guarantee is immaterial to both (a) the firm or the member of the audit team and the immediate family member, and (b) the client.

290.122 Similarly, if the firm or a member of the audit team, or a member of that individual's immediate family, makes or guarantees a loan to an audit client, the self-interest threat created would be so significant that no safeguards could reduce the threat to an acceptable level, unless the loan or guarantee is immaterial to both (a) the firm or the member of the audit team and the immediate family member, and (b) the client.

290.123 If a firm or a member of the audit team, or a member of that individual's immediate family, has deposits or a brokerage account with an audit client that is a bank, broker or similar institution, a threat to independence is not created if the deposit or account is held under normal commercial terms.

Business relationships

290.124 A close business relationship between a firm, or a member of the audit team, or a member of that individual's immediate family, and the audit client or its management, arises from a commercial relationship or common financial interest and may create self-interest or intimidation threats. Examples of such relationships include:

(a) Having a financial interest in a joint venture with either the client or a controlling owner, director, officer or other individual who performs senior managerial activities for that client.

(b) Arrangements to combine one or more services or products of the firm with one or more services or products of the client and to market the package with reference to both parties.

(c) Distribution or marketing arrangements under which the firm distributes or markets the client's products or services, or the client distributes or markets the firm's products or services.

Unless any financial interest is immaterial and the business relationship is insignificant to the firm and the client or its management, the threat created would be so significant that no safeguards could reduce the threat to an acceptable level. Therefore, unless the financial interest is immaterial and the business relationship is insignificant, the business relationship shall not be entered into, or it shall be reduced to an insignificant level or terminated.

In the case of a member of the audit team, unless any such financial interest is immaterial and the relationship is insignificant to that member, the individual shall be removed from the audit team. If the business relationship is between an immediate family member of a member of the audit team and the audit client or its management, the significance of any threat shall be evaluated and safeguards applied when necessary to eliminate the threat or reduce it to an acceptable level.

290.125 A business relationship involving the holding of an interest by the firm, or a member of the audit team, or a member of that individual's immediate family, in a closely-held entity when the audit client or a director or officer of the client, or any group thereof, also holds an interest in that entity does not create threats to independence if:

(a)   The business relationship is insignificant to the firm, the member of the audit team and the immediate family member, and the client

(b)   The financial interest is immaterial to the investor or group of investors; and

(c)   The financial interest does not give the investor, or group of investors, the ability to control the closely-held entity.

290.126 The purchase of goods and services from an audit client by the firm, or a member of the audit team, or a member of that individual's immediate family, does not generally create a threat to independence if the transaction is in the normal course of business and at arm's length. However, such transactions may be of such a nature or magnitude that they create a self-interest threat. The significance of any threat shall be evaluated and safeguards applied when necessary to eliminate the threat or reduce it to an acceptable level. Examples of such safeguards include:

(a)   Eliminating or reducing the magnitude of the transaction; or

(b)   Removing the individual from the audit team.

Family and personal relationships

290.127 Family and personal relationships between a member of the audit team and a director or officer or certain employees (depending on their role) of the audit client may create self-interest, familiarity or intimidation threats. The existence and significance of any threats will depend on a number of factors, including the individual's responsibilities on the audit team, the role of the family member or other individual within the client and the closeness of the relationship.

290.128 When an immediate family member of a member of the audit team is:

(a)   a director or officer of the audit client; or

(b)   an employee in a position to exert significant influence over the preparation of the client's accounting records or the financial statements on which the firm will express an opinion, or was in such a position during any period covered by the engagement or the financial statements, the threats to independence can only be reduced to an acceptable level by removing the individual from the audit team. The closeness of the relationship is such that no other safeguards could reduce the threat to an acceptable level. Accordingly, no individual who has such a relationship shall be a member of the audit team.

290.129 Threats to independence are created when an immediate family member of a member of the audit team is an employee in a position to exert significant influence over the client's financial position, financial performance or cash flows. The significance of the threats will depend on factors such as:

- The position held by the immediate family member; and
- The role of the professional on the audit team.

The significance of the threat shall be evaluated and safeguards applied when necessary to eliminate the threat or reduce it to an acceptable level. Examples of such safeguards include:

- Removing the individual from the audit team; or
- Structuring the responsibilities of the audit team so that the professional does not deal with matters that are within the responsibility of the immediate family member.

290.130 Threats to independence are created when a close family member of a member of the audit team is:

(a)   A director or officer of the audit client; or

(b)   An employee in a position to exert significant influence over the preparation of the client's accounting records or the financial statements on which the firm will express an opinion.

The significance of the threats will depend on factors such as:

- The nature of the relationship between the member of the audit team and the close family member
- The position held by the close family member; and
- The role of the professional on the audit team.

The significance of the threat shall be evaluated and safeguards applied when necessary to eliminate the threat or reduce it to an acceptable level. Examples of such safeguards include:

- Removing the individual from the audit team; or

- Structuring the responsibilities of the audit team so that the professional does not deal with matters that are within the responsibility of the close family member.

290.131 Threats to independence are created when a member of the audit team has a close relationship with a person who is not an immediate or close family member, but who is a director or officer or an employee in a position to exert significant influence over the preparation of the client's accounting records or the financial statements on which the firm will express an opinion. A member of the audit team who has such a relationship shall consult in accordance with firm policies and procedures. The significance of the threats will depend on factors such as:

- The nature of the relationship between the individual and the member of the audit team

- The position the individual holds with the client; and

- The role of the professional on the audit team.

The significance of the threats shall be evaluated and safeguards applied when necessary to eliminate the threats or reduce them to an acceptable level. Examples of such safeguards include:

- Removing the professional from the audit team; or

- Structuring the responsibilities of the audit team so that the professional does not deal with matters that are within the responsibility of the individual with whom the professional has a close relationship.

290.132 Self-interest, familiarity or intimidation threats may be created by a personal or family relationship between (a) a partner or employee of the firm who is not a member of the audit team and (b) a director or officer of the audit client or an employee in a position to exert significant influence over the preparation of the client's accounting records or the financial statements on which the firm will express an opinion. Partners and employees of the firm who are aware of such relationships shall consult in accordance with firm policies and procedures. The existence and significance of any threat will depend on factors such as:

- The nature of the relationship between the partner or employee of the firm and the director or officer or employee of the client

- The interaction of the partner or employee of the firm with the audit team

- The position of the partner or employee within the firm; and

- The position the individual holds with the client.

The significance of any threat shall be evaluated and safeguards applied when necessary to eliminate the threat or reduce it to an acceptable level. Examples of such safeguards include:

- Structuring the partner's or employee's responsibilities to reduce any potential influence over the audit engagement; or

- Having a professional accountant review the relevant audit work performed.

290.133 When an inadvertent violation of this section as it relates to family and personal relationships occurs, it is deemed not to compromise independence if:

(a) The firm has established policies and procedures that require prompt notification to the firm of any breaches resulting from changes in the employment status of their immediate or close family members or other personal relationships that create threats to independence

(b) The inadvertent violation relates to an immediate family member of a member of the audit team becoming a director or officer of the audit client or being in a position to exert significant influence over the preparation of the client's accounting records or the financial statements on which the firm will express an opinion, and the relevant professional is removed from the audit team; and

(c) The firm applies other safeguards when necessary to reduce any remaining threat to an acceptable level. Examples of such safeguards include:

    (i) Having a professional accountant review the work of the member of the audit team; or

    (ii) Excluding the relevant professional from any significant decision-making concerning the engagement. The firm shall determine whether to discuss the matter with those charged with governance.

Supplementary reading: Annex 1 290.134 to 290.194

Employment with an audit client

290.134 Familiarity or intimidation threats may be created if a director or officer of the audit client, or an employee in a position to exert significant influence over the preparation of the client's accounting records or the financial statements on which the firm will express an opinion, has been a member of the audit team or partner of the firm.

290.135 If a former member of the audit team or partner of the firm has joined the audit client in such a position and a significant connection remains between the firm and the individual, the threat would be so significant that no safeguards could reduce the threat to an acceptable level. Therefore, independence would be deemed to be compromised if a former member of the audit team or partner joins the audit client as a director or officer, or as an employee in a position to exert significant influence over the preparation of the client's accounting records or the financial statements on which the firm will express an opinion, unless:

(a) The individual is not entitled to any benefits or payments from the firm, unless made in accordance with fixed pre-determined arrangements, and any amount owed to the individual is not material to the firm; and

(b) The individual does not continue to participate or appear to participate in the firm's business or professional activities.

290.136 If a former member of the audit team or partner of the firm has joined the audit client in such a position, and no significant connection remains between the firm and the individual, the existence and significance of any familiarity or intimidation threats will depend on factors such as:

- The position the individual has taken at the client

- Any involvement the individual will have with the audit team

- The length of time since the individual was a member of the audit team or partner of the firm; and

- The former position of the individual within the audit team or firm, for example, whether the individual was responsible for maintaining regular contact with the client's management or those charged with governance.

The significance of any threats created shall be evaluated and safeguards applied when necessary to eliminate the threats or reduce them to an acceptable level. Examples of such safeguards include:

- Modifying the audit plan

- Assigning individuals to the audit team who have sufficient experience in relation to the individual who has joined the client; or

- Having a professional accountant review the work of the former member of the audit team.

290.137 If a former partner of the firm has previously joined an entity in such a position and the entity subsequently becomes an audit client of the firm, the significance of any threat to independence shall be evaluated and safeguards applied when necessary to eliminate the threat or reduce it to an acceptable level.

290.138 A self-interest threat is created when a member of the audit team participates in the audit engagement while knowing that the member of the audit team will, or may, join the client sometime in the future. Firm policies and procedures shall require members of an audit team to notify the firm when entering employment negotiations with the client. On receiving such notification, the significance of the threat shall be evaluated and safeguards applied when necessary to eliminate the threat or reduce it to an acceptable level. Examples of such safeguards include:

- Removing the individual from the audit team; or

- A review of any significant judgements made by that individual while on the team.

Audit clients that are public interest entities

290.139 Familiarity or intimidation threats are created when a key audit partner joins the audit client that is a public interest entity as:

(a) A director or officer of the entity; or

(b) An employee in a position to exert significant influence over the preparation of the client's accounting records or the financial statements on which the firm will express an opinion.

Independence would be deemed to be compromised unless, subsequent to the partner ceasing to be a key audit partner, the public interest entity had issued audited financial statements covering a period of not less than twelve months and the partner was not a member of the audit team with respect to the audit of those financial statements.

290.140 An intimidation threat is created when the individual who was the firm's Senior or Managing Partner (Chief Executive or equivalent) joins an audit client that is a public interest entity as:

(a)   An employee in a position to exert significant influence over the preparation of the entity's accounting records or its financial statements; or

(b)   A director or officer of the entity. Independence would be deemed to be compromised unless twelve months have passed since the individual was the Senior or Managing Partner (Chief Executive or equivalent) of the firm.

290.141 Independence is deemed not to be compromised if, as a result of a business combination, a former key audit partner or the individual who was the firm's former Senior or Managing Partner is in a position as described in paragraphs 290.139 and 290.140, and:

(a)   The position was not taken in contemplation of the business combination

(b)   Any benefits or payments due to the former partner from the firm have been settled in full, unless made in accordance with fixed predetermined arrangements and any amount owed to the partner is not material to the firm

(c)   The former partner does not continue to participate or appear to participate in the firm's business or professional activities; and

(d)   The position held by the former partner with the audit client is discussed with those charged with governance.

Temporary staff assignments

290.142 The lending of staff by a firm to an audit client may create a self-review threat. Such assistance may be given, but only for a short period of time and the firm's personnel shall not be involved in:

(a)   Providing non-assurance services that would not be permitted under this section; or

(b)   Assuming management responsibilities.

In all circumstances, the audit client shall be responsible for directing and supervising the activities of the loaned staff. The significance of any threat shall be evaluated and safeguards applied when necessary to eliminate the threat or reduce it to an acceptable level. Examples of such safeguards include:

- Conducting an additional review of the work performed by the loaned staff

- Not giving the loaned staff audit responsibility for any function or activity that the staff performed during the temporary staff assignment; or

- Not including the loaned staff as a member of the audit team.

Recent service with an audit client

290.143 Self-interest, self-review or familiarity threats may be created if a member of the audit team has recently served as a director, officer, or employee of the audit client. This would be the case when, for example, a member of the audit team has to evaluate elements of the financial statements for which the member of the audit team had prepared the accounting records while with the client.

290.144 If, during the period covered by the audit report, a member of the audit team had served as a director or officer of the audit client, or was an employee in a position to exert significant influence over the preparation of the client's accounting records or the financial statements on which the firm will express an opinion, the threat created would be so significant that no safeguards could reduce the threat to an acceptable level. Consequently, such individuals shall not be assigned to the audit team.

290.145 Self-interest, self-review or familiarity threats may be created if, before the period covered by the audit report, a member of the audit team had served as a director or officer of the audit client, or was an employee in a position to exert significant influence over the preparation of the client's accounting records or financial statements on which the firm will express an opinion. For example, such threats would be created if a decision made or work performed by the individual in the prior period, while employed by the client, is to be evaluated in the current period as part of the current audit engagement. The existence and significance of any threats will depend on factors such as:

- The position the individual held with the client

- The length of time since the individual left the client; and

- The role of the professional on the audit team.

The significance of any threat shall be evaluated and safeguards applied when necessary to reduce the threat to an acceptable level. An example of such a safeguard is conducting a review of the work performed by the individual as a member of the audit team.

Serving as a Director or Officer of an audit client

290.146 If a partner or employee of the firm serves as a director or officer of an audit client, the self-review and self-interest threats created would be so significant that no safeguards could reduce the threats to an acceptable level. Accordingly, no partner or employee shall serve as a director or officer of an audit client.

290.147 The position of Company Secretary has different implications in different jurisdictions. Duties may range from administrative duties, such as personnel management and the maintenance of company records and registers, to duties as diverse as ensuring that the company complies with regulations or providing advice on corporate governance matters. Generally, this position is seen to imply a close association with the entity.

290.148 If a partner or employee of the firm serves as Company Secretary for an audit client, self-review and advocacy threats are created that would generally be so significant that no safeguards could reduce the threats to an acceptable level. Despite paragraph 290.146, when this practice is specifically permitted under local law, professional rules or practice, and provided management makes all relevant decisions, the duties and activities shall be limited to those of a routine and administrative nature, such as preparing minutes and maintaining statutory returns. In those circumstances, the significance of any threats shall be evaluated and safeguards applied when necessary to eliminate the threats or reduce them to an acceptable level.

290.149 Performing routine administrative services to support a company secretarial function or providing advice in relation to company secretarial administration matters does not generally create threats to independence, as long as client management makes all relevant decisions.

Long association of senior personnel (including partner rotation) with an audit client

General provisions

290.150 Familiarity and self-interest threats are created by using the same senior personnel on an audit engagement over a long period of time. The significance of the threats will depend on factors such as:

- How long the individual has been a member of the audit team

- The role of the individual on the audit team

- The structure of the firm

- The nature of the audit engagement

- Whether the client's management team has changed; and

- Whether the nature or complexity of the client's accounting and reporting issues has changed.

The significance of the threats shall be evaluated and safeguards applied when necessary to eliminate the threats or reduce them to an acceptable level. Examples of such safeguards include:

- Rotating the senior personnel off the audit team

- Having a professional accountant who was not a member of the audit team review the work of the senior personnel; or

- Regular independent internal or external quality reviews of the engagement.

Audit clients that are public interest entities

290.151 In respect of an audit of a public interest entity, an individual shall not be a key audit partner for more than seven years. After such time, the individual shall not be a member of the engagement team or be a key audit partner for the client for two years. During that period, the individual shall not participate in the audit of the entity, provide quality control for the engagement, consult with the engagement team or the client regarding technical or industry-specific issues, transactions or events or otherwise directly influence the outcome of the engagement.

290.152 Despite paragraph 290.151, key audit partners whose continuity is especially important to audit quality may, in rare cases due to unforeseen circumstances outside the firm's control, be permitted an additional year on the audit team as long as the threat to independence can be eliminated or reduced to an acceptable level by applying safeguards. For example, a key audit partner may remain on the audit team for up to one additional year in circumstances where, due to unforeseen events, a required rotation was not possible, as might be the case due to serious illness of the intended engagement partner.

290.153 The long association of other partners with an audit client that is a public interest entity creates familiarity and self-interest threats. The significance of the threats will depend on factors such as:

- How long any such partner has been associated with the audit client

- The role, if any, of the individual on the audit team; and

- The nature, frequency and extent of the individual's interactions with the client's management or those charged with governance.

The significance of the threats shall be evaluated and safeguards applied when necessary to eliminate the threats or reduce them to an acceptable level. Examples of such safeguards include:

- Rotating the partner off the audit team or otherwise ending the partner's association with the audit client; or

- Regular independent internal or external quality reviews of the engagement.

290.154 When an audit client becomes a public interest entity, the length of time the individual has served the audit client as a key audit partner before the client becomes a public interest entity shall be taken into account in determining the timing of the rotation. If the individual has served the audit client as a key audit partner for five years or less when the client becomes a public interest entity, the number of years the individual may continue to serve the client in that capacity before rotating off the engagement is seven years less the number of years already served. If the individual has served the audit client as a key audit partner for six or more years when the client becomes a public interest entity, the partner may continue to serve in that capacity for a maximum of two additional years before rotating off the engagement.

290.155 When a firm has only a few people with the necessary knowledge and experience to serve as a key audit partner on the audit of a public interest entity, rotation of key audit partners may not be an available safeguard. If an independent regulator in the relevant jurisdiction has provided an exemption from partner rotation in such circumstances, an individual may remain a key audit partner for more than seven years, in accordance with such regulation, provided that the independent regulator has specified alternative safeguards which are applied, such as a regular independent external review.

Provision of non-assurance services to audit clients

290.156 Firms have traditionally provided to their audit clients a range of non-assurance services that are consistent with their skills and expertise. Providing non-assurance services may, however, create threats to the independence of the firm or members of the audit team. The threats created are most often self-review, self-interest and advocacy threats.

290.157 New developments in business, the evolution of financial markets and changes in information technology make it impossible to draw up an all-inclusive list of non-assurance services that might be provided to an audit client. When specific guidance on a particular non-assurance service is not included in this section, the conceptual framework shall be applied when evaluating the particular circumstances.

290.158 Before the firm accepts an engagement to provide a non-assurance service to an audit client, a determination shall be made as to whether providing such a service would create a threat to independence. In evaluating the significance of any threat created by a particular non-assurance service, consideration shall be given to any threat that the audit team has reason to believe is created by providing other related non-assurance services. If a threat is created that cannot be reduced to an acceptable level by the application of safeguards, the non-assurance service shall not be provided.

290.159 Providing certain non-assurance services to an audit client may create a threat to independence so significant that no safeguards could reduce the threat to an acceptable level. However, the inadvertent provision of such a service to a related entity, division or in respect of a discrete financial statement item of such a client will be deemed not to compromise independence if any threats have been reduced to an acceptable level by arrangements for that related entity, division or discrete financial statement item to be audited by another firm or when another firm re-performs the non-assurance service to the extent necessary to enable it to take responsibility for that service.

290.160 A firm may provide non-assurance services that would otherwise be restricted under this section to the following related entities of the audit client:

(a) An entity, which is not an audit client, that has direct or indirect control over the audit client

(b) An entity, which is not an audit client, with a direct financial interest in the client if that entity has significant influence over the client and the interest in the client is material to such entity; or

(c) An entity, which is not an audit client, that is under common control with the audit client, if it is reasonable to conclude that (a) the services do not create a self-review threat because the results of the services will not be subject to audit procedures and (b) any threats that are created by the provision of such services are eliminated or reduced to an acceptable level by the application of safeguards.

290.161 A non-assurance service provided to an audit client does not compromise the firm's independence when the client becomes a public interest entity if:

(a) The previous non-assurance service complies with the provisions of this section that relate to audit clients that are not public interest entities

(b) Services that are not permitted under this section for audit clients that are public interest entities are terminated before or as soon as practicable after the client becomes a public interest entity; and

(c) The firm applies safeguards when necessary to eliminate or reduce to an acceptable level any threats to independence arising from the service.

Management responsibilities

290.162 Management of an entity performs many activities in managing the entity in the best interests of stakeholders of the entity. It is not possible to specify every activity that is a management responsibility. However, management responsibilities involve leading and directing an entity, including making significant decisions regarding the acquisition, deployment and control of human, financial, physical and intangible resources.

290.163 Whether an activity is a management responsibility depends on the circumstances and requires the exercise of judgement. Examples of activities that would generally be considered a management responsibility include:

- Setting policies and strategic direction

- Directing and taking responsibility for the actions of the entity's employees

- Authorising transactions

- Deciding which recommendations of the firm or other third parties to implement

- Taking responsibility for the preparation and fair presentation of the financial statements in accordance with the applicable financial reporting framework; and

- Taking responsibility for designing, implementing and maintaining internal control.

290.164 Activities that are routine and administrative, or involve matters that are insignificant, generally are deemed not to be a management responsibility. For example, executing an insignificant transaction that has been authorised by management or monitoring the dates for filing statutory returns and advising an audit client of those dates is deemed not to be a management responsibility. Further, providing advice and recommendations to assist management in discharging its responsibilities is not assuming a management responsibility.

290.165 If a firm were to assume a management responsibility for an audit client, the threats created would be so significant that no safeguards could reduce the threats to an acceptable level. For example, deciding which recommendations of the firm to implement will create self-review and self-interest threats. Further, assuming a management responsibility creates a familiarity threat because the firm becomes too closely aligned with the views and interests of management. Therefore, the firm shall not assume a management responsibility for an audit client.

290.166 To avoid the risk of assuming a management responsibility when providing non-assurance services to an audit client, the firm shall be satisfied that a member of management is responsible for making the significant judgements and decisions that are the proper responsibility of management, evaluating the results of the service and accepting responsibility for the actions to be taken arising from the results of the service. This reduces the risk of the firm inadvertently making any significant judgements or decisions on behalf of management. The risk is further reduced when the firm gives the client the opportunity to make judgements and decisions based on an objective and transparent analysis and presentation of the issues.

Preparing accounting records and financial statements

General provisions

290.167 Management is responsible for the preparation and fair presentation of the financial statements in accordance with the applicable financial reporting framework. These responsibilities include:

- Originating or changing journal entries, or determining the account classifications of transactions; and

- Preparing or changing source documents or originating data, in electronic or other form, evidencing the occurrence of a transaction (for example, purchase orders, payroll time records, and customer orders).

290.168 Providing an audit client with accounting and bookkeeping services, such as preparing accounting records or financial statements, creates a self-review threat when the firm subsequently audits the financial statements.

290.169 The audit process, however, necessitates dialogue between the firm and management of the audit client, which may involve:

- The application of accounting standards or policies and financial statement disclosure requirements

- The appropriateness of financial and accounting control and the methods used in determining the stated amounts of assets and liabilities; or

- Proposing adjusting journal entries. These activities are considered to be a normal part of the audit process and do not, generally, create threats to independence.

290.170 Similarly, the client may request technical assistance from the firm on matters such as resolving account reconciliation problems or analysing and accumulating information for regulatory reporting. In addition, the client may request technical advice on accounting issues such as the conversion of existing financial statements from one financial reporting framework to another (for example, to comply with group accounting policies or to transition to a different financial reporting framework such as International Financial Reporting Standards). Such services do not, generally, create threats to independence provided the firm does not assume a management responsibility for the client.

Audit clients that are not public interest entities

290.171 The firm may provide services related to the preparation of accounting records and financial statements to an audit client that is not a public interest entity where the services are of a routine or mechanical nature, so long as any self-review threat created is reduced to an acceptable level. Examples of such services include:

- Providing payroll services based on client-originated data

- Recording transactions for which the client has determined or approved the appropriate account classification

- Posting transactions coded by the client to the general ledger

- Posting client-approved entries to the trial balance; and

- Preparing financial statements based on information in the trial balance.

In all cases, the significance of any threat created shall be evaluated and safeguards applied when necessary to eliminate the threat or reduce it to an acceptable level. Examples of such safeguards include:

- Arranging for such services to be performed by an individual who is not a member of the audit team; or

- If such services are performed by a member of the audit team, using a partner or senior staff member with appropriate expertise who is not a member of the audit team to review the work performed.

Audit clients that are public interest entities

290.172 Except in emergency situations, a firm shall not provide to an audit client that is a public interest entity accounting and bookkeeping services, including payroll services, or prepare financial statements on which the firm will express an opinion or financial information which forms the basis of the financial statements.

290.173 Despite paragraph 290.172, a firm may provide accounting and bookkeeping services, including payroll services and the preparation of financial statements or other financial information, of a routine or mechanical nature for divisions or related entities of an audit client that is a public interest entity if the personnel providing the services are not members of the audit team and:

(a)   The divisions or related entities for which the service is provided are collectively immaterial to the financial statements on which the firm will express an opinion; or

(b)   The services relate to matters that are collectively immaterial to the financial statements of the division or related entity.

Emergency situations

290.174 Accounting and bookkeeping services, which would otherwise not be permitted under this section, may be provided to audit clients in emergency or other unusual situations when it is impractical for the audit client to make other arrangements. This may be the case when (a) only the firm has the resources and necessary knowledge of the client's systems and procedures to assist the client in the timely preparation of its accounting records and financial statements, and (b) a restriction on the firm's ability to provide the services would result in significant difficulties for the client (for example, as might result from a failure to meet regulatory reporting requirements). In such situations, the following conditions shall be met:

(a)   Those who provide the services are not members of the audit team

(b)   The services are provided for only a short period of time and are not expected to recur; and

(c)   The situation is discussed with those charged with governance.

Valuation services

General provisions

290.175 A valuation comprises the making of assumptions with regard to future developments, the application of appropriate methodologies and techniques, and the combination of both to compute a certain value, or range of values, for an asset, a liability or for a business as a whole.

290.176 Performing valuation services for an audit client may create a self-review threat. The existence and significance of any threat will depend on factors such as:

- Whether the valuation will have a material effect on the financial statements.

- The extent of the client's involvement in determining and approving the valuation methodology and other significant matters of judgement.

- The availability of established methodologies and professional guidelines.

- For valuations involving standard or established methodologies, the degree of subjectivity inherent in the item.

- The reliability and extent of the underlying data.

- The degree of dependence on future events of a nature that could create significant volatility inherent in the amounts involved.

- The extent and clarity of the disclosures in the financial statements.

The significance of any threat created shall be evaluated and safeguards applied when necessary to eliminate the threat or reduce it to an acceptable level. Examples of such safeguards include:

- Having a professional who was not involved in providing the valuation service review the audit or valuation work performed; or

- Making arrangements so that personnel providing such services do not participate in the audit engagement.

290.177 Certain valuations do not involve a significant degree of subjectivity. This is likely the case where the underlying assumptions are either established by law or regulation, or are widely accepted and when the techniques and methodologies to be used are based on generally accepted standards or prescribed by law or regulation. In such circumstances, the results of a valuation performed by two or more parties are not likely to be materially different.

290.178 If a firm is requested to perform a valuation to assist an audit client with its tax reporting obligations or for tax planning purposes and the results of the valuation will not have a direct effect on the financial statements, the provisions included in paragraph 290.191 apply. Audit clients that are not public interest entities.

290.179 In the case of an audit client that is not a public interest entity, if the valuation service has a material effect on the financial statements on which the firm will express an opinion and the valuation involves a significant degree of subjectivity, no safeguards could reduce the self-review threat to an acceptable level. Accordingly a firm shall not provide such a valuation service to an audit client.

Audit clients that are public interest entities

290.180 A firm shall not provide valuation services to an audit client that is a public interest entity if the valuations would have a material effect, separately or in the aggregate, on the financial statements on which the firm will express an opinion.

Taxation services

290.181 Taxation services comprise a broad range of services, including:

- Tax return preparation
- Tax calculations for the purpose of preparing the accounting entries
- Tax planning and other tax advisory services; and
- Assistance in the resolution of tax disputes.

While taxation services provided by a firm to an audit client are addressed separately under each of these broad headings; in practice, these activities are often interrelated.

290.182 Performing certain tax services creates self-review and advocacy threats. The existence and significance of any threats will depend on factors such as:

- The system by which the tax authorities assess and administer the tax in question and the role of the firm in that process
- The complexity of the relevant tax regime and the degree of judgement necessary in applying it
- The particular characteristics of the engagement; and
- The level of tax expertise of the client's employees.

Tax return preparation

290.183 Tax return preparation services involve assisting clients with their tax reporting obligations by drafting and completing information, including the amount of tax due (usually on standardised forms) required to be submitted to the applicable tax authorities. Such services also include advising on the tax return treatment of past transactions and responding on behalf of the audit client to the tax authorities' requests for additional information and analysis (including providing explanations of and technical support for the approach being taken). Tax return preparation services are generally based on historical information and principally involve analysis and presentation of such historical information under existing tax law, including precedents and established practice. Further, the tax returns are subject to whatever review or approval process the tax authority deems appropriate. Accordingly, providing such services does not generally create a threat to independence if management takes responsibility for the returns including any significant judgements made.

Tax calculations for the purpose of preparing accounting entries

Audit clients that are not public interest entities

290.184 Preparing calculations of current and deferred tax liabilities (or assets) for an audit client for the purpose of preparing accounting entries that will be subsequently audited by the firm creates a self-review threat. The significance of the threat will depend on:

(a) The complexity of the relevant tax law and regulation and the degree of judgement necessary in applying them

(b) The level of tax expertise of the client's personnel; and

(c) The materiality of the amounts to the financial statements.

Safeguards shall be applied when necessary to eliminate the threat or reduce it to an acceptable level.

Examples of such safeguards include:

- Using professionals who are not members of the audit team to perform the service

- If the service is performed by a member of the audit team, using a partner or senior staff member with appropriate expertise who is not a member of the audit team to review the tax calculations; or

- Obtaining advice on the service from an external tax professional.

Audit clients that are public interest entities

290.185 Except in emergency situations, in the case of an audit client that is a public interest entity, a firm shall not prepare tax calculations of current and deferred tax liabilities (or assets) for the purpose of preparing accounting entries that are material to the financial statements on which the firm will express an opinion.

290.186 The preparation of calculations of current and deferred tax liabilities (or assets) for an audit client for the purpose of the preparation of accounting entries, which would otherwise not be permitted under this section, may be provided to audit clients in emergency or other unusual situations when it is impractical for the audit client to make other arrangements. This may be the case when (a) only the firm has the resources and necessary knowledge of the client's business to assist the client in the timely preparation of its calculations of current and deferred tax liabilities (or assets), and (b) a restriction on the firm's ability to provide the services would result in significant difficulties for the client (for example, as might result from a failure to meet regulatory reporting requirements). In such situations, the following conditions shall be met:

(a) Those who provide the services are not members of the audit team

(b) The services are provided for only a short period of time and are not expected to recur; and

(c) The situation is discussed with those charged with governance.

Tax planning and other tax advisory services

290.187 Tax planning or other tax advisory services comprise a broad range of services, such as advising the client how to structure its affairs in a tax efficient manner or advising on the application of a new tax law or regulation.

290.188 A self-review threat may be created where the advice will affect matters to be reflected in the financial statements. The existence and significance of any threat will depend on factors such as:

- The degree of subjectivity involved in determining the appropriate treatment for the tax advice in the financial statements

- The extent to which the outcome of the tax advice will have a material effect on the financial statements

- Whether the effectiveness of the tax advice depends on the accounting treatment or presentation in the financial statements and there is doubt as to the appropriateness of the accounting treatment or presentation under the relevant financial reporting framework

- The level of tax expertise of the client's employees

- The extent to which the advice is supported by tax law or regulation, other precedent or established practice; and

- Whether the tax treatment is supported by a private ruling or has otherwise been cleared by the tax authority before the preparation of the financial statements.

For example, providing tax planning and other tax advisory services where the advice is clearly supported by tax authority or other precedent, by established practice or has a basis in tax law that is likely to prevail does not generally create a threat to independence.

290.189 The significance of any threat shall be evaluated and safeguards applied when necessary to eliminate the threat or reduce it to an acceptable level. Examples of such safeguards include:

- Using professionals who are not members of the audit team to perform the service

- Having a tax professional, who was not involved in providing the tax service, advise the audit team on the service and review the financial statement treatment

- Obtaining advice on the service from an external tax professional; or

- Obtaining pre-clearance or advice from the tax authorities.

290.190 Where the effectiveness of the tax advice depends on a particular accounting treatment or presentation in the financial statements and:

- The audit team has reasonable doubt as to the appropriateness of the related accounting treatment or presentation under the relevant financial reporting framework; and

- The outcome or consequences of the tax advice will have a material effect on the financial statements on which the firm will express an opinion.

The self-review threat would be so significant that no safeguards could reduce the threat to an acceptable level. Accordingly, a firm shall not provide such tax advice to an audit client.

290.191 In providing tax services to an audit client, a firm may be requested to perform a valuation to assist the client with its tax reporting obligations or for tax planning purposes. Where the result of the valuation will have a direct effect on the financial statements, the provisions included in paragraphs 290.175 to 290.180 relating to valuation services are applicable.

Where the valuation is performed for tax purposes only and the result of the valuation will not have a direct effect on the financial statements (that is, the financial statements are only affected through accounting entries related to tax), this would not generally create threats to independence if such effect on the financial statements is immaterial or if the valuation is subject to external review by a tax authority or similar regulatory authority. If the valuation is not subject to such an external review and the effect is material to the financial statements, the existence and significance of any threat created will depend upon factors such as:

- The extent to which the valuation methodology is supported by tax law or regulation, other precedent or established practice and the degree of subjectivity inherent in the valuation.

- The reliability and extent of the underlying data.

The significance of any threat created shall be evaluated and safeguards applied when necessary to eliminate the threat or reduce it to an acceptable level. Examples of such safeguards include:

- Using professionals who are not members of the audit team to perform the service

- Having a professional review the audit work or the result of the tax service; or

- Obtaining pre-clearance or advice from the tax authorities.

Assistance in the resolution of tax disputes

290.192 An advocacy or self-review threat may be created when the firm represents an audit client in the resolution of a tax dispute once the tax authorities have notified the client that they have rejected the client's arguments on a particular issue and either the tax authority or the client is referring the matter for determination in a formal proceeding, for example before a tribunal or court. The existence and significance of any threat will depend on factors such as:

- Whether the firm has provided the advice which is the subject of the tax dispute

- The extent to which the outcome of the dispute will have a material effect on the financial statements on which the firm will express an opinion

- The extent to which the matter is supported by tax law or regulation, other precedent, or established practice

- Whether the proceedings are conducted in public; and

- The role management plays in the resolution of the dispute.

The significance of any threat created shall be evaluated and safeguards applied when necessary to eliminate the threat or reduce it to an acceptable level. Examples of such safeguards include:

- Using professionals who are not members of the audit team to perform the service

- Having a tax professional, who was not involved in providing the tax service, advise the audit team on the services and review the financial statement treatment; or

- Obtaining advice on the service from an external tax professional.

290.193 Where the taxation services involve acting as an advocate for an audit client before a public tribunal or court in the resolution of a tax matter and the amounts involved are material to the financial statements on which the firm will express an opinion, the advocacy threat created would be so significant that no safeguards could eliminate or reduce the threat to an acceptable level. Therefore, the firm shall not perform this type of service for an audit client. What constitutes a 'public tribunal or court' shall be determined according to how tax proceedings are heard in the particular jurisdiction.

290.194 The firm is not, however, precluded from having a continuing advisory role (for example, responding to specific requests for information, providing factual accounts or testimony about the work performed or assisting the client in analysing the tax issues) for the audit client in relation to the matter that is being heard before a public tribunal or court.

Supplementary reading: Annex 1 290.195 to 290.222

Internal audit services

General provisions

290.195 The scope and objectives of internal audit activities vary widely and depend on the size and structure of the entity and the requirements of management and those charged with governance. Internal audit activities may include:

- Monitoring of internal control – reviewing controls, monitoring their operation and recommending improvements thereto

- Examination of financial and operating information – reviewing the means used to identify, measure, classify and report financial and operating information, and specific inquiry into individual items including detailed testing of transactions, balances and procedures

- Review of the economy, efficiency and effectiveness of operating activities including non-financial activities of an entity; and

- Review of compliance with laws, regulations and other external requirements, and with management policies and directives and other internal requirements.

290.196 Internal audit services involve assisting the audit client in the performance of its internal audit activities. The provision of internal audit services to an audit client creates a self-review threat to independence if the firm uses the internal audit work in the course of a subsequent external audit. Performing a significant part of the client's internal audit activities increases the possibility that firm personnel providing internal audit services will assume a management responsibility. If the firm's personnel assume a management responsibility when providing internal audit services to an audit client, the threat created would be so significant that no safeguards could reduce the threat to an acceptable level. Accordingly, a firm's personnel shall not assume a management responsibility when providing internal audit services to an audit client.

290.197 Examples of internal audit services that involve assuming management responsibilities include:

- Setting internal audit policies or the strategic direction of internal audit activities

- Directing and taking responsibility for the actions of the entity's internal audit employees

- Deciding which recommendations resulting from internal audit activities shall be implemented

- Reporting the results of the internal audit activities to those charged with governance on behalf of management

- Performing procedures that form part of the internal control, such as reviewing and approving changes to employee data access privileges

- Taking responsibility for designing, implementing and maintaining internal control; and

- Performing outsourced internal audit services, comprising all or a substantial portion of the internal audit function, where the firm is responsible for determining the scope of the internal audit work and may have responsibility for one or more of the matters noted in (a)–(f).

290.198 To avoid assuming a management responsibility, the firm shall only provide internal audit services to an audit client if it is satisfied that:

(a) The client designates an appropriate and competent resource, preferably within senior management, to be responsible at all times for internal audit activities and to acknowledge responsibility for designing, implementing, and maintaining internal control

(b) The client's management or those charged with governance reviews, assesses and approves the scope, risk and frequency of the internal audit services

(c) The client's management evaluates the adequacy of the internal audit services and the findings resulting from their performance

(d) The client's management evaluates and determines which recommendations resulting from internal audit services to implement and manages the implementation process; and

(e) The client's management reports to those charged with governance the significant findings and recommendations resulting from the internal audit services.

290.199 When a firm uses the work of an internal audit function, ISAs require the performance of procedures to evaluate the adequacy of that work. When a firm accepts an engagement to provide internal audit services to an audit client, and the results of those services will be used in conducting the external audit, a self-review threat is created because of the possibility that the audit team will use the results of the internal audit service without appropriately evaluating those results or exercising the same level of professional scepticism as would be exercised when the internal audit work is performed by individuals who are not members of the firm. The significance of the threat will depend on factors such as:

- The materiality of the related financial statement amounts

- The risk of misstatement of the assertions related to those financial statement amounts; and

- The degree of reliance that will be placed on the internal audit service.

The significance of the threat shall be evaluated and safeguards applied when necessary to eliminate the threat or reduce it to an acceptable level. An example of such a safeguard is using professionals who are not members of the audit team to perform the internal audit service.

Audit clients that are public interest entities

290.200 In the case of an audit client that is a public interest entity, a firm shall not provide internal audit services that relate to:

(a) A significant part of the internal controls over financial reporting

(b) Financial accounting systems that generate information that is, separately or in the aggregate, significant to the client's accounting records or financial statements on which the firm will express an opinion; or

(c) Amounts or disclosures that are, separately or in the aggregate, material to the financial statements on which the firm will express an opinion.

IT systems services

General provisions

290.201 Services related to information technology (IT) systems include the design or implementation of hardware or software systems. The systems may aggregate source data, form part of the internal control over financial reporting or generate information that affects the accounting records or financial statements, or the systems may be unrelated to the audit client's accounting records, the internal control over financial reporting or financial statements. Providing systems services may create a self-review threat depending on the nature of the services and the IT systems.

290.202 The following IT systems services are deemed not to create a threat to independence as long as the firm's personnel do not assume a management responsibility:

(a) Design or implementation of IT systems that are unrelated to internal control over financial reporting

(b) Design or implementation of IT systems that do not generate information forming a significant part of the accounting records or financial statements

(c) Implementation of 'off-the-shelf' accounting or financial information reporting software that was not developed by the firm if the customisation required to meet the client's needs is not significant; and

(d) Evaluating and making recommendations with respect to a system designed, implemented or operated by another service provider or the client.

Audit clients that are not public interest entities

290.203 Providing services to an audit client that is not a public interest entity involving the design or implementation of IT systems that (a) form a significant part of the internal control over financial reporting or (b) generate information that is significant to the client's accounting records or financial statements on which the firm will express an opinion creates a self-review threat.

290.204 The self-review threat is too significant to permit such services unless appropriate safeguards are put in place ensuring that:

(a)   The client acknowledges its responsibility for establishing and monitoring a system of internal controls

(b)   The client assigns the responsibility to make all management decisions with respect to the design and implementation of the hardware or software system to a competent employee, preferably within senior management

(c)   The client makes all management decisions with respect to the design and implementation process

(d)   The client evaluates the adequacy and results of the design and implementation of the system; and

(e)   The client is responsible for operating the system (hardware or software) and for the data it uses or generates.

290.205 Depending on the degree of reliance that will be placed on the particular IT systems as part of the audit, a determination shall be made as to whether to provide such non-assurance services only with personnel who are not members of the audit team and who have different reporting lines within the firm. The significance of any remaining threat shall be evaluated and safeguards applied when necessary to eliminate the threat or reduce it to an acceptable level. An example of such a safeguard is having a professional accountant review the audit or non-assurance work.

Audit clients that are public interest entities

290.206 In the case of an audit client that is a public interest entity, a firm shall not provide services involving the design or implementation of IT systems that (a) form a significant part of the internal control over financial reporting or (b) generate information that is significant to the client's accounting records or financial statements on which the firm will express an opinion.

Litigation support services

290.207 Litigation support services may include activities such as acting as an expert witness, calculating estimated damages or other amounts that might become receivable or payable as the result of litigation or other legal dispute, and assistance with document management and retrieval. These services may create a self-review or advocacy threat.

290.208 If the firm provides a litigation support service to an audit client and the service involves estimating damages or other amounts that affect the financial statements on which the firm will express an opinion, the valuation service provisions included in paragraphs 290.175 to 290.180 shall be followed. In the case of other litigation support services, the significance of any threat created shall be evaluated and safeguards applied when necessary to eliminate the threat or reduce it to an acceptable level.

Legal services

290.209 For the purpose of this section, legal services are defined as any services for which the person providing the services must either be admitted to practice law before the courts of the jurisdiction in which such services are to be provided or have the required legal training to practice law. Such legal services may include, depending on the jurisdiction, a wide and diversified range of areas including both corporate and commercial services to clients, such as contract support, litigation, mergers and acquisition legal advice and support and assistance to clients' internal legal departments. Providing legal services to an entity that is an audit client may create both self-review and advocacy threats.

290.210 Legal services that support an audit client in executing a transaction (for example, contract support, legal advice, legal due diligence and restructuring) may create self-review threats. The existence and significance of any threat will depend on factors such as:

- The nature of the service
- Whether the service is provided by a member of the audit team; and
- The materiality of any matter in relation to the client's financial statements.

The significance of any threat created shall be evaluated and safeguards applied when necessary to eliminate the threat or reduce it to an acceptable level. Examples of such safeguards include:

- Using professionals who are not members of the audit team to perform the service; or
- Having a professional who was not involved in providing the legal services provide advice to the audit team on the service and review any financial statement treatment.

290.211 Acting in an advocacy role for an audit client in resolving a dispute or litigation when the amounts involved are material to the financial statements on which the firm will express an opinion would create advocacy and self-review threats so significant that no safeguards could reduce the threat to an acceptable level. Therefore, the firm shall not perform this type of service for an audit client.

290.212 When a firm is asked to act in an advocacy role for an audit client in resolving a dispute or litigation when the amounts involved are not material to the financial statements on which the firm will express an opinion, the firm shall evaluate the significance of any advocacy and self-review threats created and apply safeguards when necessary to eliminate the threat or reduce it to an acceptable level. Examples of such safeguards include:

- Using professionals who are not members of the audit team to perform the service; or

- Having a professional who was not involved in providing the legal services advise the audit team on the service and review any financial statement treatment.

290.213 The appointment of a partner or an employee of the firm as General Counsel for legal affairs of an audit client would create self-review and advocacy threats that are so significant that no safeguards could reduce the threats to an acceptable level. The position of General Counsel is generally a senior management position with broad responsibility for the legal affairs of a company, and consequently, no member of the firm shall accept such an appointment for an audit client.

Recruiting services

General provisions

290.214 Providing recruiting services to an audit client may create self-interest, familiarity or intimidation threats. The existence and significance of any threat will depend on factors such as:

- The nature of the requested assistance; and

- The role of the person to be recruited.

The significance of any threat created shall be evaluated and safeguards applied when necessary to eliminate the threat or reduce it to an acceptable level. In all cases, the firm shall not assume management responsibilities, including acting as a negotiator on the client's behalf, and the hiring decision shall be left to the client.

The firm may generally provide such services as reviewing the professional qualifications of a number of applicants and providing advice on their suitability for the post. In addition, the firm may interview candidates and advise on a candidate's competence for financial accounting, administrative or control positions.

Audit clients that are public interest entities

290.215 A firm shall not provide the following recruiting services to an audit client that is a public interest entity with respect to a director or officer of the entity or senior management in a position to exert significant influence over the preparation of the client's accounting records or the financial statements on which the firm will express an opinion:

- Searching for or seeking out candidates for such positions; and
- Undertaking reference checks of prospective candidates for such positions.

Corporate finance services

290.216 Providing corporate finance services such as:

- assisting an audit client in developing corporate strategies
- identifying possible targets for the audit client to acquire
- advising on disposal transactions
- assisting finance raising transactions; and
- providing structuring advice
- may create advocacy and self-review threats. The significance of any threat shall be evaluated and safeguards applied when necessary to eliminate the threat or reduce it to an acceptable level. Examples of such safeguards include:
- Using professionals who are not members of the audit team to provide the services; or
- Having a professional who was not involved in providing the corporate finance service advise the audit team on the service and review the accounting treatment and any financial statement treatment.

290.217 Providing a corporate finance service, for example advice on the structuring of a corporate finance transaction or on financing arrangements that will directly affect amounts that will be reported in the financial statements on which the firm will provide an opinion may create a self-review threat. The existence and significance of any threat will depend on factors such as:

- The degree of subjectivity involved in determining the appropriate treatment for the outcome or consequences of the corporate finance advice in the financial statements
- The extent to which the outcome of the corporate finance advice will directly affect amounts recorded in the financial statements and the extent to which the amounts are material to the financial statements; and

- Whether the effectiveness of the corporate finance advice depends on a particular accounting treatment or presentation in the financial statements and there is doubt as to the appropriateness of the related accounting treatment or presentation under the relevant financial reporting framework.

The significance of any threat shall be evaluated and safeguards applied when necessary to eliminate the threat or reduce it to an acceptable level. Examples of such safeguards include:

- Using professionals who are not members of the audit team to perform the service; or

- Having a professional who was not involved in providing the corporate finance service to the client advise the audit team on the service and review the accounting treatment and any financial statement treatment.

290.218 Where the effectiveness of corporate finance advice depends on a particular accounting treatment or presentation in the financial statements and:

(a) The audit team has reasonable doubt as to the appropriateness of the related accounting treatment or presentation under the relevant financial reporting framework; and

(b) The outcome or consequences of the corporate finance advice will have a material effect on the financial statements on which the firm will express an opinion.

The self-review threat would be so significant that no safeguards could reduce the threat to an acceptable level, in which case the corporate finance advice shall not be provided.

290.219 Providing corporate finance services involving promoting, dealing in, or underwriting an audit client's shares would create an advocacy or self-review threat that is so significant that no safeguards could reduce the threat to an acceptable level. Accordingly, a firm shall not provide such services to an audit client.

Fees

Fees – Relative size

290.220 When the total fees from an audit client represent a large proportion of the total fees of the firm expressing the audit opinion, the dependence on that client and concern about losing the client creates a self-interest or intimidation threat. The significance of the threat will depend on factors such as:

- The operating structure of the firm

- Whether the firm is well established or new; and

- The significance of the client qualitatively and/or quantitatively to the firm.

The significance of the threat shall be evaluated and safeguards applied when necessary to eliminate the threat or reduce it to an acceptable level. Examples of such safeguards include:

- Reducing the dependency on the client

- External quality control reviews; or

- Consulting a third party, such as a professional regulatory body or a professional accountant, on key audit judgements.

290.221 A self-interest or intimidation threat is also created when the fees generated from an audit client represent a large proportion of the revenue from an individual partner's clients or a large proportion of the revenue of an individual office of the firm. The significance of the threat will depend upon factors such as:

- The significance of the client qualitatively and/or quantitatively to the partner or office; and

- The extent to which the remuneration of the partner, or the partners in the office, is dependent upon the fees generated from the client.

The significance of the threat shall be evaluated and safeguards applied when necessary to eliminate the threat or reduce it to an acceptable level. Examples of such safeguards include:

- Reducing the dependency on the audit client

- Having a professional accountant review the work or otherwise advise as necessary; or

- Regular independent internal or external quality reviews of the engagement.

Audit clients that are public interest entities

290.222 Where an audit client is a public interest entity and, for two consecutive years, the total fees from the client and its related entities (subject to the considerations in paragraph 290.27) represent more than 15% of the total fees received by the firm expressing the opinion on the financial statements of the client, the firm shall disclose to those charged with governance of the audit client the fact that the total of such fees represents more than 15% of the total fees received by the firm, and discuss which of the safeguards below it will apply to reduce the threat to an acceptable level, and apply the selected safeguard:

- Prior to the issuance of the audit opinion on the second year's financial statements, a professional accountant, who is not a member of the firm expressing the opinion on the financial statements, performs an engagement quality control review of that engagement or a professional regulatory body performs a review of that engagement that is equivalent to an engagement quality control review ('a pre-issuance review'); or

- After the audit opinion on the second year's financial statements has been issued, and before the issuance of the audit opinion on the third year's financial statements, a professional accountant, who is not a member of the firm expressing the opinion on the financial statements, or a professional regulatory body performs a review of the second year's audit that is equivalent to an engagement quality control review ('a post-issuance review').

When the total fees significantly exceed 15%, the firm shall determine whether the significance of the threat is such that a post-issuance review would not reduce the threat to an acceptable level and, therefore, a pre-issuance review is required. In such circumstances a pre-issuance review shall be performed.

Thereafter, when the fees continue to exceed 15% each year, the disclosure to and discussion with those charged with governance shall occur and one of the above safeguards shall be applied. If the fees significantly exceed 15%, the firm shall determine whether the significance of the threat is such that a post-issuance review would not reduce the threat to an acceptable level and, therefore, a pre-issuance review is required. In such circumstances a pre-issuance review shall be performed.

Supplementary reading: Annex 1 290.223 to 290.514

Fees – Overdue

290.223 A self-interest threat may be created if fees due from an audit client remain unpaid for a long time, especially if a significant part is not paid before the issue of the audit report for the following year.

Generally the firm is expected to require payment of such fees before such audit report is issued. If fees remain unpaid after the report has been issued, the existence and significance of any threat shall be evaluated and safeguards applied when necessary to eliminate the threat or reduce it to an acceptable level. An example of such a safeguard is having an additional professional accountant who did not take part in the audit engagement provide advice or review the work performed. The firm shall determine whether the overdue fees might be regarded as being equivalent to a loan to the client and whether, because of the significance of the overdue fees, it is appropriate for the firm to be re-appointed or continue the audit engagement.

Contingent fees

290.224 Contingent fees are fees calculated on a predetermined basis relating to the outcome of a transaction or the result of the services performed by the firm. For the purposes of this section, a fee is not regarded as being contingent if established by a court or other public authority.

290.225 A contingent fee charged directly or indirectly, for example through an intermediary, by a firm in respect of an audit engagement creates a self-interest threat that is so significant that no safeguards could reduce the threat to an acceptable level. Accordingly, a firm shall not enter into any such fee arrangement.

290.226 A contingent fee charged directly or indirectly, for example through an intermediary, by a firm in respect of a non-assurance service provided to an audit client may also create a self-interest threat. The threat created would be so significant that no safeguards could reduce the threat to an acceptable level if:

(a)   The fee is charged by the firm expressing the opinion on the financial statements and the fee is material or expected to be material to that firm

(b)   The fee is charged by a network firm that participates in a significant part of the audit and the fee is material or expected to be material to that firm; or

(c)   The outcome of the non-assurance service, and therefore the amount of the fee, is dependent on a future or contemporary judgement related to the audit of a material amount in the financial statements.

Accordingly, such arrangements shall not be accepted.

290.227 For other contingent fee arrangements charged by a firm for a non-assurance service to an audit client, the existence and significance of any threats will depend on factors such as:

- The range of possible fee amounts

- Whether an appropriate authority determines the outcome of the matter upon which the contingent fee will be determined

- The nature of the service; and

- The effect of the event or transaction on the financial statements.

The significance of any threats shall be evaluated and safeguards applied when necessary to eliminate the threats or reduce them to an acceptable level. Examples of such safeguards include:

- Having a professional accountant review the relevant audit work or otherwise advise as necessary; or

- Using professionals who are not members of the audit team to perform the non-assurance service.

Compensation and Evaluation policies

290.228 A self-interest threat is created when a member of the audit team is evaluated on or compensated for selling non-assurance services to that audit client. The significance of the threat will depend on:

- The proportion of the individual's compensation or performance evaluation that is based on the sale of such services

- The role of the individual on the audit team; and

- Whether promotion decisions are influenced by the sale of such services.

The significance of the threat shall be evaluated and, if the threat is not at an acceptable level, the firm shall either revise the compensation plan or evaluation process for that individual or apply safeguards to eliminate the threat or reduce it to an acceptable level. Examples of such safeguards include:

- Removing such members from the audit team; or

- Having a professional accountant review the work of the member of the audit team.

290.229 A key audit partner shall not be evaluated on or compensated based on that partner's success in selling non-assurance services to the partner's audit client. This is not intended to prohibit normal profit-sharing arrangements between partners of a firm.

Gifts and Hospitality

290.230 Accepting gifts or hospitality from an audit client may create self-interest and familiarity threats. If a firm or a member of the audit team accepts gifts or hospitality, unless the value is trivial and inconsequential, the threats created would be so significant that no safeguards could reduce the threats to an acceptable level. Consequently, a firm or a member of the audit team shall not accept such gifts or hospitality.

Actual or threatened litigation

290.231 When litigation takes place, or appears likely, between the firm or a member of the audit team and the audit client, self-interest and intimidation threats are created. The relationship between client management and the members of the audit team must be characterised by complete candour and full disclosure regarding all aspects of a client's business operations. When the firm and the client's management are placed in adversarial positions by actual or threatened litigation, affecting management's willingness to make complete disclosures, self-interest and intimidation threats are created. The significance of the threats created will depend on such factors as:

- The materiality of the litigation; and

- Whether the litigation relates to a prior audit engagement.

The significance of the threats shall be evaluated and safeguards applied when necessary to eliminate the threats or reduce them to an acceptable level. Examples of such safeguards include:

- If the litigation involves a member of the audit team, removing that individual from the audit team; or

- Having a professional review the work performed.

If such safeguards do not reduce the threats to an acceptable level, the only appropriate action is to withdraw from, or decline, the audit engagement.

Paragraphs 290.232 to 290.499 are intentionally left blank.

Reports that include a restriction on use and distribution

Introduction

290.500 The independence requirements in Section 290 apply to all audit engagements. However, in certain circumstances involving audit engagements where the report includes a restriction on use and distribution, and provided the conditions described in paragraphs 290.501 to 290.502 are met, the independence requirements in this section may be modified as provided in paragraphs 290.505 to 290.514.

These paragraphs are only applicable to an audit engagement on special purpose financial statements (a) that is intended to provide a conclusion in positive or negative form that the financial statements are prepared in all material respects, in accordance with the applicable financial reporting framework, including, in the case of a fair presentation framework, that the financial statements give a true and fair view or are presented fairly, in all material respects, in accordance with the applicable financial reporting framework, and (b) where the audit report includes a restriction on use and distribution. The modifications are not permitted in the case of an audit of financial statements required by law or regulation.

290.501 The modifications to the requirements of Section 290 are permitted if the intended users of the report (a) are knowledgeable as to the purpose and limitations of the report, and (b) explicitly agree to the application of the modified independence requirements. Knowledge as to the purpose and limitations of the report may be obtained by the intended users through their participation, either directly or indirectly through their representative who has the authority to act for the intended users, in establishing the nature and scope of the engagement. Such participation enhances the ability of the firm to communicate with intended users about independence matters, including the circumstances that are relevant to the evaluation of the threats to independence and the applicable safeguards necessary to eliminate the threats or reduce them to an acceptable level, and to obtain their agreement to the modified independence requirements that are to be applied.

290.502 The firm shall communicate (for example, in an engagement letter) with the intended users regarding the independence requirements that are to be applied with respect to the provision of the audit engagement.

Where the intended users are a class of users (for example, lenders in a syndicated loan arrangement) who are not specifically identifiable by name at the time the engagement terms are established, such users shall subsequently be made aware of the independence requirements agreed to by the representative (for example, by the representative making the firm's engagement letter available to all users).

290.503 If the firm also issues an audit report that does not include a restriction on use and distribution for the same client, the provisions of paragraphs 290.500 to 290.514 do not change the requirement to apply the provisions of paragraphs 290.1 to 290.232 to that audit engagement.

290.504 The modifications to the requirements of Section 290 that are permitted in the circumstances set out above are described in paragraphs 290.505 to 290.514. Compliance in all other respects with the provisions of Section 290 is required.

Public interest entities

290.505 When the conditions set out in paragraphs 290.500 to 290.502 are met, it is not necessary to apply the additional requirements in paragraphs 290.100 to 290.232 that apply to audit engagements for public interest entities.

Related entities

290.506 When the conditions set out in paragraphs 290.500 to 290.502 are met, references to audit client do not include its related entities. However, when the audit team knows or has reason to believe that a relationship or circumstance involving a related entity of the client is relevant to the evaluation of the firm's independence of the client, the audit team shall include that related entity when identifying and evaluating threats to independence and applying appropriate safeguards.

Networks and Network firms

290.507 When the conditions set out in paragraphs 290.500 to 290.502 are met, reference to the firm does not include network firms. However, when the firm knows or has reason to believe that threats are created by any interests and relationships of a network firm, they shall be included in the evaluation of threats to independence.

Financial interests, loans and guarantees, close business relationships and family and personal relationships

290.508 When the conditions set out in paragraphs 290.500 to 290.502 are met, the relevant provisions set out in paragraphs 290.102 to 290.145 apply only to the members of the engagement team, their immediate family members and close family members.

290.509 In addition, a determination shall be made as to whether threats to independence are created by interests and relationships, as described in paragraphs 290.102 to 290.145, between the audit client and the following members of the audit team:

(a) Those who provide consultation regarding technical or industry specific issues, transactions or events; and

(b) Those who provide quality control for the engagement, including those who perform the engagement quality control review.

An evaluation shall be made of the significance of any threats that the engagement team has reason to believe are created by interests and relationships between the audit client and others within the firm who can directly influence the outcome of the audit engagement, including those who recommend the compensation of, or who provide direct supervisory, management or other oversight of the audit engagement partner in connection with the performance of the audit engagement (including those at all successively senior levels above the engagement partner through to the individual who is the firm's Senior or Managing Partner (Chief Executive or equivalent)).

290.510 An evaluation shall also be made of the significance of any threats that the engagement team has reason to believe are created by financial interests in the audit client held by individuals, as described in paragraphs 290.108 to 290.111 and paragraphs 290.113 to 290.115.

290.511 Where a threat to independence is not at an acceptable level, safeguards shall be applied to eliminate the threat or reduce it to an acceptable level.

290.512 In applying the provisions set out in paragraphs 290.106 and 290.115 to interests of the firm, if the firm has a material financial interest, whether direct or indirect, in the audit client, the self-interest threat created would be so significant that no safeguards could reduce the threat to an acceptable level. Accordingly, the firm shall not have such a financial interest.

Employment with an audit client

290.513 An evaluation shall be made of the significance of any threats from any employment relationships as described in paragraphs 290.134 to 290.138. Where a threat exists that is not at an acceptable level, safeguards shall be applied to eliminate the threat or reduce it to an acceptable level.

Examples of safeguards that might be appropriate include those set out in paragraph 290.136.

Provision of non-assurance services

290.514 If the firm conducts an engagement to issue a restricted use and distribution report for an audit client and provides a non-assurance service to the audit client, the provisions of paragraphs 290.156 to 290.232 shall be complied with, subject to paragraphs 290.504 to 290.507.

Supplementary reading: Annex 1 291.1 to 291.138

Section 291

INDEPENDENCE – OTHER ASSURANCE ENGAGEMENTS

CONTENTS

Structure of section

A conceptual framework approach to independence

Assurance engagements

Assertion-based assurance engagements

Direct reporting assurance engagements

Reports that include a restriction on use and distribution

Multiple responsible parties

Documentation

Engagement period

Other considerations

Application of the conceptual framework approach to independence

Financial interests

Loans and Guarantees

Business relationships

Family and personal relationships

Employment with assurance clients

Recent service with an assurance client

Serving as a Director or Officer of an assurance client

Long association of senior personnel with assurance clients

Provision of non-assurance services to assurance clients

Management responsibilities

Other considerations

Fees

    Fees – Relative size

    Fees – Overdue

    Contingent fees

Gifts and Hospitality

Actual or threatened litigation

Structure of section

291.1 This section addresses independence requirements for assurance engagements that are not audit or review engagements. Independence requirements for audit and review engagements are addressed in Section 290. If the assurance client is also an audit or review client, the requirements in Section 290 also apply to the firm, network firms and members of the audit or review team. In certain circumstances involving assurance engagements where the assurance report includes a restriction on use and distribution and provided certain conditions are met, the independence requirements in this section may be modified as provided in paragraphs 291.21 to 291.27.

291.2 Assurance engagements are designed to enhance intended users' degree of confidence about the outcome of the evaluation or measurement of a subject matter against criteria. The International Framework for Assurance Engagements (the Assurance Framework) issued by the International Auditing and Assurance Standards Board describes the elements and objectives of an assurance engagement and identifies engagements to which International Standards on Assurance Engagements (ISAEs) apply. For a description of the elements and objectives of an assurance engagement, refer to the Assurance Framework.

291.3 Compliance with the fundamental principle of objectivity requires being independent of assurance clients. In the case of assurance engagements, it is in the public interest and, therefore, required by this Code of Ethics, that members of assurance teams and firms be independent of assurance clients and that any threats that the firm has reason to believe are created by a network firm's interests and relationships be evaluated. In addition, when the assurance team knows or has reason to believe that a relationship or circumstance involving a related entity of the assurance client is relevant to the evaluation of the firm's independence from the client, the assurance team shall include that related entity when identifying and evaluating threats to independence and applying appropriate safeguards.

A conceptual framework approach to independence

291.4 The objective of this section is to assist firms and members of assurance teams in applying the conceptual framework approach described below to achieving and maintaining independence.

291.5 Independence comprises:

(a) Independence of mind

The state of mind that permits the expression of a conclusion without being affected by influences that compromise professional judgement, thereby allowing an individual to act with integrity and exercise objectivity and professional scepticism.

(b) Independence in appearance

The avoidance of facts and circumstances that are so significant that a reasonable and informed third party would be likely to conclude, weighing all the specific facts and circumstances, that a firm's, or a member of the assurance team's, integrity, objectivity or professional scepticism has been compromised.

291.6 The conceptual framework approach shall be applied by professional accountants to:

(a) Identify threats to independence

(b) Evaluate the significance of the threats identified; and

(c) Apply safeguards when necessary to eliminate the threats or reduce them to an acceptable level.

When the professional accountant determines that appropriate safeguards are not available or cannot be applied to eliminate the threats or reduce them to an acceptable level, the professional accountant shall eliminate the circumstance or relationship creating the threats or decline or terminate the assurance engagement.

A professional accountant shall use professional judgement in applying this conceptual framework.

291.7 Many different circumstances, or combinations of circumstances, may be relevant in assessing threats to independence. It is impossible to define every situation that creates threats to independence and to specify the appropriate action. Therefore, this Code establishes a conceptual framework that requires firms and members of assurance teams to identify, evaluate, and address threats to independence. The conceptual framework approach assists professional accountants in public practice in complying with the ethical requirements in this Code. It accommodates many variations in circumstances that create threats to independence and can deter a professional accountant from concluding that a situation is permitted if it is not specifically prohibited.

291.8 Paragraphs 291.100 and onwards describe how the conceptual framework approach to independence is to be applied. These paragraphs do not address all the circumstances and relationships that create or may create threats to independence.

291.9 In deciding whether to accept or continue an engagement, or whether a particular individual may be a member of the assurance team, a firm shall identify and evaluate any threats to independence. If the threats are not at an acceptable level, and the decision is whether to accept an engagement or include a particular individual on the assurance team, the firm shall determine whether safeguards are available to eliminate the threats or reduce them to an acceptable level. If the decision is whether to continue an engagement, the firm shall determine whether any existing safeguards will continue to be effective to eliminate the threats or reduce them to an acceptable level or whether other safeguards will need to be applied or whether the engagement needs to be terminated. Whenever new information about a threat comes to the attention of the firm during the engagement, the firm shall evaluate the significance of the threat in accordance with the conceptual framework approach.

291.10 Throughout this section, reference is made to the significance of threats to independence. In evaluating the significance of a threat, qualitative as well as quantitative factors shall be taken into account.

291.11 This section does not, in most cases, prescribe the specific responsibility of individuals within the firm for actions related to independence because responsibility may differ depending on the size, structure and organisation of a firm. The firm is required by ISQCs to establish policies and procedures designed to provide it with reasonable assurance that independence is maintained when required by relevant ethical standards.

Assurance engagements

291.12 As further explained in the Assurance Framework, in an assurance engagement the professional accountant in public practice expresses a conclusion designed to enhance the degree of confidence of the intended users (other than the responsible party) about the outcome of the evaluation or measurement of a subject matter against criteria.

291.13 The outcome of the evaluation or measurement of a subject matter is the information that results from applying the criteria to the subject matter. The term 'subject matter information' is used to mean the outcome of the evaluation or measurement of a subject matter. For example, the Framework states that an assertion about the effectiveness of internal control (subject matter information) results from applying a framework for evaluating the effectiveness of internal control, such as COSO1 or CoCo2 (criteria), to internal control, a process (subject matter).

291.14 Assurance engagements may be assertion-based or direct reporting. In either case, they involve three separate parties: a professional accountant in public practice, a responsible party and intended users.

291.15 In an assertion-based assurance engagement, the evaluation or measurement of the subject matter is performed by the responsible party, and the subject matter information is in the form of an assertion by the responsible party that is made available to the intended users.

291.16 In a direct reporting assurance engagement, the professional accountant in public practice either directly performs the evaluation or measurement of the subject matter, or obtains a representation from the responsible party that has performed the evaluation or measurement that is not available to the intended users. The subject matter information is provided to the intended users in the assurance report.

1   'Internal Control-Integrated Framework' The Committee of Sponsoring Organisations of the Treadway Commission.

2   'Guidance on Assessing Control – The CoCo Principles' Criteria of Control Board, The Canadian Institute of Chartered Accountants.

Assertion-based assurance engagements

291.17 In an assertion-based assurance engagement, the members of the assurance team and the firm shall be independent of the assurance client (the party responsible for the subject matter information, and which may be responsible for the subject matter). Such independence requirements prohibit certain relationships between members of the assurance team and (a) directors or officers, and (b) individuals at the client in a position to exert significant influence over the subject matter information.

Also, a determination shall be made as to whether threats to independence are created by relationships with individuals at the client in a position to exert significant influence over the subject matter of the engagement. An evaluation shall be made of the significance of any threats that the firm has reason to believe are created by network firm3 interests and relationships.

291.18 In the majority of assertion-based assurance engagements, the responsible party is responsible for both the subject matter information and the subject matter. However, in some engagements, the responsible party may not be responsible for the subject matter. For example, when a professional accountant in public practice is engaged to perform an assurance engagement regarding a report that an environmental consultant has prepared about a company's sustainability practices for distribution to intended users, the environmental consultant is the responsible party for the subject matter information but the company is responsible for the subject matter (the sustainability practices).

291.19 In assertion-based assurance engagements where the responsible party is responsible for the subject matter information but not the subject matter, the members of the assurance team and the firm shall be independent of the party responsible for the subject matter information (the assurance client). In addition, an evaluation shall be made of any threats the firm has reason to believe are created by interests and relationships between a member of the assurance team, the firm, a network firm and the party responsible for the subject matter.

Direct reporting assurance engagements

291.20 In a direct reporting assurance engagement, the members of the assurance team and the firm shall be independent of the assurance client (the party responsible for the subject matter). An evaluation shall also be made of any threats the firm has reason to believe are created by network firm interests and relationships.

Reports that include a restriction on use and distribution

291.21 In certain circumstances where the assurance report includes a restriction on use and distribution, and provided the conditions in this paragraph and in paragraph 291.22 are met, the independence requirements in this section may be modified. The modifications to the requirements of Section 291 are permitted if the intended users of the report (a) are knowledgeable as to the purpose, subject matter information and limitations of the report and (b) explicitly agree to the application of the modified independence requirements. Knowledge as to the purpose, subject matter information, and limitations of the report may be obtained by the intended users through their participation, either directly or indirectly through their representative who has the authority to act for the intended users, in establishing the nature and scope of the engagement. Such participation enhances the ability of the firm to communicate with intended users about independence matters, including the circumstances that are relevant to the evaluation of the threats to independence and the applicable safeguards necessary to eliminate the threats or reduce them to an acceptable level, and to obtain their agreement to the modified independence requirements that are to be applied.

291.22 The firm shall communicate (for example, in an engagement letter) with the intended users regarding the independence requirements that are to be applied with respect to the provision of the assurance engagement. Where the intended users are a class of users (for example, lenders in a syndicated loan arrangement) who are not specifically identifiable by name at the time the engagement terms are established, such users shall subsequently be made aware of the independence requirements agreed to by the representative (for example, by the representative making the firm's engagement letter available to all users).

See paragraphs 290.13 to 290.24 for guidance on what constitutes a network firm.

291.23 If the firm also issues an assurance report that does not include a restriction on use and distribution for the same client, the provisions of paragraphs 291.25 to 291.27 do not change the requirement to apply the provisions of paragraphs 291.1 to 291.159 to that assurance engagement. If the firm also issues an audit report, whether or not it includes a restriction on use and distribution, for the same client, the provisions of Section 290 shall apply to that audit engagement.

291.24 The modifications to the requirements of Section 291 that are permitted in the circumstances set out above are described in paragraphs 291.25 to 291.27. Compliance in all other respects with the provisions of Section 291 is required.

291.25 When the conditions set out in paragraphs 291.21 and 291.22 are met, the relevant provisions set out in paragraphs 291.104 to 291.134 apply to all members of the engagement team, and their immediate and close family members. In addition, a determination shall be made as to whether threats to independence are created by interests and relationships between the assurance client and the following other members of the assurance team:

(a)   Those who provide consultation regarding technical or industry specific issues, transactions or events; and

(b)   Those who provide quality control for the engagement, including those who perform the engagement quality control review.

An evaluation shall also be made, by reference to the provisions set out in paragraphs 291.104 to 291.134, of any threats that the engagement team has reason to believe are created by interests and relationships between the assurance client and others within the firm who can directly influence the outcome of the assurance engagement, including those who recommend the compensation, or who provide direct supervisory, management or other oversight, of the assurance engagement partner in connection with the performance of the assurance engagement.

291.26 Even though the conditions set out in paragraphs 291.21 to 291.22 are met, if the firm had a material financial interest, whether direct or indirect, in the assurance client, the self-interest threat created would be so significant that no safeguards could reduce the threat to an acceptable level.

Accordingly, the firm shall not have such a financial interest. In addition, the firm shall comply with the other applicable provisions of this section described in paragraphs 291.113 to 291.159.

291.27 An evaluation shall also be made of any threats that the firm has reason to believe are created by network firm interests and relationships.

Multiple responsible parties

291.28 In some assurance engagements, whether assertion-based or direct reporting, there might be several responsible parties. In determining whether it is necessary to apply the provisions in this section to each responsible party in such engagements, the firm may take into account whether an interest or relationship between the firm, or a member of the assurance team, and a particular responsible party would create a threat to independence that is not trivial and inconsequential in the context of the subject matter information.

This will take into account factors such as:

- The materiality of the subject matter information (or of the subject matter) for which the particular responsible party is responsible; and

- The degree of public interest associated with the engagement.

If the firm determines that the threat to independence created by any such interest or relationship with a particular responsible party would be trivial and inconsequential, it may not be necessary to apply all of the provisions of this section to that responsible party.

Documentation

291.29 Documentation provides evidence of the professional accountant's judgements in forming conclusions regarding compliance with independence requirements. The absence of documentation is not a determinant of whether a firm considered a particular matter nor whether it is independent.

The professional accountant shall document conclusions regarding compliance with independence requirements, and the substance of any relevant discussions that support those conclusions. Accordingly:

(a) When safeguards are required to reduce a threat to an acceptable level, the professional accountant shall document the nature of the threat and the safeguards in place or applied that reduce the threat to an acceptable level; and

(b) When a threat required significant analysis to determine whether safeguards were necessary and the professional accountant concluded that they were not because the threat was already at an acceptable level, the professional accountant shall document the nature of the threat and the rationale for the conclusion.

Engagement period

291.30 Independence from the assurance client is required both during the engagement period and the period covered by the subject matter information. The engagement period starts when the assurance team begins to perform assurance services with respect to the particular engagement. The engagement period ends when the assurance report is issued. When the engagement is of a recurring nature, it ends at the later of the notification by either party that the professional relationship has terminated or the issuance of the final assurance report.

291.31 When an entity becomes an assurance client during or after the period covered by the subject information on which the firm will express a conclusion, the firm shall determine whether any to independence are created by:

(a) Financial or business relationships with the assurance client during or after the period covered by the subject matter information but before accepting the assurance engagement; or

(b) Previous services provided to the assurance client.

291.32 If a non-assurance service was provided to the assurance client during or after the period covered by the subject matter information but before the assurance team begins to perform assurance services and the service would not be permitted during the period of the assurance engagement, the firm shall evaluate any threat to independence created by the service. If any threat is not at an acceptable level, the assurance engagement shall only be accepted if safeguards are applied to eliminate any threats or reduce them to an acceptable level. Examples of such safeguards include:

- Not including personnel who provided the non-assurance service as members of the assurance team

- Having a professional accountant review the assurance and non-assurance work as appropriate; or

- Engaging another firm to evaluate the results of the non-assurance service or having another firm re-perform the non-assurance service to the extent necessary to enable it to take responsibility for the service.

However, if the non-assurance service has not been completed and it is not practical to complete or terminate the service before the commencement of professional services in connection with the assurance engagement, the firm shall only accept the assurance engagement if it is satisfied:

(a) The non-assurance service will be completed within a short period of time; or

(b) The client has arrangements in place to transition the service to another provider within a short period of time.

During the service period, safeguards shall be applied when necessary. In addition, the matter shall be discussed with those charged with governance.

Other considerations

291.33 There may be occasions when there is an inadvertent violation of this section. If such an inadvertent violation occurs, it generally will be deemed not to compromise independence provided the firm has appropriate quality control policies and procedures in place equivalent to those required by ISQCs to maintain independence and, once discovered, the violation is corrected promptly and any necessary safeguards are applied to eliminate any threat or reduce it to an acceptable level. The firm shall determine whether to discuss the matter with those charged with governance.

Paragraphs 291.34 to 291.99 are intentionally left blank.

Application of the conceptual framework approach to independence

291.100 Paragraphs 291.104 to 291.159 describe specific circumstances and relationships that create or may create threats to independence. The paragraphs describe the potential threats and the types of safeguards that may be appropriate to eliminate the threats or reduce them to an acceptable level and identify certain situations where no safeguards could reduce the threats to an acceptable level. The paragraphs do not describe all of the circumstances and relationships that create or may create a threat to independence. The firm and the members of the assurance team shall evaluate the implications of similar, but different, circumstances and relationships and determine whether safeguards, including the safeguards in paragraphs 200.11 to 200.14 can be applied when necessary to eliminate the threats to independence or reduce them to an acceptable level.

291.101 The paragraphs demonstrate how the conceptual framework approach applies to assurance engagements and are to be read in conjunction with paragraph 291.28 which explains that, in the majority of assurance engagements, there is one responsible party and that responsible party is the assurance client. However, in some assurance engagements there are two or more responsible parties. In such circumstances, an evaluation shall be made of any threats the firm has reason to believe are created by interests and relationships between a member of the assurance team, the firm, a network firm and the party responsible for the subject matter. For assurance reports that include a restriction on use and distribution, the paragraphs are to be read in the context of paragraphs 291.21 to 291.27.

291.102 Interpretation 2005–01 provides further guidance on applying the independence requirements contained in this section to assurance engagements.

291.103 Paragraphs 291.104 to 291.120 contain references to the materiality of a financial interest, loan, or guarantee, or the significance of a business relationship. For the purpose of determining whether such an interest is material to an individual, the combined net worth of the individual and the individual's immediate family members may be taken into account.

Financial interests

291.104 Holding a financial interest in an assurance client may create a self-interest threat. The existence and significance of any threat created depends on:

(a) The role of the person holding the financial interest

(b) Whether the financial interest is direct or indirect, and

(c) The materiality of the financial interest.

291.105 Financial interests may be held through an intermediary (for example, a collective investment vehicle, estate or trust). The determination of whether such financial interests are direct or indirect will depend upon whether the beneficial owner has control over the investment vehicle or the ability to influence its investment decisions. When control over the investment vehicle or the ability to influence investment decisions exists, this Code defines that financial interest to be a direct financial interest.

Conversely, when the beneficial owner of the financial interest has no control over the investment vehicle or ability to influence its investment decisions, this Code defines that financial interest to be an indirect financial interest.

291.106 If a member of the assurance team, a member of that individual's immediate family, or a firm has a direct financial interest or a material indirect financial interest in the assurance client, the self-interest threat created would be so significant that no safeguards could reduce the threat to an acceptable level. Therefore, none of the following shall have a direct financial interest or a material indirect financial interest in the client: a member of the assurance team; a member of that individual's immediate family member; or the firm.

291.107 When a member of the assurance team has a close family member who the assurance team member knows has a direct financial interest or a material indirect financial interest in the assurance client, a self-interest threat is created. The significance of the threat will depend on factors such as:

- The nature of the relationship between the member of the assurance team and the close family member; and

- The materiality of the financial interest to the close family member.

The significance of the threat shall be evaluated and safeguards applied when necessary to eliminate the threat or reduce it to an acceptable level. Examples of such safeguards include:

- The close family member disposing, as soon as practicable, of all of the financial interest or disposing of a sufficient portion of an indirect financial interest so that the remaining interest is no longer material

- Having a professional accountant review the work of the member of the assurance team; or

- Removing the individual from the assurance team.

291.108 If a member of the assurance team, a member of that individual's immediate family, or a firm has a direct or material indirect financial interest in an entity that has a controlling interest in the assurance client, and the client is material to the entity, the self-interest threat created would be so significant that no safeguards could reduce the threat to an acceptable level. Therefore, none of the following shall have such a financial interest: a member of the assurance team; a member of that individual's immediate family; and the firm.

291.109 The holding by a firm or a member of the assurance team, or a member of that individual's immediate family, of a direct financial interest or a material indirect financial interest in the assurance client as a trustee creates a self-interest threat. Such an interest shall not be held unless:

(a) Neither the trustee, nor an immediate family member of the trustee, nor the firm are beneficiaries of the trust

(b) The interest in the assurance client held by the trust is not material to the trust

(c) The trust is not able to exercise significant influence over the assurance client; and

(d) The trustee, an immediate family member of the trustee, or the firm cannot significantly influence any investment decision involving a financial interest in the assurance client.

291.110 Members of the assurance team shall determine whether a self-interest threat is created by any known financial interests in the assurance client held by other individuals including:

- Partners and professional employees of the firm, other than those referred to above, or their immediate family members; and

- Individuals with a close personal relationship with a member of the assurance team.

Whether these interests create a self-interest threat will depend on factors such as:

- The firm's organisational, operating and reporting structure; and

- The nature of the relationship between the individual and the member of the assurance team.

The significance of any threat shall be evaluated and safeguards applied when necessary to eliminate the threat or reduce it to an acceptable level. Examples of such safeguards include:

- Removing the member of the assurance team with the personal relationship from the assurance team

- Excluding the member of the assurance team from any significant decision-making concerning the assurance engagement; or

- Having a professional accountant review the work of the member of the assurance team.

291.111 If a firm, a member of the assurance team, or an immediate family member of the individual, receives a direct financial interest or a material indirect financial interest in an assurance client, for example, by way of an inheritance, gift or as a result of a merger, and such interest would not be permitted to be held under this section, then:

(a) If the interest is received by the firm, the financial interest shall be disposed of immediately, or a sufficient amount of an indirect financial interest shall be disposed of so that the remaining interest is no longer material, or

(b) If the interest is received by a member of the assurance team, or a member of that individual's immediate family, the individual who received the financial interest shall immediately dispose of the financial interest, or dispose of a sufficient amount of an indirect financial interest so that the remaining interest is no longer material.

291.112 When an inadvertent violation of this section as it relates to a financial interest in an assurance client occurs, it is deemed not to compromise independence if:

(a)   The firm has established policies and procedures that require prompt notification to the firm of any breaches resulting from the purchase, inheritance or other acquisition of a financial interest in the assurance client

(b)   The actions taken in paragraph 291.111(a)–(b) are taken as applicable; and

(c)   The firm applies other safeguards when necessary to reduce any remaining threat to an acceptable level. Examples of such safeguards include:

  –   Having a professional accountant review the work of the member of the assurance team; or

  –   Excluding the individual from any significant decision-making concerning the assurance engagement.

The firm shall determine whether to discuss the matter with those charged with governance.

Loans and Guarantees

291.113 A loan, or a guarantee of a loan, to a member of the assurance team, or a member of that individual's immediate family, or the firm from an assurance client that is a bank or a similar institution, may create a threat to independence. If the loan or guarantee is not made under normal lending procedures, terms and conditions, a self-interest threat would be created that would be so significant that no safeguards could reduce the threat to an acceptable level. Accordingly, neither a member of the assurance team, a member of that individual's immediate family, nor a firm shall accept such a loan or guarantee.

291.114 If a loan to a firm from an assurance client that is a bank or similar institution is made under normal lending procedures, terms and conditions and it is material to the assurance client or firm receiving the loan, it may be possible to apply safeguards to reduce the self-interest threat to an acceptable level. An example of such a safeguard is having the work reviewed by a professional accountant from a network firm that is neither involved with the assurance engagement nor received the loan.

291.115 A loan, or a guarantee of a loan, from an assurance client that is a bank or a similar institution to a member of the assurance team, or a member of that individual's immediate family, does not create a threat to independence if the loan or guarantee is made under normal lending procedures, terms and conditions. Examples of such loans include home mortgages, bank overdrafts, car loans and credit card balances.

291.116 If the firm or a member of the assurance team, or a member of that individual's immediate family, accepts a loan from, or has a borrowing guaranteed by, an assurance client that is not a bank or similar institution, the self-interest threat created would be so significant that no safeguards could reduce the threat to an acceptable level, unless the loan or guarantee is immaterial to both the firm, or the member of the assurance team and the immediate family member, and the client.

291.117 Similarly, if the firm, or a member of the assurance team, or a member of that individual's immediate family, makes or guarantees a loan to an assurance client, the self-interest threat created would be so significant that no safeguards could reduce the threat to an acceptable level, unless the loan or guarantee is immaterial to both the firm, or the member of the assurance team and the immediate family member, and the client.

291.118 If a firm or a member of the assurance team, or a member of that individual's immediate family, has deposits or a brokerage account with an assurance client that is a bank, broker, or similar institution, a threat to independence is not created if the deposit or account is held under normal commercial terms.

Business relationships

291.119 A close business relationship between a firm, or a member of the assurance team, or a member of that individual's immediate family, and the assurance client or its management arises from a commercial relationship or common financial interest and may create self-interest or intimidation threats.

Examples of such relationships include:

- Having a financial interest in a joint venture with either the client or a controlling owner, director or officer or other individual who performs senior managerial activities for that client.

- Arrangements to combine one or more services or products of the firm with one or more services or products of the client and to market the package with reference to both parties.

- Distribution or marketing arrangements under which the firm distributes or markets the client's products or services, or the client distributes or markets the firm's products or services.

Unless any financial interest is immaterial and the business relationship is insignificant to the firm and the client or its management, the threat created would be so significant that no safeguards could reduce the threat to an acceptable level. Therefore, unless the financial interest is immaterial and the business relationship is insignificant, the business relationship shall not be entered into, or shall be reduced to an insignificant level or terminated.

In the case of a member of the assurance team, unless any such financial interest is immaterial and the relationship is insignificant to that member, the individual shall be removed from the assurance team.

If the business relationship is between an immediate family member of a member of the assurance team and the assurance client or its management, the significance of any threat shall be evaluated and safeguards applied when necessary to eliminate the threat or reduce it to an acceptable level.

291.120 The purchase of goods and services from an assurance client by the firm, or a member of the assurance team, or a member of that individual's immediate family, does not generally create a threat to independence if the transaction is in the normal course of business and at arm's length. However, such transactions may be of such a nature or magnitude that they create a self-interest threat. The significance of any threat shall be evaluated and safeguards applied when necessary to eliminate the threat or reduce it to an acceptable level. Examples of such safeguards include:

- Eliminating or reducing the magnitude of the transaction; or

- Removing the individual from the assurance team.

Family and personal relationships

291.121 Family and personal relationships between a member of the assurance team and a director or officer or certain employees (depending on their role) of the assurance client, may create self-interest, familiarity or intimidation threats. The existence and significance of any threats will depend on a number of factors, including the individual's responsibilities on the assurance team, the role of the family member or other individual within the client, and the closeness of the relationship.

291.122 When an immediate family member of a member of the assurance team is:

(a)   A director or officer of the assurance client, or

(b)   An employee in a position to exert significant influence over the subject matter information of the assurance engagement, or was in such a position during any period covered by the engagement or the subject matter information, the threats to independence can only be reduced to an acceptable level by removing the individual from the assurance team. The closeness of the relationship is such that no other safeguards could reduce the threat to an acceptable level. Accordingly, no individual who has such a relationship shall be a member of the assurance team.

291.123 Threats to independence are created when an immediate family member of a member of the assurance team is an employee in a position to exert significant influence over the subject matter of the engagement. The significance of the threats will depend on factors such as:

- The position held by the immediate family member; and

- The role of the professional on the assurance team.

The significance of the threat shall be evaluated and safeguards applied when necessary to eliminate the threat or reduce it to an acceptable level. Examples of such safeguards include:

- Removing the individual from the assurance team; or

- Structuring the responsibilities of the assurance team so that the professional does not deal with matters that are within the responsibility of the immediate family member.

291.124 Threats to independence are created when a close family member of a member of the assurance team is:

- A director or officer of the assurance client; or

- An employee in a position to exert significant influence over the subject matter information of the assurance engagement.

The significance of the threats will depend on factors such as:

- The nature of the relationship between the member of the assurance team and the close family member

- The position held by the close family member; and

- The role of the professional on the assurance team.

The significance of the threat shall be evaluated and safeguards applied when necessary to eliminate the threat or reduce it to an acceptable level. Examples of such safeguards include:

- Removing the individual from the assurance team; or

- Structuring the responsibilities of the assurance team so that the professional does not deal with matters that are within the responsibility of the close family member.

291.125 Threats to independence are created when a member of the assurance team has a close relationship with a person who is not an immediate or close family member, but who is a director or officer or an employee in a position to exert significant influence over the subject matter information of the assurance engagement. A member of the assurance team who has such a relationship shall consult in accordance with firm policies and procedures. The significance of the threats will depend on factors such as:

- The nature of the relationship between the individual and the member of the assurance team

- The position the individual holds with the client; and

- The role of the professional on the assurance team.

The significance of the threats shall be evaluated and safeguards applied when necessary to eliminate the threats or reduce them to an acceptable level. Examples of such safeguards include:

- Removing the professional from the assurance team; or

- Structuring the responsibilities of the assurance team so that the professional does not deal with matters that are within the responsibility of the individual with whom the professional has a close relationship.

291.126 Self-interest, familiarity or intimidation threats may be created by a personal or family relationship between (a) a partner or employee of the firm who is not a member of the assurance team and (b) a director or officer of the assurance client or an employee in a position to exert significant influence over the subject matter information of the assurance engagement. The existence and significance of any threat will depend on factors such as:

- The nature of the relationship between the partner or employee of the firm and the director or officer or employee of the client

- The interaction of the partner or employee of the firm with the assurance team

- The position of the partner or employee within the firm; and

- The role of the individual within the client.

The significance of any threat shall be evaluated and safeguards applied when necessary to eliminate the threat or reduce it to an acceptable level. Examples of such safeguards include:

- Structuring the partner's or employee's responsibilities to reduce any potential influence over the assurance engagement; or

- Having a professional accountant review the relevant assurance work performed.

291.127 When an inadvertent violation of this section as it relates to family and personal relationships occurs, it is deemed not to compromise independence if:

(a) The firm has established policies and procedures that require prompt notification to the firm of any breaches resulting from changes in the employment status of their immediate or close family members or other personal relationships that create threats to independence

(b) The inadvertent violation relates to an immediate family member of a member of the assurance team becoming a director or officer of the assurance client or being in a position to exert significant influence over the subject matter information of the assurance engagement, and the relevant professional is removed from the assurance team; and

(c) The firm applies other safeguards when necessary to reduce any remaining threat to an acceptable level. Examples of such safeguards include:

- Having a professional accountant review the work of the member of the assurance team; or

- Excluding the relevant professional from any significant decision-making concerning the engagement.

The firm shall determine whether to discuss the matter with those charged with governance.

Employment with assurance clients

291.128 Familiarity or intimidation threats may be created if a director or officer of the assurance client, or an employee who is in a position to exert significant influence over the subject matter information of the assurance engagement, has been a member of the assurance team or partner of the firm.

291.129 If a former member of the assurance team or partner of the firm has joined the assurance client in such a position, the existence and significance of any familiarity or intimidation threats will depend on factors such as:

- The position the individual has taken at the client

- Any involvement the individual will have with the assurance team

- The length of time since the individual was a member of the assurance team or partner of the firm; and

- The former position of the individual within the assurance team or firm, for example, whether the individual was responsible for maintaining regular contact with the client's management or those charged with governance.

In all cases the individual shall not continue to participate in the firm's business or professional activities. The significance of any threats created shall be evaluated and safeguards applied when necessary to eliminate the threats or reduce them to an acceptable level. Examples of such safeguards include:

- Making arrangements such that the individual is not entitled to any benefits or payments from the firm, unless made in accordance with fixed pre-determined arrangements

- Making arrangements such that any amount owed to the individual is not material to the firm

- Modifying the plan for the assurance engagement

- Assigning individuals to the assurance team who have sufficient experience in relation to the individual who has joined the client; or

- Having a professional accountant review the work of the former member of the assurance team.

291.130 If a former partner of the firm has previously joined an entity in such a position and the entity subsequently becomes an assurance client of the firm, the significance of any threats to independence shall be evaluated and safeguards applied when necessary, to eliminate the threat or reduce it to an acceptable level.

291.131 A self-interest threat is created when a member of the assurance team participates in the assurance engagement while knowing that the member of the assurance team will, or may, join the client sometime in the future. Firm policies and procedures shall require members of an assurance team to notify the firm when entering employment negotiations with the client. On receiving such notification, the significance of the threat shall be evaluated and safeguards applied when necessary to eliminate the threat or reduce it to an acceptable level. Examples of such safeguards include:

- Removing the individual from the assurance team; or

- A review of any significant judgements made by that individual while on the team.

Recent service with an assurance client

291.132 Self-interest, self-review or familiarity threats may be created if a member of the assurance team has recently served as a director, officer, or employee of the assurance client. This would be the case when, for example, a member of the assurance team has to evaluate elements of the subject matter information the member of the assurance team had prepared while with the client.

291.133 If, during the period covered by the assurance report, a member of the assurance team had served as director or officer of the assurance client, or was an employee in a position to exert significant influence over the subject matter information of the assurance engagement, the threat created would be so significant that no safeguards could reduce the threat to an acceptable level. Consequently, such individuals shall not be assigned to the assurance team.

291.134 Self-interest, self-review or familiarity threats may be created if, before the period covered by the assurance report, a member of the assurance team had served as director or officer of the assurance client, or was an employee in a position to exert significant influence over the subject matter information of the assurance engagement. For example, such threats would be created if a decision made or work performed by the individual in the prior period, while employed by the client, is to be evaluated in the current period as part of the current assurance engagement.

The existence and significance of any threats will depend on factors such as:

- The position the individual held with the client
- The length of time since the individual left the client; and
- The role of the professional on the assurance team.

The significance of any threat shall be evaluated and safeguards applied when necessary to reduce the threat to an acceptable level. An example of such a safeguard is conducting a review of the work performed by the individual as part of the assurance team.

Serving as a Director or Officer of an assurance client

291.135 If a partner or employee of the firm serves a director or officer of an assurance client, the self-review and self-interest threats would be so significant that no safeguards could reduce the threats to an acceptable level. Accordingly, no partner or employee shall serve as a director or officer of an assurance client.

291.136 The position of Company Secretary has different implications in different jurisdictions. Duties may range from administrative duties, such as personnel management and the maintenance of company records and registers, to duties as diverse as ensuring that the company complies with regulation or providing advice on corporate governance matters. Generally, this position is seen to imply a close association with the entity.

291.137 If a partner or employee of the firm serves as Company Secretary for an assurance client, self-review and advocacy threats are created that would generally be so significant that no safeguards could reduce the threats to an acceptable level. Despite paragraph 291.135, when this practice is specifically permitted under local law, professional rules or practice, and provided management makes all relevant decisions, the duties and activities shall be limited to those of a routine and administrative nature, such as preparing minutes and maintaining statutory returns. In those circumstances, the significance of any threats shall be evaluated and safeguards applied when necessary to eliminate the threats or reduce them to an acceptable level.

291.138 Performing routine administrative services to support a company secretarial function or providing advice in relation to company secretarial administration matters does not generally create threats to independence, as long as client management makes all relevant decisions.

Supplementary reading: Annex 1 291.139 to 291.159

Long association of senior personnel with assurance clients

291.139 Familiarity and self-interest threats are created by using the same senior personnel on an assurance engagement over a long period of time. The significance of the threats will depend on factors such as:

- How long the individual has been a member of the assurance team
- The role of the individual on the assurance team
- The structure of the firm
- The nature of the assurance engagement
- Whether the client's management team has changed; and
- Whether the nature or complexity of the subject matter information has changed.

The significance of the threats shall be evaluated and safeguards applied when necessary to eliminate the threats or reduce them to an acceptable level.

Examples of such safeguards include:

- Rotating the senior personnel off the assurance team
- Having a professional accountant who was not a member of the assurance team review the work of the senior personnel; or
- Regular independent internal or external quality reviews of the engagement.

Provision of non-assurance services to assurance clients

291.140 Firms have traditionally provided to their assurance clients a range of non-assurance services that are consistent with their skills and expertise. Providing non-assurance services may, however, create threats to the independence of the firm or members of the assurance team. The threats created are most often self-review, self-interest and advocacy threats.

291.141 When specific guidance on a particular non-assurance service is not included in this section, the conceptual framework shall be applied when evaluating the particular circumstances.

291.142 Before the firm accepts an engagement to provide a non-assurance service to an assurance client, a determination shall be made as to whether providing such a service would create a threat to independence. In evaluating the significance of any threat created by a particular non-assurance service, consideration shall be given to any threat that the assurance team has reason to believe is created by providing other related non-assurance services. If a threat is created that cannot be reduced to an acceptable level by the application of safeguards the non-assurance service shall not be provided.

Management responsibilities

291.143 Management of an entity performs many activities in managing the entity in the best interests of stakeholders of the entity. It is not possible to specify every activity that is a management responsibility. However, management responsibilities involve leading and directing an entity, including making significant decisions regarding the acquisition, deployment and control of human, financial, physical and intangible resources.

291.144 Whether an activity is a management responsibility depends on the circumstances and requires the exercise of judgement. Examples of activities that would generally be considered a management responsibility include:

- Setting policies and strategic direction

- Directing and taking responsibility for the actions of the entity's employees

- Authorising transactions

- Deciding which recommendations of the firm or other third parties to implement; and

- Taking responsibility for designing, implementing and maintaining internal control.

291.145 Activities that are routine and administrative, or involve matters that are insignificant, generally are deemed not to be a management responsibility. For example, executing an insignificant transaction that has been authorised by management or monitoring the dates for filing statutory returns and advising an assurance client of those dates is deemed not to be a management responsibility. Further, providing advice and recommendations to assist management in discharging its responsibilities is not assuming a management responsibility.

291.146 Assuming a management responsibility for an assurance client may create threats to independence. If a firm were to assume a management responsibility as part of the assurance service, the threats created would be so significant that no safeguards could reduce the threats to an acceptable level. Accordingly, in providing assurance services to an assurance client, a firm shall not assume a management responsibility as part of the assurance service. If the firm assumes a management responsibility as part of any other services provided to the assurance client, it shall ensure that the responsibility is not related to the subject matter and subject matter information of an assurance engagement provided by the firm.

291.147 To avoid the risk of assuming a management responsibility related to the subject matter or subject matter information of the assurance engagement, the firm shall be satisfied that a member of management is responsible for making the significant judgements and decisions that are the proper responsibility of management, evaluating the results of the service and accepting responsibility for the actions to be taken arising from the results of the service. This reduces the risk of the firm inadvertently making any significant judgements or decisions on behalf of management. This risk is further reduced when the firm gives the client the opportunity to make judgements and decisions based on an objective and transparent analysis and presentation of the issues.

Other considerations

291.148 Threats to independence may be created when a firm provides a non-assurance service related to the subject matter information of an assurance engagement. In such cases, an evaluation of the significance of the firm's involvement with the subject matter information of the engagement shall be made, and a determination shall be made of whether any self-review threats that are not at an acceptable level can be reduced to an acceptable level by the application of safeguards.

291.149 A self-review threat may be created if the firm is involved in the preparation of subject matter information which is subsequently the subject matter information of an assurance engagement. For example, a self-review threat would be created if the firm developed and prepared prospective financial information and subsequently provided assurance on this information. Consequently, the firm shall evaluate the significance of any self-review threat created by the provision of such services and apply safeguards when necessary to eliminate the threat or reduce it to an acceptable level.

291.150 When a firm performs a valuation that forms part of the subject matter information of an assurance engagement, the firm shall evaluate the significance of any self-review threat and apply safeguards when necessary to eliminate the threat or reduce it to an acceptable level.

Fees

Fees – Relative size

291.151 When the total fees from an assurance client represent a large proportion of the total fees of the firm expressing the conclusion, the dependence on that client and concern about losing the client creates a self-interest or intimidation threat. The significance of the threat will depend on factors such as:

- The operating structure of the firm

- Whether the firm is well established or new; and

- The significance of the client qualitatively and/or quantitatively to the firm.

The significance of the threat shall be evaluated and safeguards applied when necessary to eliminate the threat or reduce it to an acceptable level. Examples of such safeguards include:

- Reducing the dependency on the client
- External quality control reviews; or
- Consulting a third party, such as a professional regulatory body or a professional accountant, on key assurance judgements.

291.152 A self-interest or intimidation threat is also created when the fees generated from an assurance client represent a large proportion of the revenue from an individual partner's clients. The significance of the threat shall be evaluated and safeguards applied when necessary to eliminate the threat or reduce it to an acceptable level. An example of such a safeguard is having an additional professional accountant who was not a member of the assurance team review the work or otherwise advise as necessary.

Fees – Overdue

291.153 A self-interest threat may be created if fees due from an assurance client remain unpaid for a long time, especially if a significant part is not paid before the issue of the assurance report, if any, for the following period. Generally the firm is expected to require payment of such fees before any such report is issued. If fees remain unpaid after the report has been issued, the existence and significance of any threat shall be evaluated and safeguards applied when necessary to eliminate the threat or reduce it to an acceptable level. An example of such a safeguard is having another professional accountant who did not take part in the assurance engagement provide advice or review the work performed. The firm shall determine whether the overdue fees might be regarded as being equivalent to a loan to the client and whether, because of the significance of the overdue fees, it is appropriate for the firm to be reappointed or continue the assurance engagement.

Contingent fees

291.154 Contingent fees are fees calculated on a predetermined basis relating to the outcome of a transaction or the result of the services performed by the firm. For the purposes of this section, fees are not regarded as being contingent if established by a court or other public authority.

291.155 A contingent fee charged directly or indirectly, for example through an intermediary, by a firm in respect of an assurance engagement creates a self-interest threat that is so significant that no safeguards could reduce the threat to an acceptable level. Accordingly, a firm shall not enter into any such fee arrangement.

291.156 A contingent fee charged directly or indirectly, for example through an intermediary, by a firm in respect of a non-assurance service provided to an assurance client may also create a self-interest threat. If the outcome of the non-assurance service, and therefore, the amount of the fee, is dependent on a future or contemporary judgement related to a matter that is material to the subject matter information of the assurance engagement, no safeguards could reduce the threat to an acceptable level. Accordingly, such arrangements shall not be accepted.

291.157 For other contingent fee arrangements charged by a firm for a non-assurance service to an assurance client, the existence and significance of any threats will depend on factors such as:

- The range of possible fee amounts

- Whether an appropriate authority determines the outcome of the matter upon which the contingent fee will be determined

- The nature of the service; and

- The effect of the event or transaction on the subject matter information.

The significance of any threats shall be evaluated and safeguards applied when necessary to eliminate the threats or reduce them to an acceptable level. Examples of such safeguards include:

- Having a professional accountant review the relevant assurance work or otherwise advise as necessary; or

- Using professionals who are not members of the assurance team to perform the non-assurance service.

Gifts and Hospitality

291.158 Accepting gifts or hospitality from an assurance client may create self-interest and familiarity threats. If a firm or a member of the assurance team accepts gifts or hospitality, unless the value is trivial and inconsequential, the threats created would be so significant that no safeguards could reduce the threats to an acceptable level. Consequently, a firm or a member of the assurance team shall not accept such gifts or hospitality.

Actual or threatened litigation

291.159 When litigation takes place, or appears likely, between the firm or a member of the assurance team and the assurance client, self-interest and intimidation threats are created. The relationship between client management and the members of the assurance team must be characterised by complete candour and full disclosure regarding all aspects of a client's business operations. When the firm and the client's management are placed in adversarial positions by actual or threatened litigation, affecting management's willingness to make complete disclosures self-interest and intimidation threats are created. The significance of the threats created will depend on such factors as:

- The materiality of the litigation; and
- Whether the litigation relates to a prior assurance engagement.

The significance of the threats shall be evaluated and safeguards applied when necessary to eliminate the threats or reduce them to an acceptable level. Examples of such safeguards include:

- If the litigation involves a member of the assurance team, removing that individual from the assurance team; or
- Having a professional review the work performed.

If such safeguards do not reduce the threats to an acceptable level, the only appropriate action is to withdraw from, or decline, the assurance engagement.

Interpretation 2005–01 (Revised July 2009 to conform to changes resulting from the IESBA's project to improve the clarity of the Code)

Application of Section 291 to Assurance Engagements that are Not Financial Statement Audit

Engagements

This interpretation provides guidance on the application of the independence requirements contained in Section 291 to assurance engagements that are not financial statement audit engagements. This interpretation focuses on the application issues that are particular to assurance engagements that are not financial statement audit engagements. There are other matters noted in Section 291 that are relevant in the consideration of independence requirements for all assurance engagements. For example, paragraph 291.3 states that an evaluation shall be made of any threats the firm has reason to believe are created by a network firm's interests and relationships. It also states that when the assurance team has reason to believe that a related entity of such an assurance client is relevant to the evaluation of the firm's independence of the client, the assurance team shall include the related entity when evaluating threats to independence and when necessary applying safeguards. These matters are not specifically addressed in this interpretation.

As explained in the International Framework for Assurance Engagements issued by the International Auditing and Assurance Standards Board, in an assurance engagement, the professional accountant in public practice expresses a conclusion designed to enhance the degree of confidence of the intended users other than the responsible party about the outcome of the evaluation or measurement of a subject matter against criteria.

Assertion-based assurance engagements

In an assertion-based assurance engagement, the evaluation or measurement of the subject matter is performed by the responsible party, and the subject matter information is in the form of an assertion by the responsible party that is made available to the intended users. In an assertion-based assurance engagement independence is required from the responsible party, which is responsible for the subject matter information and may be responsible for the subject matter.

In those assertion-based assurance engagements where the responsible party is responsible for the subject matter information but not the subject matter, independence is required from the responsible party. In addition, an evaluation shall be made of any threats the firm has reason to believe are created by interests and relationships between a member of the assurance team, the firm, a network firm and the party responsible for the subject matter.

Direct reporting assurance engagements

In a direct reporting assurance engagement, the professional accountant in public practice either directly performs the evaluation or measurement of the subject matter, or obtains a representation from the responsible party that has performed the evaluation or measurement that is not available to the intended users. The subject matter information is provided to the intended users in the assurance report. In a direct reporting assurance engagement independence is required from the responsible party, which is responsible for the subject matter.

Multiple responsible parties

In both assertion-based assurance engagements and direct reporting assurance engagements there may be several responsible parties. For example, a public accountant in public practice may be asked to provide assurance on the monthly circulation statistics of a number of independently owned newspapers.

The assignment could be an assertion based assurance engagement where each newspaper measures its circulation and the statistics are presented in an assertion that is available to the intended users. Alternatively, the assignment could be a direct reporting assurance engagement, where there is no assertion and there may or may not be a written representation from the newspapers.

In such engagements, when determining whether it is necessary to apply the provisions in Section 291 to each responsible party, the firm may take into account whether an interest or relationship between the firm, or a member of the assurance team, and a particular responsible party would create a threat to independence that is not trivial and inconsequential in the context of the subject matter information.

This will take into account:

(a) The materiality of the subject matter information (or the subject matter) for which the particular responsible party is responsible; and

(b) The degree of public interest that is associated with the engagement.

If the firm determines that the threat to independence created by any such relationships with a particular responsible party would be trivial and inconsequential it may not be necessary to apply all of the provisions of this section to that responsible party.

Example

The following example has been developed to demonstrate the application of Section 291. It is assumed that the client is not also a financial statement audit client of the firm, or a network firm.

A firm is engaged to provide assurance on the total proven oil reserves of 10 independent companies. Each company has conducted geographical and engineering surveys to determine their reserves (subject matter). There are established criteria to determine when a reserve may be considered to be proven which the professional accountant in public practice determines to be suitable criteria for the engagement.

The proven reserves (in thousands of barrels) for each company as at December 31, 20X0 were as follows:

- Company 1 – 5,200
- Company 2 – 725
- Company 3 – 3,260
- Company 4 – 15,000
- Company 5 – 6,700

- Company 6 – 39,126
- Company 7 – 345
- Company 8 – 175
- Company 9 – 24,135
- Company 10 – 9,635
- **Total – 104,301**

The engagement could be structured in differing ways:

Assertion-based engagements

A1 Each company measures its reserves and provides an assertion to the firm and to intended users.

A2 An entity other than the companies measures the reserves and provides an assertion to the firm and to intended users.

Direct reporting engagements

D1 Each company measures the reserves and provides the firm with a written representation that measures its reserves against the established criteria for measuring proven reserves. The representation is not available to the intended users.

D2 The firm directly measures the reserves of some of the companies.

Application of approach

A1 Each company measures its reserves and provides an assertion to the firm and to intended users. There are several responsible parties in this engagement (Companies 1–10). When determining whether it is necessary to apply the independence provisions to all of the companies, the firm may take into account whether an interest or relationship with a particular company would create a threat to independence that is not at an acceptable level. This will take into account factors such as:

- The materiality of the company's proven reserves in relation to the total reserves to be reported on; and

- The degree of public interest associated with the engagement (paragraph 291.28).

For example Company 8 accounts for 0.17% of the total reserves, therefore a business relationship or interest with Company 8 would create less of a threat than a similar relationship with Company 6, which accounts for approximately 37.5% of the reserves.

Having determined those companies to which the independence requirements apply, the assurance team and the firm are required to be independent of those responsible parties that would be considered to be the assurance client (paragraph 291.28).

A2 An entity other than the companies measures the reserves and provides an assertion to the firm and to intended users.

The firm shall be independent of the entity that measures the reserves and provides an assertion to the firm and to intended users (paragraph 291.19). That entity is not responsible for the subject matter and so an evaluation shall be made of any threats the firm has reason to believe are created by interests/relationships with the party responsible for the subject matter (paragraph 291.19). There are several parties responsible for the subject matter in this engagement (Companies 1–10). As discussed in example A1 above, the firm may take into account whether an interest or relationship with a particular company would create a threat to independence that is not at an acceptable level.

D1 Each company provides the firm with a representation that measures its reserves against the established criteria for measuring proven reserves. The representation is not available to the intended users.

There are several responsible parties in this engagement (Companies 1–10). When determining whether it is necessary to apply the independence provisions to all of the companies, the firm may take into account whether an interest or relationship with a particular company would create a threat to independence that is not at an acceptable level. This will take into account factors such as:

- The materiality of the company's proven reserves in relation to the total reserves to be reported on; and

- The degree of public interest associated with the engagement (paragraph 291.28).

For example, Company 8 accounts for 0.17% of the reserves, therefore a business relationship or interest with Company 8 would create less of a threat than a similar relationship with Company 6 that accounts for approximately 37.5% of the reserves.

Having determined those companies to which the independence requirements apply, the assurance team and the firm shall be independent of those responsible parties that would be considered to be the assurance client (paragraph 291.28).

D2 The firm directly measures the reserves of some of the companies. The application is the same as in example D1.

Effective date

This code is effective on January 1, 2011. Early adoption is permitted. The Code is subject to the following transitional provisions:

Public interest entities

1   Section 290 of the Code contains additional independence provisions when the audit or review client is a public interest entity. The additional provisions that are applicable because of the new definition of a public interest entity or the guidance in paragraph 290.26 are effective on January 1, 2012. For partner rotation requirements, the transitional provisions contained in paragraphs 2 and 3 below apply.

Partner rotation

2   For a partner who is subject to the rotation provisions in paragraph 290.151 because the partner meets the definition of the new term 'key audit partner,' and the partner is neither the engagement partner nor the individual responsible for the engagement quality control review, the rotation provisions are effective for the audits or reviews of financial statements for years beginning on or after December 15, 2011. For example, in the case of an audit client with a calendar year-end, a key audit partner, who is neither the engagement partner nor the individual responsible for the engagement quality control review, who had served as a key audit partner for seven or more years (that is, the audits of 2003–2010), would be required to rotate after serving for one more year as a key audit partner (that is, after completing the 2011 audit).

3   For an engagement partner or an individual responsible for the engagement quality control review who immediately prior to assuming either of these roles served in another key audit partner role for the client, and who, at the beginning of the first fiscal year beginning on or after December 15, 2010, had served as the engagement partner or individual responsible for the engagement quality control review for six or fewer years, the rotation provisions are effective for the audits or reviews of financial statements for years beginning on or after December 15, 2011. For example, in the case of an audit client with a calendar year-end, a partner who had served the client in another key audit partner role for four years (that is, the audits of 2002–2005) and subsequently as the engagement partner for five years (that is, the audits of 2006–2010) would be required to rotate after serving for one more year as the engagement partner (that is, after completing the 2011 audit).

Non-assurance services

4   Paragraphs 290.156–290.219 address the provision of non-assurance services to an audit or review client. If, at the effective date of the Code, services are being provided to an audit or review client and the services were permissible under the June 2005 Code (revised July 2006) but are either prohibited or subject to restrictions under the revised Code, the firm may continue providing such services only if they were contracted for and commenced prior to January 1, 2011, and are completed before July 1, 2011.

Fees – Relative size

5   Paragraph 290.222 provides that, in respect of an audit or review client that is a public interest entity, when the total fees from that client and its related entities (subject to the considerations in paragraph 290.27) for two consecutive years represent more than 15% of the total fees of the firm expressing the opinion on the financial statements, a pre- or post-issuance review (as described in paragraph 290.222) of the second year's audit shall be performed. This requirement is effective for audits or reviews of financial statements covering years that begin on or after December 15, 2010. For example, in the case of an audit client with a calendar year end, if the total fees from the client exceeded the 15% threshold for 2011 and 2012, the pre- or post-issuance review would be applied with respect to the audit of the 2012 financial statements.

Compensation and evaluation policies

6   Paragraph 290.229 provides that a key audit partner shall not be evaluated or compensated based on that partner's success in selling non-assurance services to the partner's audit client. This requirement is effective on January 1, 2012. A key audit partner may, however, receive compensation after January 1, 2012 based on an evaluation made prior to January 1, 2012 of that partner's success in selling non-assurance services to the audit client.

Mock Assessment

Chapter learning objectives

This section is intended for use when you have completed your study and initial revision. It contains a complete mock assessment.

This should be attempted as an exam conditions, timed mock. This will give you valuable experience that will assist you with your time management and examination strategy.

Certificate Level

Fundamentals of Ethics, Corporate Governance and Business Law

Instructions: attempt all 85 questions.

Time allowed 2 hours.

Test your understanding 1

Which of the following describes the aim of corporate governance?

A   To ensure that companies are well run in the interests of their shareholders and the wider community

B   To ensure the wealth of companies contributes to the health of the economies where their shares are traded

C   To ensure that companies have a positive impact on the environment, stakeholders and the wider society

D   None of the above

Test your understanding 2

Which corporate governance report focused specifically on the role of non-executive directors?

A   Greenbury report

B   Turnbull report

C   Higgs report

D   Smith report

Test your understanding 3

In which one of the following instances will misrepresentation generally not be recognised?

A   The contract contains half-truths

B   In a contract of the utmost good faith, full disclosure is not made

C   Information ceases to be accurate because of changed circumstances

D   A party fails to disclose material facts

Test your understanding 4

The following advertisement appeared in a farming magazine.

'Plough for sale. Little used, very good condition £1,000.'

How would this statement be defined at law?

A   Advertising puff

B   Offer to sell

C   Invitation to treat

D   Invitation to buy

Test your understanding 5

An offer was made by A to sell goods on the 1st April for £2,000. B the offeree telephoned A on the 5th April offering to pay £1,800 for the goods. On the 8th April, A offered to sell the goods to C for £1,900, and C accepted this offer on the same day. On the 7th April, B sent a letter to A which was received on the 10th April agreeing to pay the £2,000, the asked price for the goods.

A   There is a contract between A and B created on the 7th April

B   There is a contract between A and B created on the 10th April

C   There is a contract between A and C

D   There is no contract created

Test your understanding 6

A coat was displayed in a shop window with a price tag attached which read £10. The price tag should have read £100. X who saw this went into the shop and demanded the coat for £10.

Which one of the following is correct?

A   As the window display is an offer, X can demand the coat at £10

B   The window display is merely an invitation to treat and the shopkeeper does not have to sell the coat to X

C   The shopkeeper can refuse to sell the coat for £10, but cannot refuse to sell the coat to X for £100 if X was prepared to pay this sum

D   The shopkeeper would be bound to sell the coat to any customer prepared to pay this £100

Test your understanding 7

Which of the following statement/s is/are correct?

1   A contract term can be implied by statute

2   A contract term can be implied by a court on the basis of trade custom

A   1 only

B   2 only

C   Both 1 and 2

D   Neither 1 or 2

Test your understanding 8

Which one of the following statements is correct?

A   In a contract, a breach of a condition will result in the contract being terminated

B   In a contract, a breach of a condition is a breach of a term of fundamental importance to the contract

C   In a contract, a breach of warranty entitles the injured party to terminate the contract

D   In a contract, a breach of warranty can terminate a contract, but only on the basis of equity

Test your understanding 9

Which of the following statement/s is/are correct?

1   A limited liability partnership has legal personality

2   Individual members of a limited liability partnership will have contractual liability to creditors of the partnership

A   1 only

B   2 only

C   Both 1 and 2

D   Neither 1 or 2

Test your understanding 10

To which type of company is the UK Corporate Governance Code primarily directed?

A   All companies

B   All public companies

C   All private and public companies

D   All listed public companies

Test your understanding 11

Which of the following is not a recommendation of the UK Corporate Governance Code?

A   The board should ensure that workforce policies and practices are consistent with the company's values

B   The board should promote short-term profitability for the shareholders

C   There should be an annual evaluation of the board

D   No director should be involved in setting their own pay

Test your understanding 12

The two-tier board structure comprises a Supervisory Board and what other organ?

A   A board representing the employees

B   A board majority of non-executive directors

C   An all-executive board

D   A management board

Test your understanding 13

Which of the following is not an accurate description of what a company's code of ethics is likely to achieve?

A   It tells employees what is expected of them in terms of behaviour

B   It explains the approach and outlook of the organisation

C   It encourages employees to take a consistent approach to ethical issues

D   It eliminates the need for legislation

Test your understanding 14

Which of the following actions by a company would not encourage employees to speak up if they encounter potentially serious cases of unprofessional or unethical behaviour?

A   Introduce an employee helpline for ethics-related queries

B   State in the company's code of ethics that employees have a duty to speak up

C   Stress the importance of employees working together to meet ambitious sales targets

D   Develop a culture where it is safe and acceptable for employees to raise concerns

Test your understanding 15

Which of the following does not specifically relate to business ethics?

A   The financial viability of a business

B   The behaviour of the business and its employees

C   How a business conducts its relationships with its stakeholders

D   How a company does business, rather than what it does

Test your understanding 16

Which of the following is not one of the five personal qualities that CIMA expects of its members?

A   Reliability

B   Respect

C   Responsibility

D   Reflection

Test your understanding 17

While reviewing the work of one of your colleagues, you discover that he has made some extremely serious mistakes. When you discuss this with him, it becomes clear that he does not have the understanding of financial matters that he requires to be a competent accountant. This violates CIMA's fundamental principle of:

A   Integrity

B   Objectivity

C   Professional competence and due care

D   Confidentiality

Test your understanding 18

Where a transaction has been completely missed out from the ledger account what is this known as?

A   Error of principle

B   Error of commission

C   Error of omission

D   None of the above

Test your understanding 19

You are working abroad and find yourself in a situation where a particular element of the country's legislation is in conflict with the IFAC Code of Ethics. In this situation, you should:

A   Obey the law because it is mandatory to comply with legislation

B   Obey the ethics code because it is internationally binding

C   Obey the law because you have a public duty to uphold the law, but not to uphold ethics

D   Obey the ethics code because it is a requirement of your profession

Test your understanding 20

Which of the following relates specifically to accountability?

A   Taking responsibility for one's work and conclusions

B   Maintaining clear records that provide evidence to back up conclusions

C   Being answerable to queries in relation to one's work

D   All of the above

Test your understanding 21

Which of the following relates to an ethical issue?

A   Moving into a larger office as part of a plan to expand your business

B   Introducing a new monthly reporting process to maximise efficiency

C   Introducing a new IT system to ensure confidentiality of customer information

D   Recruiting a new finance director

Test your understanding 22

Which of the following would be of the least help in developing an effective corporate ethics programme?

A   Having a chairman and chief executive who champion ethics at every opportunity

B   Providing copies of the company's code of ethics to trusted personnel only to avoid the document falling into the hands of competitors

C   Incorporating ethical issues into new employee induction programmes

D   Talking to the company's key stakeholders about the social and environmental issues they believe to be important

Test your understanding 23

Which of the following correctly states the composition of an audit committee?

A   Executive directors only

B   Non-executive directors only

C   Executive directors and internal auditors

D   Non-executive directors and internal auditors

Test your understanding 24

In tackling ethical dilemmas, which of the following would not help you to find a solution?

A   Establishing the facts and the ethical issues involved

B   Referring to the CIMA and/or your company's code of ethics

C   Following an established internal procedure

D   Choosing to postpone tackling the issue due to pressure of deadlines

Test your understanding 25

One of your colleagues has just been passed over for promotion for the third time. She shows you evidence that only a small number of women have ever been promoted to positions of seniority within your company. This, she says, is an issue of:

A   Harassment

B   Discrimination

C   Conflict of interest

D   Bribery and corruption

Test your understanding 26

Which of the following is not an ethical issue for a bank?

A   Providing accurate information about terms and conditions when advertising interest rates for customer loans

B   Launching a premium account service for customers who are willing to pay a monthly charge for improved service

C   Money laundering

D   Disabled access to bank branches

Test your understanding 27

Which of the following ethical issues is most likely to be affected by new developments in information technology?

A   Data protection

B   Gifts and hospitality

C   Harassment

D   Health and safety

Test your understanding 28

In contract law, a misrepresentation is which one of the following?

A   An untrue statement of fact or opinion which induces another to contract

B   An untrue statement of fact, opinion or intention which induces another to contract

C   An untrue statement of fact which induces another to contract

D   An untrue statement of fact or intention which induces another to contract

Test your understanding 29

When deciding on whether a solution to an ethical dilemma is appropriate, which of the following questions is irrelevant?

A   Do I feel comfortable about others knowing about my decision?

B   Have I considered all parties who may be affected by my decision?

C   Would a reasonable third party consider my decision fair?

D   Is this the most appropriate decision considering my career aspirations?

Test your understanding 30

Which of the following board has members which are elected by shareholders at the annual general meeting?

A   Management board only

B   Supervisory board only

C   Both the management and supervisory board

D   Neither the management or supervisory board

Test your understanding 31

What is the objective of an external audit?

A   To protect the interests of minority shareholders

B   To detect fraud and other irregularities

C   To assess the effectiveness of the company's performance

D   To provide assurance on the directors' assertions about the financial statements

Test your understanding 32

Which of the following correctly describes the composition of a unitary board?

A   Executive directors only

B   Non-executive directors only

C   Both executive and non-executive directors

D   Non-executive directors and internal auditors

Test your understanding 33

Which of the following is incorrect in relation to the Sarbanes-Oxley Act ('the Act')?

A   The Act created the Public Company Accounting Oversight Board ('PCAOB')

B   The Act requires all US listed companies to have an audit committee

C   The Act restricts the additional services that an auditor can provide to an audit client

D   The Act requires directors to be professionally qualified to act as directors of public companies

Test your understanding 34

Who is ultimately responsible for ensuring that the financial statements are prepared in accordance with relevant legislation?

A   The external auditors

B   The internal auditors

C   The board of directors

D   The shareholders

Test your understanding 35

In relation to the UK Corporate Governance Code which of the following statements is correct?

A   The Code contains principles which, if broken, may give rise to civil liability only

B   The Code contains principles which, if broken, are punishable by relatively small fines

C   The Code contains principles which, if broken, only oblige the board to disclose the reasons for the breach

D   The Code contains principles which, if broken, have no consequences whatsoever

Test your understanding 36

Which one of the following statements is incorrect in relation to the interaction of corporate governance with business ethics and company law?

A   Corporate governance is primarily concerned with the effective control business efficacy and accountability of the management of public listed companies

B   Corporate governance does not affect private companies

C   Corporate governance business ethics and company law are made up of entirely separate principles

D   The term 'stakeholders' is wider than shareholders and employees

Test your understanding 37

Which of the following is not a principle of the OECD framework of governance?

A   Disclosure and transparency

B   Innovation and adaptability

C   Responsibilities of the board

D   Shareholders' rights of ownership

Test your understanding 38

Which of the following error/s would affect calculation of profit?

1 Error of commission

2 Error of principle

A 1 only

B 2 only

C Both 1 and 2

D Neither 1 or 2

Test your understanding 39

What is ethical conduct for a CIMA accountant?

A Doing what you think is right for society

B Thinking that what you are doing is socially right

C Thinking about the social consequences of what you do before you do it

D Doing things that you believe comply with the CIMA Code

Test your understanding 40

What is detection risk?

A That the company's control system will fail to detect and correct material errors in the processing of transactions

B That the auditor's procedures will not detect material errors which exist in the financial statements

C The susceptibility of financial statement transactions and balances to material errors which may or may not be detected

D None of the above

Test your understanding 41

Which of the following is a correct statement about CIMA's Code of Ethics?

A   It covers all ethical eventualities

B   It covers unusual situations in practice which are unlikely to give rise to ethical problems

C   It gives the general principles to guide behaviour, rather than any specific guidance on how to act in particular circumstances

D   It can only be understood if read in conjunction with the IFAC Code

Test your understanding 42

Which of these is correct?

The importance of the ethical rule is to be judged by the:

A   cost of breach to the individual bound by that rule

B   social consequences for breach of the rule

C   impact on the profession of the rule

D   the context within which it is applied

Test your understanding 43

Which of these is not a fundamental ethical principle?

A   Integrity

B   Objectivity

C   Professional competence and due care

D   Independence

Test your understanding 44

A project that your manager is keen on looks set to have problems showing a profit in the first year. Thereafter, it is projected to make a healthy margin. You are aware of the way in which the system has gaps, which could hide the weak performance in the first year and could be disguised, and your manager asks you what they are and whether you can implement them. Do you:

A   Tell him that the company systems do not permit any variance from the accounting method that would show up the weakness?

B   Say that you know how to help him, but you can't because you don't think it's right to give false information?

C   Prepare the financial reports in the way he requests, but get him to send you an e-mail confirming he asked you for this unrepresentative report?

D   Do what he says, because he's the client?

Test your understanding 45

Which of the following is not one of the personal qualities and virtues specifically sought by CIMA?

A   Courtesy

B   Timeliness

C   Respect

D   Selflessness

Test your understanding 46

Which of the following statement/s is/are correct in relation to CIMA's proposals for better corporate governance?

1   There should be more disclosure

2   There should be better disclosure

3   Disclosure should be adapted to the circumstances of the company

A   1 and 2

B   1 and 3

C   2 and 3

D   3 only

Test your understanding 47

Your employer is having liquidity problems and has reached its overdraft limit. The finance director has asked you to review the company's accounting policies to see if a change could improve the presentation of the financial accounts, which are supplied on a monthly basis to the bank. From an ethical perspective, what is the most appropriate action for you to take?

A   Seek advice from your professional body

B   Do as requested and seek advice afterwards

C   Do as requested

D   Go off sick

Test your understanding 48

Which of the following is not one of the Seven Principles of Public Life issued by the Committee on Standards in Public Life?

A   Courtesy

B   Openness

C   Integrity

D   Leadership

Test your understanding 49

Why should an accountant continually develop?

A   Because management accounting changes so fast that you need to keep up with it to stay marketable for employment

B   Because continual development means that the client always gets a better service every time he or she uses your services

C   Because professional competence rests on checking what you do know, adding to knowledge and skills and challenging habitual working practices

D   Because management accounting needs to reflect the evolving climate in business and finance

Test your understanding 50

You believe that one of your colleagues has knowingly provided misleading information. If your belief is true, which of CIMA's fundamental principles has your colleague breached?

A   Professional competence and due care

B   Integrity

C   Objectivity

D   Confidentiality

Test your understanding 51

Which of these is a good indicator of accountability:

A   Having regular reviews with your line manager to explain how you are working

B   Keeping accurate records in an orderly way

C   Always explaining your decisions when you make them

D   Being an able accountant

Test your understanding 52

Which is the best explanation of social responsibility?

A   Social responsibility means the accountant is responsible to all of society equally

B   Social responsibility means that the accountant should do additional things to support social initiatives

C   Social responsibility means that the accountant has to be squeaky clean in his or her social as well as professional life

D   Social responsibility means that the accountant should always be aware of the broader social consequences of his actions

Test your understanding 53

In relation to a value for money audit, which term does the following statement define?

'Achievement of objectives'.

A   Economy

B   Efficiency

C   Effectiveness

D   Efficacy

Test your understanding 54

An accountant who answers accusations that their work has failed to meet professional standards demonstrates which concept?

A   Accountability

B   Reliability

C   Social responsibility

D   Independence

Test your understanding 55

Which of the following is not a board committee?

A   Audit committee

B   Remuneration committee

C   Nomination committee

D   Corporate social responsibility committee

Test your understanding 56

Which is a correct statement?

A   The IFAC Codes of conduct deal with accountants working internationally, while CIMA only applies to business done in Britain

B   The CIMA Code is inferior to IFAC's Code

C   The IFAC Code reflects the standards laid down by CIMA

D   The IFAC Code is reflected in the CIMA Code

Test your understanding 57

Which of the following is not an advantage of a company limited by shares?

A   The company is liable on its own contracts

B   The member's liability is limited to the amount he agreed to pay for his shares

C   The company is not affected by any change in members

D   There are less disclosure requirements than for a sole trader

Test your understanding 58

Why do we need codes of professional ethics?

A   To resolve disputes

B   To punish bad accountants

C   To protect the reputation of the profession

D   To improve the quality of service to the public

Test your understanding 59

Which statement is the most accurate of the statements?

A   Laws can never be broken, even if they breach ethics

B   Ethical breaches always have to be justified, even if they result from the breach of a law

C   Legal breaches often result in ethical breaches

D   Ethical breaches often result in legal breaches

Test your understanding 60

The articles of association are a contract between:

A   The company and its members

B   The company and its stakeholders

C   The company and third parties

D   None of the above

Test your understanding 61

Which of the following statements most accurately expresses different approaches to ethical regulations?

A   Breaches of ethics have less serious consequences than breaches of the criminal law

B   Ethical frameworks let the individual decide about how they should act in particular situations

C   Regulations provide a 'thou shall not' approach to behaviour, whereas framework approaches encourage positive behaviour in support of ethical conduct

D   The framework approach is best suited to practical problem-solving in ethics

Test your understanding 62

How does the framework-based approach to ethics differ from the rules-based approach?

A   The framework-based approach uses legal language

B   The framework-based approach requires a detailed rule book

C   The framework-based approach sets out rules covering all eventualities

D   The framework-based approach sets out general guidelines

Test your understanding 63

Which of the following would not need to be provided to form a company?

A   The proposed name of the company

B   The type of company

C   The proposed start date of trading

D   Details of the registered office

Test your understanding 64

What is meant by the expression 'lifting the veil of incorporation'?

A   The company is treated as if it were fully liable for all its debts

B   The shareholders are treated as though they were carrying on business in partnership

C   The directors are treated as partners and are fully liable for the company's debts

D   The company is treated as if it were not a separate person at law

Test your understanding 65

Which of the following is not a type of stakeholder?

A   Associated

B   Internal

C   Connected

D   External

Test your understanding 66

In which one of the following instances will it be deemed to be an automatic unfair dismissal?

A   Where an employee brings a court action against the employer in good faith to enforce a statutory right, where no right in fact exists

B   Where an employee is selected for redundancy contrary to an agreed arrangement of custom, without good reason

C   Where an employee fails to comply with orders on the basis of valid health and safety grounds

D   Where an employee is pregnant

Test your understanding 67

Which of the following use a rules-based approach to corporate governance?

1   King III

2   UK Corporate Governance Code

3   Sarbanes-Oxley

A   1 and 2

B   2 and 3

C   1 and 3

D   3 only

Test your understanding 68

Where a dismissed employee claims wrongful dismissal, which of the following statement/s is/are correct?

1   The claim can be based on dismissal without proper notice

2   The claim will essentially be for breach of contract

A   1 only

B   2 only

C   Both 1 and 2

D   Neither 1 or 2

Test your understanding 69

Employers owe certain implied duties to employees. In which of the following instances, does a duty to provide work not exist?

A   Where the employee's remuneration depends upon the work done

B   Where the employee needs work to maintain reputation

C   Where the employee needs work to maintain familiarity with technical change

D   Where the employee is participating in an ongoing staff training programme

Test your understanding 70

In which country was King III introduced?

A   UK

B   USA

C   South Africa

D   Canada

Test your understanding 71

Which of the following is invalid consideration?

1   A promise to perform an existing contractual obligation

2   A promise to perform an existing statutory obligation

A   1 only

B   2 only

C   Both 1 and 2

D   Neither 1 or 2

Test your understanding 72

Which of the following focused on directors' remuneration in the UK?

A   Hampel report

B   Turnbull report

C   Greenbury report

D   Tyson report

Test your understanding 73

Ria writes to Sarah offering to buy Sarah's boat for £500. In her letter, she writes 'If I don't hear from you, I shall consider it mine and pick it up on Friday'. Which of the following best describes the legal position as to whether or not a contract exists?

A   There is a contract because Ria waived the need for acceptance

B   There is a contract because Sarah complied with Ria's terms exactly

C   There is a contract because acceptance can be inferred from Sarah's conduct

D   There is no contract because there is no positive act to indicate acceptance

Test your understanding 74

Which of the following constitute misrepresentation?

A   Failure to disclose full material facts

B   Failure to communicate changed circumstances

C   Failure to communicate fully relevant information, although that which is communicated is accurate

D   All of the above

Test your understanding 75

Which of the following statement/s is/are correct?

1   An external audit report has a formal reporting structure

2   An internal audit report has a formal reporting structure

A   1 only

B   2 only

C   Both 1 and 2

D   Neither 1 or 2

Test your understanding 76

Which one of the following is incorrect?

A   A condition is a term that the parties intended to be of fundamental importance

B   A warranty is a term that the parties did not intend to be of fundamental importance

C   If a condition is breached, the contract is automatically terminated

D   If a warranty is breached, the innocent party cannot treat the contract as discharged

Test your understanding 77

In relation to whistleblowing to whom can a disclosure only be made in extreme circumstances?

A   Legal adviser

B   Government minister

C   Media

D   Internal department

Test your understanding 78

Which of the following is not an advantage of a company outsourcing its internal audit function?

A   There will always be a reduction in costs

B   Provides access to specialist skills

C   Can provide access to an internal audit team immediately

D   Reduced management time in administering an in-house department

Test your understanding 79

If you are offered an expensive gift from a client which threat arises?

A   Intimidation

B   Advocacy

C   Self-review

D   Self-interest

Test your understanding 80

Which of the following is correct in relation to a company limited by shares?

A   A company has management of the company separate from ownership

B   A company does not have perpetual succession

C   A private company is not a separate legal person distinct from its shareholders

D   None of the above

Test your understanding 81

Which of the following business organisation is appropriate for a high-risk business?

A   Sole trader

B   General partnership

C   A company limited by shares

D   None of the above

Test your understanding 82

Which of the following is/are an element of audit risk?

1   The risk that the financial statements contain a material misstatement

2   The risk that the auditor fails to detect any misstatement

A   1 only

B   2 only

C   Both 1 and 2

D   Neither 1 or 2

Test your understanding 83

Which of the following statement/s is/are correct?

1   A company may enter into any contract in its own name

2   A company has restrictions on its business purpose

A   1 only

B   2 only

C   Both 1 and 2

D   Neither 1 or 2

Test your understanding 84

Which of the following statement/s regarding off-the-shelf companies is/are correct?

1   They may be cheaper and simpler than incorporating a new company

2   They cannot enter into contracts immediately

A   1 only

B   2 only

C   Both 1 and 2

D   Neither 1 or 2

Test your understanding 85

Which of the following should be included in an audit engagement letter?

1   Objective and scope of the audit

2   Results of previous audits

3   Management's responsibilities

A   1 and 2

B   1 and 3

C   2 and 3

D   2 only

Test your understanding answers

Test your understanding 1

A

Test your understanding 2

C

Test your understanding 3

D

Test your understanding 4

C

Test your understanding 5

C

Test your understanding 6

B

Test your understanding 7

C

Test your understanding 8

B

Test your understanding 9

A

Test your understanding 10

D

Test your understanding 11

B

Test your understanding 12

D

Test your understanding 13

D

Test your understanding 14

C

Test your understanding 15

A

Test your understanding 16

D

Test your understanding 17

C

Test your understanding 18

C

Test your understanding 19

A

Test your understanding 20

D

Test your understanding 21

C

Test your understanding 22

B

Test your understanding 23

B

Test your understanding 24

D

Test your understanding 25

B

Test your understanding 26

B

Test your understanding 27

A

Test your understanding 28

C

Test your understanding 29

D

Test your understanding 30

B

Test your understanding 31

D

Test your understanding 32

C

Test your understanding 33

D

Test your understanding 34

C

Test your understanding 35

C

Test your understanding 36

C

Test your understanding 37

B

Test your understanding 38

B

Test your understanding 39

D

Test your understanding 40

B

Test your understanding 41

C

Test your understanding 42

D

Test your understanding 43

D

Test your understanding 44

B

Test your understanding 45

D

Test your understanding 46

C

Test your understanding 47

A

Test your understanding 48

A

Test your understanding 49

C

Test your understanding 50

B

Test your understanding 51

C

Test your understanding 52

D

Test your understanding 53

C

Test your understanding 54

A

Test your understanding 55

D

Test your understanding 56

D

Test your understanding 57

D

Test your understanding 58

D

Test your understanding 59

A

Test your understanding 60

A

Test your understanding 61

D

Test your understanding 62

D

Test your understanding 63

C

Test your understanding 64

D

Test your understanding 65

A

Test your understanding 66

D

Test your understanding 67

D

Test your understanding 68

C

Test your understanding 69

D

Test your understanding 70

C

Test your understanding 71

C

Test your understanding 72

C

Test your understanding 73

D

Test your understanding 74

D

Test your understanding 75

A

Test your understanding 76

C

Test your understanding 77

C

Test your understanding 78

A

Test your understanding 79

D

Test your understanding 80

A

Test your understanding 81

C

Test your understanding 82

A

Test your understanding 83

A

Test your understanding 84

A

Test your understanding 85

B

How to access your on-line resources

Kaplan Financial students will have a MyKaplan account and these extra resources will be available to you online. You do not need to register again, as this process was completed when you enrolled. If you are having problems accessing online materials, please ask your course administrator.

If you are not studying with Kaplan and did not purchase your book via a Kaplan website, to unlock your extra online resources please go to www.en-gage.co.uk (even if you have set up an account and registered books previously). You will then need to enter the ISBN number (on the title page and back cover) and the unique pass key number contained in the scratch panel below to gain access.

You will also be required to enter additional information during this process to set up or confirm your account details.

If you purchased via the Kaplan Publishing website you will automatically receive an e-mail invitation to register your details and gain access to your content. If you do not receive the e-mail or book content, please contact Kaplan Publishing.

Your code and information

This code can only be used once for the registration of one book online. This registration and your online content will expire when the final sittings for the examinations covered by this book have taken place. Please allow one hour from the time you submit your book details for us to process your request.

Please scratch the film to access your unique code.

Please be aware that this code is case-sensitive and you will need to include the dashes within the passcode, but not when entering the ISBN.